"Marsha Coleman-Adebayo clearly and engagingly tells us Americans a truth that we might not want to hear but should."

—**DAL LAMAGNA**, author of *Raising Eyebrows: A Failed Entrepreneur Finally Gets It Right*

"Dr. Coleman-Adebayo presents the public a trenchant critique of how the US government too often not only turns a blind eye, but also enables the worst kinds of human rights practices by its multinational corporations abroad. Her unique insider position and her principled commitment were what made her dangerous to the federal bureaucracy. Thankfully, she did not give up. This book is a must-read if you're concerned with government accountability and want a rare inside look at the toll willful government negligence can take on individuals, families, and communities."

—**DANIELLE BRIAN**, president, Project on Government Oversight (POGO)

"I take my hat off to Marsha Coleman-Adebayo, who had the guts to challenge her superiors. . . . How I wish my fellow governments of Africa would emulate her good example. Her contribution in exposing the wrongdoings by a South African company in dealing with dangerous toxins will serve as a lesson for would-be investors in the future."

—**HONORABLE BANTU HOLOMISA**, member of Parliament, South Africa, and president of the United Democratic Movement

"This is the story of Marsha Coleman-Adebayo's courageous struggle against vested interests and an obdurate bureaucracy to ensure that US government agencies and officials conduct themselves in a manner consistent with the high ideals embodied in the US Constitution—and in ours."

—**RICHARD SPOOR, ESQ.**, human rights advocate and employment attorney, South Africa

"Marsha has, through her memoirs, demonstrated no fear of serving and protecting the integrity of her country, whatever the price she paid. . . . This book should enable an internal cleansing of the EPA. A must-read."

— **JACOB NGAKANE**, former union official,
Congress of South African Trade Unions

"Dr. Marsha Coleman-Adebayo approached our community with an urgent request to investigate the poisoning of defenseless residents of the vanadium mining city of Brits, South Africa. Barnard, with its tradition of producing strong and responsible women leaders, rose to the challenge. The students and two professors who accompanied Dr. Coleman-Adebayo experienced a life-changing opportunity to provide insightful research and leadership to this critical problem."

— **DR. JUDITH SHAPIRO**, former president,
Barnard College

NO FEAR

A WHISTLEBLOWER'S TRIUMPH OVER CORRUPTION AND RETALIATION AT THE EPA

MARSHA COLEMAN-ADEBAYO

FOREWORD BY NOAM CHOMSKY

AFTERWORD BY REV. WALTER E. FAUNTROY

Lawrence Hill Books

Chicago

Library of Congress Cataloging-in-Publication Data
Coleman-Adebayo, Marsha.
  No fear : a whistleblower's triumph over corruption and retaliation at the EPA /
Marsha Coleman-Adebayo ; foreword by Noam Chomsky ; afterword by Walter
Fauntroy.
      p. cm.
  Includes bibliographical references and index.
  ISBN 978-1-55652-818-7
  1. Coleman-Adebayo, Marsha. 2. United States. Environmental Protection
Agency—Officials and employees—Biography. 3. Political scientists—United
States—Biography. 4. African American political scientists—United States—Biog-
raphy. 5. United States. Environmental Protection Agency—Trials, litigation, etc. 6.
Whistle blowing—United States. 7. Vanadium industry—Corrupt practices—South
Africa. 8. Social responsibility of business. 9. United States. Notification and Federal
Employee Antidiscrimination and Retaliation Act of 2002. I. Title.
  TD140.C65A3 2011
  363.7092—dc23
  [B]
                                    2011016723

Interior design: Sarah Olson

Published by Lawrence Hill Books
An imprint of Chicago Review Press, Incorporated
814 North Franklin Street
Chicago, Illinois 60610
ISBN 978-1-55652-818-7
Printed in the United States of America
5 4 3 2 1

The Lord is my light and my salvation. . . . Whom shall I fear?

—Psalm 27

IIIIIIIIIIIIIIIIII

I do not believe, based on the transcript, what I have seen of
the transcript, she was treated by her colleagues with the
respect any employee deserves.

—Carol Browner (then EPA administrator)
in testimony before the House Science Committee

IIIIIIIIIIIIIIIIII

This time it has to be different. This time we cannot fail, nor can
we be lulled into complacency. . . . That's why I'm naming Carol
Browner to a new position in the White House to coordinate energy
and climate policy. . . . She brings the unmatched experience of
being a successful and longest-serving administrator of the EPA. She
will be indispensable in implementing an ambitious and complex
energy policy. . . . We can't afford complacency
nor accept more broken promises.

—President Barack Obama's introduction of Carol Browner

Contents

|||||||||||||

Foreword

IIIIIIIIIIIII

by Noam Chomsky

Dr. Marsha Coleman-Adebayo wrote to me in 1996 expressing her deep frustration with the US Environmental Protection Agency's "cover-ups" and attempt to use her to execute what she perceived to be its back-channel deception in South Africa. She wrote: "We had promised to assist a community center that also doubles as an orphanage for children who lost their parents during the revolution." That facility, which wanted to train students in environmental waste management, was about to close, according to Marsha, "because of EPA's neglect." Offering another example of EPA's disregard for the local population, she reported that "hundred[s] of people [have reportedly] died due to water contamination. EPA agreed in July to send a team of scientists to the Brits area [a mining community] to test the water. . . . Again, EPA reneged on its commitment and then tried to force me to 'cover up' its lies to the EPA Administrator's Office and the Vice President's Office by stating that a 'dairy cow' assessment . . . was in fact related to the request by the Brits Community. When one talks about 'cover-ups' and racist policies by US policy makers towards African countries I can't think of a better case study than the EPA example. The Agency has knowingly withheld assistance that could have saved lives and decreased misery."

With Marsha Coleman-Adebayo's book, we now have the benefit of the records she kept as an insider within the seat of power from about the mid-nineties, as well a US federal court transcript that put US foreign policy makers under oath at trial. We also have her account of progressing from the politically organized working class in Detroit of the 1960s through her undergraduate education at Barnard College and her doctoral studies at MIT, during which I sat on her dissertation committee. Her professional working experience includes fieldwork for the United Nations, senior policy analysis for international affairs for the Congressional Black Caucus, work as a senior social scientist for Africa at the World Wildlife Fund, and senior policy analysis for the Environmental Protection Agency. Her activism was intertwined with a professional career spanning from the latter part of the civil rights movement as a high school student, to the environmental movement of the eighties, through her activism in the antiapartheid movement in the nineties.

Dr. Coleman-Adebayo was the US official to whom the first reports of illness and death relating to vanadium mining were given by black South African union leaders and later by the new environmental leadership within the Nelson Mandela government. As she discusses, the US government ignored these reports, choosing to protect the American-owned and multinational corporations that were operating in South Africa. The reports included instances of tongues turning green, bronchitis, asthma, bleeding from nearly every orifice of the body, and impotence in young, healthy male workers. Even after the US–South Africa Binational Commission (BNC) agreed that a team of experts from the United States would investigate these reports, no serious investigation ever occurred. Instead, EPA dispatched a single veterinarian to care for its new, black African partners, as the United States focused all its serious efforts and resources on developing a private sector project.

Had Marsha's memoir simply explored this time period, it would merit serious consideration for its rich contributions. What truly distinguishes her account, however, is that she represents the antithesis of what could easily have been the all-American story of a young African American woman whose hard work and dedication paid big dividends— if only she would look the other way while White House–appointed policy makers and colleagues in the US government turned blind eyes to exploitative multinational corporations and the reported atrocities against the indigenous populations of South Africa that had just thrown off the bitter yoke of apartheid.

Marsha was uniquely qualified among EPA's delegation to win the confidence of her black South African counterparts. For her doctorate in African political affairs and development, her area of specialization was Southern Africa. She was also an activist who had marched against apartheid for a year as a part of the antiapartheid movement at the South African embassy in Washington, DC. If the US government wanted a thorough investigation into what was happening at the Vametco vanadium mining operation in Brits, South Africa, they had the right person for the job. As the agency's liaison to the White House, Marsha—the executive secretary of the Environment Working Group to BNC, commonly known as the Gore-Mbeki Commission—was expected to deliver US pitchmen to unsuspecting black South Africans in order to facilitate private industry.

If these crimes had been perpetrated by the former Soviet Union or Venezuela, it is unlikely that a single eyebrow would have been raised about the way a gifted and dedicated civil servant from either country was abused by her own government when she blew the whistle on corruption and the atrocities that she encountered in South Africa. It is easier to ascribe deplorable behavior to political systems we reject than to admit they occurred within our own government. However, the excesses that Marsha documents occurred within our own federal system. That we are even minimally aware of Marsha's history is owed to her having won a civil case in the federal court system, which made her story newsworthy. In a system where legal obstacles are so insurmountable that only 2 to 3 percent of the tens of thousands of total plaintiffs prevail, Marsha's court victory should have received banner headlines in every major newspaper in America, as a victory for all federal workers. But the media prefer to present Marsha's case as an isolated example. Missing from their reporting is any analysis of the logical compulsion for the federal system to retaliate against whistle-blowers. Protecting business interests over human beings must remain unchallenged; thus whistleblowers are routinely publicly discredited. By portraying Marsha as a noble, heroic individual who stood up to a few bad apples, the media perform a complicit role of ignoring the larger trend of oppression that is systemic and designed to maintain control within the ranks.

Her case was brought under the protections of the 1964 Civil Rights Act. For tactical reasons the case was limited to the jurisdiction of Title VII. Excluded therefore was any substantial analysis of the underlying cause that drove her to the courts: the systematic abuse, endangerment, and, through deliberate neglect, injury and manslaughter—if not murder—of predominantly black mine workers. These workers are subjected to toxic and potentially lethal working environments without proper protective equipment, without best practices for working with hazardous materials, without competent or uncompromised medical care, and without legal recourse to seek remedies. These corporate-overseen crimes leave fingerprints.

Whether the agenda-setting media bother to look there or not, the trial transcript is part of the public record. It contains a diagram of the crime scene, in the form of sworn testimony by federal employees, Senior Executive Service federal managers, political appointees who were presidentially selected and congressionally approved to carry out the policies of the Clinton-Gore administration, along with names, dates, rationales, official dissembling, and corroborative testimony that convinced a jury that the EPA had systematically discriminated against Marsha and maintained a hostile work environment. There is significant testimony regarding the mining of vanadium. We may recall that Union Carbide was at the heart of the Bhopal, India, disaster that killed several thousand Indians in their sleep. Union Carbide's legal representation was adroit in minimizing financial liability for the company and justice for its victims. Only recently were seven Indian officials of Union Carbide found guilty of criminal conduct for their roles in the disaster. Still, no Americans have ever been brought to justice.

Vanadium helped fuel the Industrial Revolution and is listed as a strategic mineral by the US Central Intelligence Agency because it strengthens the ability of steel to withstand temperature extremes of heat and cold and is critical to the functioning of machinery—not to mention advanced weaponry. Perhaps this explains the government's reluctance to look too closely at the human and environmental devastation wrought by vanadium mining.

Marsha Coleman-Adebayo's two-decade struggle with the Environmental Protection Agency is a valuable micro-example of what a much larger body of evidence reveals: in matters of business, defense, and social welfare, official US policy has remarkable consistency, with only modest differences, whether Democrats or Republicans control the Congress or the White House. Marsha's case illustrates how the government seeks to use Trojan horses to generate business.

Dr. Coleman-Adebayo's work, furthermore, analyzes how the government looks from the inside. Despite the government's resorting to standard formulas to crush yet another whistleblower, Marsha refused to submit to the pressures that were brought to bear against her in 1996, defiantly writing to her supervisors after she was reprimanded for not delivering South African markets, saying: "I will not distort the facts about the South Africa program. I will not lie to the public about the EPA program in South Africa and I will not provide false information."

Vice President Al Gore said of the BNC, "I reaffirm that the people of the United States of America are committed to the strongest possible partnership with the citizens of South Africa." His counterpart, Thabo Mbeki, then deputy president of South Africa, proclaimed that he appreciated "this relationship of support and engagement for creating a better life for the people of this country." CNN reported that a further goal of the BNC was to hold regular trade talks and cooperate in the fight against international terrorism.

Although Nelson Mandela went on to win the Nobel Peace Prize, his name remained on the official US list of terrorists until 2008, twenty years after the Reagan administration declared his African National Congress to be one of the world's "more notorious terrorist groups" for its resistance to the brutal apartheid regime that Washington was supporting. Meanwhile, multinational corporations continued to enjoy impunity for major crimes, illustrating yet again how profits are placed over people.

According to CNN, "South Africa is the United States' most important trading partner in Africa. . . . The United States exported $3 billion worth of goods to South Africa in 1997 and imported South African goods worth $2.5 billion," including imports of strategic value to the United States such as magnesium, gold, diamonds, and vanadium.[1]

The BNC was established under the leadership of presidents Bill Clinton and Nelson Mandela on March 1, 1995, to (among other things) "launch a new era in cooperation between the two countries by establishing permanent and vigorous institutional partnerships" and to "explore areas for cooperation based on shared values and experiences."

Furthermore, "every project approved by the co-chaired committee must then be approved by the South African Government."[2]

The narrative prepared about Marsha for public consumption depicted her courageous effort in pursuing justice in the courts (*Coleman-Adebayo v. Carol Browner*) and presenting her case to Congress as proof of the need for federal employee whistleblower and civil rights protection. Such prestigious publications as *Time* referred to Marsha as "the Rosa Parks of the 21st century," and *Good Housekeeping* magazine named her its Woman of the Year in 2003.[3] Congress, incensed by the record of Marsha's mistreatment, mandated protection into law with the No FEAR Act of 2002 (Notification and Federal Employee Antidiscrimination and Retaliation Act). The legislation passed both houses of Congress unanimously, with Marsha's case mentioned in its introductory language. The president honored Marsha at the signing, as it was the first civil rights and whistleblower protective legislation of the twenty-first century.

There is, however, more to the story. Marsha's personal story played out against the background of the neoliberal policies that were being implemented during this period, designed to secure investor rights while the interests of people were deemed incidental. The severe human costs of these measures are downplayed in media reporting and commentary in favor of themes of liberated masses of black South Africans and the bright future that awaited all of them.

We have now lived long enough in that "bright" future to assess its accomplishments. Since 1994, when the ANC took power, the number of people who live on under a dollar a day in South Africa has doubled from two to four million; the unemployment rate for black Africans has more than doubled; of the thirty-five million black citizens, five thousand earn more than $60,000 a year while for whites the number is twenty times higher; the ANC has built 1.8 million homes, while at the same time, two million have lost their homes; one million people were evicted from their farms in the first decade of democracy; the number of shack dwellers has increased by half; in 2006 more than one in four lived in shantytowns, many without running water or electricity. The US Department of State reports that in 2008, South African exports to the United States had risen to $9.9 billion. The United States was the second largest source of foreign direct investment in South Africa after the UK, and the largest portfolio investor, at $51.6 billion.

One can only marvel at how the "benefits" have managed to elude the huddled masses.[4]

The impetus to pass the No FEAR Act was bottom up, with masses of federal workers risking their jobs to demand protection from their superiors. Now that Marsha has turned a vanadium-clad mirror on the inner workings of what she calls the federal envirotaucracy and their witting accomplices the envirocrats, others may use her achievement to help find a way to approach their government without fear. International readers—particularly the citizens of developing countries—should feel chilled by this narrative and be wary of investors bearing gifts. In Marsha's case we see a rare instance of the victim who becomes the victor. But it is important to remember that she did not act alone. It is only when ordinary people act in accordance with their decent impulses and work to improve the world that, quoting the ANC Freedom Charter, "the people shall govern."

Preface and Acknowledgments

In the summer of 1996, two harsh facts were revealed. First, a US-based multinational corporation had been and was still actively poisoning entire communities around its South African vanadium mining operation. Second, despite its commitment to investigate the vanadium tragedy, the United States, under the Clinton-Gore administration, had no intention of following through with this agreement.

Much of the story I detail in this book has received some coverage in the press. Almost all of that coverage has focused on my victory in court over the Environmental Protection Agency in a claim brought under Title VII of the 1964 Civil Rights Act, and the subsequent passage of the No FEAR Act of 2002, which became the first civil rights and whistle-blower law of the twenty-first century. That law grew out of my court victory. But almost no mention of the plight of vanadium mining communities has found its way into the mainstream media. The vanadium story has been obscured by the domestic civil rights implications of my case and its impact on US law and has not been told before now. That missing story is told here from an insider's view. It illuminates how US foreign policy masquerades as aid while it bludgeons developing countries for the benefit of American business.

The bulk of the material about South Africa in these pages was taken from interviews I conducted with miners and their family members during several trips there and during study tours that I oversaw at the Massachusetts Institute of Technology (MIT) and Howard University with South African delegations receiving environmental instruction in the United States. I also relied heavily on transcripts of sworn US federal court testimony and congressional hearings, contemporaneous records, correspondence, e-mails, and other documentation I accrued over the period. I drew from video recordings, roundtable discussions, and symposia held in South Africa and at Barnard College. Representatives of the affected South African communities were invaluable in confirming the accuracy of the narrative. I have compared my personal recollections against sworn testimony at both my trial and congressional hearings, which corroborate the events described in these pages. Perhaps equally important was the role that Barnard College played; this small, elite women's college stepped forward to document the impact of vanadium pollution on an embattled community after the US government reneged on its commitments.[1]

Nearly all of the interviews, both in the United States and South Africa, took place in person, during recordings that often lasted several hours. I spoke with nearly everyone identified in the book, except for a few who declined to participate or, because of adversarial positions, were unapproachable, or were unavailable. Many provided me information they had in the form of e-mails, photographs, memos, relevant notes, recordings, calendars, and other sundry documentation.

Significant interviews with people still employed within the federal system were executed on a confidential basis; to protect those individuals' identities, their names have been changed in the book. This was done to shield them from retribution from the US government, which had shown itself to be particularly vindictive in my own case and which has grown markedly more hostile to whistleblowers with each successive administration. Confidentiality was also critical in encouraging frankness from government employees who were otherwise reluctant to divulge their insights. Predominantly, I interviewed colleagues and associates I had known professionally and with whom I had developed trust.

I took painstaking efforts to compare my recollections with testimonies about the same events. Transcripts were most useful in this. Where possible, I have reconstructed dialogue with the help of the principals. This was a meticulous process. In instances where the principals' participation was not available to me, I relied on sworn testimony by those participants for corroboration. Dialogue presented in the text, largely within quotation marks, is meant to indicate the general content of conversations rather than serve as verbatim accounts of what exactly was said. Comparisons between notes, transcripts, eyewitness accounts, and personal memory served to authenticate the accuracy of those portrayals. Where this was not possible, I paraphrased, attempting to create an accurate summary of the sense of each statement, without claiming the paraphrase as the exact wording.

Predictably, principal figures in the book will object to their portrayal herein. How could it be otherwise? I have not concerned myself with seeking approval from those who engaged in environmental misconduct or resorted to harassment and retaliation. As my mother counseled me on more than several occasions, "You do not need, nor should you seek, the approval of your abuser."

Another comforting realization is that distance and time have taken some of the sting out of the events I lived through, and abundant information is publicly available for review that I had no hand in creating. I was able to draw extensively from the body of that independent information to find a voice that was plaintive where appropriate, passionate when it needed to be, and ultimately factual overall. Many documents that are referenced throughout this book were entered into evidence during the federal trial. This book represents the first in-depth analysis of the public record.

A Yoruba proverb says that it takes more than one broom straw to sweep the ground clean. When I extrapolate that proverb to my own life, I recognize that it took a family, a community, colleagues, and dedicated activists to fill the pages of this memoir. Prominent in capitalist society is the myth of the individual's supremacy. Hopefully, this memoir strikes a blow to that myth and instead celebrates the myriad groups and people who stepped forward to create a better society than existed before their sacrifice.

Before there was a No FEAR Coalition there was EPA Victims Against Racial Discrimination, a group of courageous, in-your-face activists determined to bring the plight of federal employees, particularly those working at EPA, to the attention of the American public. These employees risked their careers and their families, and endured harassment, but never surrendered their integrity. I speak of Dwight Welch, former president of National Treasury Employees Union Chapter 280, Selwyn Cox, Theresa Fleming-Blue, Anita Nickens, the late

Patricia Lawson, and a host of others throughout the nine regions of the federal government.

From the EPA Chicago office, I would like to thank Michael Bland for his friendship and wisdom, along with Christine Urban, and acknowledge the work of the late Alfred Krause. Both veterans, Michael and Dwight brought finely honed skills that inspired others through their leadership. I would like to recognize Dr. Alan Abramson, an exceptional EPA supervisor, who encouraged a creative workplace and scientific integrity with zero tolerance for a hostile work environment. He sustained me when I needed it most.

The No FEAR Coalition was established after Congressman F. James Sensenbrenner and Congresswoman Sheila Jackson Lee introduced the No FEAR legislation. It was their stellar bipartisan leadership in concert with Senator John Warner and Senator Joseph Lieberman that led to the unanimous passage of the No FEAR Act in both houses of Congress. Enormous appreciation goes to Senators Warner and Lieberman, Senator Russell Feingold, and Congresswoman Connie Morella. Beth Sokul, legislative director for Congressman Sensenbrenner, was undaunted and tactically astute.

The coalition evolved beyond its EPA-centric origins to embrace all federal employees and civic and faith-based organizations. Tanya Ward Jordan, Janet Howard, Joyce Megginson, Blair Hayes, Woody Hatcher, Altheria Myers, Norris McDonald, Arthuretta Martin, Quinton Lynch, Matthew Fogg, Penny Kriesch, Dawn Johnson, Cathy Harris, Marsha Bishop, Dennis Young, Evan Vallianatos, Steven Spiegel, Phillip Newsome, Mary Bass, Rawle King, Macani Toungara, Muyiwa Oni, Dorothy Picard, Robert Smith, Kris Kolesnic, Gretchen Helm, Eyvone Petty-Callier, Ronald Harris, Clarence Day, and Dana Hawkins comprised the heart and soul of the original coalition. Jon Grand deserves special mention for the extraordinary price he paid for honoring his pledge to uphold, protect, and defend the Constitution against all enemies foreign and domestic. Many hundreds of others threw themselves into the battle. I cringe to think that overlooking some truly brave souls is inevitable, but not for lack of appreciation for their spirit and contribution.

The No FEAR Coalition worked closely with the NAACP Federal Sector Task Force under the leadership of Leroy Warren, a former member of the organization's national board of directors. Leroy's leadership, both at the grassroots level and in congressional circles, was crucial in our ability to navigate the shark-infested political waters. Leroy, Ira Patterson, and Linda Plummer provided solace and comfort for hundreds of battered federal employees. Support from Blacks in Government (BIG) was essential to the struggle and passage of the No FEAR Act. Hundreds of dedicated BIG members marched with us to register their protest against discrimination and retaliation in the government. I also wish to thank Lawrence Lucus, John Boyd, and Black Farmers for their enduring support.

Twentieth-century civil rights heroes, both dead and alive, were front and center in the persons of the Southern Christian Leadership Conference's Dr. Ruby Reese Moone and Rev. Walter E. Fauntroy. Dr. Moone was a stalwart in difficult times, having endured much more severe challenges in her native segregated Georgia. Rev. Fauntroy's mark on history carries forward with his counsel to the No FEAR Institute, where he has worked relentlessly on behalf of whistleblowers and victims of discrimination. His wisdom and moral clarity were steeled by suffering alongside Dr. Martin Luther King Jr. as they braved the violence of American apartheid, attack dogs, and water hoses.

I thank Dick Gregory, one of America's true treasures: Gregory was a whistleblower before the word was coined. Joe Madison's generosity in providing the coalition the reach of his syndicated radio show to push for the passage of No FEAR was invaluable.

Rev. Al Sharpton was the X factor, leading the demonstration to the Senate that broke through the final barrier to the No FEAR Act's passage.

How does one acknowledge the generosity of spirit and depth of heroism of Jacob Ngakane, General Bantu Holomisa, and the late Peter Mokaba and Sis. Bessie Mdoda? I was honored to be the recipient of their confidence and the repository of their stories of life under apartheid. Jacob Ngakane has remained a dear friend throughout the years and continues to fight for the day when "the people will govern." General Holomisa epitomized integrity and commitment to his people. Within US foreign policy circles, this South African official is considered beyond reproach. My time with Mokaba was brief but insightful. He possessed the toughness, dedication, and love it took to give birth to a new nation. After losing her son to the liberation struggle, Sis. Bessie's one-woman crusade in the cause of orphans and impoverished children became a tour de force that influenced many lives. Her legacy will last generations.

When I arrived at MIT to study political science, my goal was to acquire the skills to become a scholar-activist. I had the great privilege to learn by example from two men whose names are synonymous with brilliance and devotion to social activism: Noam Chomsky and Willard Johnson. These humanitarian scholars, perhaps more than anyone else outside of my family, set me on the journey that made it inevitable that I would not look the other way when I learned about what was happening inside EPA and the vanadium mines of South Africa.

I would like to acknowledge the wonderful contributions of the late Drs. Ronald Walters and Robert Cummings of Howard University to the South African study tours. Both men poured their ample intellectual wealth and, more important, their hearts, into each student.

Great appreciation goes to Dr. Joanne Godley and her daughter Juanita Godley Losier, Dr. Caroline Wyatt and her late daughter Holly, and my children, Olusina and Folasade, for traveling to South Africa to investigate the plight of vanadium mine workers.

I have loved and continue to cherish the women I grew up with on the seventh floor at Barnard College. Our love has grown through sharing the seminal moments in our lives: weddings, births, and the loss of loved ones.

Barnard College accepted my proposal and sent their Mellon Mays and GE undergraduate fellows (MMUF) to aid an embattled community in South Africa: Hayley Holness, Alexandra Severino, Kendra Tappin, and Alexandria Wright, and Professors Diane Dittrick and Timothy Halpin-Healy. Tim's son, Tyler, accompanied the group. Thanks go also to past president Judith Shapiro for her support of the South African mission. Dr. Vivian Taylor, associate dean of the college, and professor of history Rosalind Rosenberg, coordinators of the Barnard MMUF, enabled the funding of the mission. Thanks also to Provost Elizabeth Boylan, Dean of the College Dorothy Denburg, Dean of Studies Karen Blank, and former director of the Alumnae Center Marilyn Chin. Barnard women threw themselves into the research, gaining respect and admiration from government officials and the community. They were the last line of defense for the vanadium mining community. Vanadium victim Benedict Sebone said of the Barnard team: "We thought the world had forgotten us, and then you came to our rescue." Thanks also to fellow alum Barbara Dreyfus for reading early drafts of the book and giving tons of great advice.

David Shapiro and Richard Swick provided brilliant legal representation. I would also like to thank Richard Renner, Steve Kohn, Michael Kohn, and David K. Colapinto of the National Whistleblowers Center, who provided not only legal support but also office space, pencils, pens, paper, and the moral support that facilitated the passage of No FEAR. Thanks also go to Tom Devine, Doug Hartnett of the Government Accountability Project, Danielle Bryant of the Project on Government Oversight, and Jeff Ruch of Public Employees for Environmental Responsibility. Norris McDonald, among the cofounders of the No FEAR Coalition and president of the African American Environmentalist Association, provided invaluable advice and guidance.

Federal employees from across the United States placed themselves at considerable risk by testifying and standing with whistleblowers. Thank you, Dr. Bradford Brown, Kathy Washburn, Nora Magee, Inga Barnett, Franklin Moore, Kenneth Thomas, Marty Falls, and Martha Shimkin for demonstrating true courage. Aretha Brockett offered her friendship during a particularly difficult time at the agency.

Dr. William (Bill) Ellis gave his considerable intellectual insight and analysis. His research skills are unparalleled. Joseph Opala was always available for midnight calls when writer's block prevented me from resting—many thanks! Paul Ruffins's editing helped sentences jump off the page.

Dr. Pamela Ransom helped me relive the Beijing Conference and reanimate the role of Bella Abzug. I thank Jack White of *Time* magazine for his coverage of the struggle for the No FEAR Act.

My deep appreciation goes to my extended family: Bolaji and Remi Aluko and their children Seye, Moyo, Toni, Jumi, and Sope. We were blessed with "people's historian" Dr. Jeanne Toungara of Howard University. I must also thank the University of the District of Columbia for their in-kind contributions.

I can never sufficiently extol my greatest and most precious support base, my church family: Macedonia Baptist Church led by Pastor Sterling King, and his wife, Dr. Rosalyn King. Rev. King, a son of the South, endured American apartheid while growing up in segregated Arkansas. This sensitivity informed the entire church family, who provided prayers and supplications on behalf of victims of government repression. I am deeply indebted to all of the members of this church community for their support and love.

After years of struggle, I became ill, and Drs. Martin Kanovsky, James Davis, and Stephen Rojcewicz Jr. came to my aid. They wrote countless letters to the agency pleading for officials to provide a reasonable accommodation for my health and to respect the law. They symbolize the most noble and compassionate representatives of their profession.

I thank Yuval Taylor, my editor at Lawrence Hill Books, for his straightforward and sometimes painfully truthful critique in guiding the direction of this book. Yuval's steady editorial hand was invaluable in providing an objective review of very sensitive material. My deep and abiding appreciation goes to my agent, Jim McCarthy of Dystel and Goderich Literary Management, for his kindness, patience, support, and guidance throughout this process. Jim was always available to read and react to various drafts of the manuscript and to provide provocative and challenging perspectives on my work. In particular, I am very grateful that Jim recommended that I choose to publish this book with Chicago Review Press.

Thanks to Kevin Berends, a renaissance man who seems to hold competency in so many spheres of endeavor. Our paths crossed, and the narrative was greatly enriched by Kevin's precious and gentle nudges to tone down a given section and to invest more emotional energy in others. Two other paths crossed mine via Kevin's lifelong friendship with Bill Davison, who, along with Bill's friend Julie Gordon, read early drafts of the manuscript and slayed many of its dragons.

On first hearing of my situation at the EPA and the plight of vanadium workers, actor and activist Danny Glover said he would like to produce a motion picture exposing these injustices. Glover provided a film crew and production team that documented the Barnard students' interviews with the South African vanadium miners. I am grateful also to Louverture Films cofounder Joslyn Barnes, a screenwriter and Emmy Award–nominated producer, who oversaw Louverture's on-location unit and coordinated with the South African production team.

African American family histories arise out of a rich oral tradition. My great-aunt, Bessie Woods Chapman, my grandmother, Olivia Cornelia Woods Thompson, and my grandfather, the Rev. George Lee Thompson, told me the family stories recounted in this narrative. I come from a small family that packs love and commitment into each hug and caress. Farmers hailing from Dublin, Georgia, my family joined other African Americans during the great migration to the North in the 1930s, relocating to Detroit, Michigan, to escape the state-sanctioned violence of the South, and seeking opportunities in the emerging auto industry. My cousins Mary Woods Harper and Thomas Chapman aided in reconstructing our family history. My paternal grandparents, Samuel and Lilee Coleman deserve enormous gratitude for sharing their lives and collective memories with me.

There are people without whom this work would not have been possible. My aunt Ruth Woods Thompson Whitley, a constant source of love and caring, has always played a dual role in my life as an aunt and second mother. It is with great love and devotion that I thank her for her lifetime of mentoring me. Her husband, Troy Whitley, has been her support and mine throughout this journey.

My mother, Majestice Woods Thompson Coleman Prater, was the rock of my life and is the standard by which I measure honor, grace, and dignity. She departed this life on March 1, 2006, but her spirit and legacy continue. Her abundant love and teaching by example set into motion my desire to fight for those who couldn't fight for themselves and inspired me to assist federal government workers and South Africa's vanadium victims. When I called to report the federal jury verdict, my mother's response reflected her deep faith: "Our God neither sleeps nor slumbers!" Her love sustains me, her grandchildren, and her son-in-law, Segun.

How does one write about a man who has filled your life like a second breath? Over half of our lives have been intertwined. Segun's integrity and courage are without equal. I was the beneficiary of his underpinning, his unflinching prayers to God, and a cheerful disposition that even battling EPA for over a decade could not quash. Every step of the way, every battle, every strategy exhibits Segun's indelible fingerprints. He is the most brilliant man I have ever met, yet his brilliance is only surpassed by his humility. As a pastor, professor, husband, and father, Segun's life has been about service to his community and his family. This book would have been a collection of blank pages without his intellectual, spiritual, and moral compass.

Finally, I thank my children for teaching me how to appreciate each day as a wonderful and spectacular opportunity to embrace joy with abandon.

Introduction

They came to me complaining of green tongues. They told me about bleeding from every orifice. Their husbands could no longer perform. The sheet on his side of the bed would be black in the morning from whatever it was that oozed from his pores while he tried to sleep. Some had only photographs of their husbands who had died at the age of fifty but had looked like ninety-five. There were reports of many dead and more dying. The company would not help. The company would not even let them see their own X-rays. It was an American company, so they had come to me. For them, I was America. I worked for the United States Environmental Protection Agency, and America had sent me to them in joy and celebration at the end of apartheid. America had come to help them and to help their new government succeed.

These were the miners' stories in Brits, South Africa. It was 1995, and I was representing the EPA as the executive secretary of the United States–South Africa Binational Commission (BNC) Environment Working Group to the White House. Also known as the Gore-Mbeki Commission, the effort was convened in Pretoria to aid in the transition to the new government of Nelson Mandela, in the years following the suffering, brutality, and crimes that had been committed against blacks by whites in pursuit of the abundant minerals that enabled industrialism and produced prodigious capital. In Brits, this pursuit came in the form of the mining of vanadium, a mineral that when added to steel enabled enhanced physical properties, much more strength, and many

1

more products. The victims were only so much collateral damage. There were millions more available in the townships.

The company allegedly responsible for the crimes reported to me was Union Carbide, which had decades of experience in disregard for human life. It had become adept in morphing itself into different legal entities since it had killed thousands of Indians in their sleep with a poisonous cloud in what has become known as the Bhopal disaster. Union Carbide had been astute in slipping liability and feinting beneath jurisdictions, while maintaining the same location for its corporate headquarters in Danbury, Connecticut.

The Dow Chemical Company, with legal problems of its own after providing the US military with oceans of Agent Orange during the Vietnam War, looked fondly on the proposed acquisition of Union Carbide in 2001 and became its proud new parent. Perhaps it was diplomatic insensitivity that brought IBM and Dow into the Binational process[1]— both companies would later face criminal charges in US courts for having supported the apartheid regime.[2]

The motive, whatever it was, was well beyond my pay grade. But it now appears that an ulterior design for the environment committee of the BNC was to provide cover for the same US multinational companies that had participated in the repression of South Africans during apartheid. Under a new green banner, they were seeking to continue the previous relationships they had enjoyed while Nelson Mandela had languished in prison for three decades.

At the time, I was sure my EPA supervisors would feel the same outrage, would be as eager to help, and would want as much as I did to make Union Carbide come clean this time. This was our watch. In seeming contrast to US policy all through the apartheid years, America now had a progressive president in Bill Clinton. This was America under the watchful environmental eyes of Al Gore. The BNC's mission was to make things right this time and to get the United States on the right side of history.

So I was stupefied when my superior told me to shut up—when it was suggested that, instead of trying to help these people who had turned to America expecting our best, I should turn my attention to better pursuits. I could decorate my office, for instance.

In 2000, I testified about the plight of vanadium victims and whistle-blowers before a House Science Committee hearing, convened after a jury had found in my favor in a Title VII complaint against the EPA about abuses that had taken place under Carol M. Browner's watch and with her knowledge.[3] Tearful and contrite, Browner sat before Congress and said, "I am deeply, deeply troubled by what is in the transcript." Turning to me, she said, "It was rubbish. I'm sorry." But instead of enforcing a commitment the EPA had made to investigate vanadium poisoning and rather than firing the managers named in my case, Browner never lifted a finger. She had been briefed about the situation several times by me, my attorney, and many leaders of environmental justice NGOs.[4] She knew. Even the White House knew.[5]

On the American side of the Atlantic, many federal employees of color were finding the culture inside the EPA so toxic that they were becoming sick. Hypertension, stress-related autoimmune disorders, and heart diseases were taking a heavy toll. There were fault lines beyond which people of color—and women, especially—did not move. Senior Executive Service (SES) positions were dominated by white males. These same white, male managers coveted their privilege and defended it in a turf war that used every means of intimidation, harassment, discrimination, and retaliation imaginable.

In the post-civil rights federal government, surely the Civil Rights Office of the EPA—the most enlightened of all federal agencies—would feel the same outrage that I felt when I informed them that I had experienced all of these things. But again I was shocked when those at the highest levels of government turned a blind eye to a pervasively hostile work environment.

⁣⁣⁣⁣⁣⁣⁣⁣⁣⁣⁣⁣

So this book is about whistleblowing. It is about the harrowing position employees find themselves in when, at some point in their careers, policies, procedures, and practices run afoul of common human decency and the powerful victimize the powerless. In my case, in South Africa, I came across evidence of systematic poisoning of whole communities that under any circumstance would be difficult not to see as criminal.

And within the borders of my own country, inside the structure of my own government, I encountered a regressive racism on par with the worst elements of Jim Crow. In both instances I blew the whistle, and in both I experienced the full force of systematic governmental retaliation.

At its deepest level this is a story of betrayal. Much has been written about the betrayal of the South African revolution that brought about the end of apartheid. Significant, incontrovertible data show that, twenty years after the fall of the apartheid regime, living conditions for the majority of black South Africans have gotten considerably worse. Naomi Klein and others have analyzed the mechanisms that abandoned the majority of black South Africans and maintained the status quo for whites—English and Afrikaner—leaving control of economic power within the hands of the minority.[6]

I was at the negotiating table and saw firsthand how America played a supporting role in that betrayal, while paying lip service to the principles of liberty, democracy, and freedom.[7] At the end of the day, the BNC was merely an instrument of neoliberalism, beholden to business interests and bottom lines while waving the banner of a green flag.[8]

I sought recourse in the only two venues that were available to me: the federal courts and the streets. I was tempted to see legislation as my second recourse; but, as a people, we have never been given anything by government that we haven't first won in hard-fought battles in the streets.

My personal battle was a two-staged attack: In the complaint I filed under Title VII of the 1964 Civil Rights Act in federal court, *Coleman-Adebayo v. Carol Browner*, a jury found in my favor, validating my charges of race, sex, and color discrimination and affirming that the EPA tolerated a sexually and racially hostile work environment.[9] This victory provided the underpinning for the second stage—the fight for whistleblower protection legislation—that was passed unanimously in both houses of Congress with the No FEAR Act of 2002.

‖‖‖‖‖‖‖‖‖‖

We have only to look at the Wall Street bailouts, the health care "debate," and the fate of whistleblowers sounding the alarm on governmental malfeasance to see where the United States government places its allegiance today. In all three examples, the government has sided with industry over the best interests and consent of the people.

In the absence of real, mandated protection, "whistleblowing" is just another name for public suicide. Had there been significant whistleblower protection in place in the decade before the financial meltdown, it is likely the severity of the crisis would have been diminished, if not averted. Likewise, if common employees within the health care industry felt adequately protected, the shenanigans foisted upon the public through denial of coverage and wasteful spending could have been exposed and remedied long ago. This raises the even more ominous prospect of what our government is capable of doing to its own citizens, should we organize and insist on the implementation of our wishes.

⁗⁗⁗⁗

Historians of South Africa since the end of apartheid have not been kind to the West's treatment of the postapartheid leadership. The process I witnessed used black faces to legitimize the white face of neo-apartheid. This would signal a new metamorphosis we would see repeated not only in South Africa but also in the United States, where the old instruments of oppression began to wear a smiling black face.

But if we know our history, if we pay attention to those instances when the American people stood up to tyranny, whether during slavery or in the midst of the women's rights, civil rights, or labor movements, our history abounds with examples of the people triumphant over cold-blooded business and its treacherous political allies.

This book documents one instance of saying no, with a lot of help and support from like-minded people. It will take that same kind of determination and solidarity to reclaim our sovereignty as a people from the culture of fear that business—in collusion with politicians—prefers to a constitutional republic.

⁗⁗⁗⁗

After playing by the rules, attending the best institutions of learning in America, and earning advanced degrees, I was virtually assured the American dream. When powerless South African people looked on me as the face of an environmental protector, my superiors expected their pantomime could add my smiling black face. When black South Africans and their new black representatives asked me to help people whose tongues were turning green, silence was not an option—ever.

Not this American.

Not on my watch.

And, it is my hope, not on yours.

Welcome to EPA: Consider Yourself an Honorary White Man

I burst into the women's room. An older black woman was sitting in a chair inside, smoking. I waved at the cloud of smoke.

"I wish you'd do that outside." I had seen her around the office. She was an executive secretary. I closed the stall door.

"You working on air quality or something?"

"If you don't care about your own health, you could at least be considerate of others. Secondhand smoke kills. You should know that, working here."

"Oh, I know what kills."

I emerged from the stall and went to the sink, the woman assessing me.

"How's Inga working out for you?" she asked.

"She's very capable, thank you."

"I trained her. I trained all the good secretaries."

"And you are . . . ?" I looked at her in the mirror.

"Lillian Pleasant."

"Marsha Coleman-Adebayo." I turned back to my image. I looked like hell.

"When are you due?"

"Excuse me?"

"You told them yet?"

I shut the faucet off, walked toward the paper towels, dried my hands, and patted perspiration from my face with the damp towel. "I haven't told anyone yet, except my family. Why?"

Lillian shrugged. She struggled to her feet and stubbed out her cigarette. She turned her face toward me, smiling as she leaned on the door. "I'll smoke outside from now on."

Checking my profile in the mirror, I smoothed down my dress.

।।।।।।।।।।।।

The hope and optimism of the sixties had been instilled in us as a people. And for those of us who came of age when hope summoned our intelligence and our sense of duty, it still remained. Long after the assassinations, still believing, as the song had told us, that we would overcome, we entered the workplace skeptical but optimistic. If there were any meaning that could begin to temper the loss, it was the example of the nascent power of the common people when they organize. This was the torch passed to my generation. I was determined to carry that torch forward and hand it, improved, to the next.

But in my earliest days at the EPA in 1990, I was struck by the stark disparities that ran—over twenty-five years after the civil rights movement—along clear fault lines. The pay disparities in the system ranged from, in government vernacular, GS-1 to GS-15 (at the high end). Above this was the Senior Executive Service—the elite of all federal workers— few in number but heavily dominated by white men. The makeup of the lower grades became more populated by African Americans and women in a descending scale of pay and rank.[1]

Right at the outset there were alarming signals that the culture within the Office of International Activities was a far cry from enlightened. The most jarring of these came the day of my first weekly staff meeting after returning from maternity leave. Another African American employee, Franklin Moore, joined me at the meeting.

I arrived at the conference room ahead of Franklin where the other members of our section, who were all white, were already seated around a table. On seeing me in the doorway, my supervisor, Alan Sielen, called out to me.

"Come on in, Marsha. We'll make you an honorary white man so you can join us."

Those around the table burst into laughter. I was stupefied. I felt humiliated. I felt belittled. I felt attacked and not a little angry. Having never been in a similar situation, I was at a complete loss as to an appropriate response to the rush of emotions washing over me—but I also knew that a strong response could be catastrophic to my career. This was the first time I had felt the powerful forces that rise up inside a person subjected to prejudicial ridicule. There were opposing urges to hide and to fight, and a tremendous desire to yell that I knew everyone who was laughing was well aware of how difficult it was for me. Worst of all, I was keenly aware of the fact that I had blinked in this first encounter with racism at EPA. They had no dogs. They had no hoses or guns. But with only a single chorus of laughter, I had caved. Then Franklin Moore walked in and was welcomed with the same greeting. Only this time, I was seated among them.

I wanted to crawl under the floorboards and hide. Franklin's face went from open and kind to blank as he stood in the barrage of laughter. I wanted to run to him and hold him, but his face now bore the expression of a warrior. Franklin moved forward slowly and calmly, placing his briefcase on the table before addressing Sielen directly.

"Do you have any idea what you just said to me?" Franklin's face was stone. "Before you answer that, let me tell you something. I have traveled to South Africa extensively. I travel as a United States citizen. I carry a United States passport. Everywhere else that means something. But when I went to South Africa, a US passport wasn't good enough. I had to stand and watch some white fool stamp Honorary White on my passport before I could enter their country." He paused to collect himself. "I'll be damned if I'm going to let you do that to me here."

"Now calm down, cowboy. Let's not overreact here." Sielen's back was up.

"Overreact?"

"That's right, overreact. I know a thing or two about racism. I went to the same school as Jackie Robinson, for Chrissake."

Had I not witnessed it with my own eyes and ears, I would not have believed it if someone had told me that Alan Sielen had extolled the virtues of having gone to the same school as Jackie Robinson—or how impervious the man had been while everyone else in the room had been aghast by his going on and on about it. Franklin didn't even feign listening. He sat shaking his head in disbelief.

About a week later I went to Alan Sielen's office for my annual performance review. During my maternity leave, Paul Cough had been given a noncompetitive promotion, making him my supervisor, although Paul had neither my experience nor my educational background. When I mentioned this to Sielen, he was incredulous.

"There you go again," Sielen said, "complaining. Look, you're an intelligent woman. You know how to prevent pregnancy. How can you let yourself get pregnant and still expect to compete with a man?" He wasn't done. "No wonder people think you're hard to get along with. People around here are starting to think you're uppity."

"Uppity, Alan? Do you know what that means?"

"Yes, I know what it means."

"Who have you heard say that they think I'm uppity?"

"The other day Alan Hecht told me he thinks you're uppity."

Alan Hecht was Sielen's boss. He hardly even knew me.

I didn't think it could get worse, but it did.

"Marsha!" Hecht said furiously later that month when I walked into his office in the executive suite that he shared with Bill Nitze, a Clinton appointee and the assistant administrator of EPA Office of International Activities (OIA). "Why don't you just go down to the office of civil rights and file a complaint?" I wasn't sure if I was interrupting the rantings of a lunatic or if I was an invisible visitor in a conversation Hecht was having with himself. Hecht was yelling at the top of his lungs and banging his fist on the table he sat behind.

"Alan, what are you talking about?" I repeatedly asked. I felt ambushed, paralyzed, trapped. I couldn't get enough air in my nostrils, and I felt like I had taken a punch to my solar plexus. He was so absorbed in his own conversation that I don't think he heard me ask what was he talking about. I cautiously sat down, looking around the room for a window or any alternative route of escape, hoping that one of the secretaries would open the door to investigate the shouting and banging in Hecht's office.

"We didn't have these kinds of problems until *you* people came here," he said.

"What are you talking about? I have no idea—" I tried to interject, but his yelling intensified, his face getting closer and closer to mine. I could feel the heat radiating from his skin, and I could smell and feel particles of recently injested tuna. His eyes were bulging, and his face had turned a bright red. He had worked himself into a state of self-induced frenzy. Pounding the table, he yelled again, "Just file a complaint! I'm sick of this!"

"Stop shouting at me!" I demanded with equal force, using every nerve in my body to steady my voice. I stared him down. "Get out of my face," I said slowly but firmly.

He moved back, and I could finally breathe for the first time since entering his office.

"Marsha, one of your colleagues told me that you made an inappropriate comment at the last Africa team meeting. This kind of behavior will not be tolerated; do you understand?" His voice had started to rise again.

"Alan, you've got the wrong black person. Franklin attended that meeting, not me." I quickly picked up my notepad and headed for the door. "The next time you decide to call someone in and yell at them, I suggest you get the right person, because we don't all look alike!" Franklin was over six foot two, and a man.

I reached my office reeling from a cocktail of disbelief and anger. I contemplated calling the police but worried that my colleagues would consider this akin to treason. I would be seen as weak, bitching, and unprofessional—definitely a career ender. But what I knew without any hesitation was that I would never allow myself to be alone in a room with that man again.

I called Segun. It was difficult to tell him what had just happened between my sobs and hyperventilation. There was a pause, deep breathing, and then silence.

"Just come home, Marsh, come home."

‖‖‖‖‖‖‖‖‖

In 1993, backed by President Clinton, who was on record as a champion of women's rights and justice, Vice President Al Gore's former legislative director, Carol M. Browner, confidently strode into this environment as the new EPA administrator.

With Carol Browner's selection, an excitement came that I had not felt in the agency before. Early on we paid close attention to her every move for signs indicating what kind of manager she would be, what mattered to her, and how she would implement policy. A telling rumor circulated at the time: The new administrator had called a meeting of senior staff. Upon walking into the conference room, she was greeted by the clatter of men rising on her arrival. Browner strode to her place at the conference table, looked around the room, and seeing no other women present snapped, "There are no women department heads at this table. This is unacceptable."

So it was panache that swirled into the agency when Browner addressed the staff in the customary welcoming ceremony. Gone was the staid, Eddie Bauer, wing-tips-with-pinstripes style of her predecessor, Bill Riley. Carol had style, color, vigor. And where Riley was of the old school, blue-blooded Bostonian mold, Browner's pedigree—though not her airs—was far more modest. Her posture, the bored disdain she leveled at subordinates, gave the impression of stature. This was a woman who had been through the trenches, throwing elbows with the best of them. She thrived there. She was above all else confident, holding forth on her duty, first and foremost, to protect and serve the interests of the people.

There was a different atmosphere around her that left me unsettled—something bordering on contempt. Was it for the staff? Or was it some deep disdain for the process itself, which required cheerleading when she preferred bare knuckles?

Two quick appointments sent a stir through the agency. Both were department heads. Both were women. Carol Browner was signaling her support for women's place at the table. Yet I was not the only one to note another signal. Both women were white. By 1993 it was inconceivable that the vetting process for EPA department heads would proceed without considering racial minority representation for senior management positions.

Still, I found myself with a certain empathy for how lonely a place at the head of the United States Environmental Protection Agency might be for someone who had not cut her teeth on caviar. I could understand the toughness one might have to exude and imagined Administrator Browner's aloofness to be a sort of personal triage. Don't show them you hurt there—that's too vulnerable. Don't let them get too close—they'll discover your modest lineage. While everything about Carol Browner dripped with arrogance, I consoled myself with believing that sometimes the best defense is a good offense.

By this time I had already felt many early rumblings of a house destined to fall. It gave itself away with shivers and groans under the weight of social issues I thought had long since been put to bed—women's rights, civil rights, human rights, environmental conservation. All of these topics sent shudders through the agency like waves down a length of rope. Having come to EPA from the United Nations, I found this to be quite a departure from the progressive environment of the UN, where new approaches were not only welcomed but encouraged.

Yet even within what many people consider the most enlightened of all federal agencies, certain topics could raise red flags about one's career trajectory. One supervisor chastised me for raising issues of women's health at every possible opportunity. Don't we all breathe the same air? Drink the same water? Yes, we do, but we may not metabolize these elements in the same way, and with the standard for risk assessment being a 160-pound white man, as late as the 1990s women and children were left out of the protections of environmental toxicity assessments. Women who questioned this model risked being labeled angry or unserious or being called women's libbers.

Well before the arrival of Carol Browner, the writing on the wall about the direction for the agency was clear. After the watershed 1992 United Nations Conference on Environment and Development held in Rio, the EPA was coming to grips with the reality that it was no longer a strictly domestic agency. The Rio conference was the twentieth anniversary reaffirmation of the original UN Conference on the Human Environment held in Stockholm in 1972. The intervening twenty years had not been kind to the status quo of governments laying down the law behind closed doors.

It was anticipation of Rio, in fact, that in 1990 prompted the EPA's Office of International Activities to begin hiring a team of experts—which included me—to engage this new dynamic. EPA was interested in broadening its global reach and effectiveness via the NGO sector.

My experience, both academically and through my clinical work in the field for the UN, were well known within the agency. In fairly short order, my expertise and my familiarity with the lay of the land inside the UN were seen to fit the bill, and I became the Environmental Protection Agency liaison to the United Nations. The briefing for an upcoming trip to New York to propose collaboration between the two organizations was the first time the project's team was assembled in one room. This was also my first face-to-face interaction with Administrator Browner.

I had been working on an environmental impact assessment tool since my days in Africa, where as a UN program officer I had seen firsthand the ravages of drought and famine on the people of Ethiopia. Such a tool could provide the means to measure, monitor, and begin to significantly reduce environmental degradation. I suggested that we join forces with the UN to monitor environmental data with this tool. A nearly immediate global impact could result from such a program's implementation. My role was to move the project forward, arranging meetings between Carol Browner and the United Nations Development Program administrator, William Draper III. Draper was the son of a banker and diplomat, Yale educated, with family ties to the first venture capital firm on the West Coast. During his tenure with the UNDP, Draper oversaw nearly ten thousand international aid projects. Carol Browner and I worked to bring Draper's acumen to bear in implementing the environmental impact assessment tool. When that effort succeeded, I walked away knowing my work at EPA could have an impact. I had worked closely with the administrator, who had proved to be a skilled negotiator and a delight to work with.

||||||||||||

I was beginning to hear about preparations for the Fourth World Conference on Women that was to be held in Beijing, China, in September of 1995.[2] My contacts at the UN were abuzz, and several colleagues in other federal agencies were beginning to gear up for their participation in the summit. This seemed an ideal opportunity to leverage the agency's efforts with the UN within another dynamic, multinational constellation of highly skilled and motivated people. But when I ran the idea past my boss, he doused it with ice water.

"Why do we need to be limiting ourselves to a summit with women?" He was annoyed. Whether aware of it or not, he repeated the standard reasoning: "Don't we all drink the same water? Breathe the same air?"

I resisted saying, "There you go again, Alan." I had made a conscious effort to avoid any confrontations with him after my earlier "honorary white" experience. I was reluctant to press the issue, but I remembered how violated I had felt then. I vowed that the next time I would be prepared to engage him. "This is not a women-only issue, Alan. The women attending this event will be doctors, lawyers, wives, mothers. They represent families, entire communities, professions, and governments. Madeleine Albright will be there. Hillary Clinton." I have no idea why I thought this might impress him.

"Oh, come on, Marsha. You can walk down the street to have tea with them. We don't have the resources to be sending people halfway around the world for stuff like that."

I didn't even float Arundhati Roy.

⅏⅏

The agency employed thousands of dedicated workers, scientists, and specialists—quirky environmentalists who couldn't help but care about what science taught them concerning the perils facing the planet. Many worked with an insular focus, jammed anywhere a desk could be made to fit. But there were other scientists whose lifelessness showed no spark of curiosity was left in them. Whether impassioned or lifeless, they were all linked through networks and telephones and cables in clusters between offices where the managers presided. The eggheads I could deal with. They accepted convincing arguments. But the boys' club mentality of the senior management at OIA I could do without.

Most of them had attended state universities and were regular Americans. Some had fought their way in, inch by inch, bringing that mentality to management positions. But they were not the stuff of political appointees. Those positions were reserved for the best of the best— the best connected, the best groomed. Others were wired in politically. There was a certain backstory about America that was only taught at the best schools, understanding that all of this talk about human rights and justice was fine for the riffraff. It kept them occupied. But the real roots of power, the real source of wealth and its generation was the stuff of a certain ilk that was prized for its scarcity. The cream rises to the top, they liked to say. And liking so much how it felt at the top, they said it again: Cream rises to the top. Cream, and a lot of other stuff.

⅏⅏

"All of that women's lib crap, we don't have to take it."

Lillian and I looked at each other. I was walking past her desk.

"If it happens out there, that's one thing. Nothing you can do about that. But inside?"

It wasn't uncommon to hear a manager lay down the law just loud enough to be overheard. Lillian mouthed, Let's talk.

We decided to meet under the canopy of trees, as the wind tripped through the place and birds flew overhead, the susurrus of leaves sounding like applause. These were the things the Environmental Protection Agency was intended to protect, its raison d'être. These very things had drawn me here in the first place. But delight had not drawn us to the park that day. We were not drawn but pushed, by need of distance and privacy. The park was our safety.

There were active eyes and ears and tongues inside the EPA. Lillian didn't want to be overheard. She couldn't afford to have anyone repeat what she was about to say. I didn't understand it then. I had come into the agency as a GS-14. But Lillian, after years of hard work and diligence at the agency, had worked her way up from the secretarial pool to the equivalent of an executive secretary for a deputy assistant administrator. This was no small accomplishment for a woman with a high school education. It came with the perk of having her own office in the executive suite; though a small thing, it recognized Lillian's work ethic.

I was moving with purpose, my heels hitting hard on the walk. I saw Lil before she noticed me. She popped a pill into her mouth and threw her head back to swallow it, nodding to acknowledge me as I approached.

"You all right?"

After swallowing hard, Lillian's eyes widened. "Are you?"

Catching myself, I tried to calm down.

"My boss's been appointed an ambassador," Lillian said.

"Well, that's OK, isn't it?"

"For him. He's going to Europe." Lillian squinted at the distance. "They're sending me somewhere colder'n that. I'll be working for Pat Koshel." She looked back at me, rolled her eyes, and shook her head slowly and emphatically.

"Pat's a little quirky, but she's not going to overwork you."

Lillian looked at me with a smile. "I've never minded working hard." She closed her eyes against the breeze, head tilted back.

"I don't know what to say, Lil. I'm so sorry."

We wanted to be outside in the open, the wind riffling our hair. Yet Lillian's hands shook as she opened her purse and crossed her legs. It seemed difficult for her to sit still.

||||||||||||||

The Beijing women's conference was to be the largest-ever gathering of its kind, bringing together some seventeen thousand registered participants from some two hundred nations. Four thousand representatives of nongovernmental organizations and well over 3,200 representatives from the world's media convened in Beijing. State and other US departments were attending. So why not the EPA?

I decided to give Sielen another try.

I told him of the serious environmental issues surrounding the prevalence of breast, cervical, and ovarian cancer in women. It would really make sense for us to have a presence in Beijing.

"You are already so busy. The office has so much going on. I can't spare you."

I caught the hint: drop the issue—but I couldn't. Not with a woman like Carol Browner at the helm of EPA. I felt sure that Carol would support the agency's involvement in the women's conference.

||||||||||||||

I saw Carol going into the building ahead of me. I ran to catch up to her, just as she was stepping into the elevator. "Carol, have you heard of the UN's World Conference on Women that's coming up in Beijing?

"No, I haven't."

I told her what it was and that I would love to work on an EPA presentation about women and the environment that we could share with the world at the conference. "It would be a wonderful way for us to leverage our risk assessment work with the UN."

Carol looked at me and smiled. "Send me an e-mail and put an outline together and send it to my special assistant, Kim."

What a difference a woman makes, I thought.

As the elevator door closed behind me on my floor a few moments later and I headed toward my office, I had a sickening thought: I just

committed a major faux pas. Bringing this to the administrator's attention would be seen as an end run. There would be hell to pay.[3]

I immediately informed Alan Sielen that I had bumped into Carol
Browner, that we had talked about the Beijing Conference, and that the
administrator had asked for a one-page summary of how the agency
could benefit from participating. I expected him to hit the ceiling.

"Then prepare a one-pager if she asked for one."

I thought he was being magnanimous.

||||||||||||||

On April 28, 1994, in a memorandum to all EPA employees, Browner
named me the coordinator for the Beijing Conference and instructed
program offices "to identify environmental factors that disproportion-
ately impact the health and safety of women."[4]

It turned out that, once initiated, there was unprecedented excitement agency-wide for the summit—especially among EPA's women. I
was soon overrun by requests to include information about environmental links to women-specific cancers from all corners of the agency.
The task force collated research and became a clearinghouse for information on women's health issues.

Because of the ad hoc nature of the assignment, I had as-needed
direct access to the administrator, and we met frequently. It became
clear that I needed staff. EPA staff members were recruited from program offices and detailed to work on this project as part of what became
the EPA Task Force on Women. I soon got my first taste of magnanimity.

One US Preparatory Conference for Beijing was scheduled to be held
in Oakland, California.[5] EPA successfully fought to focus the conference's attention on the relationship between women's health and the
environment, so it became a kind of dress rehearsal for what we would
present at Beijing. EPA and the Department of Labor were the primary
sponsors. Administrator Browner asked me to coordinate the agency's
effort.

Around this time I became the target of small territorial skirmishes.
For example, complaints were leveled against me that seemed motivated more by questions of turf and ego than by propriety. One male
supervisor complained that now every time he met with Administrator
Browner, he was sitting behind me.

In the weeks leading up to Oakland, I learned with horror that the staff that had been working with me was no longer available. I appealed directly to Carol Browner, saying it looked to me like my efforts to pull the work together for the Beijing Conference were being deliberately sabotaged. I had to remind Alan Hecht, the principal assistant administrator in the office, that in an earlier memo Browner had already weighed in with a handwritten declaration—"I really want this!"—before they backed off and restaffed the Task Force.[6]

As she approached the podium at the Oakland Convention Center ballroom at the close of the conference, Carol Browner looked unburdened, wearing a collarless lavender jacket with striking black trim and smiling broadly as the applause flooded the room.[7]

"It is so wonderful," she began, "to be in a room with so many women." She smiled broadly at the hoots and claps bursting out in support. "I spend most of my days in rooms where I am the only woman in the room. And so to find a room that is filled with all of you who care so much, who have done so much, and are so committed to fighting the tough fight, to making the tough decisions, is really wonderful."

After thanking her colleagues at the Departments of Commerce, Energy, and Labor and noting the hundreds of hours the people at EPA had dedicated to the project, Browner said, "One of them has been involved at every turn, and we owe her a special thanks for her commitment and for her leadership for making this possible, and I would like to ask Marsha Coleman-Adebayo to stand so we can thank her."

Wonderful indeed.

At the end of the day, no one needed to know about the sniping. No one had to know anything beyond the information we had brought to Oakland. We had expanded the debate from traditional women's issues to examining how persistent organic pollutants (POPs) could trigger cancers in women. There was growing interest in POPs, the organic compounds that are resistant to environmental degradation and are capable of long-range transport and bioaccumulation in human and animal tissues and food chains.

The EPA's insistence on placing the environment on the Beijing agenda was not received without resistance from some colleagues in the international community. You environmentalists have convened in Stockholm and Rio. Now you are trying to make Beijing a conference about the environment, our detractors argued. I traveled to UN planning meetings in several countries advocating for linking worldwide increases of cancer in women with exposure to pesticides and toxic chemicals. Given the supporting evidence, women the world over rallied around the idea.

I drew enormous comfort knowing that Browner had shown real courage in going to the wall for women's issues. In fact OIA had approved a small grant to Women's Environment and Development Organization (WEDO), founded by Bella Abzug, legendary feminist and former congresswoman, to attend the conference to provide leadership from within the NGO community.

||||||||||||||

It shouldn't have surprised me so, but it did. There was so much work to do for Beijing that there was no way to get through it. I had vented some worry about it one day to Lillian Pleasant, and she had said, "Just give it to me. If all you need's the typing, I can tear through it in no time." Later I stopped by Lillian's office to see how she was progressing. There she was, language for the conference to one side, craning her neck the other way to read the small print in her dictionary. I could hear her reading a definition under her breath.

"Hi, Lil."

"Oh, hi, Miss Marsha."

"You don't have to worry about the spelling, Lil. I can run a spell check once it's keystroked."

Lillian looked up and smiled. "I was just trying to figure out what a hormone mimicker is. Just a habit. I never let a word slip past me before I know its meaning."

The spine of the book was frayed, the pages dark along the edges.

A day later, as I was walking back across the outdoor plaza to EPA headquarters from a Beijing preparatory meeting with Hillary Clinton at the White House, I heard someone sobbing. Peering around a pillar I found Lillian, crumpled in a corner.

"Lillian? Lil, what's wrong? What's the matter?" I went to her and put my arm around her.

"They've taken everything away from me," Lillian sobbed, "my dignity, my self-respect . . ."

"Oh no, Lillian! Nobody can do that. Come on. You're just tired." I hugged her. "Come now. Don't cry."

"All of my years of service, and she put me back in there with the girls fresh out of high school."

"What? Who did that?"

"My supervisor did that," Lillian wept. "Oh, Lord! I feel so bad."

She was trembling. "Lil, you have to go home. Rest."

"If I go home, the office will mark me down as AWOL, and that will give them another excuse."

"Lillian," I said, "I know you have high blood pressure. You're very upset. This cannot be good for your health. Please, you must go to the health clinic." I helped her to her feet. "Look, we can take this to someone higher up, but you have to take care of yourself first."

"You think I should file with Civil Rights?"

"I don't know, Lil. Why don't you talk with your minister? Fortify your spirit and then decide."

Lillian nodded. "I know, I know. But don't you think—"

My cell phone rang. "That's my husband. I've got to go." I held Lillian's face between my hands and then patted her eyes. "Promise me that you will go to the health clinic?"

Lillian nodded her head yes.

When Lillian stopped by my desk, it was two hours later.

"What on earth are you still doing here?" She was trembling worse than before.

"They told me that I can't leave until I finish my work."

"Well, didn't the clinic give you something to release you?"

"I gave it to them! They still won't sign off on me leaving."

"OK, Lillian. It's OK. You need to go home. Call your doctor, Lil. Take care of yourself. That's the most important thing."

Still later Lillian came back. "I can't get anyone to sign off on my leave."

‖‖‖‖‖‖‖‖

The weather was nice enough not to need coats. With my Leo blood, it's always so much better when the weather doesn't require coats. I had let the warm breeze get the better of me and loitered as long as I could before resigning myself to entering the building. With the scent of fresh air on my clothes, things seemed so different. It was a good hair day, a day to enter the office feeling pretty.

Inga stood up when I came in, tears streaming down her face.

"Inga, what's wrong?"

"It's Lillian." She dropped her head, her shoulders quaking as she spoke. "She died this morning getting ready for work!" Inga looked up again. "I didn't want to tell you over the phone."

I looked at Inga.

"It was a massive heart attack."

I turned and walked out of the office. As I passed the cubicle Lillian had been demoted to, I stopped and looked at her desk. Two just-so stacks of paper stood in neat piles between the phone and her dictionary, the pages smudged along the edges like an old deck of cards.

The woman who had taken such pride in discovering buried meanings between its pages was now dead.

The Fourth UN World Conference on Women, Beijing: "Call Me Bella"

"This is Bella Abzug from WEDO. Where the hell is our money?"

My close friend and schoolmate from MIT, Dr. Pamela Ransom, had been my contact person with WEDO. I had been in touch with Pam constantly since beginning to coordinate and collate as much data as I could find nationwide inside the agency about linkages between environmental pollutants and their health affects on women. Pam was WEDO's breast cancer expert. She told me what a hoot Bella was to work for.

The EPA had committed to funding a small grant to WEDO in advance of the Fourth World Conference on Women. I was the point person between the two organizations and had been trying to ease the dollars out of the managers' clenched fists ever since they had agreed to fund the program. I'd been a long-distance admirer of Abzug's since first hearing a wonderful tirade she had loosed on Richard Nixon, but I never dreamed I'd be on the receiving end.

"Oh, hello, Ms. Abzug."

"Only my enemies call me Ms. Abzug. You can call me Bella."

"Thank you, Bella. Yes. Well, as you probably know, the agency has protocols and procedures in place, and I have been assured that the funds—"

"Look, cut the bureaucratic bullshit. I didn't just get off some boat. It's been over three months since the money was green-lighted. We've got a lot of work to get done here in advance of the Women's Conference. We can't do it on a wing and a prayer. Pam tells me you're a straight shooter. What gives?"

I was trying to play one of my feminist heroes? She was close to reaching through the phone and taking my eyes out. I liked her immediately. "I'm sorry, Bella. I should have known better. The truth is, there is a raft of testosterone in this place that thinks women would be better off if we remembered who walked on the moon. They've been stonewalling the money, and, quite frankly, I haven't been able to get anywhere with them."

"Well, why don't I call Carol Browner then?"

"That's probably an excellent idea. Carol has been very supportive of the conference and would hit the ceiling if she knew what was going on. If I went to Browner directly I'd be cutting through channels. But you have every right as a concerned citizen to call her."

"Thank you, dear. I'll do that."

Click.

It didn't take long.

"Well, Bella was Bella!" Pamela called from WEDO the very next day. "Bella talked to Carol Browner yesterday," she said. "My understanding is that we're back on track."

I was impressed. Bella had lived up to her reputation as a no-nonsense, driven powerhouse of a personality.

When the UN agreed to include the environment as part of the Beijing Conference agenda, Bella called me to congratulate the EPA team. "Finally," she said, "we have an EPA that gets women's issues. But," she asked, "is EPA really prepared to take on the chemical and pesticide industries?" Before I could answer, she continued, "Whatever. I'm looking forward to fighting them in the trenches with you when we get to Beijing."

The next sound I heard was the dial tone. It would take some getting used to Bella not saying good-bye before she was on to her next battle.

||||||||||||

Beijing. I had grown up calling this great and ancient city Peking. Second only to Shanghai, Beijing was the hub for the People's Republic of

China, not only as the landing point for foreign travelers but also as the center of Chinese culture, education, and politics. With massive walls and ornamental gates that date to the first millennium, Beijing straddled the architecture of modern Western cities and the pagodas of its own ancient roots. Its massive art treasures and universities burst with history, tradition, and time.

I arrived a month prior to the conference to work with Pam on the WEDO presentation for the NGO portion of the conference and to network. I delighted in Beijing's people, food, and abundance—literally, with over twelve million metro Beijingers—and in the people's generous warmth and spirit. Having lived in New York City, I was no stranger to population density. But Beijingers' hearts weren't barnacled over in the way I felt New Yorkers' hearts were. There was a simplicity in Beijing that seemed to link the urban dwellers to their rural roots.

The preparation for the conference was in some ways Kafkaesque. I felt aligned with the masses of common people who, but for their appearance and language, were close spiritually to their counterparts whom I'd grown up with in Detroit. Yet here I was, planning for conferences that would include First Lady Hillary Rodham Clinton; Dr. Madeleine Albright, US ambassador to the United Nations; Geraldine Ferraro, former vice presidential candidate and congresswoman; and Donna Shalala, secretary of health and human services. There had been several meetings in the White House like the one held on August 7, 1995, with Mrs. Clinton and some or most of the others attending. Yet for all the photo ops, beaming smiles, and colorful phrasings, I had yet to find a comfort level with any of the US officials that was even remotely reminiscent of a feeling I'd associate with home.

Of all of the women in the higher echelons of Washington society, there was only one who reminded me of family. She was rough, crude, loud—traits that would have had my mother flinching—and she always wore a big hat: Bella Abzug. Somehow, for all of her foibles, Bella reminded me of family.

Perhaps it was because she had been voted out of Congress and didn't run with that crowd anymore. But even as a congresswoman she had always been a renegade. Or maybe it was that, unlike so many others who had whisked through the revolving door of government only to later take up lucrative positions in lobbying firms, Bella Abzug had turned her immense energy and passion toward a different lobby. She lobbied for the people, cofounding WEDO and focusing her energies on what had long been her passion—women's issues, coupled with a fervent desire to identify the linkages between environmental toxins that were manufactured by infamous multinational corporations including Union Carbide and Monsanto and the women-specific maladies of breast, uterine, cervical, and ovarian cancers.

It wasn't until much later that I would realize that these diseases were more than a theoretical pursuit. I learned that Bella Abzug herself had survived a brush with breast cancer—she had skin in the game. That went a long way in explaining why she didn't have time for niceties, why she could be so brusque, why she didn't say good-bye when she hung up. When you have cancer, there is no such thing as time to waste. Bella was always, enthusiastically, in the moment.

But at the time, all I knew was that, despite her sharp edges and penchant for cursing that at times could rival the soundtrack of a Mississippi men's room, I was drawn to Bella Abzug's humanity.

When I met her in person in Beijing, I was expecting the barnstorming intimidator I had seen so many times on television, so animated and forceful while addressing a crowd, pivoting from side to side behind a microphone. But those images were from twenty years earlier. Though not a tall woman, Bella had always come across as imposing. In China, I didn't expect to see her so aged—and never would I have expected a wheelchair. But there she was when first I laid eyes on her, the signature hat like a canopy over a now-diminutive Bella Abzug.

But one should not conflate Bella Abzug in a wheelchair with Bella being wheelchair bound. Far from it. Beijing became the culmination of the body of work she had amassed since departing Congress in 1977. As she recorded in a journal from 1972, the Beijing Bella still spent plenty of time "figuring out how to beat the machine and knock the crap out of the political power structure." After leaving Congress, Bella had traveled the world and championed the cause of women and children in developing countries where human trafficking, forced prostitution, brutalization, and the blackballing of women from governmental office were still prevalent.

Hobbled or no, Abzug was in the thick of the independent and parallel Non-Governmental Organization Forum to the official UN Women's Conference held in Huairou, China, from August 30 to September 8, 1995. Convened in conjunction with the official conference, the NGO

Forum boasted upward of thirty thousand participants. Even physically diminished, Bella still possessed the fire that had impelled her over two decades earlier to introduce a resolution against the Vietnam War as her first act—on her first day—as a freshman congresswoman from New York.

I would see her in action on the floor, where, unlike other NGO representatives, Bella had gained entry to the conference by virtue of her connections within the assembled governments and the UN, and by the sheer force of her personality. A high-ranking US official had been resisting efforts by the NGOs to get language included in the platform that was critical of corporations operating with impunity in the developing world. Abzug took this middle-aged woman aside on the conference floor and lit into her with invective, in a voice that Norman Mailer had once said could boil the fat off a cab driver's neck. I couldn't read the headline in the Chinese newspaper the next day, but it would not have surprised me if it translated: US BUREAUCRAT BLUDGEONED BY WHEELCHAIR-WIELDING ABZUG.

"Marsha," Bella confided in me later, "I was sorry that I had to take her on in public, but what the hell! I can't stand it when our government blatantly sides with the chemical and pesticides industries. These people never think anyone is going to call them on it. Well, she got an earful from me. Didn't I ask you earlier if EPA was really going to side with women over the chemical industry?"

It was with particular pride that this emphasis appeared in the "Platform for Action," the final document released from the Women's Conference in Beijing, as Section K. It became a benchmark for women's health all around the world.

During the plenary session of the UN/NGO Forum on Women, Bella addressed women from around the world.

"We are bringing women into politics to change the nature of politics, to change the vision, to change the institutions. Women are not wedded to the policies of the past. We didn't craft them. They didn't let us." Wearing a deep purple suit and signature hat, also purple, with an embroidered gold band, Abzug held forth with calm, with humor, with force. "We are challenging all corporations to play by the rules and all governments to ensure that the rules are fair."

"Women's rights are human rights, and human rights are women's rights!" declared Hillary Clinton. This quote would be repeated over and over in the media and would do a great deal in bringing women's issues to the forefront of discussion. They would also be remembered as instrumental in Clinton's stepping out of her husband's shadow. But for me, her words echoed the insight that recognized a political leader as someone who identified the inevitable and then got out in front of it.

The poor women, the nameless women, the women who had witnessed the ravages of war, who had seen their daughters carried off to be raped or sold, the women who could very well face caning for having come as individuals to Beijing—the acts, the deeds, the small rebellions and affirmations of those women touched my soul.

And before I knew it, it was time to leave.

||||||||||||||

As with any extended trip abroad, coming back stateside took some getting used to. There was the immediate joy of reuniting with family, smelling my children's hair, feeling their skin. There was reconnecting with my husband, Segun, and rediscovering what I love so much about him. There was so much to tell. But there was also jet lag, weariness, and guilt that I could measure the time I was away by how much Sina and Sade had grown. I felt the need to curl up in bed and sleep for at least three times as long as I had been away, but of course that wasn't possible. I was back inside the agency the next day.

Everyone who travels across several time zones knows the queer place the next few days or even weeks can represent. There are stories shared about it being worse to travel east to west than vice versa, and sympathy offered for the returning traveler, in her strung-out state. Perhaps the most beneficial byproduct of extended stays in other cultures is the perspective it gives you on returning: a Tocquevillian view of America and Americans. You notice the joylessness of the American street—and how most Americans walk around inside a bell jar.

It was clear on my arrival back in the agency that the men who had taken so much exception to the pertinence of the Women's Conference had not spent the month on more pressing matters at the expense of punishing me. On the latter they'd been busy. It didn't matter that I had gotten commendation letters from Hillary Clinton and Madeleine Albright. It didn't matter that Administrator Browner had singled me out for praise about my performance as the front person or that the conference had been a raving success.

On my return I found that my office had been the target of small acts of sabotage: weeks-old lunches left on my desk, newspapers flung on the floor. My desk had been ransacked. I put all this down to arrested pubescent development. Boys, as obnoxious as it is, will be boys. But I discovered too that I was the only program officer in my branch not given an annual bonus. The two secretaries and I, all black females, were the only employees excluded. This was no longer prankster-level behavior. This was serious. They were hitting me where they knew it would hurt, and it was clear from the snickering I heard through the grapevine that everyone in my branch knew it. They were trying to humiliate me, and they were sending a message about just exactly who was really running the shop.

"I have decided to give you an 'exceeds expectations' rating, Marsha," said Paul Cough, my new boss.

"You must be kidding, Paul! Everyone—including you—knows that I deserve an 'outstanding.' Everyone in the government is applauding my leadership in Oakland and Beijing—the First Lady and Madeleine Albright! Even Administrator Browner! We got the environment successfully placed into the women's agenda, negotiated language all over the world, and helped organize a major conference on women and the environment where the administrator delivered the keynote!"

"My decision is final. I have the backing of both the Alans and Bill on this," he said, invoking the name of Bill Nitze, the assistant administrator.

I studied him. He seemed to be enjoying our exchange. "Paul, you and the Alans may be in agreement, but I know Bill cannot approve of this action. You and the Alans have tried to sabotage this effort from the very beginning. You have never supported the idea of putting agency resources behind a women's health agenda."

"You're wasting your breath." He was almost smiling. This must be what it would have been like to have an older brother taunt me. "By the way," he added, as though it were an afterthought, "I've also decided not to award you a bonus. You simply didn't cut the mustard. Too many of us had to help you with the conference."

"Paul, I will go to the administrator's office with this. This is patently unfair and unjust."

"We all know how much you like to hide behind the administrator, but the conference is over. You're back here with us now. We'll see how fast Browner comes running to your rescue with the TV lights off."

But I was just strung out enough from the Women's Conference to take it to them like I'd told Paul I would. This might not have been literal foot binding, but it was that and more symbolically. I had learned early in life from my mother that letting a pressing issue fester only compounds the problem, increasing tensions and making one's ability to confront the perpetrator more difficult. The anticipation, my mother often said, is the ordeal. I decided to bring the issue up with Assistant Administrator Bill Nitze.

On hearing my protest, Nitze was almost comically dismissive. "Oh, come on, Marsha! What do you care about a bonus? It's a pittance. What difference does it make? You couldn't even buy one decent dress for the increase that would give you over an entire year."

"That's not the point, Bill. I worked hard over the last year. Very hard."

"Yes, you did, and it has been duly noted."

"Wait a minute, Bill. What do I look like to you? I worked hard. Harder than any of the people who were given bonuses, and without a single acknowledgement."

"Marsha, Marsha, Marsha." I watched his eyes glaze over in front of me. "These types need their merit badges," he said while gesturing with his hand like it was a whiskbroom. "That's what's important in the bush leagues, but not to you. You have a future here. That's your reward."

"Bill, you promised me you'd give me a promotion when I got back."

"Well, Marsha. I know I said that, but I've decided to change my policy on promotions. No one will get promotions this year. There is work to be done that will require sacrifices. This is public service. 'Ask not what your country,' etcetera, etcetera." The whiskbroom again, but with a tumbling motion.

"Give me a break, Bill. No one is going to get a promotion? You just promoted Paul Cough without any competition. Maybe that's the way white men promote each other. Was I not supposed to notice that? Then, you know what, Bill? Keep the high-profile, eighteen-hour-a-day assignments. Give me a nine-to-five like everybody else. That's what I want."

"You're just jet-lagged, Marsha. And it's awful. You'll feel better about it in a week." He looked at me over his glasses. "Now, if you'll excuse me?"

"I filed a complaint, Bill."

"What's that?" he said, not looking up from his desk. "Oh yes, the complaint."

"The complaint, Bill. I mean it."

"Try to be serious, Marsha. A complaint? Where did you learn that, in civics class in high school?"

"No, Bill. I learned it in Beijing. I am dead serious. I'm not taking it anymore. Eighteen-hour days, I'm constantly disrespected, and the men who used my office as a dumpster get bonuses! I spent too much time learning about the systemic poisoning of women on every level imaginable to just waltz back in here and tolerate the same old, same old."

I lay in bed later that night thinking—or not really thinking so much as having impressions wash over me. Impressions of the feel of the air in China, tingling with hope and anticipation. Impressions of the stifling atmosphere inside OIA. I kept coming back to Bella and what she had said at the plenary.

"Some wonder how I have kept going for so long and how I manage to remain optimistic. . . . Conditions for women on factory floors did not change. Women died in childbirth and in their homes. Hunger gnawed at the bellies of millions. The world went on, in its downward spiral we all know all too well."

Bella was speaking not only as a woman but also as a mother. That's what it was. A mother understands the risks and dangers surrounding her children that the men at OIA did not understand. The thought of one of them engaging the Beijing women was laughable. In the disquieting presence of so much hostility in the agency, I took comfort in Bella's pluck.

"In the face of so much pain," she had said, "I remain an incurable optimist. I am fueled by the passion of the women I have been privileged to meet and work with, buoyed by their hope for peace, justice, and democracy. . . . I wish each of you well and sustainable optimism for the days ahead. Never underestimate the importance of what we are doing here. Never hesitate to tell the truth. And never, ever give in or give up."

Much later the world would learn that a doctor had told Bella's daughter that anyone else in her condition would have died by going to that UN Conference on the other side of the world. Bella's health was failing; her cancer had returned. It would have been perfectly understandable for her to seek peace and rest far from the rigors of the Beijing Conference. But in sickness, as in health, Bella Abzug took comfort in the fight, providing guidance and grace to women everywhere, including me.

Ultimatum to Public Service

A burst of waterfront air. Fish. A sense of the sea. I walked across a lawn toward the bay and then past the boat vendors with steamed shrimp, the oceanfront boats, and the restaurants with waterfront windows. It was not common practice for the assistant administrator, the president's eyes and ears at the EPA, to do lunch with a member of his staff. This must have something to do with how they had treated me after the Women's Conference in Beijing, I thought. I'll bet he's going to weigh in on the complaint.

The Yacht restaurant was actually a converted boat. It sat moored in the river and moved with the waves. It was a favorite for many in the office, but I never liked crossing the gangplank, which was only wide enough for one person at a time. I didn't like the feel of the ropes, the sway. Looking down, I could see the iridescence on the water slapping against the wood, the dark buildup on the hull, bobbing up and down with all of that strangeness. The interior design consisted of paneling with nautical clocks, compasses, and spools of rope to capture the feel of a yacht, but to me the restaurant felt closed in. The blue napkins and blue tablecloths were too confining. I felt a little queasy.

Why me?

Bill Nitze served under Carol Browner. He ran my office. But saying that he worked under Browner would be like saying Genghis Khan was involved in a few skirmishes. Nitze hailed from DC and Colorado political royalty. A landmark building in Washington and a battleship bear his family name. Given the flying elbows I had caught in the agency after the Beijing Conference, I thought at the very least he would be conciliatory, even if the flak had come from much further down the food chain. I was by then beginning to believe I could expect elbows from a certain caliber of career civil servants—but not at the upper levels and certainly not at EPA. Administrator Browner herself had been nothing but respectful and supportive of me. She'd gone to the mat for me against some of these same people. Bill Nitze knew what I had done for Administrator Browner. He knew what I had taken for it. And everyone had heard about it when I'd filed my complaint.

Nitze was the face of the Clinton administration on international environmental issues and the agency I was still dedicated to. It was going to take some order of magnitude to resurrect the agency in my eyes after being called uppity by senior management, but I still wanted to believe that EPA was the good agency.

"I did the work of three people for Beijing, Bill. And when I got back, what did I get for it? Nothing! No raise, no promotion. Except for harassment, I got nothing," I said to Bill.

After the humiliation of that experience, I was going to control this conversation with the assistant administrator for a while. If he wanted something from me, he was going to have to work for it.

"Against my better judgment, I'm going to order the bisque," Nitze said. "Yes, yes . . . eighteen-hour workdays, daughter on the floor beside you, Chinese in paper bags and cardboard boxes. I know, I know."

"Come on, Bill! I've had it. I won't stand for this."

Nitze had heard just about enough. "Look, Marsha, I know you've had problems in your branch. Forget about them."

"You just don't get it, Bill."

"Marsha." He leaned forward. "You are the perfect candidate. We've all seen what you have done and what you can do. Eighteen-hour days, and you're still productive. The administrator has noticed. I have noticed. You are really quite gifted." He sat back in his seat as the waiter brought our lunch. "You did a magnificent job in Beijing. Carol couldn't be happier. I couldn't be happier."

He lowered his face toward the bisque, closed his eyes, and wafted the steam rising from the bowl toward his face as he breathed in deeply. "This smells wonderful. I'm very excited about what I have to tell you.

The vice president himself wants the best person we've got for a commission we're heading up in South Africa. It will be fashioned after the model we established with Gorbachev and the implementation of glasnost.

"This isn't some Sunday brunch at the Smithsonian, Marsha. This is the big leagues. I need someone to make me and the agency look good, and that someone is you."

He took a first taste of the bisque, closing his eyes and breathing in through his nose. "Oh, this is really quite impressive. Almost Nantucket."

I was trying to clear my head from the jet lag and anger and insults. But I was listening.

"The transition of power in South Africa from the apartheid regime to the government of Nelson Mandela is under way. His deputy president, Thabo Mbeki, and Al Gore are going to head the Gore-Mbeki Commission to look at ways the United States can assist them in that transition. I am going to make you liaison to the White House. You will be coordinating policy between Washington and Pretoria. There is no one else with credentials even close to yours. The person we have there now can't touch your Africa background. You went to MIT. And Barnard, for Chrissake!" The way he buttered me up, I worried there wouldn't be any left for the bisque.

"Do you know what you're asking me to give up after Beijing? The agency is committed to doing serious investigative work into environmentally related illness in women—that's huge. And the work is just getting started. I made commitments to the women I worked with in Beijing, Bill. I've never seen such courage. I feel very strongly about the work we've begun."

"Think about the connections you'll make in the White House, Marsha. I'm giving you your stepping-stone. All of those marches you were in for Mandela, your dissertation on Steve Biko, your previous work on the continent . . ." He looked up from his soup. "You will be in the room at a pivotal moment in history."

"I was treated like dirt when I got back, Bill."

"Forget that stuff, Marsha. I'm offering you the career opportunity of a lifetime. Think about it. Even if you only take it for the Rolodex you'll have afterwards, you should do it. It's that good. Executive Secretary to the Environment Working Group Marsha Coleman-Adebayo, PhD

MIT, Africanist. In two years you'll know every important person in government." He leaned forward. "How do you think it will feel to be sitting in the room as a senior policy analyst for the United States while Nelson Mandela hammers out a new government?"

Nitze knew where to land his punches. I had marched against apartheid in front of the South African embassy every day for over one year until Nelson Mandela's release from prison. But for the time being, I stuck to my guns.

"No. I've heard promises before, Bill. You know what I hear now? I hear a six-hour time difference between Washington and Pretoria. I hear getting up at four in the morning to make phone calls to South Africa before their offices close. Why me?"

"Because it's right up your alley. Because you're perfect for it. This is a new day in South Africa, Marsha. You could take an active role in that. What better face for a new American relationship with South Africa than Dr. Coleman-Adebayo?"

No matter how deeply I looked into Nitze's eyes, I could not see Nelson and Winnie Mandela pumping their fists triumphantly through the streets of Cape Town after Mandela's release. I saw oil rigs. I saw a family fortune that owed a lot to its coziness with a succession of US government administrations. I saw invisible doors magically opened by pedigree.

"I don't know, Bill. I'm really invested professionally with the Women's Task Force, to say nothing about emotionally. Plus, I just spent the better part of a year away from my kids. There's a part of me that's thinking that I may just want a J-O-B like everyone else around here. Especially after the way I was treated."

Nitze stiffened. It was my turn to listen. He patted his mouth with his napkin while leaning in so close I could smell the bisque on his teeth.

"Let me put it this way, Marsha. There is one job and one job only that you can do for me that will make me happy, and that is taking on the assignment as the executive secretary for the Environment Working Group." He looked over the top of his wire-rimmed glasses. "You"—he paused and looked around the restaurant—"will do it with the same enthusiasm that you brought to Beijing, and you will make me look as good in South Africa as you made Carol Browner look in China." I realized that Nitze was authorized to speak for the administration.

He sat back in his chair, glutted.

I sat chastened. "So, has this conversation been authorized by the president and the vice president?"

"Take a couple days." His attention was strictly on his lunch now. "I'm sure the proportions of this will occur to you when you come to your senses."

Message delivered.

iiiiiiiiiiiiii

I still had not responded to Nitze's lunchtime ultimatum. I knew that he expected my answer within a week—but I sensed there was something wrong. Why the urgency for me to take on this assignment? And what about the Women's Task Force?

I called Dr. Clarice Gaylord. We had developed a relationship at the agency, and Clarice had been my mentor. She was the highest-ranking black woman at EPA. Clarice was astute in her assessments and a good listener.

"I am really torn. On the one hand I can't believe what an opportunity this represents to make a difference in South Africa. On the other, with all the work we did on the Women's Conference—I don't have to tell you how important this effort is. The last year in my kids' lives is never coming back. And you know Nitze reneged on his promise to promote me. I'm being used, Clarice. I don't know what to do."

"I just don't think you have a choice, Marsha. If your AA wants you to do it, you have to do it. If you don't, it will be your first step out of the office."

iiiiiiiiiiiiii

My Beijing jet lag may have messed with my sleep, but the thought of being in South Africa as a senior policy analyst during the transition to the Mandela government had visions of sugarplums dancing in my head. The position that Nitze wanted me to accept would be during the implementation of the Freedom Charter, the ANC's equivalent of the US Declaration of Independence, that had been so instrumental in sealing Mandela's fate three decades earlier when the ANC had insisted that South Africa's natural resources belonged to the people and would therefore be nationalized. This accomplishment would be the crowning achievement of the liberation struggle and would have far-reaching ramifications for the entire continent, still struggling to emerge from the oppression of European colonialism.

By 1995, the power struggle between the departing National Party government and the emerging ANC was already well under way, with the integrity of the Freedom Charter in the crosshairs. Vice President Al Gore would be heading the US delegation to the Binational Commission. Gore's counterpart, Deputy President Thabo Mbeki, was already leading the much lower-profile economic negotiations between the ANC and the National Party, and had stripped much of the nationalization language out in favor of a neoliberal agenda that was more in keeping with his beliefs as a self-described Thatcherite.[1] Economics, lacking the raw passion of the political power struggle, did not draw the attention of the ANC leadership or the media. The Freedom Charter had been writ on the hearts of the masses of black South Africans since its public reading in Kliptown in 1955. Despite enduring massacres and forced exile, and even after burying so many of their children, the majority of South Africans still clung to the hope that the charter would be realized.

My husband, Segun, never objected to anything that made me happy or satisfied me professionally. Even though my new position would mean more travel and distance, I knew he would support me. But the thought of more extended trips away from my children ripped my heart up.

||||||||||||

I called Bill Nitze when the morning came.

"Bill, I'm calling to let you know that I will accept your offer and work on South Africa. But I must be very direct with you. As an Africanist, I am well versed in US policy in Africa. We have been on the wrong side of history for a very long time, Bill. I will not participate in anything that will have an adverse effect on South Africa or its people."

"Marsha," Nitze said without hesitation, "don't worry. This project has been painstakingly designed to support the new Mandela administration. I'll get a letter over to Agriculture Secretary Glickman in the morning.[2] Welcome aboard."

The Gore-Mbeki Commission: The Sound That Freedom Makes

South Africa is renowned for many wonderful things—coastal beaches, mountains, gold, diamonds, mineral fields, amicable golfers—and one monstrosity: apartheid. The colonial governments of South Africa, from that of President F. W. de Klerk all the way back through the British domination, to the eighteenth century, when the Dutch first "discovered" South Africa's riches—and then attacked the indigenous people to get them—have been masterful at showcasing every one of South Africa's characteristics except apartheid. The Dutch were armed with the modern technology of European warfare. The Africans were armed only with traditional hunting gear. But the most lethal of the Europeans' weapons was their belief in the white man's burden to civilize African people and the corresponding brutality they therefore felt justified in inflicting upon the local people, without regard for their humanity or any worry about consequences.

The Africans never stood a chance, neither in battle nor in appealing for justice to an outside world that didn't speak their language or see the need to. Even as colonialism was being dismantled piece by piece in the rest of the world, it managed to thrive in South Africa well past the midpoint of the twentieth century by the conceits of a culture that called itself "civilized" and its masterful use of propaganda. The fascist regime had its allies. President Ronald Reagan supported the apartheid government, he explained to CBS News, because it was "a country that has stood by us in every war we've ever fought, a country that, strategically, is essential to the free world in its production of minerals."[1]

Toward the end of another long flight, this time diagonally across the Atlantic, I looked out the window as we approached the lit coastal areas near Cape Town. I tried to give flesh and fiber to the odious word, *apartheid*, that had been so much a part of my being, my thoughts, and my prayers, knowing that what I was about to encounter would not be abstract but tactile. Apartheid would no longer be something I read about, marched against, and risked arrest for. It would be the people, the vast majority of the population of South Africa, who had remained hidden to the rest of the world—by the design of an occupying government and with the collusion of most of the world's other governments.[2]

||||||||||||

The members of the US delegation to Gore-Mbeki were now in Pretoria, settled into our individual rooms at the hotel. We were all going through our various home remedies for jet lag. For some this meant sleeping. For others it meant working until they dropped. But I headed to street level to get a sense of the lay of the land. It must have been the Leo in me, because like a cat, I needed to wander my new home range. I also needed something to eat.

The hotel doors slid open like glass eyelids on the face of a city that could have been Marrakech, Buenos Aires, or any other metropolitan resort city with signature high-rises, designer clothing stores, and traffic. The thought occurred to me that since I had flown in a different direction than for my journey to China, this trip might provide the corrective needed to right my circuitry, which was still misaligned from that marathon, even six months later. I was anxious to stretch my legs and hungry for food, for American food in particular. I'd have plenty of time to experience the local cuisine, but my needs just then were primal. I sought therapeutic instant gratification. I decided to take a stroll through downtown Pretoria in search of my American birthright. It couldn't be far, but I'd still get a chance to clear my head and case my new surroundings.

My experience in other metro centers elsewhere in Africa had been that the veneer of the modern city was only the makeup that covered the abscess of the more common living conditions. One never needed to travel too far to see how the greater population lived. But Pretoria was designated a "whites only" area during apartheid, and blacks had been required to carry passes that severely limited their access to the city. Nestled among Pretoria's Western amenities was the familiar red sign of a Pizza Hut. Perfect. Fast, American, and greasy.

I was beginning to feel better already when a commotion broke out. A black man ran out of one of the little shops, racing in a direction that would bring him directly in front of me. Another black man burst out of the shop in pursuit. The first man slowed, twisting his torso around, raised a gun, and shot the second man. Then he sprinted out of sight. The second man fell to the ground like a duffel bag. Thump. No grasping his chest. No, You got me! Just thump. He was lying facedown.

My stomach was in my mouth. My heart was pounding. I felt light headed. The fallen man's arms were immobile at his sides. His face had hit the pavement hard, with nothing to break his fall. His legs still rose and fell alternately at the knees as if he was running to his death in slow motion. The legs rose and fell, but the motion got weaker, until they were only twitching.

I ran into the Pizza Hut.

"A man has just been shot! We need to call the police!"

The inside of the place was like every other Pizza Hut I'd ever seen. The white man behind the counter craned to look out the window where the shot man had fallen.

"The police will come" is all he said. He looked at me like it was just another day and I was just another customer deciding between the pan pizza and the salad bar.

"You don't understand. A man has been shot!"

"I understand," he said, pointing. "People are already coming. The police know."

There were people squatting beside the fallen man, kneeling on either side of him, calling his name. One was a woman who was holding his shoulders, one arm across his back, saying something into his ear. She straightened herself, holding her head in her hands, and screamed, throwing her arms out to her sides.

I hurried back outside and began taking pictures with the camera I always carried in my purse, thinking they would need photos. A police car pulled up behind the fallen man. Two white officers got out of the car, in no hurry; they looked in all directions while standing beside the car with the doors still open. I could see the man's legs continue to writhe in a slow rhythm; he seemed to be in pain. But the officers showed no interest in him. One of them began to draw a chalk line around the shot man's body while the other watched him and the perimeter. When the outline was finished, both officers stepped to a patch of ground beyond the man lying in the road to stand in the shade offered by a little tree, smoking cigarettes while the fallen man's legs moved with less energy and less frequency. The officers gestured and talked and had finished their smokes by the time an ambulance came.

The driver and attendant got out of the ambulance, walked to the back of it, and pulled out a gurney that they wheeled behind the fallen man's feet. One of them snapped open a sheet and draped it over the man's body before the two of them lifted him onto the gurney and then tucked the sheet in under his body, working opposite each other. When they were done they wheeled the gurney into the ambulance, climbed back inside the cab from opposite sides, and drove away. The police left directly behind them.

In the shock of the moment I had forgotten to tell the police about my pictures. They would not have been interested anyway. The silhouette of the shot man continued to bleed where he had lain.

I didn't have a clear sense of where I was in this place and whether this was the norm or the aberration. As terrible as what I had witnessed was, I didn't want to be the next victim. Franklin Moore saw me hurrying back into the hotel lobby.

"Well, I've seen some seriously jet-lagged people in my day," he joked, "but I don't think I've ever seen anything quite like how you look."

"Franklin! You cannot imagine what I just witnessed." I blurted out the story, shaking uncontrollably.

"Girl, you need a martini." He took my arm, and we headed toward the lounge. "You have to be very careful here, Marsha. The crime rate here makes South Central Los Angeles look like Disneyland. It's out of control."

I dumped the drink down my throat. I didn't care what it was.

"Whoa. I'll buy you another drink, but you've gotta be careful with those things too." He ordered a vodka martini. "You know why vodka martinis are like breasts?"

I gave him a wry smile. "No, Franklin. Why?"

"Because one's not enough, and three are too many."

He could have made millions on his laugh. It was full-throated and completely unself-conscious. I had known Franklin, who also worked in EPA's Office of International Activities, since our first days at the agency, and I knew there was nothing more to his joke than a good-hearted attempt to break the pall. Whether it was the laughter, the vodka, or both, I was feeling much better.

Franklin took a sip of his drink, shaking his head. "The Afrikaners haven't had to worry much about the conditions here until recently. And even now their only worry is PR. They don't give a damn what happens to the people here. If you control the media and access, nobody knows what you're up to. It's only been in the last decade or so that the world has gotten a glimpse behind the walls and has begun to see the full extent of the horror. Mandela is going to be in way over his eyebrows. It's going to take a miracle for anyone to put even the slightest dent in the conditions here."

Bill Nitze and Kathy Washburn, from the Department of Interior, joined Franklin and me in the lounge. Kathy was a tall, striking woman with all the airs of nobility, who, when I first met her, seemed almost standoffish. Her speech had a thoughtful and slow rhythm, with a hint of English aristocracy reminiscent of the Roosevelts. She turned out to be among the dearest, sweetest, and warmest people I knew. A human touch was just what I needed.

"I heard about what happened, Marsha. I am so sorry." She touched my forearm, nodding toward my drink to ask if I'd like another. "How are you feeling?"

"Like two martinis. Thank you. A third would be too many." I looked at Franklin. He nearly repeated the joke but caught himself. I saw him chuckling into his glass.

"You do need to be careful, Marsha," Nitze offered.

Kathy changed the subject. "I am looking forward to the program," she said, not so much pulling me aside as suggesting it. This is always a good tactic when two men and two women are together in a group. If we played our cards right, within a couple of minutes we would clear Nitze's overwhelming presence and be free to talk woman to woman. Franklin, bless him, knew what we were up to.

"So, Bill," Franklin began. He looked at me and then dragged his eyes slowly back to Nitze as a cue. This was our chance. "I was wondering what your assessment of the situation in Alexandra is."

Kathy and I had scuttled out of range by the end of his question and took an additional few steps to be safe. As Nitze launched into what would be Franklin's ordeal, Franklin lifted his glass, first to the bartender to indicate a refill, and then toward Kathy and me to indicate we owed him one. He turned back toward Bill with an almost painful smile on his face.

"Marsha, I cannot tell you how awful I feel that this happened to you. You must be sickened by it. Maybe if we talked about the agenda it will take your mind off it."

"I've been telling myself it could just as easily have happened in Detroit. But you're right—let's see if there's anything we still need to do for the commission tomorrow. Thanks."

Kathy was thorough if she was anything. She had pulled the elements together on the commission masterfully and was in full command of every detail. This would be a grand-scale event to showcase its significance. The hall itself was beautiful with monumental proportions that were symbolically equal to the political significance of relinquishing power to the South African majority. "We have the vice presidents' opening statements," she said. "If we can identify what the majority population needs and get that into the conversation without getting steamrolled by the Afrikaners, I will consider it a major accomplishment." The unity government of Mandela had left the old-guard Afrikaners in positions of power, and they still heavily influenced the agenda.

"You know, Kathy, there might be a way to drive the point home if we can give ourselves the flexibility to leave the convention hall and get out and wander around with everyday people."

She liked the idea and was quick to expand it. "You are so right. They control the environment inside the building where everything is out of sight, out of mind. They can drive any point home they want to there. Why don't we keep one eye open for opportunities tomorrow to see if at least you can get away? I won't be able to, but if you had a few hours in the late afternoon, maybe that would give us an edge."

We returned to the men. I could see by the level of his drink and his sobriety that Franklin had merely been nursing his. He drew his eyes across Kathy and me slowly. "And did you ladies have a nice chat?"

||||||||||||||

I hadn't been able to shake the execution. And, while I managed to sleep and keep myself busy enough to keep from thinking about it, still it hung in the air like ozone, invisible until it gets close enough to cloud the view and color it with its undeniable presence. All through the opening ceremony and speeches, through the prayers, and especially through the long speeches the two vice presidents made, I could hear the sound of chalk against asphalt, more abrasive than against a blackboard.

It was so much easier to concentrate when we broke into groups and had face-to-face time with real South African people. Their smiles, their diction, their clean enunciation of language, with its heightened inflections, was a refreshing break from Al Gore's mechanical and staid presentation. Now, as the day fell out of the bombast and pomp, I settled into the back seat of a car driven by Tami Sokutu, who represented the South African Department of Water Affairs and Forestry and was a delegate to the commission. During a pause in the breakout session, I had asked him if it would be possible for someone to take me to a township so I could get some other perspectives on the problems facing the people there. "I can take you this afternoon," Tami said without hesitation.

I let Kathy Washburn know that I had made arrangements to visit a township. "Good! Leave as soon as you can," she said.

I told the others in my group that I would be taking a tour of a township and excused myself, returning to my room to change into jeans and a T-shirt, and then met Tami in front of the hotel. I knew him to be a dear, sweet man, perhaps because of an upbringing by parents who had managed to escape the maw of this craven land, or maybe just by the fluke of personality. Whatever its source, he not only drove, he drew me out of my despair and into the life and vitality of South Africa.

We were on our way to find a counterpoise to the preordained— if designedly obtuse—outcome of the Gore-Mbeki Commission: the development of South Africa's vast emerging market for American goods. This is what always drives policy, no matter the public utterances. There had been ample talk and press about a new era dawning, of freedom from the scourge of apartheid and establishing a government for the people, but behind the policy were American-owned companies lined up to sell turbines and engines and vehicles and devices—not necessarily because they were needed, but because that's what they were selling. There wasn't much on the list for the sprawling wastelands in between the Westernized centers.

During the break-out sessions, it was the basic things that were mentioned time and time again, from every township, every region, every pair of pleading eyes. Water. Sanitation. Food. Medicine. Netting. There was no cry for high-tech gizmos for the multitudes. With rates of hunger, disease, and infection that would dismay the civilized world, the high-tech focus was difficult to justify.

Ascertaining basic environmental needs was my specialty. I knew from experience in Ethiopia that the apparent modernity of the cities and the conveniences offered tourists were no indication of the broader—and dire—realities confronting the masses. I needed evidence of what the general population was up against. I hoped Tami could provide a more accurate overview than what could be found in a posh downtown Pretoria conference room. Tami Sokutu made it his duty to deliver me into an area with exactly the kind of evidence I had asked for.

IIIIIIIIIIIII

"Look at these fortresses, Marsha. These are the white people's homes." He was referring to the compounds on the high ground where the Afrikaners lived. "Walls, fortifications, armed guards, barbed wire, dogs. They look like personalized prisons from here. But inside there is nothing but the best in furnishings, food, decor. Any black man who approaches them has his life balanced on his head inside a glass of water. They will shoot you for breathing their air."

Tami was a well-educated and polished man. He understood what his people needed and focused his attention and energy on that. Tami's car became my classroom. I was taking a crash course in apartheid from a man with an advanced degree in life on the pointed end of the apartheid stick.

"The people who live inside these encampments know they would be ripped to shreds without such measures," Tami continued. "It is not that the people here are savages—quite to the contrary. We have significant numbers who are fully aligned with nonviolence and Black Consciousness. It is just that there are so many people living in dire conditions."

Tami's fight against the apartheid regime was in his DNA. Although he was too young to have witnessed the early galvanizing events himself, he had grown up in South Africa and lived with all of the indignities of that environment, surrounded by the daily conversations, outbursts, demonstrations, and testimonials of thousands of people who had witnessed those pivotal moments themselves. The Sharpeville massacre, the Soweto riot of June 16, 1976. There is a famous photograph from that day of a young student, fourteen-year-old Hector Pieterson, who had been shot and was being carried by another student in a desperate attempt to save him while Hector's sister ran alongside. Hector was the first to die that day. Tami mentioned this photograph with no apparent emotion.

"It became the face of apartheid. A horrible, wrenching tragedy. Hector was the first to die. But there is also murder by memory." He looked at me quickly. "You have heard the phrase? We remember someone to forget them. The same thing is happening in the United States to the memory of Dr. King. 'I have a dream,' but not a word about 'Beyond Vietnam.' The same thing happens here routinely. In the official reports on the Soweto uprising twenty-three people were killed. 'People'—not children—as was the case. In truth they were young students. Over six hundred killed, with four thousand wounded. It takes time and diligence to bring the truth to light, but in the meantime the official account becomes accepted as the truth. Murder by memory.

"Here you see the Afrikaners with their swimming pools," Tami pointed out. Then, pointing to a shack on the other side of the road, "and there you see one of the better shelters for kaffers."

"What does *kaffers* mean, Tami?"

"Forgive me, Marsha, but I'm afraid *kaffers* means the same thing here as the word *nigger* means in America."

There was a science fiction quality to all of this, except no reassuring narrator appeared suddenly from outside the frame to remind us that this was what it would be like if everything went horribly wrong one day. Everything had gone horribly wrong. The countryside itself, the expanse of valleys and mountains, the air, was breathtaking. It was late afternoon, and the angle of the light heightened the colors and warmth. To absorb all this in any other setting would be spellbinding. But these impromptu shacks—I hesitate to call them shelters because of their flimsy, mishmash appearance—that were somewhere between tents, boxes, chicken coops, and coffins, were strewn everywhere along the drive. Where the land was fruitless and desolate, you found the townships. The prime locations—with trees, water, and loam—were home to the Afrikaners.

"What can you tell me about Black Consciousness, Tami?"

"BC? Well, I can tell you the history. I can tell you the current state of affairs. And I can tell you the likely future of the movement. Why don't I start with the future, because that we don't know." He looked at me and smiled. "It is very likely that within a decade the hope we see flashing its lightning in the imagination of the people will have become reality. We are seeing the transformation Steve Biko described, where the black man no longer sees himself as an extension of a broom or a machine, like it was under the whites. Now it is a black machine."

"I wrote my dissertation on Steve Biko. He reminds me of one of my civil rights heroes, Malcolm X."

"Oh, yes. Biko's reach has been tremendous around the world. It has been tremendous here. You and I would not be in this car, you would not be at this conference, Al Gore and Mbeki would not be discussing how the EPA can support the Mandela government, but for Steve Biko."

Biko had challenged blacks to emancipate their minds in order to fully participate in the liberation movement, whatever that would take.[3] It would not be possible to take up arms against apartheid if they were still bound to the oppression burrowed inside the word *boss*. This idea was the tectonic shift that sent tremors through the foundations of the apartheid regime and signaled the beginning of the end. Like all seismic quakes it was most deadly nearest its source, and Steve Biko was the epicenter. The Afrikaners looked up from the seismograph record, nodding their heads: Steve Biko must die.

Alexandra:
The Sacrifice Zone

Tami pointed out subtleties in the landscape that were invisible to me. The places where water ran and where there was none. We slowed from wheeling down a highway to being one of many things moving slowly through the bends and over the bumps in the road. What was endless vista on leaving Pretoria was now narrowed and obscured by a clutter of people, animals, and miserable, misshapen materials tied to trees or poles or nothing at all in what looked like a neighborhood of the absurd. The farther we got, the slower the going among clots of black Africans who looked at us like we were mad. And then it was like a bat had flown in the window and gotten caught in my throat. I was gagging, struggling to breathe, before I realized it was the smell, thick and heavy, of animal waste, human waste, rotting things.

"Oh! This is terrible, Tami! What is that smell?"

"Apartheid, Marsha." Tami's face was contorted, his mouth pulled down at the corners. "This is the smell of apartheid."

He pulled the car as close to a bush as he could get it and turned off the engine. Opening his door, he got out and looked around with his back to me before bending his head back into the car. "Welcome to Alexandra."

My throat was tightening as I got out of the car. My eyes were watering. I was trying to collect myself so I could engage the people here, while trying also to suppress my gagging. As I came around the back of

49

the car, Alexandra hit me, but this time right between my eyes. Nothing—not Ethiopia, not images of the Holocaust—nothing could have prepared me for this. Everywhere, in every direction, for as far as I could see, there swarmed people and animals and filth. The road was a slurry of a dark, mud-like substance that was a mixture of dirt, sewage, dung, and God knew what. I opened my mouth to say something but stopped because I could taste the stench. There were children playing, standing, sitting in the sludge. And flies everywhere, generating a steady hum like bicycle tires on pavement.

I felt like I was wrapped in cellophane, hot, unable to breathe. My skin felt prickly. My eyes were about to explode. I had an instant, intense headache. It smelled like someone was burning rubber very nearby, but the odor was thicker, sweeter, and stifling. I watched a woman gather water from a rut animals were standing in higher up the slow incline.

"Tami, how can this be?"

Tami said nothing. He looked at me.

There were close to a half a million people strewn here. And an equal number of animals—goats, dogs, fowl, pigs. Carcasses. The caked stains on the sides of the shelters showed what happened in the rain. It all washed downhill, mixed, swirled, and worked its way into every corner and crook. The prospect was staggering.

"There is no running water. No electricity. No sewers in many parts of this township." Tami was talking more to himself than to me. "There are no stoves. No sinks. No windows. No screens. There is nothing."

"My God, Tami! I just want to cry!"

I had never felt so powerless in all my life. I was standing in an incubator of death and disease. The scientist in me was no match for this. Yet almost instantly, I adopted the same mechanical functioning of everyone I saw mired in this open wound. I moved like I didn't believe. I asked questions like I didn't know the answers. What do you use for cooking? Where do you get your water? What do you do with your waste? Where do you go to the bathroom? What do you do with the bodies? An hour passed like an hour on the cross. Eyes looked toward me but not at me. My questions got trick answers. I get my water from puddles. I shit on the ground by the puddle. I eat on the floor with the rats. I sleep on a mat with the animals. I bury my own in the ground.

This was inconceivable, the more so because of the scale. No flood, no fire, no quake, no pestilence had brought this into being. This was the work of man. These people were as maggots to the apartheid regime. Their lives had the permanence of mist. I was so angry when we turned the car around and headed back that I was speechless. I was so crushed by the weight of it all that I had no tears. We were almost halfway back. Not a word had passed between us.

I remembered, as if inside the glass of my window, a young Ethiopian woman's beautiful, chiseled face, deferential, dignified, emaciated. Bowing slightly, she cradles a small, wrapped bundle. Of course, I will help this woman. She smiles, holding her baby forth. Reflected behind her, Tami's arms cradled the wheel as he drove.

I fold the dirty blanket back on a little girl. Laughter heaved in and out of the springs with the road jarring the van. I braced my arm against the dashboard. The woman. Her bundle. Of course I will help them. The road bumped and wound beneath the stars.

"I've seen this before." I looked at Tami. "Alexandra is a sacrifice zone."

Tami did not reply. His eyes blinked. The road churned in the headlights, Tami watching, listening. A voice entered the silence like the rumble of the road. It sounded like my voice.

"My great-great-grandmother rode away from enslavement in a place like this. On a road like this. Only her vehicle was a mule-drawn wagon. She rode inside a coffin with a corpse."

Tami watched as he listened.

"Can you imagine? Mile after mile, her uncle drove the buggy, flinching with each bump, fearing it might waken the dead. All the way out beyond the sounds of the plantation. All the way into the sounds of the woods and the breeze that almost sounded like freedom—before the clatter of hooves came with voices and whistles and whips. They tumbled them out on the ground. They tore her from her clothes. Then led her back naked for all to see."

Tami looked at me. "But she had heard the *sound* that freedom makes."

ıııııııııııı

I woke up wondering how I had slept. I woke up fearless. In another world I might not call Kathy Washburn at six in the morning, but the rules of etiquette held no currency here.

"They have to see Alexandra, Kathy." She was already awake. "It is a nightmare. There is no other way to describe it. There is no way to get Nitze to act on it without him seeing it."

"I'll make the arrangements, Marsha. Thank you."

I was so expecting opposition, I said it again. "He has to see it, Kathy. He just has to."

"I understand, Marsha. I'll make the arrangements." There was a pause. "Good morning, Marsha. I won't ask how you are."

I called Franklin Moore.

"Yeah! Let's take Nitze and Kathy Washburn. It's even worse than you describe. You can't get it all in an hour. Let's let them walk around in Alex for a day. Let them get the feel of it in their bloodstream. That's what it's going to take."

When I got in the shower, the soap stunk, even though I had just taken it out of its wrapper. My hair stunk. The water stunk. It was like I had just woken up from a bender and the thought of a drink made me want to vomit. I was suddenly aware of odors, of scents, of manufactured scent especially. I took a clean towel from the bar and smelled it. It had the chemical odor of institutionalized laundry. As I dried my hair, I placed my nostrils on the flesh of my biceps. The masking scent was even here. The room itself had the pine-scented, chemical-tinged fragrance of the sort of industrial plant that churns out oceans of camouflaging agents to help Western culture ignore its own odor and its human scents. But after Alexandra, I was hungry for the scent of the human, of healthy, clean humans. No chemical masks today. No lotions. Estée Lauder was persona non grata.

⦙⦙⦙⦙⦙⦙⦙⦙⦙⦙⦙

"We have a driver and a van." Kathy's eyes were knowing. "We can fit seven comfortably."

"Thank you so much, Kathy. I cannot overstress the importance of this. There is no way for any of us to grasp the full measure of what we're facing short of seeing a township."

"I can't say that I'm looking forward to it." She turned to me and smiled. "But I feel your urgency. We can take Bill, and Franklin, you, myself. The driver makes five."

"And Tami Sokutu. His background is crucial."

"And Tami Sokutu. That will be enough." She noticed I had nothing on my plate and smiled. Her gentleness was home. "Eat something, dear. Even if it's only some fruit."

IIIIIIIIIIIIII

Glaringly absent from any discourse on the township question had been the view of the Afrikaners. One official weighed in with me on our proposed outing to Alexandra. "What's the purpose? My family has been here for three generations, and I have never set foot inside a township. Alex is a wild and brutal place. I don't have to go there to know that." He was clearly annoyed by and dismissive of the suggestion. "Certainly you have places like Alex in the United States. I fail to see the point in going."

I considered this man, his posture and disdain, took a deep breath, and then looked him straight in the eye. "Not in my lifetime. Not since slavery has the United States had anything close to the conditions I observed here yesterday. There are nearly a half million people huddled together in squalor, with no running water, sanitation, or electricity. This township, if we are delusional enough to call it that, exists to feed industry, with victim after victim that you, and people like you, have been only too willing to sacrifice."

"You are free to move as you like about the country. But of course there are security risks."

"Understand, sir, that if you are threatening me, you are threatening the United States government."

He looked at me with a smile.

"We need to see the conditions on the ground in this country, not just the view from the clubhouse. If we're going to get that other perspective, we need to do it before we leave here late tomorrow. We are prepared to take those risks."

IIIIIIIIIIIIII

Franklin Moore made a point of positioning himself close to Bill Nitze in the van. Franklin had been to South Africa before as an agricultural economist and had a good handle on the situation. He had been to townships before. This was Franklin's opportunity to drive his points home to Nitze conceptually before the shock of the township shut Bill down. En route, Franklin also vented the steam of his passions. I positioned Tami Sokutu so he could address the rest of us. I had one ear trained on Franklin as he worked on Nitze.

"This is the fruit of bad policy, Bill. This is what air conditioners and high-rises and waitstaff conceal. There is a tangible emergency here. We must address the plight of these people."

All through the tour Nitze remained quiet and expressionless. His face was a clock with no hands. His eyes moved, his legs worked, but there was nothing to read. We got out and walked, stretching. He looked at the people, their surroundings, the inside of some of the homes, but said nothing.

Kathy was stunned and on the verge of tears, repeating one phrase into the hand she kept cupped over her lips. "Oh dear."

I avoided eye contact with her.

Tami knew a surprising number of the people there. He talked and laughed with them, instructing the driver to stop so he could get out and shake hands with friends, hugging them, trading stories. We all walked along with him and passed a bank of chemical toilets, with the van following close behind. The blue plastic stalls were knotted with material that looked like seaweed. The stench was appalling. Runoff trailed away into the furrows people gathered their drinking water from.

"This is totally unacceptable." Franklin walked slowly around the portable toilets. He was no longer addressing Nitze directly but was speaking his rage. "These facilities have not been cleaned in months. Maybe years. There are enough toxins right here to wipe out the East Coast. And there are babies here!" His voice faltered.

"Imagine this." Tami sweeps his arm across our field of vision. "After days of torrential rain, these toilets overflowing, mixing with animal feces, mixing with barefoot children. Look at the marks on the buildings there. That is how high the water rises—all of it sweeping into the homes, the tents, the huts, the sleepers. Dysentery and cholera kill even the strong. But the weak?" He pointed toward a corner that had escaped our attention. "It all leads there. Hundreds. The old. The children. Every year. In the rainy seasons hundreds will be carried there." He was pointing toward a graveyard.

Franklin's fist was pressed against his lips. "Get us out of here," he said to the driver without looking at him.

It was a long drive back to Pretoria. Franklin Moore kept hammering away. I was sitting next to Kathy, who was by the window watching the distance. "Oh my God, Marsha. Oh my God." I touched her on her forearm. "I had no idea." She shook her head. "Oh my God."

⁜

This time it was Kathy Washburn calling me early.

"Marsha, we haven't much time and a lot of ground to cover today. I just wanted to make sure that I thanked you personally for opening our eyes to the situation in the townships before we both get buried in details. I also think it's very important that we have some actionable items we can introduce as policy at the meeting today. Some kind of tangible outcome that will begin to impact the people we saw in the township yesterday."

This was music. "Wonderful, Kathy! You're so right. We have environmental assessment tools and protocols for clean water, air, solid waste, that we have a lot of experience with. We could incorporate them into a program easily."

"I'm thinking something beyond the standard fare, Marsha. Something more personal than that. I could not get those hopeless eyes out of my head last night. Hopeless. If we can really engage the new environmental leadership in an intensive program that they could internalize, they could bring skills with them wherever they are needed. The idea of study tours is already on the table, and I am really going to push it."

"I love it, Kathy. That is exactly the kind of thing to give us the most bang for the buck. We already have inroads with the best institutions in the country. We could put together a really effective program in no time."

Kathy, Franklin, Tami, and I were confident the trip to Alex was worth the gamble, not so much because we thought the brass had been moved to altruism, but because the money required to fund a study tour was less than a drop in the bucket. There would be plenty of money for the business brokers and then some. They would have to leave us some crumbs. The beauty of our plan was that even crumbs could go a long way.

We were now at the end of the commission's stay and had gotten the tour into the final report. Equally important, Franklin Moore had agreed to work with me at the conclusion of the study tours to provide the US Agency for International Development (USAID) funds to address the environmental and health crises in Alexandra. There was no doubt in my mind that we were on the right track and that we were going to make a difference. The decision on the makeup of the final South African contingent that would visit the United States was still six months away. The battle over the tour's participants could wait until we returned stateside. The working day was over. It had begun early, and I was exhausted. I decided to go back to my room and catch a nap.

Who Are You Calling a Necklacer?

Bill Nitze had asked me to join him. He was going to be meeting with Bantu Holomisa to go over some final things before the ambassador's reception scheduled for later in the night that would mark the end of this phase of the BNC. We found Holomisa in good spirits and enthusiastic about the progress that had been made between his ministry and the environment committee. When business was finished, the conversation turned more personal, with Nitze asking Holomisa about his own history and the role he had played in the antiapartheid struggle. Holomisa mentioned his upbringing in Mqanduli in the Eastern Cape. "There was not any question of what I was going to do with my life so long as apartheid was in place."

Bantu Holomisa was a statuesque general of heroic proportions among black South Africans. Holomisa was not just physically beautiful, he was regal in gait, in stance, in gravitas. He was imposing and punctual to a fault. As organized a man as had ever lived, Holomisa's life and security had depended on his being where he was supposed to be. He was also a man of his word. It was reported that, after having buried his own daughter, he spoke at another funeral that same day because he had previously made the commitment. In South Africa, when Bantu Holomisa wanted something done, it got done. In his deepest being, Holomisa was a man of the people.

He did not go into any of the details of what he had done to become the head of state in Transkei, of having overthrown Prime Minister Stella Sigcau in 1987 when Holomisa was a brigadier in the Transkei Defense Force. He did not mention anything about how the South African resistance had staged its missions from Transkei or that this had played a crucial role in weakening the apartheid regime.

"There was more than enough for me to do," he said with a smile. Nitze nodded, seeming aware of Holomisa's modesty. "I am well aware of your father's influence," Holomisa said.

Nitze smiled, saying his father, Paul Nitze, cast a long shadow indeed, but that women in his family were also descended from stellar stock, his grandmother having been the first woman congressperson elected in New York State. Nitze's uncle, he went on to say, had established the Aspen Institute and Aspen Skiing Company, both instrumental in the establishment of Aspen, Colorado. Almost embarrassed, Nitze looked at me, saying that it must be difficult for me not knowing my heritage because of my family's history of enslavement.

"Au contraire," I said. "I know quite a bit about my heritage from the vibrant stories that have been passed down through the generations. My great-great-grandmother was enslaved as a house servant in Georgia. She actually went to great lengths to save any glass that was broken in the household." Her frugality seemed to please Nitze. "She stayed up nights and ground the glass with a pestle she kept squirreled away and then added it to the salt in the enslaver's saltshakers."

Holomisa broke into laughter, clapping his hands. "Marsha, I would have loved your granny."

|||||||||||||||

After dinner, we left for the ambassador's reception, which was being held in a ponderous national park with stone buildings, nestled in an oasis of flowers, plants, and formal gardens. One could easily forget South Africa's bloody history there. An otherworldliness haunted the place. That night it was the nexus of the new South Africa. All of the characters were in place: the outgoing and angry Afrikaners; the newly invested ANC government officials, their faces fresh as the night's full moon. Some of the guests would be so passionate about their beliefs that they would refuse to speak the names of some of the others. People on both sides, who only a few months earlier would have waited in the bushes outside to pick off many of the attendees with relish, were now plucking hors d'oeuvres off silver trays hoisted on white gloves carried around the room for everyone to taste. But I knew Americans, who were oblivious to any but their own perceptions and goals, would look at the plight of the black South Africans and shrug, saying, So what? It's time to move on. The thought of impending disaster was so gripping I began to shake.

Franklin was always the freshest and best dressed of any he traveled with. His resilience and energy were unsurpassed. "Well, look at you," he said, stopping in his tracks to take me in. "And where has this radiant queen of Africa been hiding? Girl, you need to take a nap more often. And I love those earrings!"

I was delighted that Franklin was there to have fun. We were washed by the sweet scent of hibiscus and linden and bathed in moonlight, lanterns lighting the way across the grounds marked with elegant canopies housing banquets of the most delicate, sumptuous, and impeccable American and South African cuisines. There were people everywhere, guests and staff, in clusters. Tami Sokutu saw me, Kathy, Franklin, Bill, and Bradford Brown, a marine biologist on the US delegation, and joined us, addressing Nitze first.

"How are you this evening, sir? Before I forget, I would like to extend an invitation to all of you to come to an after-party that I am hosting. It will begin after the ceremonies here are completed and will be much more informal and relaxed. We would be so happy if all of you could attend." Tami shook all of our hands and excused himself, returning to join his colleagues.

Nitze watched Tami go. "I really like that man. And do you know why? Because he knows how to speak good English. You can tell a lot about how civilized a person is and how dignified they'll treat their guests by whether or not they use proper English."

"You know what, Bill?" Franklin was pissed. "You should realize that, as a black American, I learned everything I know about hospitality from my grandmother, who had a third-grade education. I have never been more insulted in my life! Particularly coming from an American from our culture who can stand here and say they believe there is a relationship between the ability to speak proper English and being hospitable to friends and guests."

Bill excused himself and asked Kathy to accompany him.

Franklin watched them walk away for a moment. "Keep your boss away from me, Marsha!" He said it without looking at me. He was seething. All of his earlier joy was gone. "Good English!" His knees buckled as he laughed. "Good English?" There was a boyish playfulness in his affectations.

It was so good to see such buoyancy. Franklin was never far from humor—or pain.

We had reached a side entrance to the room where the reception would be held. Franklin, a tall man, surveyed the room.

"I don't know who organized this invite list, Marsha." He was standing on his toes. "But whoever it was either has a fantastic sense of humor or delights in throwing cherry bombs into crowds. This ought to be v-e-r-y interesting," he said with his eyes wide. "Come on. I need to find me a drink!"

As we entered the hall, he spotted a station where someone was fixing drinks. He pointed to it, with his eyebrows raised. "That's me. I won't be too far if you get into trouble."

On his way to the station he stopped to chat with a small group of people. "Hello, my name is Franklin Moore. I'm here as part of the environmental contingent from the United States."

The teams of people, though not in uniforms, collected in knots like people will do when the only others they know are the people they came with. If it had not been for newspapers and television it would have been impossible at first glance to tell the big cheeses from the small fries. Or perhaps, had I been from South Africa, I would have known which huddles represented the big names from this country and continent. Apart from the officers with epaulettes, the room was full of uniforms unfamiliar to me, some South African, some Western. The only certainty was that there were no common folk in the room.

Both the evening and the trip were coming to a close. Everything was winding down. Mercifully, the speeches would soon be over, the protocols would have been met. I had opened as many new avenues as I could have hoped. I had seen the face of the humanitarian crisis. I had strengthened my bond with Bantu Holomisa, whom I was coming to see as a major force in the political future of the disenfranchised. Holomisa was a key figure, willing to confront US policy makers who were not accustomed to dealing with an African leader who could not be compromised.

I was looking for Franklin again. I wanted to be standing next to him during the speeches. I knew I could use his sense of humor once they began. I saw him standing in a small group of people including Secretary Hazel O'Leary, Ambassador Bill Richardson, Nitze, and Ken Thomas. I hadn't seen Ken, an attorney, since meeting him at the initial Gore-Mbeki conference in Washington. Ken was a handsome, slender man, with dark eyes, hair, and mustache. His kindness and grace were endearing.

By the time I made it over to them, Ken had disappeared. Bill Richardson and Bill Nitze were talking along with Franklin Moore and Peter Mokaba, the fiery leader of the ANC Youth League, who was said to have coined the phrase, "Kill the Boer, kill the farmer," at the April 1993 funeral of assassinated South African Communist Party leader Chris Hani. Peter was the confidant of Winnie Madikizela-Mandela. As I approached, Mokaba shook hands with Richardson, Nitze, and Franklin and then blended into the crowd.

Nitze turned to Richardson. "Do you know who that was? He is one of the lions of the African unity movement. You know, a necklacer."

Necklacing was the practice, performed by some in the resistance movement, of singling out a black informant, placing a tire around his or her neck to immobilize the person's arms, and then lighting the tire.

Richardson's eyebrows jumped, and Franklin almost jumped out of his shoes. "How can you say that, Bill? How can you accuse someone of murder in front of the US ambassador to the UN?"

"I was merely trying to give the ambassador a sense of the flavor of some of the people here."

"The flavor! Flavor's fine, Bill. But that's a very serious accusation, and you need proof. You tell me one documented instance of Peter Mokaba ever necklacing someone. One credible report. One verdict."

Before Bill could respond, there was the tinkling of silverware tapping crystal, a signal to gain everyone's attention. Franklin saw me, turned away from Nitze, and headed my way, shaking his head. The closing speeches were about to begin.

While the vice presidents were making their final remarks, an Afrikaner I did not know approached me. "Excuse me. Before you leave I wanted to make sure you know that we have seen your interference with the program."

I was stunned. I had watched this man from a distance, standing with a group of other Afrikaners, all of them sneering, looking down their noses at the black South Africans.

"You are so biased in favor of black South Africans you cannot possibly represent our concerns. We have a story also. I want you to know how displeased we are and that we have registered our displeasure with Deputy President Mbeki. It is my fervent hope that you will take to heart this information I'm giving you in confidence before you come back here again on your crusade."

The man turned and walked away before I could respond.

There was nothing for an Afrikaner like this man to be worried about. Former President F. W. de Klerk, dubbed "the smiling face of apartheid" by some ANC members, had secured the economic future of people like him during negotiations with Mandela. De Klerk was the same man who, it was reported, in the dying throes of apartheid, stepped up the savagery against black South Africans and armed everyone he could find who was opposed to the ANC.

Naomi Klein states in *The Shock Doctrine* that the economic costs of these negotiations were severe. All apartheid-era civil servants were guaranteed their jobs. Those retiring would receive lifelong pensions. Going forward, 40 percent of the government's annual debt payments would be committed to the country's enormous pension fund, the vast majority of the beneficiaries being former apartheid employees.

With breathtaking insolence, the man who had just walked away from me could count on the people of townships like Alexandra to pay his pension. Even more, white businesses that had wallowed in profits from black labor during apartheid would be free of the obligation to pay reparations—while the victims of apartheid were legally bound to pay retirement to their former victimizers.

The actual cost of all of this would be to forfeit the well-being of future black South Africans for generations to come—in denial of health care, education, and environmental protection—to the peace-at-any-price euphoria of those new postapartheid days.

||||||||||||||

The previous day had been my first day off in ten straight, and it could hardly be called a day off, except that I did get some much needed sleep.

Aside from that, I had to pack for the late-night flight out of Pretoria, strategize about the implementation of the study tour, and consult and commiserate with colleagues. I had thought I might take in the wonders of the city, but there simply wasn't time.

I wrestled my luggage out of the hotel to a cab, and a strong man flipped the unwieldy cases into the trunk while I climbed into the backseat, trying to get my left arm back into its socket. The flight was timed to arrive in DC as though to add our passengers to the morning traffic flow. An eighteen-hour flight is close to my definition of hell. With secretaries of the Departments of the Interior and Energy, several SES staff, the media, military, and security all clamoring to get their seats, their drinks, and their sleeping arrangements, I was one of the peons. There were protocols and a chain of command. At that point, I'd have settled for anything short of sleeping in the landing gear.

Even Air Force Two couldn't accommodate some of the egos wedged in the fuselage. It seems the vice president would not be traveling with us. Thus, a big, comfy, king-sized bed awaited the senior officer on board. The contenders were Secretary of Interior Bruce Babbitt and Secretary of Energy Hazel O'Leary.

"Look. I've got meetings tomorrow, I've got work I still have to do tonight before I'm done, and I must get a good night's sleep," O'Leary said, adding that she was sure Babbitt understood, as she headed for the vice-presidential suite.

"Well, now, wait a minute," said Babbitt. "Far be it from me to deny you your sleep, Madam Secretary, but I have meetings in the morning, I've got work that still needs to be done, and I need a good night's sleep too. So if you'll excuse me, I believe I'll be sleeping in the vice president's compartment."

Our lucky stars put a protocol officer on board. She was a dear and, like all librarians, tidy and fastidious. Tasked with determining who was the ranking officer, she had died and gone to heaven. "Give me a few minutes, and I'll get back to you both."

All the heads in the movie section turned toward the protocol officer as this drama unfolded. Let's see, does a secretary of the interior trump a secretary of energy?

The guy next to me leaned in. "If Interior is in her direct line of command, my money's on Interior."

The protocol manual snapped closed. The officer and the pronounce-ment returned to the movie compartment. You could have heard a ker-nel of corn pop.

"Since the Department of Energy was established in 1977 and the Department of the Interior was established in 1849, the secretary of interior is the ranking officer on board. The vice presidential suite is to be used at the pleasure of the secretary of the interior."

Babbitt threw out his hands—voila. "Good night, Hazel," he said and headed toward the suite.

||||||||||||

With all of the quartering arrangements made, the commission's entou-rage was settled in for the long flight home. Some were sleeping, some reading, but most were chatting with their colleagues. I was seated near the rear of the plane.

Bill Nitze was forward in the same compartment, talking with his colleagues. We were a few hours into the flight when Nitze came down the aisle and sat in the empty seat across from me.

"You know, Marsha, you have to keep your emotions in control. What you've seen is very disturbing, but there are convergences. We need to keep our priorities right." He lowered his voice even further. I could just hear him above the engines. "The Afrikaners are not happy with you. You should try to lower the heat on them."

"I'm trying to lower the heat on the people dying, Bill. They are liv-ing in concentration camps. The Afrikaners put them there in the first place. You saw Alexandra."

"Look, Marsha, you are an intellectual, and you are passionate. I like that about you. But I have to help the private sector."

"You're talking about trinkets, Bill. When do we get to talk about the public health side? How about we save some lives first?"

"When we get back, I want to have Mark Kasman work with you." I had always thought of Mark as a colleague, perhaps even a friend, so I knew that his field of expertise was in Asia and not in Africa.

"Why Mark? What does he know about South Africa?"

"That's my decision, Marsha."

Nitze got up and walked back to the front. The message was clear: since I wouldn't steer the project toward business first, Mark Kasman would.

||||||||||||

Flight sleep is like drunk sleep: neither is worth a damn. I managed a few naps, but each just seemed successively less restful. It was now early morning DC time, and most of the people on board were sleeping. I noticed the protocol officer was up, so I approached her.

"Excuse me. I was wondering . . . would it be permissible for me to make a phone call to my family?"

"Of course. No one else is using the phone. Be my guest."

It was still early enough that Sade, Sina, and Segun were probably still in their midmorning wrangling, if not asleep. Since my mother has always been a crack-of-dawner, I decided she'd get the honors.

"Hi, Mom. Guess where I'm calling from."

"Oh, Marsha, you're home!"

"Not quite, Mom. We're still about an hour out of DC. I'm calling from Air Force Two."

"Air Force Two! Well, I never. And where's the vice president? Is he up there too?"

"No, no. He's on another flight. But I just wanted to call and say hi."

"Thank you, dear. You have a good rest of your trip."

Next was the call home. I had to steel myself for this call because, for some reason, whenever I was traveling and called home, I would get overwhelmed by an urge to cry. With as little sleep as I'd had it would take something extra to keep it together when I heard my children's early-morning voices. It would be harder to fool Segun.

"Hello, Segun. How are you, sweetheart? I'm almost home."

"Hello, Marsh! Where are you?"

"I'm on Air Force Two!"

"Really?" He laughed. "So I am talking to the big shot, Marsha, not my sweetheart, Marsh."

He had me. I had to regroup—but so did he. I laughed through my tears. "Where are the kids? Please tell me they're still home."

I could hear him say, "It's Mommy," as he handed the phone to Sina.

"Hi, Mom! Comin' home today?"

"Yes, sweetie. I won't be home in time to see you before you leave for school, but I'll be there when you get home."

"They got a big movie screen up there?"

"Yes, a big one. A real big one, but lousy movies. Is Sade there? I can't talk long. Put Sade on, sweetie. Mommy loves you."

This was the toughest one.

"Hi, Mommy!"

"Hello, sweetheart! How are you?"

"I don't like the way Daddy makes eggs, and my dress is all wrinkled."

"Oh no! Don't you have another one?"

"Yeah, but I want to wear this one, and Daddy won't iron it."

"I'm sure Daddy would iron it for you if he had the time, but you have to go to school, and Daddy has to go to work." Her fussing made me miss her more. "Mommy has to go now, baby. Could you put Daddy back on the phone?"

"Bye!"

After finally hanging up, I thanked the protocol officer for use of the phone and the Kleenex she handed me, smiling.

"You're welcome, Marsha. It's been a long flight. We've still got about an hour in the air. Why don't you try to get some more sleep?"

Maybe it was that my children sounded so healthy that just wouldn't let go. I returned to my seat and leaned against the window with my back toward the aisle. The pillow absorbed what my closed eyes couldn't conceal.

Sleep

It is early morning.

The old boards whisper and crack, still settling through the years.

I am awake in a space neither here nor South Africa.

Inside this house in Bethesda that is full of deep breathing.

Segun's foot taps his dreaming with light flutters that woke me from peculiar sleep, and now I wander through the house like I have moved through our years, while everything—the plants, the furniture—sleeps.

My movement through the hushed rooms here is no different than the early air in Alexandra—heavy with the images it keeps of the hungry, the dying, the dead.

I am whisked back, first to my son, my Sina, my Olusina, firstborn, and I see that he is soon a man, asleep in the strength that is building.

Then to my Sade, Folasade, my only daughter, whose sleep is troubled from a place I have not known, but I know it will be calmed by how fully she's sunk into her sheets. And then Segun, always Segun, this man who has been so gentle and so kind.

I have seen.

I have smelled.

I have witnessed.

I am trying to get back.

Why Waste MIT on People Like That?

When Bill Nitze had first informed me that I would be working with Mark Kasman, I had taken great offense, realizing Nitze's intent to turn an environmental and humanitarian mission into a business venture. Mark took the lead of a program called US Environmental Training Institute (USETI or ETI) whose stated goal as reported in the September 1992 EPA document titled "International Update" included "to increase U.S. competitiveness in the environmental market overseas and . . . the sale of U.S. products and services."[1] The South African government, and in particular Bantu Holomisa, deputy minister of environmental affairs—in accord with the protocols as specified in an unclassified cable from the American Embassy, Pretoria, dated August 25, 1995, regarding USAID funding for exchanges to support the United States– South Africa Binational Commission—had rejected any notion of the Gore-Mbeki Commission masquerading as a front to promote American business that would directly compete with South African domestic industries:

> Exchanges under the business development committee of the BNC supported by the proposed agreement must be of a general nature, not oriented to increasing the competitiveness or

financial advantages of any individual, company, or group of companies over its competitors.[2]

Addressing the environmental and public health crisis was paramount to Deputy Minister Holomisa. From a perspective sympathetic to conditions in the townships, it would be crude in the extreme to exploit this crisis to sell American goods. There were, however, significant obstacles to mitigating the conflicting interests. As part of the negotiated settlement between the Mandela government and the outgoing administration, many Afrikaners had remained in managerial positions. These managers acted as gatekeepers and defenders of the status quo. An early instance of their influence came when I received a list of study tour participants, submitted by Afrikaner holdovers. The list looked like a who's who of the Greater Pretoria Country Club. There were only two black South Africans included, with all other names being strictly Afrikaner. This seemed suspiciously like Afrikaner overreach. My colleague Kathy Washburn noted this problem in a memo to the BNC dated November 12, 1995: "The U.S. has expected the three to four visits to the U.S. that have occurred to date to include both blacks and whites from South Africa. . . . The South Africans have only sent white officials." She added, "If we are not able to get the white South Africans on board with this issue we may have to have Vice President Gore talk with Deputy President Mbeki privately."[3]

The black South African official who would be in charge of environmental matters after the transition was Bantu Holomisa. I e-mailed Holomisa months later to confirm that the list represented the position of the incoming government.

Within twenty-four hours, on February 21, 1996, Ken Thomas, deputy counselor to the US mission in Pretoria, and I received a new list of study tour participants via e-mail:

Marsha,

I believe this list represents the new environmental leadership of South Africa. If I can be of further assistance, please do not hesitate to ask. Good luck.

Bantu Holomisa[4]

We were interested in providing sound scientific training during the study tour. I had inroads with the most renowned science educators in the world at MIT. It would also make eminent sense to enlist the services of Howard University, as its African Studies program was second to none. The proximity to the EPA could not have been more convenient, and I also had strong connections to the faculty there.

But when I suggested this to the agency, there was a mixed reaction. It was seen as a good strategy, but there would be a problem finding the funding to support it. Whose budget had the luxury of hiring MIT faculty? And, it was noted, the tour members Bantu Holomisa had suggested would have mixed educational backgrounds.

"Why would the agency want to waste MIT on people like that?" Pat Koshel, my supervisor in the office, commented. "Why not just send them to our people in Philadelphia, Region III?"

"I don't have the budget for anything like that," Nitze had said, "but if you can come up with the money, it's a very good idea."

I did not raise objections at the time, despite how offensive I had found Pat's statement. Instead, I scoured my Rolodex for any contacts who could put me on the money trail. Some colleagues suggested the Rockefeller Foundation. It turned out to be good advice. The foundation accepted the proposal and agreed to help fund the study tour.

Pat, however, sent me an e-mail ordering me to have four EPA offices sign off before I could send out the letters of invitation:

> Secure formal sign off on the letters and the list of participants for the EPA study tour from OECA [Office of Enforcement and Compliance Assurance], Francesca for Region III, and the Office of Environmental Justice. The final letters and the description . . . should then be sent through me for sign off by the Allans [sic] and Bill before the letters go out.[5]

Translation: your study tour is dead. Fortunately, Bill Nitze overruled Pat's bureaucratic red tape, and the letters were sent out.

So there I was, looking at the entourage arriving at Logan Airport in Boston to attend study tour courses I had arranged at MIT, through the generous cooperation of my former doctoral mentor, Willard Johnson. Bantu Holomisa had provided much-needed background information on the participants, beyond their names, including employment status, educational background, and their areas of interest in environmental matters. Using this information, Willard Johnson was able to link the participants with various experts in related fields on the MIT staff. I had grown to trust Holomisa's instincts and his keen understanding of South African needs, so I was looking forward to greeting the contingent as they disembarked. The first person through the gate was a dark, handsome man, wearing a light blue blazer with a white shirt and black pants. He had a shoulder pack and walked straight toward me like he was marching, looking past me, and if I hadn't moved, he would have marched right through me. He stopped and extended his hand.

"My name is Jacob Ngakane." His voice was a little raspy, distinguished. He rolled his r's. His eyes were close to possessed, intense and unblinking. "I represent the Vametco mine workers in Brits, South Africa, who have been and continue to be poisoned by the process of extracting the mineral vanadium from the earth. I will consider this trip, my entire experience while I am in America, a total failure if you do not agree to help us."

"Hello, Mr. Ngakane," I said, stunned. "My name is Marsha Coleman-Adebayo. I represent the Environmental Protection Agency."

My Name Is Jacob Ngakane

I could just see General Bantubonke Harrington Holomisa smiling as he hit the send button. Be careful what you ask for, Marsha. The question was whether this assertive, intense black South African man standing before me was the embodiment of what Steve Biko called the "new man," unleashed from the chains of slavery, or a potentially difficult member of the study tour. A critical assessment of Jacob Ngakane would have to wait until after I returned from the airport, after the day's welcoming activities were finished, and perhaps even until after the study tour had been completed and he was on a plane back to South Africa.

We had built a program that would keep Jacob and his colleagues busy for two weeks. But my gut reaction was that I liked him. First impression: he cut to the chase, whether impulsively or because he had been sitting in his seat forty thousand feet up at 650 miles per hour, rehearsing his introductory comments. As I greeted and shook hands with the others in the delegation, the thought that he was first, his message specific, and his call for action clear, had premeditation written all over them. But why this man? And what was that mineral he mentioned?

I made a point of accompanying Jacob out of Logan; I filled him in on our itinerary and asked about the flight. "Now, Jacob, what was it you said about a mineral, something about mining?"

"The mineral is vanadium. The mining company is Vametco, a United States owned multinational. You remember Bhopal?" He looked at me.

"Thousands poisoned in their sleep in India by Union Carbide? That is the same company. Vanadium is used to strengthen metal. Metal that is repeatedly heated becomes brittle. Vanadium solves that problem. It is used in motors, ovens, automobiles. It was in the airplane I just came across in. It is in weapons. There are vast reserves of it in South Africa. It is mined in pits. Open, gaping wounds are carved into the earth, and the vanadium extracted."

"And why are you so adamant that we have to help you? What do you mean?"

"The workers in the mines are being poisoned by this process. Young, strong men are reduced to feeble. They cannot breathe. They bleed from their eyes, their noses, their genitals, their colons. These same young men become impotent from working in the mines. Their tongues turn green."

"This is more than we can talk about right now, Jacob. We are on a tight schedule today and for the rest of your stay. Can you get me more information on this? I will need documentation and evidence."

Jacob had already reached into his shoulder pack and produced a notebook. "It is all there. The company. The names. The victims. People are dying as a direct result of working in the mines. They bring vanadium home to their families on their clothing, in their hair, under their fingernails. Everyone and everything is poisoned, and the company denies it exists. Their doctors deny it exists. It is an American company. You have jurisdiction. You must help us." He paused, smiling. "Please."

I shook Jacob Ngakane's hand as he boarded the bus, and then welcomed and assisted the other participants. I had no idea what the notebook I now held in my hand represented—or whether I should thank or curse Bantu Holomisa.

Jacob Ngakane was born in Randfontein, forty-five kilometers from Johannesburg, the seventh of eleven children. Thus, like his older siblings, he could remember when his father had worked in the Aranda Textile Mill. He could remember his father coming home from the grueling, filthy work, belittled in his own eyes. He could remember his father's anger at his treatment and at the pitiful existence his family knew because of the insult of his pay. But for Jacob, as for his four younger siblings, it was easier to remember his father after he had stopped working at the mill. That was easier than trying to remember his father when he had been whole—not spiritually, Jacob could never recall his father as a whole man spiritually—but physically, before his right hand was devoured by a machine.

Jacob could recall the horror of that day and of seeing his father come home with a white bandage where his hand had been, and the deep, maroon stain that had spread as the night wore on. He could describe the ceiling he had watched above his bed in another corner of the same room as howls kept him awake in the night, his father shrieking in delirium. He could tell about his father learning to put on his shoes and pants, button his shirt, with one hand. Jacob could recite in great detail the process of shock, the shame he felt when he left the house and saw the faces turned toward him and heard the hushed tones, if not the actual comments, of neighbors and friends.

He could tell you how at first there were sympathy and offers of help. People brought food. They stood and listened as his father described the accident, how it was waiting to happen really when you thought of the clutter and darkness and sheer volume of work, and how he had always relied on his quickness and reflexes to avoid it. At first they had stood, nodding, and listened to him relive how that day there had been something small and hard, a stone maybe, under his foot. And when it had been time for his quickness to avoid the machine, the stone had slipped—his torso lurched, and, before he even felt it, his hand was gone.

Jacob remembered how his father's need to relive and retell his story had increased, while the availability of those willing to listen had subsided. Or they listened to the voices inside their own heads, cautioning them to shuffle their feet while they worked and to kick loose anything underfoot, while Jacob's father recounted what had happened. Even though he could not pinpoint when, it became clear to Jacob that at some point the others stopped pretending to listen, stopped coming by to see how his father was doing, and started looking the other way when he or Jacob passed by.

It was easy for Jacob to locate the pain he felt knowing his father felt diminished and slighted. On top of everything, the company denied Jacob's father benefits or compensation. This, Jacob Ngakane retold in the context of his primary school, where his teacher had given the class the assignment of writing about what they wanted to be when they grew up. Jacob had sat for hours and considered his options before the first words wrote themselves out on the page. Of all the occupations he could imagine, he saw himself as a lawyer who took Aranda Textile to court, who took pains in selecting a jury so that his father would have a fair hearing. He took to describing the way he would put the plant manager himself on the docket and have him repeat under oath what he had said to Jacob's father, face to face in front of others, including the company doctor, that Jacob's father had deliberately thrust his hand into the machine so he could claim compensation.

Jacob poured his heart into writing—the way he would challenge the doctor to explain how the angle of the wound itself suggested that his father was falling down when the accident had happened; how he would subpoena the South African Health and Safety officials who had ruled in favor of the company and denied his father any compensation, demanding an explanation as to how any of them could so maim themselves for money. Have you any idea how easy it would be to hate all of you? Jacob would demand. Do you know how every one of the South Africans who have heard this story is living for a day of revenge? Have you the slightest inkling of the amount of commitment and devotion and spiritual refocusing it has required of me to relinquish my hatred of all whites?

Ngakane's teacher was so taken by the content and style of his writing that she read it to her senior classes, revealing—to Jacob's dismay— his deepest suffering and pain before all of his classmates and calling on him to describe what had prompted his writing.

"Ma'am, this is what happened to my father and to my family." Jacob could say no more. His body heaved as he fought his tears.

As a teenager Jacob could write about moving beyond his anger and hate. Reality, however, would test those ideals, beginning with the immediate effect on his own family. Most of his siblings had to leave school early and take low-paying, futureless jobs. They could not provide for their own children's college or university educations. The company and the supporting government policy treated their father like so much chattel, thereby reaching with their bloody hands well into the future. Jacob freely told of how this fueled his own anger and the all-consuming hatred he felt toward all whites, about how the thought of revenge was addictive and cruel.

He admitted how every report of assaults on whites filled him with a vicarious delight that only frustrated his desire to exact more vengeance of his own. By 1967 the white apartheid regime had declared that Afrikaans—a language derived from the form of Dutch brought to the Cape by Protestant settlers in the seventeenth century—was the only language besides English to be used in the classroom. Black South Africans were enraged and saw this as yet another form of racial annihilation, an attempt to break linguistic connections to their non-European cultural and national identities in the most profoundly personal and psychologically devastating way. The very languages of the oppressor were to be the only languages allowed in black South African ears.

This led to the mass actions and resistance in Soweto. The township was ablaze as the students attacked and destroyed all symbols of apartheid. The regime's response was swift and brutal. Police attacked students with gunfire that killed at least six hundred and wounded over four thousand. During the Soweto revolt many students fled the country to join the ANC, the Pan African Congress military wings, and other exiled parties. Jacob Ngakane was captured.

The Afrikaners beat and tortured him, applying electrodes to his genitals. Jacob was sixteen years old. There is no irony to his saying that his first night of imprisonment was the easiest. They flung him into a cell that was a darkened room with no windows. The stench was unbearable. Jacob slipped whenever he moved. He could not see and kept falling down, so he decided to stay still in one corner of the room. The next morning, as day broke and daylight found its way through the boards and under the door, Jacob watched the contours of the room and its ghastly contents take form. He had been thrown into a makeshift morgue, where the bodies of his fellow students, killed during the uprising, had been stacked. The floor was thick with the blood that had drained out of the bodies.

They held him for six months.

"I still cannot look upon a dead body to this day," said Jacob twenty years later. "After the first night it only got worse."

I learned all this over the two weeks by listening to Jacob. He bared his soul as though he were talking about someone else, and in many ways he was. He had a quality that is easy to imagine would have fit the role of a shaman in another time or place. His intensity was strangely low key. His voice was soft and articulate. It was hard to imagine this man as a warrior, while somehow at the same time, it was impossible to think he was not.

Jacob answered every question as though he were addressing history itself and his words would be judged by eternity, as though he were an oracle and he knew that the person seated beside him would also pass. And yet his flesh—the injured voice, the eyes that seemed to see everything present, past, and future—was calming, while gripping the soul. I was aware that these were not the sort of observations a scientist would accept; I could hear in the back of my head a voice, persistent like the sound of a trapped miner banging on a pipe, the only signal to an outside world that he was still alive.

I could already hear the objections, which I anticipated would come from the EPA, about the veracity of his claims. I knew I could count on Segun to look into this with a cold, dispassionate, just-the-facts clarity—to investigate the claim and also watch my back. But I knew that the scientist in Segun was also alive to the possibilities of the unexplained and intuitive. And on more than one occasion Segun had consoled me with his advice to follow my instincts. I found myself listening to my intuitions while I listened to this man. I was drawn to him, not because I believed him yet but because of his passion in telling me these things. I would believe him because he was earnest. And I would believe him because he was only going to be in town for two weeks. There would be plenty of time after he left to investigate his allegations.

Back to MIT

It was good to be back at MIT. The open, collegial environment, the receptivity to ideas, and the nearness of friends I had not seen for years were all a welcome respite from the closed, biased, hostile culture within EPA. As I was coordinating the study tour with former colleagues at the Insitute, it occurred to me for the first time since joining the agency that I might have been suffering from some form of Stockholm syndrome. I noticed this during a conversation with Willard Johnson when I broached the idea of bringing the South African delegation to MIT.

"Of course! Fantastic idea," Willard had said.

I launched into an immediate justification of the collaboration and the relationship it would establish between MIT and EPA, along with an analysis of the costs and benefits for the new South African government.

"I agree, Marsha," Willard reiterated. "I already said let's do it."

|||||||||||||

Jacob Ngakane didn't hesitate during our first study tour session.

"Why are we wasting time, energy, and resources on the pursuit of rudimentary discussions?" he blurted out when I began. "There is a systematic, verifiable, environmentally devastating operation going on in Brits, South Africa, that is poisoning mineworkers, contaminating every leaf, every blade of grass, every tributary that the dust from this operation settles upon. The government knows it, the company knows it, the miners know it, and now you know it.

"There are extreme obstacles in the way," Jacob continued. "Moneyed concerns who will resist our every move even to the point of our talking about vanadium. We must focus on and develop strategies that will require all of our attention and dedication. What are you going to do when you mention the word *vanadium* and the earth opens up beneath your feet and swallows you? This is where we need to focus our attention."

This was where the presence of Willard Johnson, a professor of politics who had written extensively on Africa and African Americans, was so refreshing. Even compared to the twentysomethings he was surrounded by, Willard was quick on his feet and secure enough in himself that he didn't have to run the show or be its brightest star. MIT was notorious for being stacked with brilliant minds and their accompanying outsized egos. If Willard had felt threatened by every genius who challenged his position or strategy, he would not have lasted long there. He gloried in the back-and-forth—it gave him strength. His approach was more in keeping with the classic model of mentoring, in which the student and professor are seen as educating each other. In Willard's eyes, learning significant details about South Africa from a native South African was the most sensible place to start. "You're absolutely right," he responded to Jacob. "If we can substantiate your charges, we should make vanadium a top priority."

Perhaps I'd already become enough of a bureaucrat to know to temper the discussion. "All right," I said, "I have no objection to making this a priority, but I still have a job to do, and I didn't sell this idea to anyone at the EPA as part of the curriculum for the tour. I'll help develop a working strategy to get this issue into the discussion going forward. We can't just come back to EPA and the vice president's office from left field without touching on the areas that, from their perspective, they have already committed considerable resources to."

"I do not know about a left field, but I can tell you that unless we address this aggressively and challenge the company and the leaders, it will die a very polite and unnoticed death," Jacob replied. "They will continue to murder the miners in South Africa."

I liked this man. I liked his directness. But murder was a strong accusation. "Jacob, if I go back to the BNC and tell them that an American company is 'murdering' poor South Africans, they are going to demand proof. Harmful working conditions are one thing, but murder . . ."

"What would you prefer that I call it? What is the word you have in your language for knowingly, deliberately, consistently, and repeatedly sending men to work in an environment that will result in their deaths? Do you call that an unfavorable working environment? Do you call that a health hazard? Do you call that indifference? It may be all of those things, but they are not what it is at the bottom. Underneath the denial, underneath the reports from their doctors, underneath their expressed concern for the safety of the workers is a ruthless, premeditated, calculating policy of murder. If I add arsenic to your food, in small doses, in every meal, eventually you will sicken and die." Jacob's eyes were riveting. "If I know that I am giving you these doses, that makes me your murderer. It may not be quick, like a gun. It may not be obvious. But it is still murder."

I did not dispute his argument, but I already knew from experience that convincing arguments were one thing—and getting them to inform policy was quite another. If we were going to make this case, it would have to be bulletproof. It was clear to me that Jacob was the charismatic leader of the South African delegation. This was not some pimply kid with authority issues. Jacob was talking about life and death, about criminality and justice. All eyes were on Jacob and me. Or perhaps more accurately, all eyes were on the question Jacob had just laid at the feet of the US government concerning what it was going to do about some very damning allegations from a recently empowered black South African. There was no doubt in my mind that Jacob was a force and that the entire delegation looked to his leadership.

"All right, Jacob, I have heard your allegations. I have every reason to believe you, not the least being that you come highly recommended. I have no reason to doubt that everything you have told me is the truth." There was a very real possibility that what I was about to say would create a wide array of problems for me. But it was clear that Jacob and the group needed reassurance and, more than this, if the vanadium poisoning was taking place as he described it, there was need for intercession.

"I give you my personal word, Jacob, in front of all these witnesses, that I take these charges very seriously. I will look into them. I will bring them to the attention of my supervisors inside the EPA and the White House."

|||||||||||||||||

Willard invited me to stop by his office after the class so we could catch up. Willard was a soft-spoken, stately, tall, self-composed man. If Abraham Lincoln had been black, he would have looked like Willard. Willard had the same haunted eyes that could at once be penetrating and kind. His face was deeply creased with lines, and his bone structure gave him a perpetual smile. His stride was long and loping and assigned the extra reassurance of grace to his movements, the added sense of a man in balance with himself. And Willard was the first to find humor in complexity, the first to offer himself as the brunt of a joke to take the starchiness out of an uncomfortable or unfamiliar situation. I could feel his voice inside me as I approached his office from the other side of the commons.

It had been over a decade since I last sat with him in his office, surrounded by his books, the stacks of reports and papers and journals and intellectual clutter that were a delight to scan, ask about, and search for any hint of familiarity. As a doctoral candidate I had often felt envious of his vast reserve of scholarship while browsing his office library and would console myself with the thought that, once I got established, I would have a soft, high-backed chair that would hold me in comfort while I dove into the deep waters of other minds and their experience of the world. Now that a decade had slipped under my feet, I found myself wondering about the choices I had made. I experienced a certain guilt at the compromises I'd orchestrated, knowing that my dent in the pile of scholarship had yet to begin.

What I most needed from Willard was his acceptance of all of this as simply the unexpected turns and twists in my journey. What I wanted was his understanding, a perspective from a man whose counsel I trusted, an honest assessment of where the years had led me since I had left MIT, and an evaluation offered in friendship and without judgment. I knew I could expect all of that from this abundant man. I was excited to be entering his office again. I was happy to have such a friend. And I was aware of how much I had missed this kind of confidant.

I was stepping into a sanctuary. Nothing much had changed, beyond our both looking a bit older. The clutter could have been the same old clutter buried under new. Willard had obviously been busy.

"So, Marsha, tell me what has come out of that promising mind of yours for the last fifteen years."

Good question. I wanted so much to impress Willard. Not only because he was my mentor but because I wanted him to know that all the time, energy, and passion he had put into that effort had not been wasted. In some ways I felt as though Willard were my father and as if I were now sitting in front of him as we went over my report card.

"Oh, my God, Willard. . . . Where do I start? Well, as you know, I worked in congressional offices for a while, learned the ropes, saw how it's done. Then I went to work for the World Wildlife Fund and later to the UN and did some interesting, if heartbreaking, field work in Ethiopia during the famine there. Horrible, needless, completely avoidable suffering in many instances. And then I came to the EPA. What an experience. After spending about a year cutting my teeth on the inner workings, organizational stuff, I led the EPA delegation to the fourth UN World Conference on Women, in Beijing. I was there for a month, surrounded by the most courageous and dynamic women imaginable— women from all around the world who are facing degradations and cruelty we can't even imagine, who in many cases risked their lives by daring to come to Beijing."

Willard had been at the forefront of organizing around justice issues worldwide. When I had first come to MIT, Willard and Noam Chomsky had been the standard-bearers on issues of justice. Willard was often the featured speaker at rallies against apartheid; Noam led the charge against the undeclared war in Vietnam and the covert US operations that were destabilizing grassroots efforts for democracy in Central and South America.

"And Willard, those women at the Beijing conference knew more about the civil rights movement than I did. It was their working model for their own strategies. They wanted to know what Rev. Walter Fauntroy was thinking when he organized the march in Selma, for crying out loud! At night we'd all get together and witness about the pressing issues facing women in their home societies. Afterwards we would all lock arms and sing 'We Shall Overcome.' Women from Asia, South America, Eastern Europe."

While I described these things, Willard got up from his desk and reached up to a shelf behind it, pulling down a box that he placed on his desk and opened. He reached in to pull out binders that he flipped through as I talked. I stopped, afraid that I was boring him to tears.

Willard sat down in his chair and looked at me over the top of his glasses, reading out loud: "This study investigates US prestigious newspapers' coverage of several important African crises. Situations that involve widely perceived threats to American geopolitical and economic interests . . . "

Willard's eyes had me. "Who is that? Is that something you wrote? . . . I had a bright doctoral student here once who many of us thought was looking at a brilliant future." He kept his wry smile and raised eyebrows aimed at me.

"Did I write that?"

Willard put the paper down and sat back in his chair. "Now, do you want to tell me what's really going on, Marsha? What's happened to that promising student of mine?"

Willard was no devotee of happy talk. Were it not a fair question, it would almost be too cruel to answer. "Wow. That's a much tougher question, Willard."

That was always a good way to buy myself more time when I needed to regroup. I had been running so hard, trying to hold my career together, my family. Myself. There were things I told no one. The most difficult, I didn't even tell myself. But having my own words seem as fresh to me as if they were someone else's, and feeling the distance between myself now and what I had always truly loved, were not what I'd been telling myself I had come back to MIT for. The husk I was living in had just been blown apart, and I really felt exposed. But, even as close as I was to Willard, he was not offering his shoulder for a good cry. He never had. He offered his honesty and integrity, even if it hurt. Not out of unkindness, but because he was a professional and he knew that was what I needed. So apart from the shock and the vulnerability, I was dealing with a sense of shame at trying to impress him.

"Thank you so much, Willard. I cannot tell you how badly I needed to hear that. I have been confined to writing so much one-page government-speak that always begins with 'Per your recent blah blah blah,' I want to scream. On top of that, I could save the government millions of dollars with one simple suggestion: if they want to study apartheid, they don't have to go to South Africa—they could find a perfect working model of it inside the EPA!"

"Oh no. What have they been doing to you?"

"What haven't they done is a better question. Name calling, retaliation, obstacles, denial of promotion, discrimination. I feel like I'm slowly being turned into collard greens from the heat rays emanating from upper management. It's truly unbelievable. In my worst nightmare I could not have dreamed of an environment even approximating that of the EPA. I'm engaged in hand-to-hand combat with senior management over every last inch of Jim Crow they still refuse to relinquish."

"That is not a good position to be in, Marsha. What do you plan to do about it?"

"I don't know, Willard. Being in the room, being part of the negotiations for the hammering out of the language for a new government in South Africa is not nothing. Being a part of the process to provide environmental information on water, public health, pollution is not nothing. On a deep level, it's very rewarding. But when I see the lion's share of the resources still going toward the Afrikaner old guard, the status quo, that mountains and mountains of money are being poured into the coffers of corporations that are selling trinkets to people who need the very basics to survive—it just rankles my sense of justice." I didn't mean to throw up on this man, but I hadn't see it coming. "I don't know, Willard. Do you think I should get out of the government?"

He held me with those eyes of his. "I don't presume to know what you should do, beyond knowing that you need to make a choice. But what you've described doesn't sound like it's in anyone's best interest. It does not surprise me that you have represented the United States in Beijing, in Pretoria, in Washington." Willard's image blurred as my eyes filled. "You have to decide," he continued, "about how much of a personal toll you can afford to let your current situation take, weighed against the positive contribution you can make. And then, perhaps, weigh those against what you might be able to do in another environment. There are lots of choices. The only thing you have no choice about is that you have to make one."

॥॥॥॥॥॥॥

I looked at the alarm clock. It was after 2:00 A.M. I'd thrashed around in the hotel bed, trying to sleep, with three words in my head: Willard was right. I needed to delineate the choices.

Was I immune to the allure of my six-figure income? To governmental perks? I admit that I was not. Those things are owed to all those who had come before me and fought to expand the franchise at tremendous personal risk to themselves. Now that the franchise included me, should I have been content to say that it was good enough? No. It was not enough. Not with what I had heard from women all around the world still alive in my ears. And not with what I had heard from Jacob Ngakane. It could not possibly be enough, not with what I had seen with my own eyes.

Were I to turn away from the least of these, I might as well have denied my own roots.

Breathing College Air

"Mom?" I asked carefully. The look on her face said, Don't tread on me. "Are you going somewhere?" It was 1967.

"Marsha Lynne, get your books and let's go."

When Mom used my first and middle names, it was not the time to ask questions. On arriving at school, I started heading for my homeroom.

"No. Stay with me. We're going to the principal's office!"

"Mom, what did I do?"

"Marsha, I'm too angry to talk right now. You haven't done anything." We had arrived at the office. Her voice softened. "But I need to talk with your principal. Sit down."

I sat. Majestice turned toward the secretary.

"I need to talk with the principal." The only person on earth I had ever heard Mom use that tone of voice with was me, when I was in big trouble. "Right now."

The woman looked up from her papers. Any question was not in her best interest. In a few minutes she was escorting my mother to the office. I couldn't see her, but I heard her heels hit the floor like a hammer. The door shut. My mom was generally soft-spoken, but on that day, her voice rose once, then twice, and then there were some thumps. The secretaries looked at each other. I knew they were going to call the police. I slid down in my chair.

After a few minutes, the principal emerged, sweating and flushed, and asked me to join them.

"Marsha," he said sheepishly with a nod to my mom, "your mother has brought to my attention that we have made a mistake in your high school program. It seems that we placed you in special education when in fact you belong in our college prep program." He looked at my mother. "Perhaps even our honors program."

Public education in Detroit in the 1960s provided the auto industry with a one-way conveyer to the assembly lines. I went from an all-black classroom to a nearly all-white classroom within one hour. After the drive home, dinner, and doing the dishes had lessened her anger, my mother looked at me calmly.

"I was not going to leave the principal's office until he removed you from the special education program—even if it meant getting arrested."

ııııııııııı

Worldwide, it was a time of confrontation. While the youth movement in South Africa was organizing against pass laws that required them to obtain permission to enter parts of their own cities, community organizers in Detroit were planning the largest civil rights demonstration in American history—the Great March to Freedom—designed to draw attention to employment and housing discrimination, de facto segregation in the public schools, and police brutality and to mark the twentieth anniversary of the 1943 race riots that had erupted in Detroit, as well as the hundredth anniversary of Lincoln's signing of the Emancipation Proclamation. My grandfather, the Reverend George Lee Thompson, worked closely with other ministers and Rev. C. L. Franklin in organizing the march that climaxed with Rev. Martin Luther King Jr. electrifying a packed Cobo Hall with the first public delivery of his "I Have a Dream" speech, on June 24, 1963.[1]

I called my maternal grandfather Daddy because my father had died unexpectedly at the age of twenty-seven from a rare blood disease two months before I was born. And when Daddy returned home afterward he was ecstatic.

"I have never heard such inspiration: 'a magnificent new militancy within the Negro community all across this nation.'" Daddy held the text of the speech and read it in his scorched-earth style, as if it were his own now. "'And we've got to come to see that the problem of racial injustice is a national problem.'"

Daddy looked around the room, smiling.

"'Now in the North it's different in that it doesn't have the legal sanction that it has in the South. But it has its subtle and hidden forms, and it exists in three areas: in the area of employment discrimination, in the area of housing discrimination, and in the area of de facto segregation in the public schools. And we must come to see that de facto segregation in the North is just as injurious as the actual segregation in the South.'"

"I didn't come all the way from Portsmouth, Ohio, just to listen to you repeat all that nonviolence nonsense I heard today." Grandma Lilee Coleman was never known to mince words. To me she was the father's voice that I had never heard. Daddy was my mother's father. He was educated and philosophical. My father's mother was working class and practical. "That may be the way it's done up here in civilized, unionized, and sanitized Detroit," she bellowed.

"'Love your enemies, bless them that curse you, pray for them that spitefully use you.'" Daddy was still reading from the text of King's speech, but it was a message I had heard him deliver over and over again both at home and through his fire-and-brimstone sermons at our church. "'And there is still a voice saying to every potential Peter, 'Put up your sword.'"

"In Portsmouth, they'll kill a Negro for looking the wrong way," Grandma yelled back. "You can talk that turn the other cheek stuff all you want. I'll keep my shotgun loaded and right where it is—next to my front door. Just let some white trash try to bother me."

Grandma was a staunch member of the United Negro Improvement Association founded by Marcus Garvey, who believed that all African Americans should return, of their own volition, to Africa. Grandma brandished her own copy of Dr. King's speech and read, "'Now there is a magnificent new militancy within the Negro community all across this nation. And I welcome this as a marvelous development. The Negro of America is saying he's determined to be free and he is militant enough to stand up.'"

Grandma's eyes shone with rage. The pamphlet slapped against her thigh.

"Stand up? The first thing black people need to learn about standing up is to stop referring to themselves as Negroes." She turned to me. "Don't you ever let anyone call you a Negro, Marsha. You are an African. And I predict right here and now before everybody present that you will be the first of all of us to return to Africa."

⁙⁙⁙⁙⁙⁙⁙⁙⁙

About a year earlier, in South Africa, Nelson Mandela had the same argument with the more moderate members of the ANC about nonviolent resistance and the use of force: "There are many people who feel that it is useless and futile for us to continue talking peace and nonviolence, against a government whose only reply is savage attacks on an unarmed and defenseless people," Mandela told an interviewer after the March 21, 1960, attack by the apartheid regime's forces in Sharpeville that had killed sixty-nine people and injured hundreds of others, many of whom were shot in the back.[2] The government's crackdown, together with its outlawing of the ANC, had forced Mandela into hiding. By 1961 he had become the leader of the ANC's armed wing, Umkhonto we Sizwe ("the spear of the nation"), and engaged in sabotage against military and government targets.

By the time of Dr. King's Great March to Freedom in Detroit, Nelson Mandela had already been in prison for a year—thanks, allegedly, to the cooperation of the CIA—which had tipped off the South African authorities about Mandela's location and disguise. A year after the Great March to Freedom, on June 12, 1964, Nelson Mandela was sentenced to life in prison.[3] His abandonment of nonviolent resistance in favor of military confrontation would cost him the next three decades of his life.

In America, another African American voice was gaining traction alongside that of Martin Luther King. This man, like Mandela, was souring on the prospects of nonviolence, given the history of violent and deadly suppression of black culture, albeit largely unknown to the dominant white society. This man, Detroit Red, was more widely known as Malcolm X.

Malcolm was not timid in pointing to the systematic attacks against black communities—nationwide—and rejected the then-prevalent conventional wisdom that racial hostilities were a distinctly Southern anomaly. Indeed, he argued that the repression in America was a close cousin to the more overt violence in Africa, most notably in South Africa. His argument had its rationale, with the brutal suppression of racial riots in New York City's Harlem in 1935, the aerial bombardment of a very successful black business district in what was known as Black Wall Street in Tulsa in 1921, and the crushing of the black revolt of 1943 in Detroit that the Great March to Freedom commemorated. Malcolm's message of liberation "by any means necessary" found a receptive population in Detroit that by the mid-sixties had already tamed the powerful auto industry. Yet, less than a year after the Great March, on February 12, 1965, Malcolm X was assassinated in New York City.

ıııııııııııı

The 1967 riots that shattered Detroit looked similar to the violent confrontations that were being telecast from South Africa. Inferior education of the black underclass was a key igniter of both. In direct response to the riots, I volunteered with my friends Portia James and, later, Joanne Godley to work at a free breakfast program for children sponsored by the Black Panther Party in Detroit.

I would wake up at 4:00 A.M., ride a bus forty-five minutes across town to serve breakfast to poor children in what was called Black Bottom, and then retrace my steps in time for the first bell at Mumford High School by eight o'clock. My mother had sheltered me from this part of Detroit. For the first time, I identified with people living in housing projects and subjected to police violence targeted against whole communities. Two years later, on December 4, 1969, in Chicago, Fred Hampton was drugged to sleep by an FBI informant who had infiltrated the Panthers, and at four in the morning was twice shot in the back of the head, point-blank, during a police raid—after he had already been wounded in the shoulder and left defenseless. In America, state-sponsored assassinations were well underway.

ıııııııııııı

I skip over March 16, April 4, June 6, and August 28, 1968, by design. These were the dates of the My Lai massacre, the assassinations of Martin Luther King Jr. and Robert Kennedy, and the police riots in response to the demonstrations at the Democratic National Convention in

Chicago. Though these were by no means the only instances of discord in the 1960s, the weight of these events largely defined the tumult of that period in the United States.

IIIIIIIIIIII

Over the decades during which these events unfolded I went from being a student in the largely segregated Detroit school system to sitting on the Environment Committee of the Gore-Mbeki Binational Commission. The process had begun with my mother's belief that education was the key to unlocking doors that would otherwise remain closed.

"Marsha, take deep breaths." Every Saturday after we went to the museum, Mom would drive to Wayne State University, the flagship college in the Detroit area.

"Yes, like that. Do you see how the college air smells different than other air?"

"It smells like Detroit."

"No," she said, as she put the car in park so she could take big, unrestrained lungfuls. "We'll just have to stay here until we agree on the smell." She closed her eyes, breathing deeply. "I can feel the excitement of the classrooms all the way out here on the street," she said. "Science. History. Art. There are conversations going on right now in there that are not allowed where I work. They may be having conversations about the Year of Freedom."

She opened her eyes and looked at me.

"Oh, it's a little-known African American tradition," she said, affecting erudition and patience, looking toward the campus in case I didn't take the bait.

"Some of our people count their birthdays by the number of years that have passed since the Emancipation Proclamation." She smiled. "Daddy was born twenty-three years after the Year of Freedom, on December 25, 1888, in Worth, Georgia. Grandma was born twenty-six years after the Year of Freedom, on January 30, 1891, on a farm in Dublin, Georgia. Your father was born in 1925, sixty years after the Year of Freedom. And you were born . . ."

"Eighty-seven years after the Year of Freedom!" It was infectious.

"That's right!" she laughed. "See what happens when you breathe college air?"

When I got a little older, she would find a place to park and go into the university with me to breathe college air. I had long since stopped commenting on the aroma, simply agreeing that there was indeed something sweet about the way Wayne State smelled. It was the quickest way to end our touchy-feely trip to the college. She then graduated me to standing in the corridor by myself to breathe this magical air. Anytime we were in proximity of Wayne State University, I knew the drill.

"Marsha, run and see if that door is open. Why don't you go and breathe college air for a few minutes."

"Come on, Mom! Everyone is watching me."

"Oh, don't be silly," she insisted. "Everyone does this."

After a while, I salivated like a subject in Pavlov's laboratory whenever the rotunda at Wayne State University rode along behind the trees as we approached. There was no escaping college air.

Barnard College:
The Path Sisters Take

I walked through Barnard College's wrought-iron gate wearing bell bottoms, a psychedelic shirt, and an Afro twice the size of my head, with faithful companions Mom and Aunt Ruth in tow, inspecting these New York environs for signs of safety. The gates of this prestigious college had swung open with the civil rights movement. It was love at first sight—not the least because, at a distance of six hundred miles from Detroit, Barnard meant freedom. For Majestice Coleman, who had devoted the last eighteen years of her life, her earnings, and her energy to me, Barnard represented the place where her heart and soul would grow new legs and walk away from her.

Barnard was a women's college unapologetically feminist in educational tone. As we walked to Barnard Hall, with its stone steps and grand entrance, and turned toward the dormitory, I experienced my first jolt of nervousness. We approached a young black girl sitting behind the counter and announced that I was supposed to check in to 7 Brooks. She looked up.

"You must be Marsha Coleman. My name is Karen O'Neal. I was told you were coming today." Then, with a broad and friendly smile, "Welcome."

I looked at my mom and aunt with a "Didn't I tell you so?" grin on my face. The butterflies had flown.

Seventh-floor Brooks was part of what were called the black floors, in the Brooks, Hewitt, and Reid dormitories. Barnard, until the mid-1960s, did not have a significant African American presence. Dorothy Height, the renowned president of the National Council of Negro Women, arrived at Barnard in 1929 to be told that the school had already reached its Negro quota and that she would have to come back the following year. Zora Neale Hurston, however, a writer of the Harlem Renaissance, fared better and became the first African American graduate from Morningside Heights. My class, the class of 1974, would include the largest group of African American women to ever attend and graduate from this branch of the Seven Sisters.

Our black female predecessors in the 1960s braved the stares and alienation that came with being the first African American women to be integrated among the predominantly white student body and fought for the right to live on separate floors where they would not be considered aliens or anthropologic specimens. They successfully argued that a living environment should be a place where they could relax without other women asking to touch their hair or waiting to see them walk out of the shower—to see if they were black all over. Barnard was sympathetic to these concerns. Thus, at the insistence of African American women, Barnard's black floors were born.

For the first time in my life I was given the key to my own space—Room 713. My fingers shook so that I could hardly key the lock, but eventually the door swung open and presented a long and narrow room with a sink, mirror, twin bed, and small closet. It reminded me of photographs I had seen of bedrooms in convents. But this was my own miniature mansion. The window overlooked the Chock full o'Nuts coffee shop, and when the window opened, the aroma filled our every cell. Aunt Ruth walked the length of the room—lost in the delicious possibilities for color schemes. Mom sat on the bed and watched, smiling but quiet.

There was a knock, and a small, wiry girl appeared at my door. She wore a cap that was cocked easily to one side. One leg was bent behind the other.

"Hi, my name is Deborah Thornhill, but everyone calls me Thorny. I heard you just moved in. What's your name?"

I introduced myself, Mom, and Aunt Ruth. Thorny waved from outside the room with a mischievous smile; then, seeing I hadn't settled in yet, she said she wouldn't keep me and left. A little later, giggles percolated under my door. I opened it to a small committee of girls.

"Hey! We heard you moved in."

"I'm Greta."

"I'm Happy."

"I'm Archie."

"We'll see you around or in the dining room," Greta said. "Just wanted to say hi—and welcome." Voices pregnant with joy and innocence floated down the hall, fading to whispers.

"Mom, I'm going to like this place," I said to my mother after the girls had left.

An easy smile lit her face. "I can see that," she said, before sliding right back into Mom-ness.

Mom and Ruth left for Detroit that afternoon. We all hugged and kissed and promised to call every day. It took me another thirty years, but I finally noticed the way my mother and Aunt Ruth knitted arms afterward and resumed their walk through life along the path sisters take, on the other side of me.

||||||||||||||

A little later Thorny stopped by my room again. "What are your plans?"

"I really don't have any."

Thorny eyed me up and down. "Girl, I don't know how to tell you this," she said, "but that yellow outfit?" She closed her eyes and cringed. "It's not going to work here. You see, in New York, we have our own way of dressing, more sophisticated or urban, and—how can I politely say this?" She paused for emphasis. "You look so—'bama!"

"Bama?"

"Like someone straight out of Alabama."

I suddenly forgot all about my nervousness at arriving at a new school or the fact that my mom and aunt could be hundreds of miles away by then. I had an emergency on my hands—a fashion faux pas. Thorny offered to take me downtown and help me pick out some jeans and shirts. Newly planted in New York, I had met my best girlfriend.

I grabbed my purse to follow her, but she looked at me like I had corn growing out of my ears. "Where are you taking that?"

"What? That's where I keep my money."

"I know that's where you keep your money." She looked at me. "Guess who else knows that's where you keep your money? Look, girl, you're going to get jacked if you're not careful."

Maybe they speak another language in New York?

"Jacked," she explained as she stepped out the door, "is when some-one lures you into a conversation and then steals your purse." Her voice sounded even higher in the courtyard. "Put your money in your pocket."

I couldn't tell her I had never ridden a subway before—life in Detroit seemed so 'bama now. I was beginning to miss Mom and Aunt Ruth. The only train I'd ever ridden was to visit my granny in Portsmouth. This one was packed with people, standing and sitting. The air was dank and tinged with dust. As Thorny and I chatted about Detroit and how exciting it was to be in New York, a fight broke out. Two gangs, one black and one Puerto Rican, started arguing. I had just seen *West Side Story*. This was Sharks and Jets. I sat enthralled.

"We're getting off this train," Thorny announced, pulling me out the door. "Lesson number two? When you see folks fighting, you get the hell out of their way."

||||||||||||

On waking that first morning at Barnard I realized something I had and something I lacked. I needed help. I tiptoed over to a room from which music was coming and knocked on the closed door.

"Who the hell is knocking on my door?" a gruff voice shouted sec-onds before the door swung open with enough force to tear it from the hinges. "So what do you want?"

She was tall, dark skinned, and easily the most beautiful woman I had ever seen in my life. I stood there smiling and blinking.

"Hi, my name is Marsha. Do you have," I asked cringing, "a tampon I could borrow?"

This imposing woman looked at me, expressionless. I could see the headline: STUDENT FROM DETROIT THROWN FROM 7TH FLOOR WIN-DOW. Without saying a word the woman turned and disappeared inside her room. Moments later, she returned, handing me a box of tampons. "Anything else I can help you with?"

||||||||||||

I had never seen such hair. When it passed my room—this plaited, elaborate, twisted mass, covered in string and then bent down into designs—I simply had to meet the woman brandishing it. She roomed across the hall from me, so I waited until she left her door open one day and introduced myself. She told me she was from Nigeria. She was Igbo, from the eastern part of the country. My grandfather's telling me that his enslaved mother was Igbo comprised my knowledge of the subject. This woman's name was Beatrice Egekenze. Beatrice was a mathematics major. She was quick to laugh and tell stories about her country. Her telling was the first I heard about the Nigerian-Biafran War that caused her family to flee to the United States.

Beatrice challenged me. "Why don't you take an African name?" Although I had read Malcolm with grateful amazement, I had never thought to adopt an African name. I thought of my granny in Portsmouth.

I asked, "Could you suggest an African name for me?"

"Yes," she smiled. "Let me dream about it first."

As I walked to my room, I looked back and saw Beatrice behind me, slowly nodding her head.

The next day brought a soft tapping on my door that woke me with a start. I opened the door a crack to see Beatrice standing there with a big smile on her face. "Ngozi."

"Excuse me?"

"That's the name I've decided to give you—Ngozi."

"What does it mean?"

"Blessings!" Beatrice beamed. "I've decided that you are going to be a blessing for me." From then on, everyone at Barnard called me Ngozi.

||||||||||||

I was standing in the courtyard in front of the statue of the Greek games.

"Ngozi!" someone called out. I turned and looked. It was the woman I had bothered on the seventh floor. She was with another woman I had met named Cynthia Chapman. As they walked over toward me, my heart began to sink until I noticed she was even more beautiful when she smiled.

"I heard you changed your name to Ngozi. My name's Sylvia Farrington. How are we doing today?" She looked at Cynthia. "I told you about how she introduced herself to me the other day."

Cynthia laughed. "Yes!" She touched my forearm. "We've all been there."

"So why Ngozi?" Sylvia asked. "What's wrong with Marsha?"

"Oh, there's nothing wrong with Marsha. I've always admired African names. I guess it comes from my grandmother being a staunch Garveyite."

"Get out! I'm Jamaican!" Marcus Garvey was a national hero in Jamaica. Sylvia took me by the elbow. "There's something I want you to see."

She led Cynthia and me across the courtyard and into a building on the other side of the quad.

"Do you know what happened here?"

Cynthia and I looked at each other. We were standing outside the gymnasium. "A basketball game?" Cynthia offered.

Sylvia smiled and rolled her eyes. "On the other side of those doors, Ngozi, in February of 1965, a man named Little gave an impassioned speech to a packed house. Among the things he said was that he would rather be dead than have somebody deprive him of his rights. He went on to say that 'we are living in an era of revolution, and the revolt of the American Negro is part of the rebellion against the oppression and colonialism which has characterized this era.'[1] It was the last public address Mr. Little ever made. He was shot dead three days later right down the street in Harlem."

Cynthia and I looked at each other.

"You probably know Mr. Little better as Malcolm X."

||||||||||||

It seemed like it was the next day, after immersing myself in the Barnard Organization of Soul Sisters (BOSS), making friends with women from all walks of life from the United States and all over the world, finding myself in the acute and embracing culture of Barnard's intellectual and spiritual challenges, and establishing lifelong friends on the seventh floor. But the next day, those four years were over.

"What do you plan to study when you leave Barnard?" my advisor and mentor, Dr. Inez Reid, asked. She was an attorney and held a doctorate in political science. She was one of two African American professors at the college.

"I'm interested in studying Egyptology?" I said, like it was a question. Dr. Reid looked at me.

"Are you from a wealthy family?"

"No."

"Then you will starve," she said. "If you're interested in studying Africa, why don't you study political science? You can concentrate on Africa."

Practicality, that's what I had been missing.

"I have a dear friend at MIT, Willard Johnson. You would receive a first-class education from him." As an afterthought, Inez added, "By the way—Willard is also an activist, like you."

iiiiiiiiiiiiii

"There was a curious hush come over the crowd when so many of the prestigious awards—summa cum laude, first in international affairs, most likely to succeed—went to women who lived on the seventh floor," Mom said. Her observations could be astute.

Collectively we knew the world was now within our reach. We headed out the door, expecting it.

MIT:
The Vortex of Minds and Hearts

"I call upon the board of regents to divest MIT's retirement funds immediately!"

The metallic voice belied the tall and stately gentleman who held a megaphone before his taut face as he swayed with the cadence of his phrasing. This was across from the iconic domed rotunda and Roman pillars that symbolize MIT.

Chants of "M-I-T! Divest NOW! Free Mandela NOW! Free South Africa NOW!" rose from and washed over the sea of students.

"We will not tolerate our government's criminal partnership with the fascist, antidemocratic, and brutal apartheid regime."

The man looked straight ahead—not at the waves of faces gathered in support nor farther back where the Charles River's graceful sailboats rode on calm blue water nor even to the complex of buildings sprawling above their own reflections—rather, this austere man wielded words and a deep complaint toward the powers that be in South Africa, toward all of their collaborators, and toward the expansive distance itself.

It was September 1974. Cambridge, Massachusetts. I had left my beloved friends and Barnard three months earlier. MIT was as different from Barnard as Cambridge was from New York City. Mom and Aunt Ruth accompanied me to Cambridge, again helping me settle into a new apartment—with one difference: my mother was now quite used to life in Detroit without me. She didn't have the same angst about Cambridge that she'd had about New York.

"Good evening, my name is Willard." I was standing in front of the man who had led the demonstration. The department of political science was holding a cocktail party in Building 17 to welcome its incoming doctoral students.

"Dr. Inez Reid advised me to come to MIT to study under you." I expected him to interrupt me, but he waited for me to complete my thought. "I was at the demonstration today."

"Yes! What an introduction to MIT." Johnson threw his head back.

"Well," I said, "we've had a couple of demonstrations at Columbia." We both laughed, thinking of the student takeover there. Inez had said we would have lots in common.

Dr. Johnson was an Africanist, a specialist in African political affairs and development theories of third world countries. "Have you thought about what you would like to do after you graduate?"

I had just arrived, yet my advisor already had the confidence in me to discuss my life after MIT. I liked him immediately. "My goal is to work at the United Nations. I am particularly interested in development and looking at environment, health, and politics."

"We will have a lot of time to discuss all of those issues," Johnson said. "An average student spends about six years in the program."

Six years! Did I hear him say "six years"? I was twenty-two years old. Six years was a lifetime. That meant I would almost be thirty when I graduated! I envisioned myself white haired, slowly pushing a walker across the stage to receive my diploma.

"Some students do graduate earlier," he reassured me, "but the average time is about six years, without a master's degree."

Another man approached us. "Hi, Ithiel. This is my student, Marsha Coleman. She will be studying Africa with me."

"Dr. Ithiel de Sola Pool," Willard explained after Pool had moved on to greet others, "teaches communications theory."

I later found out that Dr. Pool was credited with establishing the MIT political science department.

||||||||||||

During orientation I noticed students who appeared to be living in the library and wondered what kind of people would do that. By the end of my first month, I had moved into the all-night library, complete with toothbrush and shower cap.

"Mom, I no longer have a social life or friends. All I do is study." I felt guilty complaining. She was making enormous financial sacrifices to finance my graduate work, and she never complained.

"Marsha, it's not forever. Just buckle down and do your best." There was logic in her reasoning, but she didn't have a clue about what my daily life was like. There was a pause. "Marsha, have you decided whether you're going to move back to Detroit when you finish MIT?"

"I don't think so, Mom. I like the East Coast, and I'm probably going to find a job out here." I expected her to protest and give me a dozen reasons for coming back to Detroit.

"Well, if you're not coming back . . ." she started. I couldn't remember another time I had ever heard her voice in quite the same tone. It was soft, quiet, girl-like. "I think I'll get married this weekend."

It felt like the universe was waiting for my response. I moved through a sense of the ground lifting under me. For the first time in my life, Mom was going to have someone besides me in her life, my equal, and maybe even of more significance to her if he was not already. There was an endless instant when I was both her thankful daughter and her mother. Majestice Coleman was asking for my permission.

"Mom," I said, my voice heavy with an authority I did not know I had, "I am so glad to hear that. I am so happy for you. I want you to marry Bill. And I love you so much for all that you have done for me. You both have my blessings."

I remember her saying, "Thank you, Marsha," and how much farther away she seemed, as though she had put the phone down on the kitchen table and was talking from the other side of the room. But I don't remember anything else from the conversation. I thought about it the next day, wondering if I had made it clear enough, worried that I might not have, but deep in my heart I knew she knew. And she knew I knew.

So it was that mom married Bill Prater, the man she had started dating when I was four years old.

||||||||||||

The workload was backbreaking and ferocious. It soon became obvious that at MIT students were divided into two categories: those who had to study and those who didn't. I was among the former.

My friend, Walter Hill, had attended MIT as an undergraduate. "MIT students work hard and play hard," he said when I griped about the pace. The work part of Walter's equation was obvious. But completion of a doctoral program was not only based on performance and contingent upon competing with the best minds in the world, it also hinged on having a supportive mentor—one who essentially reserved his or her mentee a place at the table. The prospect of not making the grade became part of the stress every year. I didn't see any prospect of play at MIT.

"We're going to this party, Marsha. We've got to relax sometime." Evelyn was my roommate, and the stress from the physics program was making her crazy. "If we can't relax at this party, at least we can worry while other people have fun."

We'd been invited to a party given by some Nigerian MIT students who had studied in Russia. For my part, I'd had it with studying and needed a diversion. As we were just arriving, one of the Nigerian hosts was leaving to pick his girlfriend up at the airport, so our meeting was brief and hurried. I learned his name was Segun.

"He was cute," I told my roommate after Segun left.

"Yeah, he's one of the boy geniuses at MIT," she said. "He's working on a PhD in the Department of Aeronautics and Astronautics." She looked at me with eyebrows raised. "A certified rocket scientist."

||||||||||||

Before I had truly felt the rigors of MIT, I decided to take courses at Harvard Law School to scratch an itch I still had about becoming a lawyer. I took law school courses in the morning and attended MIT in the afternoon. As the year wound down, I was becoming passionate about my African studies with Willard but didn't feel the same pull from law school. I was, however, eligible to go on an exchange program through Harvard Law School to the University of Ghana at Legon, and decided to go.

At twenty-three, I had been able to burn the candle from both ends and the middle, keep my performance level up, begin to sour on law as a profession, and keep a spark about Africa glowing, if faintly. The flight to Europe was catch-up time for much-needed sleep. The flight from London to Ghana was endurable. The significance of the trip didn't set in until the plane landed at Kotoka International Airport in Accra. The young African American woman who had sat next to me without speaking a word in the entire ten hours since we had left Europe suddenly turned to me with tears rolling down her face. "I'm the first in my family to come back," she said.

I looked out the window and saw rolling savannah and the undiluted equatorial sunshine for the first time. Granny, I'm home.

||||||||||||

The University of Ghana campus had enormous fan palm trees gracing the entrance and an uneasy mix of colonial British architecture and tropical flair. I was assigned a dorm room in Mensah Sarbah Hall, the window laced with fragrances of mango and lemon, birdsongs, and morning groundnut hawkers.

British common law and Ghanaian traditional law were far removed from the American case method that featured dialogue between professors and students. In Ghana, the professor entered the classroom at the appointed time with his aide, lectured for one hour, and then left.

I couldn't reconcile being in Ghana with spending all of my time in a classroom. For me it was no longer Ghana—it was Africa. I was utterly distracted. Finally, I approached the professor.

"I'll take the final exam, but I won't be attending classes anymore." Clumsily as it came out, I simply couldn't take another day inside.

That afternoon, I packed some clothes in a backpack and jumped on a bus. I didn't care where it was going. Africa was a big, magical place, and for the next three weeks, I rode from one village to another, jumping off to find a place to eat or sleep, usually with an older woman taking me in. I now understood my grandmother's great yearning to live in a country where everyone looked like family and shared our standard of beauty.

Toward the end of the three weeks, I was riding on a bus next to a man who spoke Twi or Fanti. Mute companions, we didn't even try to communicate, but we felt our connection. I had dozed off against the window when he tapped on my hand and pointed to the top of a hill. It was like he had reached inside my dream and found what I was looking for. I asked the driver to stop. Jumping off the bus I found my way to what I learned was the Cape Coast Castle, the grossly inaccurately named dungeon of enslavement, and spent the rest of the day there. I so much wanted to reach out to my family members who had perished between the coast and the villages—to let them know that I had survived.

The structure itself was a glorified cave, European above ground, Neanderthal below. A curator conducted tours of the grotto-like underbelly. He was reverential and solemn in his presentation, closing the door to one of the catacombs behind us. At once there was silence and so much darkness. Then a sound like someone snapping cloth as bats stirred in the cave, its mustiness heightened by the dark. On opening the door the guide pointed out calcified fingernails, embedded in the wall.

The tour was over within an hour. Yet even after being entombed in the dark, in the feel of the place, I found connecting with the past was almost impossible. It turned out that absence—a palpable absence—was the strongest presence. This unbridgeable gulf was at first more depressing than the castle itself—where so many had suffered and died—until I realized the man on the bus was the bridge. His fingertips held the touch of the ancients. At Cape Coast, slavery took on a human face. I pondered the enormous courage my relatives had commanded to survive, knowing their DNA was alive in me like those embedded fingernails. Beatrice had christened me, but Cape Coast seared Ngozi on my soul. Ghana left me more committed than ever to finishing my degree in African studies.

iiiiiiiiiiiii

The next time I saw him, he was coming from St. Paul AME Church, near MIT.

"Hello," I said hopefully. "Do you remember me? We met briefly at your apartment."

"Not really," he said. "Were you at my party?"

I attributed the boy genius's memory loss to arrogance and decided the best way to save face was to extricate myself as quickly as possible. But I had misread Segun. The next time we met, in the Infinite Corridor, Segun was rushing off to a class when he saw me and invited me out to lunch at the student center. So he knew who I was anyway. But then our small talk felt awkward.

He told me what he was studying, and when I said I was specializing in political science, he was surprised. "I didn't know MIT had a political science department," he said.

What surprised me about the man was that he didn't have any elaborate come-ons written on his sleeve. He was direct and unaffected and had no clue how to impress me.

I was most impressed.

What I had mistaken for arrogance was shyness. Segun had just arrived in the States after receiving his bachelor's and master's degrees in the Soviet Union. I was fascinated by his accent, which was an odd mixture of Nigerian and Russian. Over lunch I found his combination of West African and Eastern European cultures fascinating.

We became good friends and over the next few months were nearly inseparable. Everyone thought we were dating, but that idea never occurred to us. We enjoyed our discussions of politics and food. The best part—on top of Segun's love of jazz and writing poetry—was that he was an excellent cook. Segun would pick me up at the all-night library, take me to his apartment where he had prepared a delicious Nigerian stew of tomatoes, okra, and chicken, and then drop me back off at the library. Nothing more than good conversation, usually on my favorite subject—Africa—from a man with deep and rich roots in the heart of the continent.

Segun had studied aeronautical engineering in Russia, arriving when he was eighteen years old. He hadn't spoken a word of Russian but had been expected not only to learn the language within a couple of months but to master complex scientific and mathematical concepts in Russian. Segun was fluent in three months. He attended the Kiev Institute of Aviation and graduated with honors at both the undergraduate and graduate levels, leaving after six years with his master's degree. At MIT he was among the gifted students. He could pick up a physics or math book, flip through it a couple of times, and understand the material. He was amazed that I had to study all the time to keep up. True to form, Segun graduated from MIT in three years and was planning to return to Nigeria to serve in the nation's air force for three years.

He had been my closest ally at MIT and a trusted confidant. I knew I was going to miss the luxury of his friendship and his cooking and that he, more than anyone, had gotten me through my roughest stretches. But even more than this, we had fallen in love.

Before he left, we decided to visit my mother. She was completely taken with him, his charm and his warmth. That night, she came into my bedroom with a smile on her face.

"Marsha, I really like him. I've always believed that, when the right man came along for you, I would know it. Has he raised the idea of marriage?"

"Mom, he's leaving for Nigeria when we return to Cambridge, but we've decided to stay in touch."

"He's the right man, Marsha. Don't let him get away!"

The next morning the air in the kitchen was buzzing. Mom had made a breakfast of homemade biscuits and eggs, which she served with a quiet and high pitch to her voice that was almost as foreign as the way Segun was acting.

"Mom," Segun said, his voice soft and serious. "What would you say if I asked for Marsha's hand in marriage?"

Mom nearly dropped her teacup. She looked at me with a straight face. "Marsha, would you like to marry Segun?"

I said, "Yes?"

Mom smiled. "You have my . . ." She started to cry. I'm sure she managed the word *blessing* eventually.

We decided to delay our marriage until Segun finished his stint in the air force and I finished school.

||||||||||||

With more than a year remaining in my doctoral program and Segun stationed in Nigeria, my favorite time every day was about ten minutes before the start of Willard Johnson's class. By arriving early I could sit and savor the solitude of the classroom, even the smell. There was a spiritual quality and suspense in the room that deepened before all of the bodies filed in.

Willard suggested I concentrate on communications theory in my dissertation, by focusing on three case studies of the press coverage of major news events in Africa: the assassination of Steve Biko; the election of Robert Mugabe in Zimbabwe; and the Cuban versus South African intervention in Angola. This would allow the integration of my interest in

culture, media, and African studies. Noam Chomsky's work on newspapers as propaganda vehicles represented another resonating possibility.

Chomsky's *For Reasons of State* is prefaced with this quote from
Michael Bakunin: "The state is the organized authority, domination,
and power of the possessing classes over the masses . . . the most fla-
grant, the most cynical, and the most complete negation of humanity."
Was this the reasoning behind what had happened to Fred Hampton? To Martin and Malcolm? Chomsky's radioactive hooks had been
set. I ingested *American Power and the New Mandarins* and later *The
Washington Connection and Third World Fascism.*[1] It was there that I
read Chomsky's indictment of the work of Ithiel de Sola Pool, who had
devised the US "hearts and minds" propaganda program for Vietnam
and promoted the notion that passivity and defeatism were necessary
for stability in third world countries.

After completing my comprehensives I was determined to meet Professor Chomsky and embark on my dissertation. I had met many professors who had egos so inflated after publishing mere pamphlets that
they would treat students like old toothpaste. I was expecting a larger-
than-life, self-absorbed, maniacal academic when I approached.

"Professor Chomsky?" I said, as he invited me into his office.

"No, please. Call me Noam."

"OK," I said softly. "I am a doctoral student working on my dissertation in the political science department in the areas of propaganda and
African studies. I have read much of your political work, and I was wondering . . ." I paused. "I was wondering if you would consider sitting on
my dissertation committee." I asked this expecting a negative response.
I imagined him saying, "I'll think about it and get back to you in a week,"
or "Sorry, I'm too busy."

"Well, I don't know that much about Africa," he said. "I'm sure Willard will take care of that." Then, without taking his eyes off me, he said,
"Yes, I'll be delighted to sit on your committee."

I was dumbfounded. I had just asked a man noted worldwide for his
brilliant mind to help usher me through the next phase of my intellectual development—and he had accepted. I was most struck by Noam's
soft kindness.

Noam had been on staff at MIT since 1955, a full professor since
1966. He had obtained the highest and most prestigious title awarded
faculty members at MIT, institute professor. With that status, Noam

acquired a unique level of freedom to pursue his research and interests across institute programs and departments. An institute professor could sit on any doctoral panel in the institute, and only twelve professors were permitted to hold that title at any time. The title conferred enormous credibility and prestige to projects or dissertations undertaken under its moniker.

In the academic and scientific community, Noam Chomsky was widely considered the father of modern linguistics. Since the early 1960s he had also become known as a political dissident and critic of American imperialism. His opposition to the Vietnam War established him as a vocal critic of US foreign and domestic policy. He was a critic of academic mandarins who developed and refined government intelligence propaganda. And at MIT this effort was led, in Vietnam particularly, by Ithiel de Sola Pool.

The announcement that Noam was going to sit on my dissertation committee was a cataclysmic moment in the environs of the political science department. Pool's books had established him as a father of twentieth-century propaganda studies and mass communications theory. He was an analyst for the CIA and intelligence-sponsored warfare studies. He vehemently opposed Noam's participation on my dissertation committee, hoping to deny him any credibility in the area of political science.

Chomsky had consistently been critical of Pool's works and of Pool's colleagues in the Chicago School who had helped develop mass-communication strategies in support of the Vietnam offensive. The two scholars were diametrically opposed in political positions and sympathies. One was a leading advocate for the US war effort in Vietnam and the other its leading opponent. Noam's wife, Carol Chomsky, had earned a doctoral degree in linguistics from Harvard University in 1968 in order to ensure that she would be able to make a living in the event that her husband was sent to jail for his active opposition to the Vietnam War.[2]

"Now that you have selected your panel and we have a topic, I'm going to ask the department secretary to schedule a date for your colloquium," Willard told me. "As you can imagine, Ithiel is not particularly pleased about you inviting Noam to sit on your panel, but I think it's going to be OK."

The colloquium was the formal announcement by the PhD candidate of the dissertation topic. The entire faculty was invited to attend, but in actual fact, colloquia were usually attended by the dissertation chairs and, if you bribed them sufficiently, your best friends. I was looking forward to the last half of my studies when rumors started flying that my dissertation was in trouble, both because of the topic and because of my bringing Chomsky into the process. It had become clear that Ithiel would be taking a stand, but Noam and Willard encouraged me to stay focused on preparing for the colloquium.

A common survival strategy employed by doctoral candidates was to choose a dissertation topic that would not draw attention. In my case, I had broken that cardinal rule. My dissertation explored whether US newspapers could be considered vehicles of propaganda. The only way to keep a topic like that under the radar was to fly the plane into the side of the mountain. Because of the very public stand Chomsky had taken protesting against the war and through his written work, word of Noam's scheduled appearance in the department of political science spread like wildfire throughout the MIT community. The mountainside was closing fast.

I stayed with a colleague, Suzanna del Mazo, the last four days before my colloquium, practicing my presentation. We role-played the question-and-answer period. Suzanna, from Mexico, was a wonderful, supportive friend whose colloquium was scheduled to take place shortly after mine.

"Where are all the voices coming from?" I looked at Suzanna. "Please tell me they're not coming from the colloquium room." The din was unnerving.

"Just stay focused. What's the worst that can happen?" Suzanna asked. I stopped in my tracks and shook my head. "Sorry," she offered with a fretful smile.

The closer we came to the room, the louder the voices. Students and faculty had arrived early to get seats, and every inch of floor space was jammed. Willard waved me to the front of the room.

"What's happening here?" I whispered to him. "I thought no one ever came to these things."

"When you have Noam Chomsky and Ithiel Pool in the same room . . ." He didn't finish the sentence. Lucky me, I thought.

Noam was late. No one was ever late for colloquia. I looked at Ithiel and the other political science faculty, who were anticipating a contrite Noam Chomsky when he arrived.

"Sorry for being late," Noam said as he walked in. "I thought the political science department was located in the School of Business." The others sat stunned and humorless.

Willard started the colloquium by introducing himself and Chomsky. He introduced me and asked me to present my dissertation topic. Suzanna later told me that my voice was shaking so much she thought I was crying. I somehow finished my statement.

It didn't take long for the fireworks. Ithiel began with a thinly veiled double entendre—asking me about the significance of my work, a fair enough question en face. The pointed implication, however, was that Noam Chomsky and Willard Johnson might not be competent to understand the significance of my research. They didn't miss the affront. First, Willard asked me to outline some of the gaps in the literature. Next, Chomsky took on the significance of an intellectual treatment of American newspapers as vehicles of propaganda. Chomsky's argument hinged on his belief, based on research, that the vast majority of newspapers worldwide—including those in the United States—had by the early 1950s been thoroughly infiltrated by government and corporate interests for the purpose of disseminating and instilling propaganda. The infiltration was further entrenched by virtue of close associations in academe, with communications theory and public relations curricula embracing and helping develop effective propaganda communication and dissemination techniques. Thus, educational systems—which, Chomsky argued, ought to be independent of ideological biases—had lost credibility, and journalism as a watchdog for governmental malfeasance was also compromised.

Pool argued that far from being instruments of propaganda, the social sciences of psychology, sociology, and communications theory were the instruments of humanizing those in power. The insights into the human condition that the social sciences provided were vital to a paradigm shift away from aloof heads of state ruling over subordinate populations and toward a more sympathetic interrelationship between those in power and the masses. This shift, in Pool's view, was born in the mid-twentieth century by virtue of a deep understanding of the social sciences.

I soon realized that the discussion was no longer about my colloquium only but about the greater issue of academic freedom, the politicization of the process. It filled two hours of intense debate between Pool, representing the school of communication and psychological warfare, and Chomsky, from the school of hegemonic ideology. The colloquium ended with political lines sharply drawn. Ithiel, Noam, and Willard had all held forth. None had backed down.

After all of the anticipation, the colloquium was finally over. I was tying up some loose ends when I saw Professor Pool coming down the hall. He was not happy about the colloquium. He asked me to come into his office.

Before I could say anything, Ithiel spoke. "You are not going to graduate from this department. If you do, it will be over my dead body."

We stood looking at each other.

"You may leave now," he said.

I was crushed. I walked down the hall in shock, feeling powerless and defeated. In three hours, I had gone from feeling like I had cleared a near-impossible hurdle to realizing I had wasted nearly six years of my life. I wanted to go back and try to reason with Professor Pool, but I also needed advice. I decided to call my mother.

"How did your colloquium go?" She couldn't wait to ask once she heard my voice.

How was I going to tell her about this roller-coaster day and its ending? I told her the colloquium had been eventful but that I thought it had gone well.

"Mom, I have to tell you what a professor said to me today."

She listened, and when I started to cry, she just let me explode on the phone. There was a long pause to make sure I was finished.

"Marsha," Mom said with a calm but firm voice, "first of all, this man is not God—he's simply a bully! I'm glad you didn't go back and talk with him. I want you to fast and pray, and I will join you. But call Noam and Willard and let them know what he said. I'm not at all concerned, except I want you to calm down. You will be fine."

I called Noam, telling him what Ithiel had said.

"I know that you're upset, but try to calm down. I need you to stay focused on your research. Willard and I can take care of the politics. Try not to worry."

The next day, Willard was concerned. "Obviously a lot of people were unhappy about the colloquium yesterday." His voice was slow and thoughtful. "What do you think about writing your dissertation outside of Cambridge? I have some contacts in California. Perhaps we could work something out."

I was still reeling from my confrontation with Ithiel. Willard and I discussed the pros and cons of a change of venue. California was a country away. The atmosphere there would be completely different. The heat of the colloquium would fade for Ithiel and his cohorts. It would be best for me to disappear for a while.

⁓⁓⁓⁓⁓

The six months it took to organize a California fellowship gave me time to work with Willard and Noam on the dissertation. Noam's schedule was relentless: classes, interviews, speaking engagements. Accompanying him to speaking events provided the only time to meet with him. We worked on the dissertation while driving places or while waiting for the events to start.

"We need to step outside for a few minutes until the police clear the area," Noam said calmly. Some democracy-loving patriot had called in a threat, and the police would have to empty the auditorium and bring in bomb-sniffing dogs. Noam didn't flinch; he didn't get angry. There were many death threats, but I never saw him complain or express any displeasure about them. He took them in stride as a natural part of the political process.

I worked closely with Willard, although the tensions within the department persisted. I accepted a fellowship at the University of California at Santa Barbara (UCSB), through their Black Studies program. Known as the American Riviera, Santa Barbara, situated on an east-west trending coastline between the Santa Ynez Mountains and the sea, had a Mediterranean feel. UCSB was another world. Either the ocean or mountains lay outside any window. This was no Cambridge pressure cooker. I taught communications theory and African politics as part of my fellowship. The rest of my time was spent completing the dissertation—whenever possible, on the beach—where I wrote in peace.

⁓⁓⁓⁓⁓

And then tragedy struck.

Mom called to tell me Bill was dying from lung cancer. Two months later, Bill was dead. Mom was devastated. After so many years of deferring her life with Bill, it had come to this. I stayed in Detroit with her as long as I could. When I returned to California after Bill's funeral, I called Segun in Nigeria to tell him about Bill. Segun and Bill had always clicked. Segun would want to know. He had also been close to Mom, and I thought he might be able to comfort her. The next day, Segun called to say that he had made travel arrangements. He arrived in Santa Barbara within two weeks.

When he climbed out of the cramped Cessna, he greeted me with a healing embrace and a jarring question. "Why don't we get married while I'm here?"

I didn't answer.

"Did you hear me?"

"Segun," I said, "Mom just lost her husband, and she's not here to witness our marriage."

We decided to table any discussion of marriage until the end of his visit. I could not wait, however, to get home and call Mom.

"Don't be silly," she said in response to my question of whether or not I should marry Segun. "I say, marry him. I promise you—you will be happy. He is my choice."

The long and the short of it is that we were married on January 19, 1981, in a simple ceremony in the office of Rev. Dana Alexander, in Santa Barbara. Two of Segun's lifelong friends, Bolaji and Remi Aluko, who happened to be living there, served as witnesses. Our honeymoon was dinner, after which we saw *9 to 5* at the movies and went home and fell asleep.

We woke up the next morning to the declaration: "I, Ronald Wilson Reagan, do solemnly swear that I will faithfully execute the office of president of the United States, and will to the best of my ability preserve, protect, and defend the Constitution of the United States."

True to form, Segun flew out alone to Detroit later that afternoon. He had planned to stay two weeks, and he wanted to spend time with Mom and Aunt Ruth before returning to Nigeria. To Segun, the idea of traveling thousands of miles to the United States and not visiting his mother-in-law—and a grieving one at that—was inconceivable. Watching his plane seemingly dissolve in the distance only added to the sense of the marriage being a mirage—married one day and Segun gone the next.

|||||||||||||

Within one month, Segun had arranged for me to arrive in Nigeria to spend more time with his family. Our first stop was to visit Segun's father, uncle, and aunt, but the highlight was a visit to his village of Igbara Oke in the mountains of southwest Nigeria to receive the blessings of the ancestors and his grandmother—Deborah Adebayo—whom we affectionately called Mama.

"Why didn't you tell me that you come from a prominent family?" I asked Segun when I saw him in Nigeria.

"Didn't think it was important," was his answer. Segun's father, Augustus, had become known throughout Nigeria as a brilliant scholar and a sought-after political advisor to presidents and military leaders. He later headed the civil service. Segun's uncle, Alex, studied architecture and helped design major government and academic structures. Segun's aunt, Comfort, took up entrepreneurial pursuits.

Mama was quite pleased about our marriage, and although we had language difficulties, she set about Yoruba bride training with a zest and fervor that belied her nearly one hundred years. She taught me how to cook Yoruba dishes, how to care for a household and my husband, and how to dress in traditional *iro ati buba*.

Early morning, around 4:00 A.M., the household was called to prayer, and promptly at 6:00 A.M. we walked to St. Paul's Episcopal Church. During my first service, Mama announced to the women in Yoruba, "This is Segun's wife from America. Her family left here when the white man came, but now Segun has brought her back to us. She is my daughter and a wife of this village."

The women in the village formed a prayer circle around me, dancing and singing praises to God. I tried to keep up, but the expert gyration of their hips and shoulders humbled me. Mama placed her hands on my head. I instinctively knew to kneel. She lifted her eyes and said:

O ni ri iponju.
You will never encounter hardship.
Jesu a se amona ati alakoso re.
Jesus will be your guide and guardian.

I knew I would one day use these prayers to bless my children.

Above our heads a bright red sun announced the dawning of a new day. A breeze crisscrossed the farmlands, releasing the newly dewed fragrance of mangoes, oranges, and papaya. I felt complete, loved, and at home.

I returned from Nigeria, excited about my new family and looking forward to concluding my research. I sent Willard and Noam the latest version of my dissertation, which I had worked on in Nigeria, fingers crossed and praying as I dropped off the document at the post office in Santa Barbara.

IIIIIIIIIIIII

"I've just spoken with Noam, and I have good news for you." It was Willard. I hadn't spoken to him in six months. It was great to hear his melodic voice. "We feel it's time for you to come back to Cambridge to discuss the final edits and schedule a defense date for your dissertation."

I was looking forward to seeing Willard and Noam in the flesh after our year apart. Returning to Cambridge under such different circumstances made the crisp New England day that much more spectacular. A man who looked vaguely familiar entered the elevator, but I could not place him. I thought better of asking if I knew him.

"Hello, Willard," I said, upon reaching his office, New England's reserve restraining both of us after the long absence.

"And how is Mrs. Coleman-Adebayo?" Willard delighted in my new last name. "It looks good on you, young lady."

We talked for a while, and then I mentioned the man in the elevator.

"Oh, yes," Willard said. "Ithiel is quite ill. He's putting up a fight. We're all hoping for the best."

I went on to successfully defend my dissertation, receiving my PhD in political science in the spring of 1982. The diversion to California had worked—but just. My run-in with forces systematically arrayed to defend and protect the status quo had come seemingly out of nowhere within a system widely regarded as a bastion of free speech, free thought, and receptivity to honest debate. I put the entire episode down to the inclinations of one man, chalking it up to experience. The prestige of MIT now bolstered my bona fides. I set myself to the task of finding a bridge to Africa.

Ethiopia:
The Good Mother

And what a bridge it was. Rather like the bridge to Key West: one gets there eventually.

Barnard and MIT had nothing to do with it. Even well placed calls to people inside weren't quite enough. As a courtesy to the contact who had recommended me I was granted a lunch with a woman of some stature at the UN. I was then treated to her chortling at the succession of no's I offered when asked whether I was an attorney, had published any books, or had written any articles.

"My advice to you, my dear," my lunch guest croaked, "is to get your JD, write some books, publish articles widely, and then come back in about ten years."

I went home and lay in bed for three days crying.

But self-pity, like the insularity of academe, also ends. Segun had secured a position at the University of the District of Columbia. Having Washington as a home base put a wide array of governmental institutions within reach. I was soon pounding the streets and found short stints teaching African and communications studies at American University and working as a senior policy analyst on Africa at the Congressional Black Caucus Foundation (CBCF). I even volunteered to be project manager for a conference on African desertification that the

UN held at Howard University, but still, I had no entrée to the United Nations. At CBCF I worked with literally hundreds of congressional offices, coordinating efforts to enact Africa-related legislation. This taught me how to build consensus and get laws passed. It was long and pressured work. I came up for air when the CBCF position ended and five years had vanished. Still, there was no UN breakthrough.

Minus the pressures of my schedule and work, this was my first opportunity since leaving MIT to relax into my marriage, sleep in mornings, and contemplate all of life's possibilities with the luxury of time. I had time to take in museums and time to put feelers out into the NGO world, carefully selected with tidbits of my interests, my credentials attached as bait, and sit back to wait for any strikes.

A peculiar, uneasy sensation came over me while I was preparing breakfast one morning. It wasn't the smell exactly. It wasn't the rather odd light. It wasn't even the countertop I hated the minute I set eyes on it. But I found myself scurrying to the bathroom and gasping for air over the sink. My oyster would have to wait. I was pregnant.

And then the phone rang.

"Good morning. This is Bertin Borna, director of the United Nations Sudano-Sahelian Office, calling. May I speak to Dr. Coleman-Adebayo?" The UN had noticed my work in Congress and the conference on deserts that I had organized. Borna offered me a job in Ethiopia and Tanzania. Africa was calling me home.

Pregnant or not, there was no way to turn this opportunity down.

The trip to the hotel in Addis Ababa by cover of night allowed for at least one night's hard, if not quite restful, sleep—the sleep of the traveler, in a strange bed. This sleep, unsatisfying as it was, would be the best I'd get on the trip.

A few hours later, daylight, a rude host, threw the morning curtain open. I saw the bleak, third-world shelters that were within spitting distance of my balcony. This image would prove much more disruptive to sleeping than the travel. The tents and rough shelters had been cobbled together from the scraps jettisoned by the society that was welcoming me as a United Nations technical expert.

It was 1987, and I was taken aback. The briefings, accounts, and photographs hadn't come close to capturing this. People were dying of starvation. How was I supposed to help them or help the communities in the northern region of the country, who were subsisting in desert conditions on chronically parched land, survive the famine? How was I to restore forestland that had been reduced to sand dunes and revive parched earth into farmland?

I had arrived as an official envoy of the United Nations fully unprepared. I had always wanted to work with the United Nations in some capacity ever since the moment I had learned that there was such a body. My insatiable appetite for all things African provided the spark for my pursuit of a career in international development. This wasted city represented the dream I had long sought to fulfill: preserving the sanctity of threatened peoples, their ancient cultures, and the wisdom they might yet impart to the rest of us.

Ethiopia was renowned for its beautiful, big-eyed, open-faced children; the entire world was watching the tragedy with doubts that the UN could act effectively to save lives. This was where I would place my shoulder to the wheel. Yet my naivete, training, and belief were not equal to what was in the air rising from those streets—not an odor exactly, but a stench that was tactile, caught in the back of my throat. It was more subtle in my room, but still it was there. Something perhaps, I thought at first, in the carpet. But on leaving the sanctuary of the hotel, there could be no more mistaking what it was.

Any exit from the hotel spilled into the presence of hundreds of people housed in makeshift wooden shacks without bathrooms or running water. Women cooked over pitiful fires fueled with broken bits of found wood. Their babies crawled around in the dirt. And those were the lucky ones. The badly sick and dying were stretched out on the parched earth, too weak and hungry to move. The sheer numbers of desperate people had my heart beating outside of my chest. This was too far beyond saving. There was no relief anywhere for such staggering misery. My head was reeling.

It might be easy for governments to look at the situation and attribute every bit of it to the natural consequences of drought, but drought was not the problem. Drought was the excuse invoked to permit such human tragedies. Drought could be dealt with. There were effective, proven strategies at our disposal. The real problem, however, was the lack of policy and the presence of war. The underlying reality was that these were poor Africans, and no one has ever cared about poor Africans.

In an instant I knew I was all wrong for the job. This wasn't what I had anticipated. I instinctively looked for a church.

||||||||||||||

Ever since I was five years old, church has fortified me. I've been a Baptist; I've been a Catholic; but there's never been a time in my life when I didn't feel God's loving hand. During times of trial, I have counted on my faith to sustain me. Near panic now, I fled back to the hotel and asked the staff if they knew where a Christian church might be. They told me the closest Christian church was an Ethiopian Orthodox Coptic church that conducted its services only in Amharic. It would have to do. While they were talking I couldn't help but notice that, even though the stench wasn't inside the hotel, it was still with me, like an aftertaste.

I hurried back outside and hailed a cab that swept me through the squalor of the adjoining streets, through a place where normal metropolitan bustle brushed its elegant hems against the moribund flesh that lay strewn here and there on mats. Here were the first people, as Ethiopians like to think of themselves for their stunning beauty, strolling through the tragic trials of other ghostly refugees who streamed in from rural areas and evaporated like vapor from a rancid dish.

The church itself was ornate and surrounded by a waist-high wall with a little swing gate that opened into its sanctuary. Once I found myself inside the coolness of the place, with an acrid burst of incense, chanting, and the prayers of the faithful, the beauty of the Mass rendered the Amharic superfluous. The priest's colorful frock gave a sense of order and authority. More than this was the presence of the eternal. Despite the reality outside, I felt at peace again. Even there, I had found solace in the familiarity of the service. I took communion and prayed to God for the strength and wisdom I'd need to make a useful contribution. Fortified by the lovely Mass, intoxicated by the Spirit, and believing that, with God, all things were indeed possible, I left the church.

Just beyond the armed guard, stationed to keep the churchyard free of beggars, I was approached by a beautiful, young Ethiopian woman with chiseled, emaciated features. She had about her an air of dignified deference. Bowing slightly, she held out a small bundle wrapped in cloth—her baby—for whose small sake she was begging.

I was so moved by this mother's plight and her courage in asking the help of a foreigner. I had left my precious year-old son, Olusina, behind to accept this assignment. Segun and I had decided that I was fortunate to be working at the United Nations, even though it meant leaving behind baby Olusina. Later, I vowed, I would bring my son along with me. Olusina was in his father's doting care, I knew, but at the sight of this mother and child, I missed him suddenly and with such intensity that I was gripped by a sharp, physical longing to hold and smell an infant. Of course, I would help this woman. Smiling, I took the baby she held out to me and began to cradle it in my arms.

It was a little girl, I saw as I folded the dirty blanket back from the child's face. Her tiny face seemed frozen, as if hunger and disease had transformed her skin into a delicate plastic wrapping. Her eyes were closed, but her wavy black hair rippled as I wrapped the blanket tenderly back around her.

Then I realized she was dead, her body stiff as ice. Her mother had come to the church to beg for money. Was it so she could give her daughter a decent burial, or was this yet another act in a theater of the grotesque, in which people desperate to survive were reduced to such horrors? There was no way to know.

I started to shake and hyperventilate. Tears rolled down my face. I'd never seen a dead person before. I never could have imagined that within twenty-four hours of arriving in Ethiopia, I'd be holding a dead baby. Why had I come to this place? What did I have to offer these devastated people? My hands were trembling so much I was afraid I'd drop the tiny corpse. I forced my arms to remain steady and handed the baby girl back to the woman. I can still see her eyes drooping, her facial lines deepening with dismay as I fled, another Westerner who couldn't deal with the fierce, terrible realities she had to face every day of her life.

My mind was racing. Where is God? How can a place like this exist in this day and age? And even more discouraging, how could anything I had learned in international development hold up to the withering pressures that were everywhere around me? As I fled via cab back toward the opulence of the hotel, the atmosphere was suffocating. I felt surrounded by the unbreathable murk of everything I had ever wanted and lost. The air in the cab was stifling. How could I ever have thought myself capable of anything meaningful or of value in the face of such staggering despair?

Back in the quiet, sterile, and sanitized air of my luxuriously appointed hotel room, I berated myself for having run from that woman's pain. Whether she was a mother who simply wanted money to bury her child or just a wraith bearing a ghostly remembrancer—I'd been too shaken to address even that. What if I had been that woman and the child had been my own? How would I have wanted to be treated?

My head, spinning with these questions, could think of only one thing to do. Like a well-to-do American, I picked up the telephone and called my mother in Detroit. It was only five in the morning there, but I needed advice. I was in a place where even motherhood could fail.

"Mom!" I cried when she picked up the phone. "I'm on my way home. I can't deal with this. I'm not strong enough to handle the pain in this place."

Mom listened. It was amazing to me how a mother thousands of miles away could rouse herself from a dead sleep and listen, with all of the weight of motherhood making the distance greater and her silent listening stronger. I poured myself into the phone, into this lifeline to sanity, into this repository of everything I had ever known, ever wanted and dreamed.

"Mom, you have no idea about the level of poverty! The people are dying on the streets!" I told her about the dead baby I'd held in my arms.

"Marsha," she said when I was through, "you have spent the last six years of your life training for this moment, working on a PhD, and now working at the UN. You have all it takes to make a difference. Pray to God for strength and then roll up your sleeves and get to work. You have no right to cut and run. Punch through the fear—stay and fight!"

Her words were exactly what I needed at that moment. That was why it hadn't mattered that I would be disrupting her sleep. I needed the maternal bond that could connect instantaneously with a daughter, deep in the throes of panic, who needed comfort, understanding, and a good boot in the ass. Mom had opened her eyes from the deepest sleep and stepped into the clarity of one who knew and trusted and believed in the daughter who was losing her nerve half a world away. She effortlessly strung together the magical sentences that are still the best advice I've ever received.

We argued, of course, she believing me better, smarter, tougher than I thought I was. She hadn't spent a lifetime as a government worker, struggling so I could earn the education she had never had the resources to pursue, just so I could underestimate my own capabilities.

"You cannot turn your back on those who need your help," she said calmly. "It won't be easy, but you will be fine."

I promised Mom I would find that young mother, and the next morning I went back to the Coptic church. But I never found her. There were so many grieving mothers surrounding the church daily, the staff had absolutely no idea which one I was talking about. And though it has been many years since the harrowing apparition of an emaciated woman bearing a cold fruit, I still feel a wave of remorse wash over me when I remember the distance that had already grown between me and the people on the African continent whose most basic needs had gone unmet for so long and whom I had so desperately wanted to assist.

IIIIIIIIIIII

During my tenure in Ethiopia I managed projects that planted over a million trees and provided employment and agricultural training. My hope and prayer was that the good mother found her way to one of these projects.

But I learned a valuable lesson that first day in Ethiopia. My fear had arisen not from the scope of the misery per se but from my own doubts about my capacity to soothe it. I had confused empathy with weakness, as so many of us do when first we encounter genuine human tragedy on a bewildering scale. But it is empathy that renders making a difference even possible—empathy, not heroism or bravery.

The first step is the simplest, if the most difficult and terrifying: it is the step that takes us from stasis, from the role of observer, to a first, tentative step toward the other, calling her—Sister!—from everything that suffers and dies. And then she is no longer other, different, anonymous. And a pathway opens before our astonished eyes from which we will never be able to waver.

Retaliation at EPA

With nearly three decades' hindsight, I now can see with humbling clarity much of what idealism, inexperience, naivete, and a healthy dash of youthful grandiosity had obscured. Although I doubt that Barnard's Dr. Inez Reid could have known how instrumental the examples of Willard Johnson and later Noam Chomsky, as activist scholars, would become for me, perhaps she was wise in knowing I was going to need these champions when my idealism ran up against a government policy that saw its own workers—like my colleague at EPA, Pat Lawson—crushed under the weight of retaliation after they had blown the whistle. Pat later died of a heart attack.[1] Without knowing the particulars, perhaps Inez knew it would take more than intellectual scholarship to confront administrators who couldn't have cared less when people on their staffs developed life-threatening health problems. But I now have no doubt that Inez knew my idealism was bound to crash against whatever reality awaited me.

Twenty-five MIT professors participated in the Gore-Mbeki study tour, teaching a variety of environmental courses such as water management, soil conservation, and waste management. Willard also persuaded MIT to offer the South Africans a highly coveted training course, Proactive Environmental Strategies for Industry.[2] World-renowned scientists and policymakers presented their research at this seminar. The South Africans were eager, quick students. After some initial skirmishes with Jacob, before he learned that he could trust some government people, and even a few more after that, when his instincts got the better of him and he had to snipe just to be sure, the curriculum I had put together proved quite effective and helpful.

Jacob's group's assessment of what they could expect on their arrival back home was limited to optimistic beliefs in a new openness in the Mandela government. Many of the participants wondered out loud how aggressive America would be in policing its own companies and what leverage this insignificant group of black South Africans could have. For a group presumed to be without sophistication by some in the EPA, the South Africans actually had a firm grasp on the importance of commerce and profit. They understood that profit was what had fueled their oppression under apartheid and that profit would fuel the new government as well as any arrangements it made with other countries. Their first priority was to make a powerful statement about their own resolve to live with dignity, irrespective of the new government's intentions or American efforts to cash in.

I could see that both the South African and US agendas were dependent on a powerless workforce. It was clear that having come from the depths of helplessness and having learned to assert their own power, black South Africans were determined to combat the forces that were aligning to strip them once again of that power. Mzwakhe Mbuli, known to black South Africans as the people's poet, captured this resolve with the line: "The bull is dying at last; the bull is kicking at random without techniques."

Everyone in the group knew the poem by heart, and they chanted it in unison. Even if apartheid was dead, there was no one in that group who believed a dead bull could not still kick. They were going to make sure it was properly dismembered, rendered, and safely disposed. Or they were going to go down themselves in the attempt.

Toward the end of that week, I was starting to hear questions about this Ngakane guy. What's all this about mining? By Friday of the first week, Jacob had been called to Region III in Philadelphia. This, it was explained, was because of Jacob's special interest in and passion about vanadium. There were people there who could help him, the managers explained. He needed to establish a rapport with them. So the next week, Jacob did not participate in my program.

For my part, I had already dispatched Segun on a vanadium fact-finding detail. I knew from watching his investigative mind in action at MIT, that, if there were anything known about vanadium, Segun would find it. His preliminaries were ominous.

"I don't think you appreciate the significance of what this man is saying to you, Marsh," Segun said, coming into the kitchen with some notes he had taken on vanadium. "I have found a few very general descriptions of some of the hazardous qualities of vanadium." He handed the notes to me. "But I think beyond the obvious effects on the miners and their families, the most important thing for you to know is that the CIA considers vanadium a strategic metal."

"Where did you find that?"

"In the CIA's World Factbook. 'Uranium, gem diamonds, platinum, copper, vanadium.'"[3]

"What does that mean?" I asked as I scanned his notes.

"It means that if you are going to step into this as a health and human rights issue, you are also going to be stepping on some very big and potentially dangerous toes."

I looked at Segun for some help.

"Sweetheart, just look around this room. The stove. The refrigerator. The pots and pans. The sink. The silverware in the sink. The car in the driveway beyond the window. The engine in the car. The transmission, axles. It's everywhere. It's in the satellites that transmit cell phone calls. It's in weaponry. The entire economy of the United States and the Western world is dependent upon vanadium. The Ford Foundation says that vanadium imported from South Africa is essential to Western industry and defense. And we are the primary beneficiaries of South African vanadium."

Segun was holding *South Africa: Time Running Out*.[4] "I quote, 'While disruption in the supply of South African gold would have significant impact on world gold prices and affect international monetary stability . . . supplies of gold are not as crucial to the West from a strategic or industrial standpoint.'"

"Oh." I tried to take it all in. "Oh, Lord!"

"Yes, sweetheart. General Motors, Westinghouse, Boeing, the army, navy, air force, and marines." He looked at me. "For starters. And then we can consider Europe, Russia, China . . ."

He paused.

"But are you ready for this? Your agency published a report that says that a probable oral lethal dose for humans is between five and fifty milligrams per kilogram or between seven drops and one teaspoonful for a 70 kilogram—150-pound—person. It's as toxic as some forms of arsenic.[5] And people with diseases like asthma or bronchitis are at greater risk. And one of the side effects of exposure to vanadium," Segun said, his voice rising, "is the high risk of developing asthma and bronchitis."

"Oh, sweet Jesus!"

After the first study tour, I planned for another tour to be conducted within about two months. Whatever denials I had consoled myself with about the foreshadowing in Jacob's being sent to Philadelphia were harder to hold on to after I learned that the second tour would not be going to MIT but had been diverted to Philadelphia Region III also. Instead of training at MIT, the tour members were now in Mark Kasman's hands. I would be the face of the agency at the airport to welcome them and see them off, but I played no role in the actual training they would receive for half of their stay in the United States.

There was some consolation for me in getting to meet Bessie Mdoda. I had first contacted her via a phone call made from my home at four in the morning to let her know that she had been selected to participate in the study tour.

"Yes, this is Bessie Mdoda." Her voice had been tentative, as if she were afraid of who I might be and what horrible news I might bear.

"I am calling from the United States to tell you that you have been selected as a participant in the Environmental Protection Agency's study tour in America, as part of the Gore-Mbeki Commission."

There was absolute silence. Then, "Are you kidding me? I'm going to America?" What followed was the most explosive hooting and hollering I have ever heard. "Ooooo whoooo whooo! Bessie Mdoda is going to America! Eee-hee-hee! I am going to America! Are you kidding me?"

As I waited at Logan, I remembered Jacob's arrival and how shocking it had been to have this man I had never even heard of come marching at me. As I waited for Bessie Mdoda, I at least knew her voice. And I had heard her exuberance—whether she looked like Kimberly Elise or Moms Mabley. In my mind's eye she was a stately woman of medium build, fairly tall. So I was surprised when she stood before me, stout, short, and considerably older than the others in her group, with graying hair. Her comportment, her gentle grace, and especially her soft and easy smile, welcomed me. I melted into her warm embrace as she spoke softly in my ear.

"Thank you so much, Marsha. It is a blessing to be in America. Bless you."

Bessie Mdoda was from the Transkei, in southeastern South Africa. She seemed to be the spokesperson for the group, whether in deference to her age or by default because of her disarming presence. No matter, Bessie shined in the role. She thanked everyone she was introduced to for their support in the struggle to end apartheid. And she drew everyone she met into her warming personality. In the brief time we were together, I watched her do this many times. She beamed, like she was the host herself. She had an inescapable, endearing, and nearly beguiling smile. And somehow, despite her benediction, there was a deep haunting about her that did not diminish her bounty but instead increased her complexity.

Bessie had opened an orphanage in her community for children whose parents had been killed in the South African struggle for liberation. Bessie confided to me that, although his body had never returned, it was most likely that her only son had been one of the casualties in the fight for liberation. I knew I would not have much time with her, and since her approach was not as direct as Jacob's had been, I moved the conversation along as much as I could. Her goal on the study tour, she told me when I asked, was to raise money to convert her center to an environmental training facility.

IIIIIIIIIIII

It was a lonely week for me while the group was in Philadelphia. On their return to Washington I was right in the mix. I met the group at the airport. Bessie's greeting, while warm, was tinged with disappointment. She told me in a hushed voice while we drove from National Airport that the people she had spoken with in South Africa who had participated in the first study tour had raved about their experience. They could not say enough about how much they had learned and the respect they had been shown.

"But this"—she looked discreetly behind herself—"this was not what I expected. I come back from the beautiful city of Philadelphia with more questions than answers."

She continued, "I do not feel as if I was educated, but rather, as if"— she dropped her voice to a whisper—"as if I was interrogated."

She looked into my eyes, nodding.

"It was as if their questions were not to learn about our needs, but like, like, like they wanted to know what we were up to." Bessie's stammering was endearing. She seemed vulnerable.

"Oh no, Bessie. I am so sorry you feel that way."

"Yes. Why were we not given the same instruction as the others? It was like we were given inferior training." She shook her head.

I didn't have any answers I could give her. I kept my hunches to myself. There was no longer any doubt that the agency was backing away from the study tour. I had already been pushed aside, and, apart from my accompanying the group to their destinations at Howard, I had no active role in the official agenda. I visited the group at night and heard many of the same questions from others—and the same disappointment.

Fortunately, the staff at Howard University was as good as it gets in African and international development studies. The campus environment could not have been more congenial. Everywhere were posters and banners from the long battle the student body and the faculty had fought to get Howard to divest of any holdings in South Africa as long as apartheid survived. Longer shadows were never cast in the field of African studies and political science than those of Drs. Robert Cummings and Ronald Walters, who took the study tour under their protective wings.

Dr. Cummings was a storyteller, gifted in the way he could humanize difficult concepts. His classes were notorious for being more like performances, with his students the audience. With the South Africans he was no different. Drawing on his vast travels to all parts of Africa and his immersion in all African cultures, Bob wove migration, national development, transportation, and labor through stories invoking black South African leaders, not as some disembodied legend but by putting the listeners in the room with Steve Biko and Nelson Mandela. Cummings's role was instrumental over the years in bringing his expertise in political strategy to the antiapartheid movement. During the first All People's Voting Campaign he organized Howard University students and faculty to act as international poll observers. The black South Africans in the group felt they owed him such a debt of gratitude that they paid him with this honor.

Dr. Ronald Walters was a respected political scientist who could bring the giants down to size, whether the larger-than-life personalities associated with movements or the overwhelming complexity of the movement itself. Dr. Walters understood that what these people needed, perhaps as much as anything else, was a sense of their being equal to the task of building a new South Africa. Walters had been the campaign director for Jesse Jackson's two presidential campaigns and had worked closely with Congressmen Charles Diggs and William Gray as a policy advisor. His gift was in helping students deconstruct complex political problems and develop workable political solutions.

After a few days of visits with Bessie, I came to call her Sis. Bessie. The participants asked me to take them to a black church. I decided on Union Temple Baptist Church. Sis. Bessie was the spokeswoman.

"Thank you for all of the help you gave to me and people like me, in the strength we took from knowing that people in America were with us in our struggle to be free. Before today you did not know me, but you helped me. You could not see me, but you saw me. You could not be with me, but you were with me. Thank you.

"There are many others I speak for. Many others like me. And most of the others are much, much younger than me. Sisters, brothers, mothers, fathers. And children. Little ones. Little ones who have seen what we pray none will ever see. Little ones who are broken—who I have not the heart to tell will never see their mother again, because their mother is dead. And I don't know how to tell them that they will never see their father again—who may be dead or may just be gone for reasons no one will ever know—but for that sweet child the truth is his father is gone forever.

"And that is my purpose now. To give that child a home and give that home the voice of that child. The clap of hands and slap of feet, the simple joys that dance in a young girl's heart. This is all I will ever have now. It is all they need now. And for them it is a start."

The outpouring of love from the congregation was tactile.

||||||||||||

Then came the gauntlet: all the institutional things that make government life maddening, seeming to slow the ascent of man, a grotesque
amount of wasted time, resources, and energy. This is not to say that
there is no value in the red tape. It standardizes processes and helps
in both communication and oversight, but it's the smothering cocoon
of red tape that got to me. I started putting breathing tubes in place by
enlisting some NGOs I knew had plenty of skin in the game by virtue of
their record of resisting apartheid, hoping to bring them into the next
BNC meeting scheduled for Washington.

Knowing that vanadium was considered a strategic metal meant
that there would be resistance from outside the agency as well, and it
would be coming from places unknown and unknowable. The only real
chance for any countervailing pressure lay outside the government.
I knew I could count on Ronald Walters and Willard Johnson, who
had worked with the antiapartheid organization TransAfrica and the
Fund for a Free South Africa and Rev. Eugene Rivers of the Ella J. Baker
House in Boston. Willard also brought Heeten Kalan, the director of
the South African Exchange Program on Environmental Justice, into
the mix. Heeten was a pioneer in the environmental justice movement.[6]
He and Willard would bring formidable resources to bear. Their collective expertise was invaluable.

I had met Eugene Rivers in Cambridge when I was a student at MIT.
Eugene had come from a hard part of Philadelphia and later started
attending classes at Yale, even though he had not been matriculated.
The faculty noticed that he was not only street smart but also brilliant
and allowed him to continue taking their classes. His work in the Boston area was centered in his deep concern for children and the bussing
problem. It made sense to bring him into the mix with the study tour.

⁣⁣⁣⁣⁣⁣⁣⁣⁣⁣⁣⁣⁣⁣⁣⁣

Kenneth Thomas, in an April 17 memo to Nitze, had thrown the weight
of the US Embassy in South Africa behind the program I championed.
The importance of this could not be underestimated. He wrote:

> I have frankly been astonished at Marsha's ability to utilize
> resources from every conceivable source, even the U.S.G. [US
> government]! In a remarkably short time she has totally changed

the focus of the committee and expanded our contacts in South Africa and the U.S.[7]

I hoped that Ken's kind words and his connection to the White House would help convince Nitze to support the recommendations of the study tour.

I presented my report on the study tour to the OIA senior staff: Bill Nitze, Pat Koshel, Alan Sielen, and Mark Kasman. Nitze informed me very late in the day before the meeting that Francesca Di Cosmo and John Armstead from Philadelphia would be joining us. This eleventh-hour message had gotten under my skin. I knew Nitze was informing me of an organizational shift and that another element was being introduced into the process. This reinforced the diversion of Jacob Ngakane to Philadelphia as the first signal. The week in Philadelphia for the second study tour had been the second. Calling the officers from Philadelphia into the Washington headquarters set off my alarms.

I began my presentation by saying there were three items that had been identified, two during the study tour and one in South Africa during the BNC, that needed EPA's immediate attention.

"The first item is the issue of vanadium poisoning, in Brits, South Africa, brought to our attention by Mr. Jacob Ngakane, a COSATU (Congress of South Africa Trade Unions) representative. He is working with vanadium miners at the Vametco mine, a subsidiary of Union Carbide, a company based in Danbury, Connecticut. According to Mr. Ngakane, there are severe—and lethal—side effects associated with the vanadium mining process that have been repeatedly brought to the company's attention for years, but the company was able to ignore the complaints during the apartheid regime."

It was hard to get a read on how the committee received the presentation. Apart from nuanced facial expressions almost designed to convey boredom and even disapproval, there were no signals of receptivity coming from any of them. Occasionally someone would turn his or her head toward another, and they'd both raise their eyebrows.

"Miners show symptoms of vanadium poisoning within months of starting to work at the mine. Among the symptoms are impotence; genital, rectal, and other bleeding; the development of green tongue syndrome; asthma; lung disease, including cancer; and other chronic illnesses. Furthermore, providing workers with rudimentary safety equipment could eliminate severe burns caused by sulfuric acid due to oral suction."

They all sat sucking their teeth.

"A second area where OIA could make a significant impact is in supporting the efforts of Bessie Mdoda, the director of the Ncediwe Community Center, who has been operating an orphanage in the Transkei. This is important to note because President Mandela, Bantu Holomisa, and Thabo Mbeki are from the Transkei and will have affinity for this effort. There is the potential for wins on multiple levels here. If we can secure funding for Bessie's facility, we can augment its functions to include environmental education and waste management, reaching younger, at-risk children and training them in the fundamentals of environmental protection that will empower them for a lifetime of positive contribution. They would be employed, as opposed to working the streets as hustlers and prostitutes. Those grim outcomes are virtually guaranteed, short of improved educational opportunities to the existing program."

There are times when silence is palpable. There was no help, no sign of agreement coming from any of them—nothing. It was awful.

"The third area of concern is in the township of Alexandra, which we visited during the Binational Commission and saw firsthand. The deplorable conditions there were beyond imagination, with the absence of running water, sewage treatment, electricity, or clean sources of energy for cooking. Rudimentary cleanup skills need to be taught and implemented in this township. The people suffer from all manner of illness related to contaminated water, including dysentery and cholera. Franklin Moore, our former colleague who is now at the Agency for International Development, has secured collateral resources to be channeled into this effort."

When I had finished, I heard a voice in my head say, Do yourself a favor, Marsha—just sit down.

I expected an assault on my conclusions, but surprisingly, the committee accepted them, with Nitze even saying that we could probably find grant money for Bessie Mdoda's Ncediwe Community Center. The ensuing discussion was short and to the point, including an agreement to present my report to the full Binational Commission for ratification.

I felt like leaping and clicking my heels together at the thought of sharing the news with Jacob, and even more so with Bessie.

"Let's not get too excited about this, Bessie," I said to her when I reached her by phone in the Transkei. My admonishment was as much to myself as to Bessie. "This is only the first hurdle of many, but it's a start. Frankly, I was not expecting any receptivity on this, so I'm guardedly optimistic. I'll keep working on my end and let you know what you can do on yours."

Jacob was a tactician, so when I called him, he wanted to know whom I considered allies and what our next steps would be. He had been engaged in infighting with bureaucrats and their corporate suitors for years.

"What is the process, Marsha? What are the obstacles?"

As with Bessie I also tried to dampen expectations with Jacob, though I knew his tenacity would take in stride whatever obstacles were thrown down.

By the time the BNC was reconvened in Washington on July 19, the mountains of preparatory work had been done. The last thing anyone would be looking for at a commission like this one was surprises, so there were regular updates between the internal and South African offices to ensure that everyone and everything was on board.

I maintained my early morning routine of calling Ken Thomas at the US Embassy in South Africa at 4:00 A.M. and Bantu Holomisa on the South African side. I also checked Sis. Bessie's progress toward finishing a thirty-thousand-dollar proposal to EPA. For the agency, such an investment was less than miniscule, but for Bessie, every penny was precious. I understood her position and tried to help her make one small step at a time.

Jacob was on top of everything and in some ways anticipated each move, either with steps he had already taken on his end or at least by strategizing and thinking things through. Franklin Moore had put together an impressive package from US Agency for International Development.

||||||||||||

The biannual BNC reconvened with Vice President Gore holding meetings with Deputy President Mbeki. Various committees of the BNC met at venues throughout Washington. The Environment Committee met at the headquarters of the National Council of Negro Women, in symbolic recognition of the mutuality of the struggles African American women and black South Africans had waged. Our host was Dr. Dorothy Height, and the meeting was chaired on her behalf by Dr. Sarah Moten. Our committee assembled the same team that had met in South Africa, with the addition of Mark Kasman and Tim Fields. Kathy Washburn represented Secretary Babbitt. The NGO representatives included Norris McDonald, president of the African American Environmentalist Association, Willard Johnson, Rev. Eugene Rivers, and Stanley Straughter, representing Rev. Leon Sullivan of the Opportunities Industrialization Center. Rev. Sullivan, as a civil and human rights leader, championed corporate responsibility in South Africa with what were known as the Sullivan Principles in his role on the board of directors of General Motors.

Bill Nitze made the introductory remarks.

"The purpose of this meeting is to finalize agreements between the United States and South Africa," Nitze explained, saying that, after meeting with South African officials in Pretoria and personally surveying the environmental conditions in some of the townships, he was pleased to present our findings, which would address the problems we had identified as priorities in three areas.

"Dr. Coleman-Adebayo will provide the background. Marsha?"

I had prepared a PowerPoint presentation outlining the recommendations of the South African study tour participants: the need to conduct an independent investigation into vanadium poisoning in the Brits area; the establishment of an environmental education program at the Ncediwe Center; and the implementation of procedures for the maintenance and cleanup of water systems, refuse, and waste in Alexandra Township.

When I finished, the applause was lively among the South Africans and energetic from my EPA colleagues. I was received enthusiastically by the invited NGO representatives. I watched for reactions on both sides. Bantu Holomisa was most animated, nodding and smiling throughout. I could see other South African government officials turning to signal one another their growing excitement. Bill Nitze looked engaged. He sat with a slight smile on his face and nodded toward Holomisa.

In response, Bantu Holomisa expressed his excitement for the three initiatives, while stating that South Africa was not interested in the Environmental Training Institute, the private sector initiative that Bill Nitze had brought Mark Kasman in to manage.

"Our priorities are with the implementation of the life-saving procedures first," Holomisa said. "There will be a point in time when we will aggressively engage ourselves with the modernization of South Africa's infrastructure. But for now, we are in dire need of basic human and environmental services with an emphasis on public health."

After a process that had begun over lunch six months earlier when Bill Nitze gave me the South African assignment, the chips were all on the table. Nitze called the issue.

"Without any objection," Nitze said, "it is agreed that the Office of International Activities will work with the South African Department of Environmental Affairs and Tourism and other relevant ministries to coordinate an independent team of scientists to investigate the problem of vanadium poisoning of miners, in converting the Ncediwe Community Center into an environmental education facility, and in the improvement of sanitation in the Alexandra Township."

My heart was leaping for joy. I could see that the South Africans were struggling to contain themselves. Bantu Holomisa was beaming. The EPA delegation was more subdued; but still, smiles and congratulatory handshakes were exchanged between both parties. This was the way the United States of America did business. It had been painstakingly slow. At times it had been frustrating. There was arm-twisting, infighting, and strategic maneuvering. But significantly, there would be improvement in the lives of black South Africans that was being directly facilitated by the hand of the US government.

Something Deeper Than Words

I actually bounced out of bed the next morning at four, almost giddy with the thought of giving Sis. Bessie the news.

"Can you believe it, Sis. Bessie? You'll be teaching them environmental skills they will carry their entire lives. Your children will have a future. I am so happy for you. Congratulations."

I was ecstatic and listened in joy as she danced and hollered and ran around her room in Umtata, while I laughed and danced in my kitchen with her, trying to muffle my enthusiasm because of the early hour.

"You will be able to buy books and supplies and hire teachers. I believe your facility will have to meet certain safety requirements."

"But I have so little money, Marsha. I cannot possibly . . . buy, buy, buy all of these things and still have enough for food."

"You will have enough for basics when the grant money comes through, Bessie. Trust me. In the short term, find a way to spend a penny in ten places. The important thing is the committee has agreed to fund it."

The conversation with Jacob was just as exciting.

"Jacob, the commission will be looking into the issue of vanadium poisoning. EPA has agreed to send a team of independent scientists to conduct an investigation."

"That is fantastic, Marsha! Thank you! Thank you! And there will be scientists to look at the mining process?"

"All of that, Jacob."

He could not have been happier. "I have waited for this day a long time, Marsha. This has been my goal and my dream. There is still much to do, but this is a very important step. Thank you."

\|\|\|\|\|\|\|\|\|\|\|

Again there was the grand ceremony, this time at the Department of State in Washington, with the vice presidents making their speeches, followed by a gala reception at the Smithsonian's National Museum of African Art. That night Bantu Holomisa spoke with the command of one who has seen injustice transformed into constructive action.

"It has been a pleasure to work closely with the United States of America," Bantu began, "to bring the principles of justice and freedom that have so informed your country and culture, together with the victories that were so hard-won, and the lessons that were so hard learned, into the process of starting a new way of life in South Africa. Jefferson's vision of truths that are self-evident, Lincoln's passion about government of, for, and by the people, and Martin Luther King's dream of equality light the way on a path that many have traveled before us. So there is the common bond between our peoples having known the darkest zones of the human heart and who have paid a heavy price in suffering, in blood, and in tears. But after it all, like the tentative first song of birds that announce the hope of a new day, long before the sun's first light breaks, in South Africa, we are singing again."

At the end of the day it was that simple.

Or not. The next weeks were consumed with contract writing and conversations with Bessie on the terms of reference and requirements that she would need to meet to qualify for the grant. What I encountered in the following months were disappointments and bureaucratic delays—more tasks, hoops, and evasions. It was impossible to coordinate with the NGOs because there was no receptivity from management to meet with them. All of my efforts were rebuffed.

When I first experienced agency brass dragging their feet, I tried to reassure Willard, Eugene, and Heeten. At first they understood how slowly these things could proceed owing to governmental inertia. I was reluctant to tell them that I was beginning to believe the agency was backing away from its commitments, and I continued trying to move the process forward.

Heeten returned from a tour of South Africa with American environmental justice activists who were excited about the US commitment to conduct an investigation into vanadium poisoning. However, as weeks passed without any investigation, they became impatient with the agency's excuses. They demanded to know whether EPA was going to move forward or not.

This was the dead end I was hoping we would not reach. I had to either give Heeten some non sequitur that he would see through immediately or declare myself and risk that, if I exposed what was happening to Heeten, it would trigger protests from the NGO community. He and the others were adept at the workings of power and would likely bring serious political heat to bear on the administration.

"I can't get to first base, Heeten, I'll be honest with you. There was never much enthusiasm in the room when I presented our ideas to the OIA, but they went along. I didn't realize at the time that so long as I was the coordinator between the White House and OIA they had no other choice. They had to at least listen at first. But they aren't even picking up the phone anymore. I've been shut out of the process, and they've handed the whole thing over to Mark Kasman and Region III. I should have seen it coming. And in reality, I guess I did, but I thought I could appeal to their better angels. I was wrong."

"So now what?"

"All I know, Heeten, is that I have received reports of deaths in South Africa, and I am duty bound to investigate this issue in my official capacity. I have gone up and down the management chain, and I am at a dead end." I paused. "Look, Heeten, this is a democracy. Perhaps you could be more successful working from the outside."

"Are you sure, Marsha? They'll have your head for that."

"If the reports of vanadium poisoning are true, I'm prepared to take that risk."

After talking with Kalan, I realized that there was a much more immediate problem. We had a deadline to meet before the availability of funding fell off the table and the agency would be off the hook for its Gore-Mbeki program commitments. It could put the failure to implement them on the NGOs—and on me. I went to Pat Koshel to get some straight answers.

"Pat, I am very concerned that management has not moved forward with the South African contracts and the clock is ticking," I began. "The

NGOs have made several attempts to get updated on the progress, and I haven't been able to get an answer from anyone. What's going on? Why aren't we moving forward on this?"

Pat looked at me like she was surprised I would even bother her with such a question.

"Nothing's going on, Marsha. If you really care about these people, you better get on the phone with them and tell them to stop spending their money."

"What do you mean, 'Nothing's going on'? We have an agreement."

Pat raised her eyebrows and shrugged. "You've got a big, new office, Marsha. Why don't you spend some time and decorate it?"

"Come on, Pat, be serious. This will devastate them. Particularly Bessie. Her entire operation is on the line here."

She gave me a mechanical smile. "Go talk to Bill. He's the boss."

I walked straight into Bill Nitze's office, breathing fire.

"I just talked to Pat about the South Africa agreements, Bill. She says the three projects aren't happening. Can you confirm that?"

Nitze continued reading a document in his hand before looking up. "Oh, hello, Marsha. And how are you today?"

"Bill. You heard me."

"There has been a change in direction. The paperwork is still being processed. You'll receive a full briefing."

I was stunned. I softened my voice, trying to appeal to the man's heart.

"Bill, do you realize what this means? Bessie will have to close the orphanage. Little boys and girls will now be put on the streets to become hustlers and prostitutes."

"I don't make the final decisions, Marsha. It's out of my hands."

"Bill, we're only talking about thirty thousand dollars, but it might as well be a billion dollars to Bessie. She has spent every penny she has based on the agreement we made. Come on, Bill. Please," I said with a prayer in my voice.

He looked at me like our exchange was getting tiresome. "The decision has already been made, Marsha. Now I suggest that, if you really care so much about these people, you pick up the phone and tell them to stop throwing their good money after bad."

IIIIIIIIIIIIII

President of the United States: The Playbook

There are few things I will wake Segun for at four in the morning. But an event on September 30, 1996, was one. The actual tremor had rocked me shortly after three. I was already up organizing the calls I had to make to South Africa. I am usually the one to initiate the calls, owing to the South African courtesy of not wanting to wake me because of the time difference. So to be the recipient of a phone call so early was jarring in itself.

"Hello, Marsha? This is Bantu Holomisa."

"Bantu! How are you? If you had waited another fifteen minutes I was going to call you."

"I wanted to call and let you know that I have been sacked."

"Sacked? What do you mean?"

"I have been removed as the deputy minister." He held his phone out into his room. I could hear the tinny sound of a news report. "It is on all of the major networks here."

"But how can that be, Bantu? Why? You've done such a wonderful job. Who will carry it through now?"

"It is a long and complicated story, Marsha. Let me just say that there are times in a man's life that define him. There are things that he says and does that give him meaning. And there are times when these defining things are more important than keeping one's position. I cannot go

It was with a lump in my throat and a heavy stone on my soul that I listened to the circuits connecting the phone from Bethesda, Maryland, to Transkei, South Africa, and heard the low trill of the ringing at the other end. I was half hoping Bessie was not there, when she picked up.

"Hello?"

"Oh, hi. Is this Bessie? This is Marsha."

"Marsha! So wonderful to hear you!"

"Sis. Bessie, I won't beat around the bush. I have terrible news. The agency has decided not to fund your community center. I am so sorry."

The scream on the other end was not a scream of joy. I could hear the receiver rattling on the floor. Bessie was shrieking in the background. "Oh my God! What am I going to do?"

Blood sport. Now we know why the tape is red.

The phone felt heavy in my hand like one of those old irons that had to be heated in an oven. It fell into the cradle like it was made of steel. I felt faint, my knees giving out. I slid to the floor with my back against the wall, collapsing, my legs going in opposite directions. I was reduced to a knot of sobbing and tears.

Bessie's voice was still in the air. It was the wail of everyone who has ever been betrayed. For the first time in my life I knew a traitor's loneliness. After all of my work, the net result was damage. Damage to those I had sought to help. I could see the results that awaited them. I could see the children's eyes darken and drain of light. I could see Sis. Bessie collapse in a heap after the last of her children slid down the drain of South Africa's despair. And I could feel her hatred of me.

This was the threshold. This, the place we all reach some impossible Wednesday, when the words of deceit find their way out of our own mouths, formed by our own lips. Whatever foul fate awaited Sis. Bessie and her children, whatever affliction began to throb in the blood cells of the miners, however many mosquitoes rubbed their hind legs together in anticipation in Alexandra, my life in America, in the government, at grade level GS-15, with seven floating holidays and accrued vacation, would be just fine.

All I needed to do was stop being me.

That's all my great-great-grandmother would have had to do to avoid the discomfort of being wedged into a coffin as a fierce means of escape. That's all it would have taken had another of my great-great-grandmothers been able to tolerate the rapes and avoid the shards that tormented

It was with a lump in my throat and a heavy stone on my soul that I listened to the circuits connecting the phone from Bethesda, Maryland, to Transkei, South Africa, and heard the low trill of the ringing at the other end. I was half hoping Bessie was not there, when she picked up.

"Hello?"

"Oh, hi. Is this Bessie? This is Marsha."

"Marsha! So wonderful to hear you!"

"Sis. Bessie, I won't beat around the bush. I have terrible news. The agency has decided not to fund your community center. I am so sorry."

The scream on the other end was not a scream of joy. I could hear the receiver rattling on the floor. Bessie was shrieking in the background. "Oh my God! What am I going to do?"

Blood sport. Now we know why the tape is red.

The phone felt heavy in my hand like one of those old irons that had to be heated in an oven. It fell into the cradle like it was made of steel. I felt faint, my knees giving out. I slid to the floor with my back against the wall, collapsing, my legs going in opposite directions. I was reduced to a knot of sobbing and tears.

Bessie's voice was still in the air. It was the wail of everyone who has ever been betrayed. For the first time in my life I knew a traitor's loneliness. After all of my work, the net result was damage. Damage to those I had sought to help. I could see the results that awaited them. I could see the children's eyes darken and drain of light. I could see Sis. Bessie collapse in a heap after the last of her children slid down the drain of South Africa's despair. And I could feel her hatred of me.

This was the threshold. This, the place we all reach some impossible Wednesday, when the words of deceit find their way out of our own mouths, formed by our own lips. Whatever foul fate awaited Sis. Bessie and her children, whatever affliction began to throb in the blood cells of the miners, however many mosquitoes rubbed their hind legs together in anticipation in Alexandra, my life in America, in the government, at grade level GS-15, with seven floating holidays and accrued vacation, would be just fine.

All I needed to do was stop being me.

That's all my great-great-grandmother would have had to do to avoid the discomfort of being wedged into a coffin as a fierce means of escape. That's all it would have taken had another of my great-great-grandmothers been able to tolerate the rapes and avoid the shards that tormented her fingers as she ground glass for the enslaver's salt. That's all that is required of any who are asked to forget their connection to their fellow human beings. It comes in many shapes. It comes in varied ways. But it comes. In my case, it came with appointments to prestigious positions. It came with letters of commendation from the White House. It came with a promise to be a part of the inevitable change for the betterment of mankind.

But it also came with a catch. Always a catch. We couldn't do it on this project because the president might object. We couldn't do it on that project because of the effect it would have on our allies. We couldn't do it on the other thing because, because, because. Next commission. Next session. Next term. We all had the look. We all had the feel. We all knew the talk. Positive. Accentuate the affirmatives. Let me get back to you on that. When a project was done, the paperwork would be filed, the trophies awarded, the press spun. Yet at the end of those very long public service days, whether any of us knew it—and even when we knew, we almost never acknowledged it—the only thing we accomplished was another layer of pretense, another layer of self-hate.

After seeing how you operate? No.

After Jacob Ngakane? No.

After Sis. Bessie? Always: no!

||||||||||||

"*Washington Post.*"

"Yes, I need to speak to a senior editor in your Washington bureau?" I was transferred to another line. "This is the Washington desk."

"Hello. My name is Marsha Coleman-Adebayo. I am a senior policy analyst at the Environmental Protection Agency. I have reason to believe the EPA is covering up crimes that are being committed by an American multinational corporation against the people of South Africa."

Something Deeper Than Words

Something happens when a person stands up one day and says,
   I refuse.
   Often it is a first: I refuse to give up my seat.
   I refuse to settle for less.
   I refuse to look the other way.
   It is beyond the day-to-day, the trendy, or the job description.
   But something deeper than words,
   beyond bullets,
   and older than anything we have ever known returns to us
in that moment.
   Large and independent,
   but still needing us,
   something comes to life in our refusal,
   and becomes the singular creed we must obey.

President of the United States: The Playbook

There are few things I will wake Segun for at four in the morning. But an event on September 30, 1996, was one. The actual tremor had rocked me shortly after three. I was already up organizing the calls I had to make to South Africa. I am usually the one to initiate the calls, owing to the South African courtesy of not wanting to wake me because of the time difference. So to be the recipient of a phone call so early was jarring in itself.

"Hello, Marsha? This is Bantu Holomisa."

"Bantu! How are you? If you had waited another fifteen minutes I was going to call you."

"I wanted to call and let you know that I have been sacked."

"Sacked? What do you mean?"

"I have been removed as the deputy minister." He held his phone out into his room. I could hear the tinny sound of a news report. "It is on all of the major networks here."

"But how can that be, Bantu? Why? You've done such a wonderful job. Who will carry it through now?"

"It is a long and complicated story, Marsha. Let me just say that there are times in a man's life that define him. There are things that he says and does that give him meaning. And there are times when these defining things are more important than keeping one's position. I cannot go

into detail now. But our paths will cross again. I will give you the comprehensive explanation when next I see you."

I placed my head on Segun's shoulder and looked at him.

"Segun, you won't believe this. Bantu was fired."

Segun woke with instant clarity.

"You know what this means," he said. "There is no one to champion the common people now."

Segun was right.

"But it could also mean something else," I said. "It could mean the US wanted him gone."

I had already been worrying. Even with Holomisa, my hopes for holding the process together had been slim. Without him they seemed nonexistent. But then, almost miraculously, the ANC chose Peter Mokaba to replace Bantu. Peter was the one who had carried the fight to the Afrikaners after Mandela and many other key freedom fighters were imprisoned. His credibility was beyond reproach, and he enjoyed wide popularity among vast numbers of black South Africans, so his appointment was very exciting.

I thought this could possibly transition into the same kind of working relationship I had enjoyed with Holomisa. Although admittedly guarded, my optimism returned. I gave the initial sting of Holomisa's removal a few days to subside before bringing up the subject of his replacement with him.

"Mokaba is serious and incorruptible," Holomisa told me. "The work I have started will be carried forward."

Then on October 17, 1996, Peter Mokaba made a formal request to Bill Nitze, sending copies to Administrator Browner and Secretary Babbitt:

I was pleased, upon assuming this position, to learn of the positive relationship between the Department of Environmental Affairs and Tourism (DEAT) and EPA. . . . In the spirit of the Binational Commission and in order for DEAT to properly follow-up on the recommendations from the study tour participants, I am looking forward to the visit to South Africa by Dr. Marsha Coleman-Adebayo, the coordinator of the study tours, to brief me on all aspects of the EPA study tour and EPA program.[1]

I needed more information on this man and was very impressed with what I found. Peter Mokaba was born in 1959 to parents who were migrant workers in and around Johannesburg. He was exposed to the inequities, injustices, and violence of the apartheid system at an early age. His family was forced to live as squatters, moving from one yard to the next around the township.

Peter distinguished himself as a high school antiapartheid student leader. In 1982 he was arrested for his membership in the ANC and for undergoing military training in Angola and Mozambique. He was released one year later, according to an ANC biography of him. "During the apartheid years," it continues, "more than a dozen attempts were made to kill Mokaba. Shots were fired at him, his home was firebombed, and a would-be assassin once confessed he had been ordered by apartheid security police to kill him."[2]

Peter was best remembered for his stirring chant of: "Kill the farmer, kill the Boer!" during the eulogy he had given for fallen freedom fighter Chris Hani in 1993.

Despite formal requests by Mokaba and Tami Sokutu as well as several requests that I submitted myself as the program officer, the agency refused to authorize my return to South Africa on four different occasions before December.

Earthquakes are always followed by aftershocks, or so I thought, with the series of events after the quake that had removed Holomisa. But then something happened that made all of those seem like just so many early tremors. These came with small slights designed to throw me off stride, to be jarring, and to serve notice that I was straddling a fault line. One of these came from Pat Koshel, instructing me to log my arrival and departure times at the office—just a small indignity to let me know I was being watched, monitored, and that any slipups would be punished.

Notwithstanding that I routinely performed uncompensated government work beginning at four in the morning, I was being singled out and treated like a time and attendance cheat. At my pay grade it was easy for me to ignore such indignity. I decided the best response to such pettiness was to ignore it.

"Good morning, Marsha," Sarah, my assistant greeted me. "You need to sign into the registry, please."

"Good morning, Sarah." I smiled, continuing to my office, where I unlocked the door and turned on the light.

At once, I could see that something was different. Stepping in, I noticed a dark blue folder sitting on my desk. I was looking at the official seal of the Executive Office of the President of the United States. My knees buckled. I knew what this meant. The folder read:

Executive Office of the President
Council on Environmental Quality
To: Sandy Hurnall
From: Peter Umhofer
Date: 10/30/96

Comments: I was asked by WH (White House) Pub. Liaison officer to review the response to Randall Robinson before it is sent. Thanks[3]

This would not be so easy to ignore.

Weeks earlier environmental and antiapartheid leaders Eugene Rivers, Heeten Kalan, Deeohn Ferris, and Randall Robinson had all written letters addressed to Administrator Carol Browner and Bill Nitze—and copied Vice President Gore and the White House. Significantly, there was only one letter inside the folder on my desk. It was the draft of a letter the White House was preparing in response to Randall Robinson's inquiry. There was no mention of the others.

Robinson was being treated differently because he had just come off a hunger strike that had drawn the world's attention to the Clinton administration's policy of intercepting Haitian boat people before they could touch American soil and claim refugee status. Contemporaneously, Clinton had reaped public relations bonanzas from embarrassing Fidel Castro by providing Cuban boat people political asylum.

Randall was the tall, stately embodiment of dignity and poise. He was the executive director of TransAfrica, an African American lobbying group that worked on behalf of Africa and the Caribbean. His commitment to the struggle of the poor was unequalled.[4]

Clinton's neoliberal policies had allowed American rice farmers to flood the Haitian market, destroying the island's rice industry. Clinton,

however, saw no PR benefit in embarrassing those American business interests whose practices were causing the Haitians to flee. Much later, in 2010, having been appointed United Nations special envoy to Haiti by President Obama after the devastating earthquake, Clinton would apologize in testimony before Congress for the very policy that had inspired Randall's hunger strike.[5]

The White House knew that to ignore Randall was to invite peril. This provided the first ray of hope that the environmental commitments could be resuscitated. I owed this hope to believing that Vice President Gore was a staunch supporter of Nelson Mandela. By supporting my efforts to have the agency represented in Beijing, Carol Browner had shown herself to be willing to challenge the status quo within EPA. In my mind, the vice president and Browner, having the power to enforce the BNC agreement, represented the last line of defense.

That this dark blue folder had materialized behind a door I had locked the last time I was there meant someone with the authority to leave the White House's calling card behind was in the mix. So the OIA's attempts to minimize the reach of the BNC and contain it within EPA had failed. The Office of the President was aware that the public sector was engaged. Worrisome for me was that the White House public liaison officer was asking for a review of the response to Randall Robinson's letter. Did this signal that damage control was engaged more than anything else?

During my discussion over lunch with Bill Nitze when he had assigned me to South Africa, he had gone on at some length about the rare opportunity South Africa's emergence from apartheid represented for the agency. This was one of those moments when we were neither American nor South African, he had said. We would have the chance to step out of our strictly EPA roles and work toward the best interests of South Africa. I had warned Nitze that I would not do anything to hurt the South Africans, and he had assured me that I would not be placed in that position.

With Randall Robinson and the White House in the mix, not only was the horse out of the barn, the barn was on fire. There was no longer any possibility of remaining in the background. I had gone to the *Post* and many other news organizations. Even though they had not picked up the story, I was now officially a whistleblower. Civil servants understand that when someone has blown the whistle, self-preservation

dictates an immediate, head-first dive into the nearest foxhole. Anyone still standing and asking questions will be mowed down. That did not bode well for me, since the first rule of whistleblowing is to remain standing.

I would soon be fired.

I did not call Willard. I did not call Eugene. Instead, I offered a prayer asking for the strength I would need for what was about to come.

I picked up the phone and called Segun.

"Hello, Segun? I'm not sure how to say this." I gathered myself. "I just got into my office, and there was a memo from the president's office waiting on my desk."

I waited to hear something but got no response.

"We've talked about what it would mean if we ever got to this point." We were no longer in the abstract. "I'm probably going to be fired. This will have consequences for everyone—you, me, and the kids. I'm scared."

"I understand, Marsh," he said. "I am scared too. We'll find a way. The children will be fine. We'll find a way to get through this."

"Thank you. I knew that before I called you. I just needed to hear you say it."

After he hung up, I held the phone until I heard the dial tone again.

⁗⁗⁗⁗⁗

Alan Sielen called me into his office about a week later.

"What's up with all these letters from NGOs, Marsha? Do you know anything about this?"

The repercussions for my admitting to knowing about the NGO letters could be severe for me. If the agency thought I was working too closely with the environmental justice community, I could be seen as a threat to the economic agenda.

"Yes, I know about the letters," I said.

Sielen watched me, waiting for more.

"As you know, Alan, all of the people who wrote letters have been involved in the study tours. They know about the findings on South African environmental issues and the agreements the agency has made to address those. I haven't been able to move on any of them. I couldn't get the authorizations I needed, and I have been completely ignored by my managers in all my communications. The deadline for the funding

came and went. I had to call Bessie Mdoda and listen to her scream after I told her the deal was off. So when Heeten and Eugene really started to press me for some straight talk, I told them I wasn't able to get anywhere because the agency had reneged on the deal."

"That is not the message we tell the public, Marsha. We tell them that the issues are very important to the agency and that we are taking steps to implement them."

"Maybe that's what *you* tell the public, Alan, but I have a problem with lying. Especially since receiving the e-mail Mark Kasman sent you. You may recall a memo dated October 8, 1996? I have a copy of it, Alan. Shall I read it to you?" I read from the paper in my hand:

> We might want to label my section on the agenda as "Environmental Technology Activities" which OGC [the Office of General Counsel] prefers to "Business Activities."[6]

"It isn't lying, Marsha—it's not airing your laundry in public. We are all in agreement with the findings of the commission. It's a process. It takes time. We'll get there."

"I'm sorry, Alan, but I simply don't believe that. If it was a process and we were all in agreement, someone would have listened to my concerns. Someone would have returned my calls. Bessie's kids wouldn't be getting put out on the streets now."

There was no going back now. "If you want to know what I think, Alan," I continued, "I think you're trying to use me. You're trying to use me because you know my history as an activist in the antiapartheid movement and you know the South Africans trust me. That's the truth of the matter. You need my credibility, and you want me to lie while you, Mark, and Bill push ETI down their throat. I'll tell you what I told Bill when I took this job—if you want to do something that's going to hurt South Africans, you can count me out!"

"No one is asking you to lie about anything, Marsha. Why does it have to be that we're asking you to lie? Have you ever been through a process that takes some negotiating skill? That takes some patience?"

"Patience? Nelson Mandela spent twenty-seven years in prison. This isn't about patience. Ronald Reagan said South Africa was strategically essential to the free world for its production of minerals. That's what this is about: 'Forget about the people in the mines—we need the vanadium.'

That's what this is about, Alan. If you want to mislead people, that's your business. But don't expect me to lie for you, because I won't."

By then we were both angry.

"You can't make policy for the agency, Marsha," Alan responded. "You don't know enough about the overall picture to be making policy decisions for the entire US government."

"You're right, I don't. But I do know there are vast numbers of poor black South Africans living in desperate conditions. I know what's happening in an orphanage in Transkei. I don't know what's going on inside the White House, but my job description requires me to act on what I know."

This showdown with Sielen did nothing to bring the BNC agreements any closer to realization. If anything, it only convinced Sielen that I was trying to force the agency to honor its own negotiated deal.

Last Obstacle to the End Run

Several nationally recognized environmental and human rights leaders had written to Vice President Gore and Administrator Browner. This, of course, would have sweeping implications for the vice president, who had so carefully orchestrated the binational process in South Africa, Russia, Mexico, and China to establish his bona fides in foreign affairs for his approaching run at the presidency. In letters dated October 28, 1996, Rev. Eugene Rivers questioned why the EPA had not "dispatched a team of vanadium experts to evaluate contamination levels,"[1] and Randall Robinson wrote, "It is difficult to understand why EPA has not been more aggressive in providing assistance in a timely manner."[2] Earlier, on October 3, Browner's chief of staff, Peter Robinson, had been notified by Lily Lee, the Environmental Justice liaison to the Office of the Administrator:

> Attached is a letter to the Administrator and the Vice President about South Africa from many of the most prominent national leaders in environmental justice (Richard Moore, Deeohn Ferris, Robert Bullard, and Beverly Wright). . . . This delegation has just returned from a mission to South Africa and they report witnessing horrendous environmental conditions.[3]

The last thing Al Gore needed on his hands was a scandal in which the fledgling government of Nelson Mandela was being victimized by the notorious Union Carbide or one of its spun-off, liability-avoiding mutations.

On one dark evening from the company's nightmare history, December 3, 1984, the Union Carbide pesticide plant in the Indian city of Bhopal in the state of Madhya Pradesh released forty-two tons of toxic methyl isocyanate, exposing more than five hundred thousand people to the toxic gas. The first official immediate death toll was 2,259. A more generally accepted figure is that eight to ten thousand people died within seventy-two hours, and it is estimated that twenty-five thousand have since died from gas-related diseases. That the company has never been held fully accountable for that disaster says as much as needs to be said about its political influence.

It also happened that the National Environmental Justice Advisory Council (NEJAC), a community-based advisory board that provides feedback to the EPA on how the agency is doing from the perspective of grassroots organizers, was about to come to Washington. Heeten Kalan, who was a council member, had written the agency in advance of the meeting specifically asking that an EPA representative attend the South African panel.

This annual meeting brings roughly three hundred environmental activists to EPA's doorstep each year. There are reasons for such partnerships, and then there are other reasons for them. OIA was aware that regarding South Africa, Heeten Kalan would not hesitate to unload on the agency if it was even slightly enabling vanadium contamination by Union Carbide. I knew the NGOs were prepared to go public if all that the agency had to offer was meetings and more lies.

Knowing this, I told Pat Koshel that I was willing to make the presentation, reasoning that since I was close to the NEJAC's viewpoints, I would not find their demands insulting or threatening.

"No," Pat said, "I'll make the presentation. They would rather hear it from senior management."

What Pat did not say was that she didn't trust me to parrot the agency line anymore, especially since I had told Alan Sielen that I wouldn't lie or misrepresent the truth and had told NEJAC that the agency had reneged on the Gore-Mbeki agreements.

I was becoming used to the bait and switch, but I still held hopes of being able to resuscitate the BNC's three commitments to the miners, orphans, and people of Alexandra. Bill Nitze agreed to meet with Heeten Kalan and Rev. Eugene Rivers in Washington to address the concerns they had laid out in their letters. To my surprise, Nitze came to the meeting with an African American man I will call John Daniels. Daniels was the executive director of an NGO from New England. I had met him during the study tour, when he was brought into the process from Region I in Boston.

Bill Nitze thanked everyone for coming, saying it was good to see them all again. After his opening remarks, Heeten spoke.

"Mr. Nitze, respectfully." Heeten's habit was to clasp his hands together under his chin while he organized his thoughts and sought to control his emotions. "As you know, the apartheid government was masterful at public pronouncements of their noble intentions while they simultaneously maintained the most barbarous of policies. Forgive me if I seem impatient. I know you are truly concerned. But unless ideals are actualized, there will be millions of black South Africans trapped in desperation."

Nitze's face was tight, his jaw set.

Eugene Rivers continued laying out the NGO position. "Everyone present here today has either been involved in the EPA study tours or with an NGO involved in South Africa. We, like our South African counterparts, are deeply perplexed and concerned about the lack of progress on the part of EPA in fulfilling its commitments made at the July Gore-Mbeki Commission."

Nitze listened, his posture and body language tense.

Heeten continued, "EPA made the following commitments during the Gore-Mbeki meeting: that $200,000 would be made available to support the programmatic initiatives of the study tour participants; that EPA would support the conversion of the Ncediwe Community Center to an environmental learning center; and that a team of EPA vanadium experts, along with independent scientists, would be sent to the Brits area to investigate the toxic nature of vanadium, and that EPA would work with USAID to develop projects in Alexandra township to address environmental pollution.

"Jacob Ngakane has told us that he is not aware of any scheduled plans for the mission," Heeten continued. "Again, Mr. Nitze, you should

be aware that we have reports of people dying or becoming ill as a result of toxic mining pollution. We promised our South African colleagues that we will do everything in our personal and organizational power to ensure that the EPA fulfills these commitments."

Nitze sat and listened stoically.

Rev. Rivers summed up the sentiments of the NGOs. "As African Americans and Americans I must say that we were extremely embarrassed that EPA is treating the study tour participants and government officials, even at the highest levels, with so much contempt. It is my understanding that Deputy Minister Peter Mokaba had written a letter to you requesting that Marsha come to South Africa to brief him. We are all extremely perplexed at how a letter from a South African cabinet member has been treated in such a careless and disrespectful manner. We vow to support the environmental goals and people of South Africa and to struggle alongside our brothers and sisters."

Nitze looked at me with lasers in his eyes. I could feel the heat coming off his body. Yet he was remarkably calm when he finally spoke. Despite the NGOs' harsh assessments of his performance, Nitze was polite.

"I appreciate the fact that you have put yourselves through considerable inconvenience in coming all the way to Washington to present your case. I can personally assure you that your concerns will get serious consideration. Marsha will still be the liaison between you and the agency. I will keep her apprised of the situation. There are still some areas to work out. Marsha will let you know what the final determination is."

He had covered his talking points and had taken the heat that was leveled at him.

"The agency is involved in an internal strategic planning exercise to determine how best to allocate resources. We know what we've agreed to. You can count on us following through on our commitments."

He looked at his watch.

"It's lunchtime. We've gone as far as we can go here. Marsha will keep you abreast of the situation as it continues to evolve."

IIIIIIIIIIII

We all left Nitze in his office and went downstairs to get lunch in the cafeteria. While we ate, John Daniels led a "brown bag," the agency term

for a presentation made over lunch. We knew next to nothing about his organization, so he described its programs and history. While Daniels was talking, I noticed Nitze's secretary milling about, looking in our direction, so I went over to her and asked if she needed to see me.

"No, Bill wants John to come to his office."

"Oh. Is there anything I can help with?"

"I'm sorry, Marsha. I've been specifically instructed to speak with no one but John Daniels."

"That's odd. Why?"

She shrugged and shook her head. "I haven't a clue."

I told John that Nitze wanted to see him.

Nitze did a double take when I walked in behind Daniels, but he did not object to my being there. "Come in, John. You're a man of action, and I'm a man of action. I can do business with you." He pressed on. "Look, John, I want to put you in charge of managing the contract for our South Africa program. We have a lot of dynamic ideas and people that need a man of action to push the process along, keep people on their toes, make sure that what is supposed to get done gets done."

Daniels accepted the offer immediately.

"Good," Nitze smiled. "We'll get the paperwork started."

That's how things got done when the agency wanted them to get done. It was extraordinary. Here was a man, who less than fifteen minutes earlier had been a stranger to the South Africa advocacy community, walking out of the assistant administrator's office with a commitment to oversee two hundred thousand dollars for the South Africa program.

After John Daniels left, I shared my astonishment with Nitze.

"Who is this man, Bill? No one even knows what he does. From what he was saying at the brown bag downstairs, he's never even been to Africa, much less South Africa. How can you turn the operation over to someone without any experience?"

"He comes very highly recommended from our office in Boston. He doesn't need Africa experience—he's done a lot of work in the poorest areas in New England. The dynamics are the same."

"Are you telling me there are places in New England like the one we visited in Alexandra, Bill? You and I stood side by side there. You saw the conditions. I had to throw my clothes away because I couldn't get the stink out of them after three washings. Where in America have you

seen people drawing their drinking water out of puddles with runoff from porta-johns?"

"Look, Marsha. I'm the boss here. You are to do as you are told. This man is going to oversee the operation. He has impeccable credentials."

It was staggering. In the course of a morning I had witnessed a meeting in which Nitze had reaffirmed the agency's support for the Gore-Mbeki process, its conclusions, and recommendations. I had helped negotiate the terms of those agreements and knew the people in South Africa who were promised funding and support. No more than an hour earlier, Eugene and Heeten had specified those same terms, and Nitze had said that they still stood. Yet here he was, handing over the responsibility and the funding to a virtual unknown. It was the Red Queen talking backward, with everything I had devoted myself to since being assigned the South Africa desk spinning out of control.

The agency, in secret, was stacking the South Africa program with people who were neither academically nor experientially qualified but, more important, who would not question policy.

It wasn't about John Daniels. It wasn't really about Bill Nitze. My central concern was that the most important participants—the South Africans themselves and their US supporters—were being excluded from the discussions and the implementation of improvements. There was something lousy going on, and black South Africans were still on the losing end.

When I got home I went directly to my bedroom and lay on our bed without even noticing if anyone else was home. When Segun came in to ask how I was, I could only muster one sentence.

"There are blows in life so cruel, I can't answer."

⁞⁞⁞⁞⁞⁞⁞⁞⁞⁞

Word reached me that Bill Nitze would be traveling to South Africa toward the end of November or early December. This news meant that, as the program officer, I should be traveling back to Pretoria with him. Stranger things have happened, but I didn't get my hopes up considering the unpredictability my position had taken on. That I even knew about it was a small miracle, considering how little I was being kept in the loop.

The trip was confirmed when I received instructions to schedule appointments for Bill with various high-level figures in the South African government. The problem was that most of the people I tried to contact were scheduled to be out of country during his visit.

There was Peter Mokaba, who at first had scheduled a meeting with Nitze around November 28 but backed out of it a few days later, citing a conflict he had with a previous commitment. He was Bill's most important counterpart and the most central to implementing any policies.

Curiously, however, the lack of official business did not deter Bill Nitze from his anticipated trip. I discovered coincidentally, when I stopped in his office after several futile attempts to book meetings for him, that there might have been ulterior motives. When I got to his office, his assistant was on the phone to South Africa, making arrangements for several members of the Nitze family to visit a wildlife refuge. I found this information puzzling. The travel date was fast approaching, but I, as the program officer, had still not received authorization to travel to South Africa. Yet with Nitze making travel arrangements for his family, the trip was definitely on. It was unheard of for a senior official to travel without the program expert during official visits.

I called Franklin to get his read on this unusual development. "Why would we be traveling to South Africa during Thanksgiving, first of all? And second, why haven't I received my clearance to travel yet?"

"South Africans don't care about our Thanksgiving. And Nitze doesn't care if you're away from your family. If you just boil it down to its simplest parts, it looks to me like Mr. Nitze's trying to get his family a free vacation."

"Get out of here," I said. "The man's got more money than the pope."

"Yeah? You think that makes him a spendthrift? Look, Marsha, this is Washington. Everyone who's anyone does it. It's one of the perks associated with being in the ruling class," Franklin said, a smirk in his tone.

||||||||||||

The good news was that I spent Thanksgiving with my family. Mokaba was on overseas travel, so whom Bill Nitze was meeting with I couldn't imagine. It was clear by then that I was the program officer in title only. The Monday before Thanksgiving brought the final confirmation, short of a pink slip:

From: ALAN HECHT
To: Kasman-Mark, Koshel-Pat, Sielen-Alan,
     Coleman-Adebayo-Marsha
Date: 11/25/96 10:45am
Subject: South Africa

Bill Nitze called this morning and things seem to be going well.
There will be no further travel to South Africa until next year. Bill
and I will talk again tomorrow.[4]

Going well indeed!
By that time the agency had reneged on all the agreements made
during Gore-Mbeki. There was no sign of movement toward a scientific
inquiry into vanadium mining. There would be no initiation of sanitation clean-up projects in Alexandra.

||||||||||||

Then some papers slid under my office door—specifically, a memo from
Mark Kasman to Bill Nitze. I had not been copied on it. The memo was
dated November 19, 1996, and concerned Nitze's trip to South Africa.
There were eyes and ears throughout the agency, and some sympathetic
individual, who had been paying attention, had slipped me this previously unseen document.
    In the memo Kasman presented Nitze with the pitch on ETI for Sid-
ney Gerber, one of the holdover Afrikaner officials in the South African Department of Environmental Affairs and Tourism (DEAT). Both
Bantu Holomisa, the former deputy minister, and Peter Mokaba, his
successor, had rejected USETI. In a startling admission, Kasman laid
out the South African concerns:

> As you are aware, DEAT officials have been resistant to the co-
> operative agreements we have signed with the U.S. Environmental
> Training Institute. . . . They have raised concerns that the involve-
> ment of the U.S. private sector in these programs threatens the
> development of South Africa's fledgling environmental industry
> and would do more to increase U.S. exports than achieve South
> African environmental and economic goals.[5]

The memo informed Nitze that Gerber "would be willing to take one more look at each of these programs before rejecting them as Gore-Mbeki sanctioned activities."[6]

The floor moved under me. If there was any question about Kasman's role being that of a back channel, this memo provided the proverbial smoking gun. Kasman's memo continued:

Kathy Washburn and Marsha Coleman-Adebayo have expressed concerns that moving ahead with these programs outside the Gore-Mbeki framework could undercut other work they are planning with DEAT under Gore-Mbeki.[7]

Kasman went on to provide Nitze with two pages of ETI's selling points for Gerber. In a stunning example of American arrogance, Kasman wrote that "we have already signed cooperative agreements with USETI . . . to work in South Africa and both organizations are anxious to begin."

Kasman continued, "EPA has held them off until we get the Gore-Mbeki issue resolved." He concluded by telling Nitze that whether or not DEAT rejected ETI, he wanted to find other outlets to "get these programs rolling." This signaled an end run around the Gore-Mbeki formal protocols if Gerber was unable to persuade Mokaba.[8]

Back-channel circumvention of the Gore-Mbeki Commission protocols was not insignificant. The Terms of Reference for the BNC Environmental Management and Pollution Working Group, Article VI, signed by the governments of the United States and South Africa stated: "The Committee will work on the basis of mutual agreement."[9]

As Ken Thomas, in his role as mission coordinator for the BNC's Environment Committee, had written:

While the BNC (Gore-Mbeki) is not a substitute for the total bilateral relationship, in those areas of committee expertise, the BNC is meant to be the primary forum or coordinating area for cooperation between the two countries.[10]

The NEJAC meeting came to Washington in the second week of December. By then, I didn't care to remind Pat of my offer to address the meeting. Now, the only thing I regretted about not making the presentation was that I hadn't brought popcorn for the show. I had been getting a steady diet of elbows, so I was actually looking forward to one of my tormentors being the one to dine on cartilage for a change. Yet Pat was oblivious to what was awaiting her. Inside her office at EPA, she was insulated from the realities—the desires and needs at the grassroots level in South Africa—because the focus in the office was on the office's perception of what the South Africans needed.

Pat started with a standard speech, enunciating the agency's efforts in helping the poorest communities in Africa. There was restlessness in the room as Pat continued in a tone that approached patronizing. When she started touting the virtues of ETI, I thought Heeten might come out of his shoes. He had heard firsthand from every level of the South African government that South Africa was not interested in whatever ETI was selling.

When Pat finished, Heeten objected, "I just returned from South Africa. I met with national leaders, regional leaders, and local leaders. Why do you come here and treat us like we are schoolchildren? This is outrageous. Why are you not holding up your end of the bargain on the Gore-Mbeki agreements? Where is the team of specialists you promised us to look into vanadium poisoning in Brits?"

Pat was caught completely flatfooted. She had not expected a knowledgeable group.

"The agency is committed to all of those areas in South Africa. But you must understand that resources are tight and there is only so much we can do."

"R-r-r-ubbish!" Heeten exclaimed. "That is pur-r-re r-r-r-ubbish! That is exactly what I mean about treating us like children. Who is this John Daniels? And why did you give a complete unknown control over the financing of the South Africa program?"

Koshel squirmed. "You may not be aware of the fact that the South African deputy minister to the commission was replaced. It has not been appropriate for EPA to release the funds without the proper chain of command in place."

Heeten put his head in his hands and shook it.

"I know Bantu Holomisa," he replied. "And I know his replacement, Peter Mokaba. Do you know either of them? This is outrageous. You are making things up as you go along. How can you come here and treat us this way? You either think we are stupid, or you hold us in utter contempt."

Pat was done. She could take no more.

"I can assure you that the agency has not reneged on any agreements with the South African government. I'm sorry that you feel that way. But there is nothing more that we can discuss here."

Pat stood up and fled the room. She would later say that I had poisoned the atmosphere against her, that I had instigated the hostility, and that the NGOs represented at NEJAC were taking my direction. But immediately upon her departure the room erupted.

Who does she think she is coming with that shit!

It's insulting!

The anger in the room was born of frustration at having fought so hard against apartheid and thinking they had won, only to find another government offering empty promises.

Heeten brought the meeting to order. "Please! Please! We have to make an evaluation to submit to NEJAC. What is your pleasure?"

Someone rose and said that the OIA's performance had been an utter failure.

Heeten scanned the room. "Without objection, is there a second?"

Several voices shouted, "Second!"

"So moved. The secretary will prepare the report and forward it to Administrator Browner."[11]

||||||||||||

Pat Koshel couldn't have hidden her black eyes if she had worn a welder's mask to work—and did she ever go to work, making known her opinion that my radioactive influence had been the source of the problem. I received my own impromptu performance rating from Pat and Nitze—unsatisfactory performance—on December 13, 1996:

> This is to notify you that your performance in OIA has been unsatisfactory since the beginning of the new fiscal year. . . . We are concerned that your unsatisfactory performance is hurting efforts to build an effective cooperative program with South Africa.[12]

Pat Koshel slid the reprimand under my office door as her last act of the day on her way out of the building after the NEJAC meeting. I went slack jawed when I picked it up first thing the next morning, not because it was surprising that I would be singled out as the problem and retaliated against, not even because it was such an incongruous rating, given that I had just received a meritorious award from the agency. It was just so predictable—it came straight out of the playbook. One month later, Nitze, adding insult to injury, would author a memorandum, dated January 13, 1997, to EPA administrator Carol Browner taking credit for the success of the very same programs he and Koshel had used to reprimand me:

> During the last year, EPA initiated a number of successful activities under the Gore-Mbeki Commission. We conducted two study tours . . . and had the opportunity to interact with faculty from MIT and Harvard [sic].[13]

The government issued unsatisfactory performance ratings like a white phosphorous flare being launched over an employee's head to let her and everyone else in the agency know that she was going to be fired. The rules of engagement were clear on this. Those rules had been developed over decades of trial and error. Decades of court trials and preliminary maneuvers over the years had rendered them bulletproof. The white flare of an unsatisfactory performance rating meant that from then on the agency's dealings with me were on autopilot. There would be no reasoning. There would be no reconsideration. There would be formulaic responses, form letters, and scripts. If there was any negotiating, it would be on the agency's terms, and it would be about just exactly what it would take to get rid of me.

‖‖‖‖‖‖‖‖‖

The more inventive playbook aficionado turned out to be Bill Nitze. After having to suffer through the NGO smackdown, Nitze went directly to the chapter titled "You Want A Negro Beneficiary? You Got A Negro Beneficiary." Apparently, part of the discretionary latitude enjoyed by disembodied assistant administrators is the option of dipping into the section called "Any Negro Will Do." This allowed for an administrative-level manager like Nitze to throw a substantial amount of money in noncompeted grants at whatever he saw fit. If NEJAC was having hissy fits about his not moving fast enough on those areas of the Gore-Mbeki specified in the agreement, well, in John Daniels he'd found himself a Negro to deflect any further criticism.

Another page out of the playbook came when Pat Koshel notified me that a doctor had been assigned to investigate vanadium toxicity in Brits. I was surprised but wanted to believe that were was still some integrity left in the process.

"I am so glad the agency has assigned you to this investigation, Doctor. We have received reports of illnesses and some deaths as a result of vanadium exposure. Would you mind sharing the range of your human exposure methodology?"

He was surprised at that question.

"I will not be studying people," he answered. "I'll be studying cows. I'm a veterinarian. I am going to South Africa to study cows' milk."

"Doctor, I'm not sure why my office gave you this assignment. I could understand studying cows' milk if we had concerns about vanadium contaminating human populations from cows or through cows' milk."

"I don't have any idea what the agency intends to do with my research. The only thing I can tell you is that I am not looking at human contamination at all. Like I said, I'm a veterinarian. My research does not extrapolate to humans."

I called Pat Koshel.

"Pat, why are we sending a veterinarian to South Africa to study cows' milk? We have a mining operation, with reports of sick employees. There isn't much question of where the poison is coming from. Why are we wasting time looking for a pathway to humans through cows? While we're doing that, people may be dying."

Pat had just ripped a page out of the "Bait and Switch" chapter of the playbook: You want a vanadium investigation? You got one. Lest anyone not employed in the public sector fall into thinking that playbook is some figure of speech, understand that there is in fact an actual playbook that was developed to circumvent all manner of regulatory attempts at curtailing discrimination and retaliation in the government.[14] But the most powerful and effective playbooks are the ones not codified in writing—the silent agreements that occur behind closed doors. These playbook strategies do not leave fingerprints or dots to connect.

IIIIIIIIIIIIIII

I called Ken Thomas at the US Embassy in South Africa to tell him that I had just received my first unsatisfactory performance report from Pat Koshel.

"What? You have to be kidding me! Everybody here is raving about you."

"Yeah, the crazy thing about it is that this is coming about a month after I received a bronze medal and an 'exceeds expectations' rating!"

"I'm a lawyer," Ken said, "and I've seen this kind of thing before. I think you need to start taking notes, because they are building a case. Keep a notebook with you at all times. Every time Alan Sielen, or Nitze, or Koshel, or any of them says, does, writes, e-mails anything to you, make a note and write a brief description of the context. You may need it to protect yourself someday, and if you do need it, you'll be glad you have it."

"What do you mean, Ken?"

"I mean they are going to go into a full-court press on you now. You should assume that every communication they make with you will be copied to your personnel folder and could have significant consequences. It could be anything that might seem innocuous—write it down. Don't let anything slide."

That seemed excessive to me at first, but after I thought about it and considered all the weird talking out of both sides of their mouths I had witnessed since coming to the agency, I thought it might not be so extreme after all. One thing I wanted to make sure they would have to put into my personnel folder was my response to Koshel and Nitze's reprimand.

They may have thought I had come to my senses and was trying to lay low, but I now realized the stakes. My career was hanging in the balance. They were building a case against me, and my response had to be precise, so I took pains making it so. I responded on March 3, 1997, in a letter to Bill Nitze, Alan Sielen, Alan Hecht, and Pat Koshel. Essentially, I said:

> Be advised that I regard the issuance of such a memorandum [alleging unsatisfactory performance] as nothing short of outrageous. . . . OIA management consistently thwarted my efforts either to fulfill the binding commitments EPA made at the [July] meeting or to advance the South Africa program. I [have] refused

your requests to falsify and "pad" reports and/or distort information being presented to the Office of the Vice President or the
Department of Interior.[15]

With so much at stake for the South Africans, it was no longer only
a matter of a career change that would make everything right for me.

If one can arrive at her spiritual center, dealing with the playbook is
not so all-consuming. Staying centered is. And staying centered when
facing a systematic process that one's superiors know very well is not
a breeze. It's like walking a balance beam with wolves nipping at your
ankles. It is much easier to lose focus than stay on the beam. This was
the terrifying place where lambs mingled with wolves. This was the
place where my belief encountered its deepest fears.

||||||||||||

Unlike the rest of the year in Washington when little gets done, the
holiday season is a time when absolutely nothing gets done. If the
Capitol were a balloon, it could be deflated between Thanksgiving and
New Year's Day. That particular holiday season was tempered with the
uneasiness that comes from not knowing. There were still other things
to drop, but the question was when.

Mercifully, I didn't have long to wait once we came back from the
holidays. Alan Sielen summoned me to his office. It might have been a
new year, but that didn't necessarily portend any new leaves. I could tell
by the poorly concealed delight on his face that this meeting was not
going to be good for me.

"Come in, Marsha." He didn't ask me to sit down. "I just spoke to Bill
Nitze. He wants me to remove you from the Gore-Mbeki project."

He didn't wait two seconds before diving into the rationale.

"We've thought long and hard about this, and it just seems like this
has been a bad fit from day one. Whether it was you launching out on
some mission to save every indigent South African on the continent,
or working at cross purposes to other members of the team, or if it
just came down to you finding fault with everything the agency has
attempted to do in good faith with the new government in South Africa,
it just seems that you are not one of us, Marsha. You seem to feel closer
to black South Africans than us."

"Who is 'us,' Alan? White men or only Americans? Does us include black South Africans? The Gore-Mbeki Commission is about support-ing the South Africans who were trampled during apartheid."

"See? That is exactly what I'm talking about. You don't even know who your friends are."

What Sielen did not say was more telling than what he did. In his November 19 memo to Nitze, Mark Kasman had said that EPA was trying to hold off its ETI friends until "we get the Gore-Mbeki issue resolved." My resistance represented the last obstacle to their end run around the BNC protocols with Sidney Gerber.

Sielen shook his head. "Well, at the risk of beating a dead horse, I'll repeat myself: you better decide whose side you're on." He looked at me for emphasis. "You are to turn your paperwork over to Mark Kasman. He'll take it from here."

||||||||||||

I made it into my office without breaking down, but only just. Once inside with the door closed, I came apart. I hadn't cried like that since the night I'd had to leave Sade in an incubator. I was crying so hard my breathing sounded asthmatic. I buried my face in my winter coat to muffle my sobs.

It had come to this.

The words my coat kept eating were: Why? Why? They couldn't. Why not? What have I done that all of it has come to this? It's not like this will bring down the empire. It won't break the bank. The dollar amounts are miniscule. If they had not been seen after Alexandra; if they had not been heard after Soweto; if Bessie Mdoda's smile had not entered these hearts—what chance do any of them have?

I forced myself to locate my breathing. I gathered myself, tucking my lung in here, finding a shoulder blade there. The blood would come out with cold water.

"Segun, they took South Africa away." I could only mumble, "Sis. Bessie, Brits, vanadium . . ."

There was a pregnant pause.

"Come home, Marsh. Just come home."

Love Will Bring Me Forth

There is an automatic zone of the brain that makes a mother lift a car off her child, and this zone has now taken over me. It knows that under the circumstances I will walk out of the building without authorization, and so it signs out for me. It knows the procedure. It knows that despite my state, the agency will categorize my actions as insubordinate. It knows this is an opportunity for them to impale me, and so it takes the proper measures and procures the proper authorizations before driving me home. It knows the way there and knows now that I am in a remote part of Bethesda, so it can loosen its grip. I can cry again. It can see through the tears. And it knows the exact distance from the door to the couch when I reach home. At the couch it deserts me and leaves me there like a pile of guts. Quaking.

There are no words. There are only the familiar hands that touch me as if I might be dead, knowing their love will bring me forth. There are no words but the gentle arms that hold me while I melt. There are no words until I have died and begin to heal.

"You did all you could do, my darling. You could have done nothing more."

It will be a while before I regain my eyes. It will be a while before I regain my voice. It will be a while before I learn to see.

When my vision returns, when I am able to look at the palm of my hand and see I have a lifeline again, when I look at Sade and I know she has survived, it comes to me. It comes to me with blinding disappointment, because we want to believe that the things that bring us down are great.

It came to me when I stepped into my home office and did not feel fear. When I stood before the drawer I had put the blue booklet in, like it was something dreadful and wrong. Like it was a snake. Like it could put an end to everything I have ever known and loved.

But holding it in my hand again, I realize now that I was only one of them. I was one of many who had seen this poorly designed logo of the brand of the president of the United States and started to shake. We all did. But it went much higher. It went to the EPA administrator. It went to the vice president. That much is so disappointingly clear that it makes me laugh now to think that for all of that power, all of those brains, all of that capability, still not one of us could bring ourselves to see the people in the mines. The children on the brink of the street.

I suppose, of all of us, I came the closest, but my seeing failed too, when I started looking toward the government for solutions and took my eyes off the people I was trying to help. Seeing them I am seeing me, imperfect, flawed, human. Simple as the tiny hand that clasps around my pinkie finger, in that purest of all human gestures: I am alive.

18

Yes, Clarice

By January 13, 1997, there was no question in the mind of anyone who worked at the EPA that the career of one Dr. Coleman-Adebayo had been made into one hell of a frightening example. I was no longer part of the OIA South Africa team. I was no longer even allowed to travel to South Africa. I had not been promoted. I had been reassigned to an area outside my expertise. My passion for solving problems in the areas of international environmental justice, particularly in Africa, had been neutered. The five pending civil rights complaints I had filed were winding their way through the agency labyrinth. And last, but by no means least, I was beginning to get threatening messages at work and at home from anonymous goons. In short, nothing could have been better.

But before I left, someone did have one last present for me. On the fourteenth, my office was broken into, and my computer files were compromised. This time I called security and filed a report. I now feared for my physical safety. The officer reported:

> Ms. Coleman-Adebayo thinks that someone from her program is out to get her in a physical manner and that they have already ostracized her in the office. She believes that while trying to gain information about possible witnesses and person [sic] named in the Legal [sic] case. Ms. Coleman-Adebayo wants her combination changed, will be accomplished [sic] by James Crump.[1]

170

Mercifully, I had one ally inside the agency who had taken me under her protective wing, the same woman I had turned to and come to trust on two other occasions: after the Beijing Conference when things had gotten testy in the office and after Bill Nitze had laid down the gauntlet regarding what he could see as a possible career path for me inside his division. She was my colleague and confidant, Dr. Clarice Gaylord, director of the Office of Environmental Justice. Clarice had been the one from the very beginning to let the egghead from MIT know that there were things we did see and things we didn't.

"I've always wanted to publish an Environmental Justice newsletter, Marsha. I needed the right person to staff it who could make the effort worth taking. What do you think? Want to work on developing an Environmental Justice newsletter?"

"But I don't know anything about publishing!"

"So what? You're a terrific writer. Think about it. Take all that talent of yours. Take all that curiosity, all those brains, and apply them to reporting Environmental Justice news."

Had this woman just fallen out of the sky from heaven or what? It would get me out of OIA, it would be a way to resurrect my career inside EPA, and I'd be working for a woman. "Just think about what you and I could do for Africa, Clarice!" I said.

She looked at me wide eyed. "Oh no, no, no. That was the one thing I said to them when I agreed to offer you this position: No Africa."

"But that's my expertise, Clarice. That's what I do for a living. That's what I love."

"And look where it has gotten you. You've been strung up, and the rope is Africa. Cool it for a while. You've got a handful of complaints in the hopper. Let them work. Don't give up on them, don't turn your back on them—just let them work. There's plenty other issues that could satisfy your sense of justice and that will keep you occupied. What you need more than anything right now is to have them call off the dogs. Your claims aren't going anywhere, girl. Just give them some oxygen. Let them work."

Sage advice. If I ever lasted in the agency beyond these fiery years and became SES, I pledged to myself, I would become the same instrument of moderation to the next generation of women of color as Clarice had been for me. Blinded by my passion, I couldn't see the damage I was doing to myself and the others who were in similar positions because I was such an idealist. She was right. My complaints were in the judicial hopper. They would work their way through the machinery, and I'd get my day in court.

My career had been languishing in a sort of purgatory for hotheads that the agency didn't know what to do with. Here was a woman who knew my passion, knew my talents, and knew a way that I could channel them into a career-saving move. I didn't have to sleep on it.

"All right, Clarice. I accept."[2]

Meanwhile, I could still hear Jacob Ngakane's horrific accounts of working conditions in Brits, South Africa. He reported that it was an environmental and human tragedy that very few people in the world knew anything about. Media coverage would have been tremendously helpful but was sporadic at best. I knew about this destruction. It had penetrated me, and it had cost me plenty to know.

||||||||||||||

Clarice's offer was at least something—it was a start. But I still couldn't shake the feeling of failure. Then I got a call. "Hello, Marsha? This is Peter."

"I'm sorry, Peter who?"

"Clearly the deputy minister of environment doesn't hold much weight in the eyes of the Environmental Protection Agency." He laughed.

"Oh! Of course, Peter Mokaba! How are you, Peter?"

"It has taken quite a commitment to track you down. I am in Washington. I would very much like to meet you. Would you have any time later this afternoon?"

I went to the hotel room thinking, So, I will finally meet Peter Mokaba. The agency had gone to great lengths to prevent this discussion from taking place. This was the man who had scoffed at roadblocks thrown across his path by the police, pushing away the gun muzzles aimed point blank at his chest, yelling: "Bug off! We can shoot too. You know we can shoot. We shot back at Cuito Canavale! One day we'll shoot back here." What kind of man has the courage to taunt South African security police by invoking the turning point in the South African Border War that had led to the withdrawal of South African troops from Angola?[3] Mokaba's legend was so much larger than life that Bill Nitze had mistakenly conflated his fierceness in battle with necklacing when pointing him out to Bill Richardson at the ambassador's party. It was like I had an appointment with Malcolm X. I paused before knocking on the door to his suite.

A stately man opened the door to a flurry of activity. The suite was set up like an office, with men working at tables piled with paperwork. One of them came forward, offering his hand.

"Marsha?"

"Yes. Peter?"

This was the man who had scoffed at death. He wasn't ten feet tall. He wasn't scowling like Mike Tyson. He looked remarkably like Segun, smiling. "I am so pleased to meet you, Marsha."

He shook my hand with both of his and then turned to the other men. His hands were healing, his voice soothing.

"Tell the others that I would like a moment in confidence with Dr. Coleman-Adebayo, please." When the room was cleared he continued. "This morning there was a meeting between the South African delegation and members of the US Environment Working Group. I wanted you to know that I asked for a moment of silence, specifically invoking your name, to thank you for all that you tried to do to help the people in Brits, in the townships."

I knew the traditions of South Africa required homage to comrades. This hadn't been to impress Nitze or the other US officials but to honor a fallen sister and sanctify the effort.

"We felt true solidarity in a non-national way. I felt it important to acknowledge that for my part, the rules have not changed."

There was a pause. "I wrote my dissertation on Steve Biko," I said. "I know you knew him. I am interested in anything you might have to offer about him."

"We lost so many. Such gifted people. Comrade Biko was fearless. He had made a conscious decision to confront fear. All South Africans carry this contribution with them now."

"I took the study tour participants to MIT."

"Yes!" Peter smiled. "That was wonderful. Not that many of us get to go to MIT. We all saw that. Minister Holomisa spoke very highly of the process and what it meant for us." I was struck by his softness. He seemed a gentle warrior.

"I have followed your career, Peter. Bantu Holomisa speaks highly of you."

"I have been fully briefed by Comrade Holomisa about the embassy marches. He tells me you fought a noble fight." His face didn't harden exactly, but the joy left it briefly. "There were so many people who worked very hard to block us from ever meeting, Marsha. On both sides. I wanted to make sure that we met personally."

His mood lightened with his broadening smile.

"They have tanks and guns. They have always had us outgunned. I have a handle on this. I am quite aware of who I am dealing with. Even though they think they can blind me with their dazzling. They cannot stop what you started. That is why it was so sad when we learned that you would be left behind."

It would almost have been better if this man were only fierce. But this kindness, his ease, caught me off guard. I began to tear up. Mokaba noticed and stood up and hugged me.

"You tried. That's all any of us can do as human beings," he said. "We will never forget that."

On driving back to the office it finally lifted. This weight I had carried from having been dismissed was suddenly gone. Bantu had a passionate replacement.

⁞⁞⁞⁞⁞⁞⁞⁞⁞⁞⁞

Maybe there was a way to use my new position to begin educating others about the South African tragedy. I believed that Clarice was sympathetic to the conditions in Africa. Despite her insistence on "nothing Africa," I hoped that learning of the plight of vanadium poisoning would change her mind. What did I know about mice and men? I knew deep down that sooner or later I had to visit South Africa, to see Jacob's allegations for myself. I just didn't know that there would be so many distractions.

The Environmental Justice position, like any new position, consumed me with learning nomenclatures, procedures, positions, and the myriad things editors need to incorporate into their skill set to keep a publication from becoming an extension of their personal diary. But I was truly loving it. If anything, Clarice was fair. She had a lot of great ideas and, because of her position, far too little time to develop their articulation. And this is where I came in. I began to ghostwrite articles for her that allowed her to keep her hand in the fire without the fire consuming her.

This also allowed me to develop a voice. It may not have been my own voice, but I learned the value of distance, of having to see and express another's perspective, and of fitting that perspective into the even larger perspective of a print publication. I found that typography was an art unto itself. Graphics, fonts, flow. In many ways it was a godsend to have taken this excursion into print heaven, and I was grateful that Clarice had not only the wisdom but also the inclination to channel me into this more constructive position.

And then, just as suddenly, what the Lord giveth, the Lord taketh away. The Environmental Justice detail was for six months, and six months is exactly how long it lasted.

ıııııııııııı

Thankfully, another sanctuary opened up for me, in the Office of Pollution Prevention and Toxics, under its director, Dr. William Sanders. Dr. Sanders had encouraged me to apply to be his special assistant on international affairs. His office was separate from OIA. With the promotion, I was back in my area of expertise, although Africa was still off limits—the OIA did not want me to work on African issues. In addition, I took on the challenge of working on mercury reduction in American hospitals. Within the first two years, I was awarded Vice President Gore's Hammer Award and other agency recognitions for this work.

While the promotion to GS-15, a six-figure income in another high-level position, was personally gratifying indeed, it had the effect of bringing me around to see that the agency did work in mysterious ways. It was in some borderline miraculous way atoning for its sins, but the South African *duende* that Jacob Ngakane had wakened in me continued to stir. I would feel its tail slide along the inside of my ribs at the most unlikely provocation: "DeBeers: because a diamond is forever," "We Are the World," my own children's normal development. The six months with Clarice Gaylord had given me time to heal, time to grow. By taking myself out of the maelstrom of OIA, I had found a way to lighten up, to let things be. But deep inside I still felt a commitment to the South Africans I had come to know and love through Gore-Mbeki. The promise of assistance I had made to Sis. Bessie was not constrained to a work duty. It was woman to woman. It was mother to mother.

With the new stability of working in Bill Sanders's office, it seemed a good time to visit some old friends. I called Jacob. I called Sis. Bessie. I shared with Segun my desire to visit South Africa. And I shared our discussion with Sina. "Sina? How would you like to go with Mommy to visit South Africa?"

Shortly after I had made my travel arrangements, Dr. Sanders called me into his office. It was a spacious office—early Howard Johnson. He got right to the point. "Is it true what I'm hearing," he asked, "that you've applied for a visa to South Africa?" He seemed incredulous, as if I'd be skiing with Adolf Hitler. My work was not security related, and the trip was not job related. I wouldn't be using government resources. I certainly didn't need the clearance of my boss to take a vacation.

I kept my voice even. "May I ask how you heard about that?"

He looked at me, ice cold, unblinking. "The US Embassy in Pretoria called the EPA to find out about the goal of your trip."

Wow, I plan a vacation, and two governments go on alert? This made no sense. "I'm going to South Africa as a tourist. A tourist."

He looked at me like a school principal tired of disciplining the same student over and over again. He'd already made his point: both governments would have their eyes on me. But that's not the kind of thing a supervisor says directly in the civil service. He phrased it as a stern set of orders. "You must make it clear to whomever you're visiting that you are not on official duty and that you most certainly are not representing the US or EPA."

I wasn't sure whether to be angry or frightened by his comment. "Bill, I'm going to South Africa on my own time, using my personal funds. Why are you questioning me like this?"

He glanced past my shoulder, as if someone were standing behind me. "Marsha, I would be careful if I were you."

There it was, ominous and clear: a blunt warning. Since meeting with Mokaba, I'd been drifting away from my time of greatest peril. Now here it was again, close at hand. I felt it, warm and dangerous, right up against my skin. I put my right hand to my forehead. I was hot to the touch.

Marsha, I would be careful if I were you.

Between an ordinary employee and boss, that could mean many things. Bill could have been worried about my traveling alone as a woman in a developing country; as a concerned supervisor, he could have worried that this vacation would leave me exhausted. But at the EPA, experience had taught me that cryptic warnings signified only one thing: the uppity woman was snooping into something again.

I looked back at him. "Are you threatening me?"

I walked out of his office when he didn't answer. I wanted to slam the door.

As soon as I got back to my office, I reached Jacob by phone in South Africa. I was afraid. I was afraid of not being strong enough to do what needed to be done.

"The US Embassy in Pretoria called EPA," I told him. "Something's happening. I'm scared."

Jacob tried to calm my fears. "Marsha, of course they are going to try and scare you. Vametco's a US-owned company. The mine used to be called the Union Carbide vanadium mine. You must be brave. Think of our struggle here. I promise you, once you arrive on South African soil, not only will you be safe, you will be free."

The Sacrifice Zone

If I have discovered nothing else at EPA it is a part of the landscape that I know many others have discovered before me, but for various reasons—family, well-being, loyalty, all of which goes by the name of human frailty—they failed themselves, their responsibility, and their progeny. Yet others reported their findings and were disemboweled for it.

But I am here to tell you that there is another stratum beyond the biosphere, atmosphere, stratosphere, and ionosphere. It is a place we might call the sacrifice zone—a place so small as to be invisible to the naked eye. It is the place where good intentions, careers, lives, principles are all drawn in, never to escape. If ever there were proof of the existence of black holes, of their invisibility, of their all-consuming nature, so dense and massive that even light cannot escape them, it is the absolute reality of the sacrifice zone.

Power accretes to its surface. Truth, honor, and courage are rent apart by its pull. It's where Malcolm and Bobby went; it's where Steve Biko and Medgar Evers went; it's where the most challenging of Martin Luther King's speeches went, hurtling down the rabbit hole, so that his birthday is celebrated in these United States with a little less enthusiasm every year, because we only remember the dream part of his speech. Gone is the interconnectivity of injustice and war, colonialism and genocide, comfort for the few and abject poverty for the many.

But lo! To discover the sacrifice zone is to court disaster. Touch it and die. Report it and die. Embrace it and die. But don't take my word for it: ask Tanya Ward Jordan, ask Janet Howard, ask Joyce Megginson, ask Dennis Young, ask Blair Hayes, ask Matthew Fogg—the list goes on and on. Each one of them a stalwart; each one a whistleblower; each one of them exiled to the sacrifice zone.

But one force is anathema to the sacrifice zone: speaking truth to power. In the beginning, there was the word. And if we remember the power of the word, once again anything is possible. We begin to remember. It may take fifty years in oblivion, but through the power of words and with the courage to say them, as a people, we begin to remember Emmett Till.

The 1998 Trip to South Africa: My Tongue Is Green

NOTE: *The following chapter is based on actual events. Because of pending litigation between South Africans affected by exposure to vanadium and its derivatives and companies producing vanadium, I have changed the names of the South Africans to protect them from retaliation and avoid jeopardizing their lawsuits.*

"Mom, do you hear people singing in the other room?" Sina asked. We could hear the melodious sound of people chanting and singing. My pulse started to race. We were finally in South Africa.

"Sina, that's the South African national anthem we used to sing at antiapartheid solidarity meetings."

Joanne and Juanita looked around to see if they could identify where the music was coming from. As we approached the door the voices became clear and loud.

Nkosi sikelel' iAfrika
Maluphakanyisw' uphondo lwayo,
Yizwa imithandazo yethu,
Nkosi sikelela, thina lusapho lwayo.

God bless Africa
May her glory be lifted high.
Hear our petitions.
God bless us, your children.

I started to sing in English. A clutch of union and human rights activists' fists punched the sweet South African air.

We were hugging and kissing everyone within reach. "Jacob, you know how to welcome people to your country!"

Jacob signaled to his friends to stop. Standing in the middle of the circle, Jacob cleared his throat.

"We are here to welcome our sisters and our brother to South Africa. They have come to investigate why our people are dying in the vanadium mines. On behalf of your brothers and sisters here in South Africa, welcome." The hugs and kisses started all over again, and the singing.

Jacob had arranged for Joanne and her daughter, Juanita; Caroline and her daughter, Holly; and me and my Sina to stay at a housing facility where one of Jacob's union members worked. Two of Jacob's colleagues, Moses and Solly, volunteered to come to our quarters each night and teach Olusina about the struggle that was waged by the young lions, as young antiapartheid activists were called in South Africa. I hoped that Sina would appreciate the import of these sessions later when faced with life's challenges. Strategically, our living quarters were not in Brits—no small detail considering that if we were easily accessible the mine would have plenty of desperate men at its mercy who would not consider it beyond the call of duty to render us into mincemeat. I had recruited my childhood friend Joanne Godley for this trip. Joanne, a gastroenterologist, had always been passionate about justice.

I had first met Joanne when we volunteered at the Black Panther breakfast program for children while we were high school students in Detroit. We lost touch with each other during our college years. Joanne was educated at Stanford and the Yale School of Medicine. We literally bumped into each other four years later, in Cambridge, at Saint Paul AME Church. She was completing her medical residency at Boston City Hospital, which was associated with Harvard. If it could be ingested, lodged, restrictive, or in any other way related to things of the digestive system, Joanne was among the best in the business in accurately diagnosing both cause and cure. She had a trained and acute eye for symptomatic indications. The second doctor was Caroline Watts, from Highland Beach, Maryland. Caroline was a family doctor, eager to lend her skills to diagnosing general medical problems, such as tuberculosis, pneumonia, asthma, and bronchitis. No veterinarian accompanied us on the trip.

That Holly didn't lord being thirteen over Juanita's and Sina's being twelve was no small matter. Our children decided that they would provide literary training to domestic workers as their contribution to South Africa. Jacob arranged classes and recruited women for this training. The kids jumped at developing a curriculum and its selected reading. To see our children's joy in contributing to the new South Africa was priceless.

In interview after harrowing interview, the decision we made before even leaving the States was confirmed: it would be unwise to take our kids to the interviews or to visit the vanadium mines. Common to every person we talked with were the patterns and symptoms of vanadium exposure, including reports of sores on the skin, shortness of breath, nausea, bleeding from the nose, eyes, genitals, rectum. Green tongues. Any mineworker who did not show symptoms was an exception. The gloves and masks the company provided as safety equipment for the workers were inadequate.

What woeful medical care was available to mining communities was offered in bad faith, Jacob said. Company doctors were suspected of malpractice by virtue of deliberate misdiagnosis of patients' illnesses, inadequate treatment and medication, and refusal to inform patients of the results of medical testing, such as what showed up in the X-rays of their lungs. The only reasonable explanation for the company even providing the appearance of medical care to the workers was for the purpose of inoculation—that is, inoculation of the company from liability. Nicely conceived diagnoses coupled with shrewd legalese and the absence of protective laws—or even any legal right for an employee to sue an employer—all conspired against the mineworkers. It soon became clear why the agency had refused to investigate the practices of this US corporation.

In the process of vanadium mining, black South African life was consumed, like gasoline, for its utility. So long as it could render profitable product from the earth, it was viewed as any other asset to the corporation. Sickness was an acceptable byproduct, so long as sickness did not reduce productivity. When it did affect productivity, the workers were no longer needed. They were released. The company could get more. The process, the company could assert, was due to the unfortunate period of apartheid that had only recently ended. It would take some time. These things don't change overnight. This was the hangover from an evil policy that had been able to take hold in a backward society that would take decades to catch up and become modern, civilized—like the United States, where Union Carbide was from.

"They couldn't get away with this in the States," Jacob insisted.

Quite apart from the anecdotal reports we had gotten when Jacob took our delegation door to door to speak with active and former miners, there had been an extant body of work by EPA scientists before vanadium was even a gleam in Jacob Ngakane's eye the day I first met him at Logan Airport. By 1977 there was substantial evidence of health risks, even potentially fatal risks, associated with vanadium. On my return from South Africa in 1998, I researched the subject of vanadium through the EPA library. A report that predated my discovery of the poisoning of vanadium miners by nearly twenty years had already identified the source of green tongue from exposure to vanadium. EPA's Agency for Toxic Substances and Disease Registry stated regarding the side effects associated with vanadium:

> Occupational exposure to vanadium, especially vanadium pentoxide, produces mainly irritation of the eyes and the upper respiratory tract, often accompanied by productive cough, wheezing, rales, chest pains, difficulty in breathing, bronchitis, questionable pneumonia, and rhinitis. There have been occurrences of green-to-black discoloration of the tongue, metallic taste, nausea, and diarrhea. Six studies have reported skin irritation.[1]

Others have also confirmed the incidence of bleeding that vanadium victims have reported:

> Other potential health effects of vanadium uptake include: cardiac and vascular disease, inflammation of stomach and intestines,

damage to the nervous system, bleeding of livers and kidneys, skin rashes, severe trembling and paralysis, nose bleeds and throat pains, weakening, headaches and dizziness.[2]

We all share the benefits of vanadium by-products—cars, refrigerators, airplanes, laptops, medical equipment, silverware, jewelry—things too numerous to list but that we all use to improve our lives. But a tiny fraction of South Africans bear most of the burden.

||||||||||||

Henry Ford knew the value of vanadium to the auto industry. It turns out that not everything that was good for Ford Motors turned out so hot for African vanadium miners. By the early 1920s, the evidence was already conclusive that vanadium was dangerous. Furthermore, significant health risks had been documented—particularly in industrial settings—where exposure to the dust created in the crushing of the raw material, or exposure to a finely ground end product that could become airborne and atomized, showed significant correlations to the illnesses Vametco miners reported.

Had any serious scientific effort been undertaken by the agency, there was ample evidence lending credence to the miners' claims. One report, published in Geneva in 1988, under the joint sponsorship of the United Nations Environment Programme, the International Labour Organization, and the World Health Organization, was rife with examples of vanadium poisoning from multiple locations worldwide and many different industrial sources of dusty and dangerous vanadium. The report was titled "Environmental Health Criteria 81: Vanadium."[3]

Even the most cursory review of data available then should have put any government official charged with protecting the environment on alert. There were enough similarities among the anecdotal evidence recorded by our ad hoc medical team, the claims made before the Gore-Mbeki Binational Commission in 1996, and earlier agency studies to merit energetic research that was on par with the urgency expressed in repeated requests from the South African government.

Still, after my dismissal from OIA in early 1997, various official EPA communications asserted several times that the agency would continue its investigation into the health effects of vanadium on workers.

But when it came to implementation, the agency's practices bore little resemblance to its promises. I was determined to do what I could to make sure that a credible investigation took place. After meeting so many suffering people, the trail could easily be traced to the mines.

In 1981, sixteen years before the South African government requested that the United States conduct an investigation into vanadium deaths, the Ford Foundation issued a report called *South Africa: Time Running Out*. The commission noted:

> South Africa has rich and varied mineral resources. . . . It has the world's largest known deposits of chromium, manganese, platinum, vanadium, and gold, all minerals which are important to the west because of their strategic, industrial, or economic uses. . . . Vanadium is used principally as an alloying element in the manufacturing of lightweight, high-strength steels for jet engines, airframes, and other transportation equipment and the large piping needed for oil and gas pipelines. South Africa is the world's largest producer of vanadium.[4]

There are substitutes, although more expensive than vanadium, such as columbium, tungsten, manganese, and titanium. More important, however, the report notes that the United States is not immune to the "effects of a stoppage of South African exports" of vanadium. The Ford Foundation report details:

> A total South African cutoff would leave worldwide production almost 25 million pounds short of demand, a shortage which could not be made up immediately by substitution or by increasing production in the US and elsewhere. . . . In the event of a stoppage, the price would rise, the US would be under considerable pressure to increase exports and share its supply, just when US domestic needs would require a reduction in exports and conservation of resources.[5]

It is likely that the strategic significance of vanadium to US national security that the Ford Foundation cites could have been the key motivating factor behind America's reneging. EPA officials chose not to conduct an independent investigation into reported deaths of vanadium victims.

Then in 2001 another report surfaced on the death of four miners from vanadium poisoning:

> Simon Taba, William Mpaketsane, Johannes Moima and Titus Letageng were fighting for compensation when they died of chronic renal failure and pneumonia or respiratory failure. Independent medical investigators have confirmed that . . . 120 workers were dismissed on medical grounds between January 1995 and September 1998, after they developed severe chemical bronchitis, bronchial hyperactivity, irritant-induced asthma, and sensorial peripheral neuropathy.[6]

A published report on the issue has National Union of Mineworkers (NUM) senior attorney Richard Spoor explaining the issue:

> The American Journal of Industrial Medicine in 1999 confirmed that some workers were exposed to 50 times the maximum limit of vanadium pentoxide, sulphur dioxide and ammonia. Company statistics shown to researchers in October 1995 indicated that 33 percent of 1,033 reported complaints at the mine's clinic related to respiratory ailments. "What more proof do they want? Is this not enough?" asked Spoor. "Our team presented original signed medical release forms granting the NUM the right to inspect the medical records. The widows all believe that their husbands died of vanadium poisoning and we have been asked to investigate the claims. But . . . other union representatives were marched from the mine by security guards. This is despite Xstrata's [Vametco's Swiss competitor] public assurance that relevant medical records are open for inspection."[7]

Since profit and national security are sacred cows that cannot under any circumstance be sacrificed, the obvious out for the agency was to ignore the vanadium poisoning issue altogether and focus its attention instead on the fundamental purpose of the Environment Committee: to invest its time, energy, and resources in further developing private sector initiatives under the ETI program. The EPA dispatched Mark Kasman and other envirocrats to South Africa as pitchmen for the ETI. The agency sought to cover up US inaction in the investigation of alleged deaths. Failure to investigate made the United States an accomplice to the crimes committed against this community.

‖‖‖‖‖‖‖‖‖‖

Jacob Ngakane introduced me to a vanadium miner named Garrison during our visit to Brits. A beefy man with a hoarse voice, he was a union leader, a member of the ANC, and one of the organizers of the strike against Vametco in 1990—for which he was fired by the company. One of his jobs at Vametco was to draw sulfuric acid through an industrial pipette—with his mouth. When a colleague missed an eight-hour shift, Garrison was required to draw the acid for two shifts. He was clearly ailing and in distress.

Despite the health risks associated with mine work, there were still lines of men queued outside the gates every day seeking work. Any miner's disloyalty could mean immediate dismissal—or worse.

Garrison asked me about the resolution passed in the Gore-Mbeki Commission, about scientists coming to South Africa to investigate why people were dying.

"I didn't know you knew about the results of the commission," I said.

"Comrade Marsha," Garrison said, bestowing the South African salutation denoting solidarity with me, "we followed the debate and resolutions very closely. In fact, when I go back to my house, I will get you a copy of the resolution." This was an encouraging sign.

Jacob spoke to the gathered miners. "Marsha and her team are not here as a part of the US government. They have come as private citizens, in solidarity with victims of vanadium poisoning."

"But where is the government team that we were promised?" Garrison demanded.

Jacob explained that the United States was not going to send the team and that now ordinary citizens had taken on the task of investigating the poisonings.

"We have two doctors, and I am a social scientist," I said. "If your community will cooperate with us, we will start a preliminary investigation and work with you and your colleagues to try and alert the international community to your plight. You are the experts on vanadium.

You work with it. We need the members of this community to tell us what is happening to your bodies, what is happening to your families, what is happening to your environment because of vanadium."

Garrison and Jacob organized a series of home visits for Joanne, Carolyn, and me to meet and conduct interviews with the miners. The first worker's name was Abel. He was hired by Vametco in 1978 and laid off in the strike.

"We wanted better working conditions, adequate gloves and masks, to protect us from the vanadium dust." He said he had permanent damage to his kidneys, lungs, and esophagus. And then he said something I didn't understand: "We demanded a pint of milk a day. The milk protects us and helps the vanadium go down."

Later we learned that company doctors used milk to "treat" the poisoning.

Joseph was hired by Vametco in 1979. He was also laid off during the strike. "I feel like there's something hot in my lungs. When I try to breathe, I feel lightheaded. I cough up blood. Sometimes I see blood in my pee. I cough all the time. I don't know when I'm going to die. I'm just waiting."

Almost everyone who testified had shortness of breath and difficulty sustaining normal conversation.[8]

As the workers noticed my questions were sincere rather than designed to shoot down their claims, they began to volunteer details. A small fellow in a lively blue-and-white-striped hat reported that he had started having breathing problems just three months after he began his job. Another spoke of masks that did not keep vanadium dust out of his mouth, but that was the only safety equipment given him. It was hard to miss the patterns. I was there as a researcher, not as a policymaker. It was my job to document cause and effect, not to pontificate. I tried to keep my observations concise and professional.

My trained objectivity began to waver, though, when a former worker, who was clearly dying, stepped up to testify. He was coughing too hard for me to catch his first name. He was embarrassed by my calling attention to his breathing troubles. I had to ask three times. A portly, pyramid-shaped man, he had a lazy eye, a pain-twisted face, and under-eye bags so deep they could have been gills. Even his hair seemed diseased, unable to grow convincingly on either head or chin. Despite the heat, he wore his entire wardrobe: ocean-blue cardigan over gray fisherman's sweater over threadbare magenta shirt over orange T-shirt. He stared at the ground, as if even being seen was too much to bear. He spoke Setswana. I scribbled notes: dynamite—mining—after kidney disease.

"When were you first diagnosed?" I asked, knowing what was coming next. The pattern didn't vary. Like so many others, my coughing new friend had been diagnosed with several major vital organ dysfunctions in a routine check-up. Since his illness was clearly occupation related, his doctor had written a report and sent it to Vametco.

"They told him," my translator said, glancing back at the man for confirmation of each detail, "there was nothing wrong with him. They told him, 'You must stop going to outside black doctors. We have our own doctors.'"

My weary brain chanted the rest of the story along with him: and then they sent him to the mines, before laying him off in the strike. The repetition of a horror does not render it any less horrifying, just less surprising.

"Thank you," I said out loud, watching him totter to his seat, coughing. I knew that even a miracle would wheeze and die with this unfortunate man.

I had thought the best way to approach the interviews was to have a set number of questions I would ask in survey style so we could use the questions themselves as a baseline and draw conclusions from that benchmark. What I discovered was that the formula was an encumbrance. It was attributing more importance to the method than the people themselves, than their answers. I found myself distracted by attempting to keep to the interview schedule. It was frustrating. It removed the human in favor of notional objectivity.

When I realized what was happening, I dumped the script. The problem was the language itself. Even when my questions were identical, the answers were all over the place. Maybe not so much in substance, but in the way people organized their responses. Generally, the men were literal with their answers, while the women sometimes hedged, reflecting how they thought their husbands would feel if they knew their wives were talking about them, about their impotence.

The men were inclined toward anger at and frustration with their powerlessness, the management structure of the mine, their impeded sexual relations with their wives, and their inability to do anything about their maladies. The wives were more concerned about providing comfort and moral support to their men and caring for their medical needs. If their men were sick, the women wanted knowledge more than anything. Widows feared becoming destitute. While in theory there were pensions and retirement benefits, in reality those benefits were systematically out of reach. What little these women had came from self-help. This was driven home during my visit with a woman whom I met on a Saturday in the living room of her home.

Joanne and I had been interviewing wives and widows of miners. We noticed a number of them reported illnesses similar to those affecting the miners—bleeding and respiratory distress.

This woman's husband had died quite recently—in 1996. Someone had told us about her, and we went to her home to see if we might talk with her. I was alive to the fact that this woman was still in the early stages of grief and that it would likely be difficult for her to talk about her late husband, but I also felt that, with the memory of his suffering still fresh in her mind, she might be able to provide some insights that may be lost over time. As horrible as the slow death from vanadium poisoning might be, for the survivor, there had to be some relief in knowing that her loved one was no longer suffering; the arduous process might even steel her for the ultimate passing.

I could not have been more wrong.

Rachel sat expressionless, motionless except for the slow rise and fall of her breathing and the slow blink of her eyes. She did not respond to any of my attempts to reach her, including asking her about her children, her siblings, her family. She might as well have been underwater. I finally asked my interpreter to see if she would allow us to take a photograph of her, for future reference, when we might come back and talk to her during a subsequent trip. She agreed and then got up and went into another part of the house, I thought to freshen herself for the photo. After some long minutes we started wondering where she had gone, if she were coming back. Then she suddenly reappeared and took her seat in a chair we had placed by a window for its ambient light. She was wearing a tattered black cloak. I looked at her daughter.

"It's what she was wearing when we buried Daddy," her daughter said.

Jacob had gotten permission for us to tour a mine. I did not ask him how. I did, however, ask him if he thought the guard who had taken my camera when we passed through security would give it back to me when we left. As was common in South Africa because of the hot climate, a table with a large canopy was situated inside the facility. The table was set with hors d'oeuvres. It seemed a nice gesture, until we got close and could see that all of the food was covered in vanadium dust.

An Afrikaner manager came out and greeted us. "I understand you are here from the United States. Welcome. I am the public relations manager."

Jacob introduced himself. "I represent COSATU. We have been receiving a lot of complaints about unsafe conditions at the mine, reports of sickness and poisoning among the workers."

"Really." The manager was ice. "We haven't had any accidents here in weeks, and there have been no reports of complaints to management by any of the workers. Perhaps you could give us their names, and we will look into their allegations."

"No, no, no!" said Jacob. "No names. We give you names, the workers will be fired."

The manager looked at me. "So you work for the EPA?"

Technically I did, although this trip had nothing to do with the agency. It was a poorly framed question. Jacob kicked my foot. "I'm here to learn about vanadium and the process of mining." That seemed good enough for him.

Comrade Violate—one of Jacob's most trusted confidants—and Joanne, along with a few other union members, finished the brief introductions. Then Jacob said, "COSATU would like to see what safety measures are being implemented in response to the workers' complaints. We need to know what you plan to do about them and how you are going to clean up your act."

And so it went, wrangling and positioning. We had notebooks and were all taking notes when my pencil fell off the table. I bent over to pick it up when something landed on the back of my hand. I thought it was some kind of a bug but recoiled when I realized a clot of blood had fallen out of my nose onto my hand. With my head below the level of the table I nudged Joanne's knee with my elbow and pointed at my hand when I got her attention. Joanne wrinkled her nose in a fierce scowl, showing her teeth. "What the hell?"

I didn't want anyone else to know I was bleeding, so I covered my face with the back of my hand and wiped the end of my nose. Joanne leaned over and whispered in my ear. "What have we gotten ourselves into here, Marsha?"

I noticed there was a tall smokestack just beyond the building beside us. "What's that smoke coming out of the stack there?" I asked the manager. He turned his head and looked.

"That," he said, "is 100 percent pure sulfuric acid." He smiled. "I know in the States you have all these command and control measures in place to prevent such things. We don't worry about that so much here."

"I would like to tour the processing facility," I said. "Do you think that could be arranged?"

"I don't know, Marsha," Joanne whispered in protest. "If I'm going inside that place I want a bubble suit or something. We don't have the slightest idea what we'll be exposed to in there."

"That can be arranged," the manager said, "but it will take some time. My concern is that if I outfit you with bubble suits, the workers are going to wonder why that would be necessary and they don't have them."

"Why don't they have them? Maybe they should." Jacob never missed a beat.

"Well, look, why don't you all in the meantime go down to the pit area over there while I'm putting the equipment together? I'll need about a half hour or so, and you can observe that part of the operation while you're waiting."

A foreman drove us to the pit in a Land Rover. In the few hundred yards from the main office building to the pit, the earth transformed from a desolate, dry landscape with misshapen vegetation to a moonscape. Erebus could just as easily have been a place like this. It was gargantuan. The only way to get a sense of the scale was to watch the trucks that crawled along its bottom. When a man approached one of the trucks, he was dwarfed by its tires. Huge mounds of black rubble heaped the entire perimeter of the pit. Terraced roads pressed along the length of each mound where the trucks drove up and back, depositing or removing material with loaders that could easily scoop a city bus into their buckets and then dumping the black material into the truck beds.

Above the entire expanse was a plume of dust hovering and drifting over the land. We stood watching the operation, awestruck by its sheer scale and by the danger it posed. Any dust, whether sawdust or radio-active dust, is dangerous because of its ability to penetrate deeply into the lungs. The dust cloud generated in the mine from conveyors, trucks, and loaders, and by the process of pulverizing the raw material, represented tons of dangerous and potentially lethal airborne material that was being dispersed by the wind. It also represented a means for the material to enter the water supply through the formation of acid rain or by simply settling on the surface of lakes, rivers, and streams.

That it would settle on dry surfaces meant it would wash off those surfaces during rain. It would settle onto food like it had coated the hors d'oeuvres. This single pit represented contamination that would affect air, water, and food supplies. The ecology was simple. The dust covered the grass. The cows ate the grass. The people ate the cows.

Our group was in the midst of discussing all these sickening possibilities when we heard the clatter of footsteps, leather, and metal approaching the pit from the direction of the office. The message that we could come back to the office came over an intercom, so we piled into the Land Rover and returned to the area where the table was set up. The plant manager was waiting for us.

"You are all ordered to leave the property immediately!" came the metallic Afrikaner voice through a megaphone.

There were several guards with the plant manager. Big, menacing guards who seemed to have come out of nowhere and stood with their arms folded across their chests. The manager came and addressed himself directly to me.

"I just got off the phone to Danbury, Connecticut, and I was told by the company president that you are to leave the premises."

"I'm here on official business," Jacob shouted. "I'm a union representative, and you can't force me to leave my people."

"I am going to ask that you leave immediately." The men with weapons started toward us.

"I am an authorized official of COSATU," Jacob protested. "I have a right to be here and to bring qualified people with me. I object in the strongest terms possible."

The more Jacob protested, the more ominous the guards looked. They got jumpy. They could take us easily.

"No, Jacob, I don't like the looks of this." I turned to Joanne. "Let's go."

All of us started toward the exit. It may have been instinct, it may have been the memory of other incidents with the mine owners, but, as we left, a sense of dread and danger swept over me. We moved quickly, rushing toward the van, just shy of panic. The guards, burly and foreboding, closed ranks and followed after us. As we drove away a miner ran out, holding my camera as he ran toward us.

"Here! Here!"

As I took the camera from him, it snapped a picture. It wouldn't be until I got back to the States that I even remembered that shot being taken. Somehow, centered in the frame, there was the miner, clear as the memory of looking back at the guards where they had stood watching us before turning to walk back to the facility, blending in with the buildings, the equipment, the haze.

"Marsha!" It was the first time I had ever heard fear in Joanne's voice. "We are covered in vanadium dust!"

I looked at my shoes and my pants. She was right. The vanadium dust was covering us. We were contaminated. Was it safe to return to the apartment? Had the vanadium penetrated our skin? Was there a way to reverse damage? We were near panic. Although our exposure was minimal, we could be in trouble. Vanadium was personal now. We showered. Washed our hair. Scrubbed our bodies of vanadium. Like workers trying to scrape the green from their tongues, we knew it was in vain.

I now understood the magic allure of milk.

The Registry of Man

Many days of listening to one person after another describe the same symptoms, the same treatment, the same humiliation tends to harden one's sensitivity. Perhaps this is what we must allow when we know there is only so much we can do in one day and that when we finish with all of these people today there will be another line waiting for us when we come back tomorrow. Call it empathy fatigue. Call it objectivity. Call it professionalism. I call it self-preservation. Otherwise, we Westerners might fall at the feet of the South African man named John—who has walked miles on his bony legs whose leanness reminds us of the legs of a deer, for the way the tendons are almost visible through the skin—and beg his forgiveness. But where a deer's legs are like cannons loaded with leaps, this man's legs are loaded with vanadium, his seventy-year-old appearance the perfect disguise for the death that trails behind him like a shadow.

John drags that death out of the countryside with him as his final accomplishment, his magnum opus to the rest of humanity to declare: This I was, a man. Try as we might it is not possible to behold the strength of that journey, across dirt roads that will forget the scratch of his feet before the next step falls. Other black South Africans have taken his place in the mines just as he took another man's place fifteen years earlier, but for various reasons—family, responsibility, desperation—none will see him as themselves. He will be the wraith that none believe.

Yet if somehow it were possible to view time-lapse images of the last seventy years on this dusty stretch of road, we would see a long progression of green-tongued, rag-and-bone men, staggering toward a world that will continue like it has always continued—without them. Collectively, they represent a body count grizzlier than that of Jonestown, all the more ghastly because the process of this poisoning remains and will remain invisible. This mummified, near-dead husk of a man is the exception to the rule of thousands of other men who, when faced with a mortal curfew, agreed with the pronouncement that reads: You will not survive to see your children grown. The rest of your miserable days will wheeze away in agony. You will not be able to provide, protect, and cherish anything you hold dear. You are nothing, you do not exist, your contribution will be easily replaced. Yet this leather-draped temporality of flesh, desire, loneliness, and bone has chosen to stand and walk one more time toward his fellows, like the first man rising from forgetfulness and shadow, to inscribe his name in the registry of man.

Death Threats and Missed Opportunities

I wondered what planet I was on when the phone rang and woke me up after I returned from South Africa.

"Get your game face ready, Marsha—it's on! We've got a court date."

"Oh my God, David! When?"

"We've got plenty of time, but I'd suggest you clear your life of anything and everything unrelated to the case. From now on, it's game time."

"Absolutely, David. Where do I begin? What can I do?" I felt like I was four years old, wrapped around my mother's leg and asking her for permission to have a playdate.

"I think the best thing you can do for yourself right now is to start thinking like a juror. Put yourself inside that jury box and inside a juror's head and try to imagine what it would be like to have someone named Marsha Coleman-Adebayo walk into the courtroom for the first time. First impression. What would you think—'you' meaning every one of the jurors, because it is their courtroom, everyone stands when they enter—if someone walked into your courtroom wearing jeans. Wearing a platinum wig. Wearing whatever. Because that impression is the most important one you're going to make during the course of the entire trial. To a juror, everything about your appearance says something about you as a person—even if they can't articulate what that is. Rich people hire consultants for this, Marsha. They go through a complete makeover so they can present themselves in the most favorable and least threatening way to a jury."

"Oh." I thought he was going to tell me to start reading through all the filings and affidavits. "You mean like my hair, my shoes."

"I didn't say anything about your hair or your shoes. I wouldn't presume to know any more than just enough to get me in trouble about any of that stuff. We all walk around in uniforms whether we know it or not. All I'm asking you to do is to start thinking about it and try to make sure that when you walk into that courtroom, not just on the first day but every day of the trial, make damn sure you've got the right uniform on. Especially that first day."

Although I didn't present it quite this way to Segun, when I told him David had called, honestly the first thing that went through my mind was this: according to my attorney, a significant shopping spree was required—by necessity. Circumstance dictated it. I would do my utmost to meet that challenge. Should I go for Angela Davis or Anita Hill? Did my braids make me too militant? I'd have to have my hair styled. Duty required nothing less.

David and I had engaged in heated arguments over how central vanadium was to my case.

"They'll tear you to shreds with it, Marsha. Believe me. We start talking vanadium, they'll start talking policy, national security, strategic minerals—we're screwed. The judge, even a sympathetic one, will throw it out."

"But David! This is a matter of justice. People are dying!"

"You want to have justice, Marsha? Win your case. Then you'll have justice. You'll have gravitas. You win in court, you'll have a platform, because the press will take you seriously. Know what you'll have if you lose your case? Nothing. A black eye, maybe, but you'll be a laughingstock. You were denied your civil rights. You were discriminated against. You were harassed, and 1964 outlawed all of that. You can win that. You talk about vanadium, you lose."

The next set of phone calls were equally dramatic and game changing.

As soon as I had filed a complaint of discrimination in 1995, opinion about me at EPA split. People at the bottom of the hierarchy—the secretaries, the janitors—were proud of me. They were rooting for me. But many of those at my pay grade, my colleagues, were afraid to be seen with me. One day I walked into the women's room humming to myself. When another woman using the toilet heard my voice, she stopped midstream, pulled up her pants, and ran out of the bathroom. Colleagues ostracized me. People stared or said mean, ugly things under their breath. It started right away.

Then came the mysterious phone calls. Someone would call me at my office and not say anything. I could hear faint breathing, but I wouldn't know who it was. "Who is this, please?" In those days, not even government phones had caller ID.

At first I thought the calls were honest mistakes—wrong numbers. I ignored them. Then a caller would say something like "Don't be surprised if you get a big bang when you put your foot on the accelerator."

So now I had to worry about being blown up in my car? The silent calls started around the time my court date was set and escalated after that. We know who you are. We don't like you—and we're watching you. I suppose, prior to the threat, we could have still considered it possible that the calls were coming from some secret admirer. But afterward? I slammed the phone down. But then what could I do? How was I to make sense of a call like that? Anonymous. Unsettling. I felt its radiation in every part of my life, because I didn't know. Did the "other" work right down the hall? It could be sitting across from me while we ate lunch together.

During the days of duck-and-cover drills, Americans knew exactly where the threat was coming from. We could understand Russians or communist nukes. But after the cold war Americans started feeling a new fear. It was no longer a tangible, nuclear threat from some country with a strange sounding language—it was now among us. The deranged gunman, the disgruntled postal worker, *The Silence of the Lambs*. What made this fear worse was its facelessness. The intruder was an affectless thing that you might find inside your home some night, with eyes so dead they would be more disturbing than the intruder's intent.

He throws a dart at a map to select his prey. Pleas for mercy make things worse. The phantom phone call was like that. My office had taken a dart and went from a routine workplace to a house of fear.

When the workplace is difficult, it is essential that home be a safe haven and sanctuary. Being afraid at night because of what happened at work is the next reality. When fear finds a way into your home, it's inescapable. Anyone could get my work number from the operator. But they couldn't get my cell. That was private. I always looked forward to a cell message because it was usually Segun or someone else I trusted. It was my secure line. The place where I could always relax.

I didn't get past message number one: I am going to fuck you so hard that I will break off my dick in your pussy.

Click.

In times of distress I called Segun, but what was I going to tell him about this call that would allay his instincts that I should drop the whole thing—not out of fear—but common sense? Segun put life and health above causes. Without even blinking I knew with this kind of threat he would ask me to terminate my lawsuit immediately. Rationally, I cared more about my life too, but it wasn't so cut and dried. This was assault. This was thuggery. The average fourteen-year-old knew better than this. This was the place where principle, common sense, and fear intersected. If I shared this ugly silencer with Segun, I feared it would be the end of the court battle. That would be capitulation because of threat. And the threats would have succeeded.

I made a calculated decision to keep the phone threats from my husband.

To deal with the dilemma of that decision, at odds with my natural inclination to confide in Segun, I sought the counsel of my pastor, the Reverend Sterling King Jr. I was most concerned about my children. Two callers had mentioned my children, noted their playing in front of the house. I stopped Sina and Sade from playing outside without my supervision after that. For a while, I wouldn't even allow them to open the outside doors. It was a terrifying time.

I couldn't chance telling Segun about these calls.

I didn't have to. In one of nature's wonderful acts of balancing unequals, especially when involving a spiritual trust, the threats were too charged to escape detection. Segun and I had identical cell phones— these were the days when cell phones were still ludicrously reminiscent of walkie-talkies in size and form—and he mistakenly took mine. Pop psychology would say I wanted him to find out and made it happen. I prefer to believe, however, that it was the attraction of polar opposites. The release of energy it produced in Segun cinched it for me. I'd never seen him so distraught. He was shaking with anger. He was incensed at the call's crude graphics. He was shocked that such bile was directed at his wife. And he was distraught that his wife had not only kept the message but had kept it from him.

"Why, Marsha? Why didn't you trust me enough to tell me about the calls? How many calls have you received like this one?"

Seeing his reaction, it was hard to remember why secrecy ever seemed a good idea. He kept asking me if I trusted him and if I really considered him my friend. I felt bad that I'd hurt him, but I tried to explain that I was dedicated to something greater than myself. I said that I knew from his perspective I was placing our family at risk.

"A marriage cannot survive without trust, Marsha. Your silence is simply not fair—especially about something so basic as threats to our physical safety."

"Segun. Sweetheart. If you had told me to stop the lawsuit or to resign from EPA—even though it would have made perfect sense—that would have been a sharp blow to something I'm dedicated to. If we give in to them now, out of common sense, out of concern for our safety, out of fear, it will be much harder on all of us until we finally stand up. It will be much harder for our children unless we stand up."

Segun looked at me fiercely.

"I would never make you do anything. And I would not let you do that alone."

I knew he was right. I agreed with him and apologized. It was an example of how isolation influences and intensifies a difficult situation. Isolation is an early chapter in the playbook: make the employee feel that she has no friends; the stress drives a wedge between couples.

Eight weeks before the trial, the next shoe dropped, right out of the playbook, a new assignment:

You have 120 days to identify all harmful chemical substances found in the human body, the primary routes of entry for these chemicals, and the current state of environmental epidemiology for these compounds.[1]

I was reading from a memo signed by Mary Ellen Weber, a manager under Bill Sanders. I immediately called Dwight Welch at the union office.

"Marsha, I'm a biologist, and I couldn't answer those questions. They know you're a political scientist. Shit! This is the typical way the agency rids itself of employees they no longer want. Look, let me call some toxicologists and see what I can do."

A few minutes later Dwight called back. "Marsha, I've spoken to some of our PhD toxicologists. Everyone agrees you're being set up. If the agency could answer those questions in 120 days, we could shut our doors.

"I've seen this a million times. First the agency gives an employee an assignment they know is impossible. When you can't deliver they will put you on a PIP [performance improvement plan]. The second step is a PAP [performance assistance plan]. It's all a game. And then comes the POP."

"Dwight, I've heard of the PIP and PAP, but what's a POP?"

"That's the sound of your heels hitting the sidewalk."

Segun's advice was more practical. "I saw Congressman James Sensenbrenner on TV grilling EPA on its environmental program. I think you should call his office."

Browner knew what was going on. My former attorney, Linda Halpern, had written to her three years earlier, on March 3, 1997, literally begging her to stop the madness in the agency. Halpern's letter cited examples of "ham-fisted and crude" retaliation. She received a response two weeks later from Browner's chief of staff, Peter Robinson, denying our request for a meeting.

I was reminded of the comment Paul Cough had made on my return from Beijing, taunting me. The conference was over, he had said. I was back in the agency now. We'd see how fast Browner would come to my rescue with the TV lights turned off.

Coleman-Adebayo v. Carol M. Browner

Day One

After a sleepless night Segun and I met David Shapiro on the steps of the Prettyman Courthouse dress in my courtroom outfit à la Ruth Bader Ginsburg. David was dressed in a blue pinstriped suit with navy socks and a meticulously selected tie. David's suits were always impeccable. Ties were his talismans. Some he chose to elicit a positive reaction from jurors. Others he wore to fortify his own mood. I was beginning to suspect that David's ties could trigger increased sunspot activity.

"I thought Wyneva would meet us here today," I said. Wyneva Johnson was the assistant United States attorney (AUSA).

David looked at me and smiled. "I told you she wouldn't be here. The government is not interested in settling." His smile quickly changed to a look of concern. He took me by the forearm. "Are you ready?"

For the first time I saw that David could be supportive, that he wasn't just consumed with law. But as soon as his foot touched the inside of the courthouse, he transformed. He was carnivorous, in fighting mode and looking forward to his interaction with Ms. Johnson.

"David," I confessed, "I'm scared. If we lose, everyone who is going to testify for me will be destroyed by the agency."

David was decidedly on. His playfulness seemed disconnected from the moment. I felt like we were entering the Colosseum—and we were the Christians. But I would soon learn that in this contest, David became giddy at the prospect of blood. He was the lion.

For a moment I was able to smile and breathe, but the fear returned, stronger than before, settling in the pit of my stomach. Somehow I found myself on the second floor of the courthouse. I stopped a moment and took a deep breath. "Segun, please pray with me before I go into the courtroom."

Segun held me for a few seconds and in Baptist style—in the center of the corridor in front of the courtroom—said out loud: "Lord, please be with my wife as she pleads her case before this judge and jury. I know that you're in the midst of this. You have kept her all of these years, and you now allow her to stand before men and declare the good news that justice rolls down like waters and righteousness like a mighty stream."

When I met my reflection in Segun's eyes, the fear, the anxiety, and the pain I had lived with left me. He handed me his large family Bible with red italics highlighting the quotes from Jesus.

Mark Twain's quip that an ethical man is a Christian holding four aces is an apt description of American justice: attorneys and judges preside over ritualized trials no one but they understand, conducted in front of common American jurors using language and procedures largely unknown to the public. But deposing the powerful has a way of redistributing the aces. Under the equalizing influence of a subpoena, the powerful are not so invincible. Suddenly they are subject to doubt. They don't know the sum total of all that is known. They don't know what others who were also under oath may have said.

Instead of toying with their subordinates with the insolence born of unfair advantage, under oath they are faced with limitation and accountability. CYA—cover your ass—kicks in big time, and where once they were immune to constraint, now they are subject to questioning that requires no deference to a chain of command.

In the deposition process I had seen what a master David Shapiro was at taking the pressure EPA managers used against their subordinates and focusing it right back between their eyes. I was told he was even better in the courtroom. As David ushered me to the plaintiff's table opposite the jury box, I was ready. He leaned over and spoke to me under his breath.

"Every trial has its challenges. You can get whipped around like a roller coaster. Our challenge is to find Dr. Gary Waxmonsky. My guy has been looking everywhere for him to serve him with a subpoena. You need to call your colleagues at EPA and find out where they're hiding him. We have to show how a similarly situated white man was treated differently than you. We need a comparator, and Gary is perfect. He has a PhD; he's head of the Gore/Russia program. We couldn't ask for a better comparator. If he testifies, I like our chances."

Judge Colleen Kollar-Kotelly walked in.

"All rise. This is Civil Case 98-CV-926 and 98-CV-1939, Marsha L. Coleman-Adebayo versus Carol M. Browner.[1] You may be seated." There was only one person seated in the large sterile courtroom, with its ancient, hard wooden benches—Segun. He sat with his legs crossed and his eyes closed in prayerful meditation.

"Counsel, please identify yourself for the record."

"Good morning, Your Honor. David Shapiro."

"Good morning, Your Honor. Wyneva Johnson on behalf of defendant. With me today is Ms. Joanne Hogan and my law clerk, Linda Tran."

Black AUSAs were statistically nonexistent before the civil rights movement had forced the Department of Justice to hire African Americans and other people of color. Ironically, all those years later, black AUSAs in the Civil Division routinely defended accused discriminators in the federal government and shredded victims of discrimination. One might think that people who had gained their foothold in society on the backs and through the blood of the heroes of civil rights movement would have had troubled consciences defending discriminators. Yet, had Frederick Douglass, Martin Luther King Jr., or Walter Fauntroy filed a complaint of discrimination against the federal government, Wyneva and her cohorts would have vigorously defended the government against their charges.

The Department of Justice, recognizing the complexity of race and gender in America, usually assigned a black AUSA when defending against the complaint of a black or Hispanic plaintiff against a white supervisor. My case was no different. Wyneva Johnson was African American, and her job was to defend federal managers accused of violating civil rights laws and to win a verdict on behalf of the government.

Washington professionals, especially federal attorneys, often have a buttoned-down, dapper appearance. Not Wyneva. She seemed untidy, sometimes leaving her slip hanging below her skirt hem or her blouse pulled out of line where it should have been tucked in. She was disheveled. During depositions I took a certain macabre delight in guessing where her gremlins of unkemptness would strike that day. But Wyneva was shrewder than her appearance might indicate. I feared this was part of a Columbo-like ploy, designed to disarm her opponents. She was backed with unlimited financial resources and a raft of attorneys. If one underestimated her, she could land a haymaker.

Shapiro was a former AUSA himself, who had left the government to form his own law firm with his partner, Richard Swick. David was known for his charm, tenacity, quick wit, and intellect. He was confident and controlled within a space he defined, both within the courtroom and out. He lost very few cases and thus was able to pick and choose his legal projects according to his interests, his passions, and the likelihood of success. While he could charm the birds from the trees, David was also known for his temper and sharp tongue, patience not being his defining virtue. A staunch Republican, David defended victims of discrimination with the same passion that he praised Ronald Reagan.

The pirouettes were over, and two Spartans—completely different in style, substance, and intensity—were about to square off in the courtroom of Judge Colleen Kollar-Kotelly.

The first day of the trial was the first time that I saw the sworn-in jury. The selection process had blurred their individual characteristics. Seated at the plaintiff's table, I could identify them as individuals, not by name certainly, but by physical traits. The jury was nearly balanced between men and women. There was one young man who worked for National Public Radio; one man worked at Howard University. Another delivered pizzas for Pizza Hut, and the last man bagged groceries at a local Safeway supermarket. The women were diverse, with one dressed like a model in stiletto heels, another in a dapper business outfit, and a third who seemed like a young professional or student. My fate would soon be in their hands. I looked at all of their faces and said a silent prayer that they would not only listen to the testimony but would also hear what was not being said. I fingered Segun's Bible, praying for comfort.

Judge Kollar-Kotelly welcomed the jury, sitting upright and straightening her black judicial robes and pearl necklace. She touched her coiffure.

"Good morning, members of the jury." She cleared her throat and described the Title VII case I had brought. "On the basis of her race, color, sex, and physical disability, [the EPA] maintained a racially and sexually hostile work environment and retaliated against her for complaining about such discrimination. Specifically, her claims include a failure to promote, removing her as EPA's South Africa program officer, denying her travel necessary to perform her duties, and subjecting her to a racially and sexually hostile work environment. The defendant denies all of the plaintiff's claims."

The judge concluded, "It is your responsibility to decide whether the plaintiff has proved her claims against the defendant by a preponderance of the evidence. We have opening statements at this point, so, Mr. Shapiro . . ."

"Thank you, Your Honor." David stood up and strolled to the podium in front of the judge and to the right of the jury. His suit fell perfectly in place. Before starting to speak, he took in a deep breath, savoring the moment.

"Well, good morning. And now we begin."

If David had been granted only thirty seconds to make his case, he would have nailed it in thirty seconds. Today, he had all the time he needed and was meticulous on every detail. I realized, watching him, that this was what David lived for. I had seen him in his office. I had seen him in public. I had seen him nearly come apart under the stress of the moment when the moment was not going well. But today I saw David Shapiro come to life. The color in his face heightened his deep blue eyes. His gestures became graceful. His voice, which at other times sounded gravelly and gruff, took on a soothing quality. There was no hesitation, no wavering—he was patient and smooth. He seemed to like the members of the jury. But above all, he seemed kind.

"This case involves a very high-level employee." There was a lot of ground to cover and many details. It occurred to me that it would be easy to overload the jury with information and lose them, but David struck an easy balance between the difficult and the everyday.

"This is a complicated world, and, as you would expect, agencies that don't seem to have anything to do with international affairs, international relations, or anything, have to have units because we have very complex relationships abroad, and this is the Environmental Protection

Agency's unit that deals with international matters. Marsha Coleman-Adebayo came there in 1990.

"Lawsuits are kind of like houses: they are not built all at once. They don't fall from the sky. They are built. And that's what testimony and documents are: pieces of evidence that build a story so that you can see what really happened. And here is what the evidence is going to show. You're going to hear that Marsha Coleman-Adebayo, a PhD in international relations, with a specialty in Africa, was on board in 1990. Now, she was brought on as a GS-14, and those of you familiar with the government know that some people start out at a GS-1 level, so GS-14 is a substantial position. The highest level is GS-15, and then Senior Executive Service, called SES. You're going to see that there were very, very few African American professionals in the Office of International Activities at EPA, the OIA. Indeed, at this time period and until Ms. Coleman-Adebayo was no longer in that office at all, there were no GS-15s who were African Americans.

"And Ms. Coleman-Adebayo, you will hear, went from [her] UN role and naturally segued because of the administrator's—that's Carol Browner, the administrator of EPA—interest in the International Women's Conference that was held in Beijing, China, in 1995. Ms. Browner was very interested in playing a lead role and having EPA play a lead role in that conference. And the assignment went to Marsha Coleman-Adebayo. I mean, even our First Lady went to China as the head of our delegation there.

"Now, obviously, everybody works for someone. And Mr. Bill Nitze, an assistant administrator, was the head of the Office of International Activities. And, of course, she worked for him. [She had] a white colleague, Paul Cough, who started, as it turned out, the same week she started. He didn't have a PhD. He was much lower educated than she was, but he was a white man, and he got a promotion, to a 15. Ms. Coleman-Adebayo asked about that. And she was told, 'Listen—'"

Wyneva Johnson rose to her feet. "Objection, Your Honor!"

"On what basis?"

"Hearsay, Your Honor."

"Overruled. You may proceed," said Judge Kollar-Kotelly.

"Now, she did a great job. She went to Beijing. Only two went from EPA, and she played a major role. But did she get anything out of it? No. In fact, when she came back she found that the white man had been selected to be her new supervisor. She had a meeting with Mr. Nitze, and he said, 'Well, I can't promote you right now, but I've got a great assignment for you—in Africa.' And this is really the nub of what happened to Ms. Coleman-Adebayo."

David then described the Gore-Mbeki Commission and how Nitze had offered me the position of executive secretary. "Now, Mr. Gore didn't just have this vice presidential-level initiative with South Africa—he had it with several other countries. Key among them, as key as South Africa, was Russia. And that was called the Gore-Chernomyrdin Commission. EPA participated in that. And they had an executive secretary, somebody from OIA, to do that work. And that person you will hear from also. He was a GS-15. His PhD is in international relations with a specialty in Russia. Just like Marsha Coleman-Adebayo was a PhD, specialty in Africa. Very able guy. Gary Waxmonsky, colleague of Marsha Coleman. Only he gets to serve it as a 15. Marsha Coleman-Adebayo gets to serve in this key role—same role, different countries, same level initiative, same area of environmental, same organization. White man, 15. Black woman, 14."

David filled the jury in about the remainder of the case. He concluded, "Like I said, the lawsuit, a case, doesn't arrive fully formed with one piece of evidence. It's built a brick at a time. It takes patience and perseverance. I thank you in advance for your applying those to this. I'll get to talk to you again at the end, and we will talk about what was shown in the evidence. For now, thank you very much."

It was now time for Wyneva Johnson to present her opening statement. David's opening was so compelling I wondered how she was going to counter. She stood up, adjusted her skirt, and stepped up to the podium. Her face held the same level of determination and focus as David's. Her voice was clear and commanding.

"May it please the court," she said. "Good morning, Ladies and Gentlemen."

She paused to gather herself.

"Now, Ladies and Gentlemen, you will hear from the government's witnesses that there is no challenge to the fact that Ms. Coleman-Adebayo has a PhD from MIT—that that's an important educational accomplishment. You're not going to hear any challenge to that, but what you're going to hear from the—the evidence will show from these managers is that even with such a degree, when one comes to work, one is to perform. The evidence will be that on some occasions Ms.

Coleman-Adebayo did outstanding work, and she received a performance rating that reflected that; but they will tell you after she received
that performance rating, her work went down.

"And then you hear [Mr. Shapiro] say that the leadership of the
office, Mr. Nitze, a white male, Dr. Hecht, Dr. Sielen, that these people attempted to prevent her from doing her job. Well, you're going to
hear Mr. Nitze tell you, Ladies and Gentlemen, that he is the one who
offered Dr. Coleman-Adebayo the assignment to South Africa because
he believed that it was important to her professional development and
that she would do a good job. But he would tell you that he was disappointed. He will tell you that in working closely with her that she did
not perform at the level that he had expected that she would perform."

The strategy was materializing. I was a good employee but incon-
sistent. She concluded, "So at the end of this case, Ladies and Gentlemen, we will have the opportunity to come back and speak with you.
After you have heard all of the evidence with regard to her performance
issues, we will be asking that you find that the defendant in this case
did not discriminate against Ms. Coleman-Adebayo because of her race,
because of her sex, because of her color, because of her alleged disability
or for any reason with regard to her employment at EPA. Thank you."

Wyneva sat down. The judge instructed David to call his first witness.

"Thank you, Your Honor. We will call the plaintiff, Dr. Coleman-
Adebayo." David turned to me with one last visual coaching. There was
confidence, reassurance, forthrightness, and nothing but business in
David's comportment. He was communicating to me that I would do
just fine. He was communicating to the jury that this was a woman he
expected them to take seriously and look upon with respect. And he
was communicating to the court that his client had nothing to hide, so
he was leading with me from the outset.

||||||||||||

I was so nervous I couldn't tell what I was communicating. No matter
how many courtroom dramas I had seen or how many imaginary cross-
examinations had run through my head, sitting in that docket was different. Its placement was different than imagined; the lighting and the
position of the jury were different. But everything mattered. This was it.
If MIT had groomed me for anything through their doctoral program,

it was performing and learning to focus on the argument, no matter the pressure.

David's general questions on my background, history, and education helped break the ice. I told the jury about my lunch with Bill Nitze and how reluctant I had been to accept his offer. "I had been promised a promotion after I worked so hard on the Beijing Women's Conference," I said. "[I did not] get the promised promotion. I was the only person [program officer] in my office that did not get a bonus; and to make matters worse, Paul Cough, who did not have my educational or experience background, had been promoted and was now my supervisor."

I told the jury about how Alan Sielen had said, "We're going to make you an honorary white man for the day," how Franklin Moore had reacted, and how Sielen had responded: "Mr. Sielen told Franklin to calm down. He said, 'Now don't get so upset. I went to the same school as Jackie Robinson. So I know black people.'" I told the jury how Sielen had told me that Alan Hecht had called me "uppity" and how he "engaged me in a conversation about why women thought they should be able to get pregnant and still compete with men."

I told them all about the study tours and the vanadium poisoning, and detailed Nitze's remarks about how you can tell how civilized someone is by how well they speak proper English. I told them how my request for the study tours had been tabled by the old-guard apartheid leadership but rescued by Bantu Holomisa. I told them how Pat Koshel had tried to bog down the process in red tape and then had sent the second group to EPA Region III in Philadelphia. "One thing was extremely clear to me," I explained, "that Ms. Koshel and Mr. Nitze had little or no respect for the new South African leadership."

Finally, I told the jury how Sielen had told me he was removing me from my position as executive secretary for the Gore-Mbeki Environment Committee and how hurt I had been.

It was now time for Wyneva Johnson to cross-examine me. She waited for David to take his seat. Wyneva came purposefully to the podium. She was all business. David had told me that she would not attack, for fear of alienating the jury. She struck me as very strict, almost like a police officer, seeking just the facts.

"You testified that Mr. Sielen told you that somebody said that you were uppity—that's what you told the ladies and gentlemen of the jury; is that correct?"

"That's correct."

"But no one ever said to you directly, 'Dr. Coleman-Adebayo, I can consider you uppity,' did they? That comment that you told him about was not made to you directly, was it?"

"No, but—"

"No. Just answer the question, please."

"No. However—"

"All right. I'll let you do the 'however,' but just answer the question first."

"Could you please repeat the question?"

"The comment that you told the ladies and gentlemen of the jury that someone called you uppity—the person that indicated to you, you said, was Dr. Sielen, is that right?"

"That's correct."

"And he told you that somebody else said it? Isn't that what you testified to the ladies and gentlemen of the jury?"

"Yes, that's correct."

"So no one said it to you directly, did they?"

"No, that's correct. However—"

"Just wait a moment. Answer my question, please. So what is the answer to the question?"

"I've already answered. I said no."

|||||||||||

The first day of court testimony was over. I was emotionally and physically exhausted. I thought I had answered the questions well, and I thought I saw some of the jurors beginning to look at me with empathy. Perhaps that is what I wanted to see. Segun and I accompanied David back to his office for a debriefing about my testimony and to prepare for the next day's session.

"Look, tomorrow is going to be a long and hectic day with Franklin Moore, Inga Barnett, and Kathryn Washburn. Get some rest," said David. "I suspect that Wyneva will try and take Franklin and Kathryn apart. My gut tells me that we have to be careful with Mark Kasman. What is he going to testify about?" David was still in courtroom mode. "There's something about Kasman that I don't like."

David leaned back in his chair, looked at me and said, "What's your take on Kasman?"

"Nitze chose Mark to take over the South Africa project when I was removed. But we have been friends for years," I told him. "I don't see him as being hostile. Mark heard Alan Sielen call me and Franklin 'honorary white men' in a management meeting. I think of him as basically honest."

David laughed and looked up at his office ceiling. "Marsha, the guy took over your position, and he is listed on both the plaintiff and defense witness lists. I would be careful whom I call a friend."

"Have you tracked down Waxmonsky yet?"

"I've placed a million calls. . . . I'm sure we'll hear something by tomorrow."

When I got home I called a colleague in the Chicago office, Michael Bland. Mike was a veteran who had suffered brutal retaliation because he had exposed corruption at the agency. He was smart, analytical, and politically savvy. I valued his judgment. Mike and I had received bronze medals for our work on reducing mercury in hospital usage. He asked me tough questions about the body language of the jurors and helped me assess some of the sidebar comments by the judge. He also promised to call around to help locate Gary Waxmonsky. The search was on.

Day Two

The day Nelson Mandela emerged from prison, the US government had seemed to embrace the new South African leadership—at least on the surface. But by the time of my trial I was beginning to believe that much of that was hype. I was looking forward to Franklin Moore's testimony. We had been friends since we had met at EPA. Franklin had navigated his way to the US Agency for International Development (USAID), deciding not to subject himself to what he saw as escalating discrimination at EPA. An early indication had come the day Bill Nitze was being introduced at a staff meeting as the new assistant administrator and had said that he was colorblind and didn't believe that racism still existed.

"He is either lying to himself or lying to us," Franklin had said, looking at me wide eyed. "Either way, I'm out of here."

In addition to Franklin, Inga Barnett, my secretary, who was African American, would testify about how our supervisor, Paul Cough, had taken her secretarial bonus of $750 and given it to a white, high-level senior official in order to top off his already generous bonus. Martha Shimkin, a white female, would testify that the same officials named in my case, Alan Sielen and Alan Hecht, had told her that she was too ambitious as a woman; she felt there was a double standard operating in the office between men and women—favoring men. According to Martha, Hecht had complained that white men were being treated as second-class citizens. The promotion Martha had worked hard for was given to Mark Kasman.

I was deeply moved that so many of my colleagues were willing to risk their careers and the financial stability of their families to speak out about the abuse we had suffered at EPA. Before I left for the courthouse, I placed some calls to close contacts in EPA to put out feelers regarding the whereabouts of Gary Waxmonsky. I picked up Segun's Bible, and we were on our way.

⁣⁣⁣⁣⁣⁣⁣⁣⁣⁣⁣

The clerk walked in from a back door in the courtroom, took her seat, adjusted her skirt, and looked around to ensure that the two counsels were in place. Judge Kollar-Kotelly, glancing first at the jury and then at counsel, was firmly in control of her courtroom. "Mr. Shapiro."

"Your Honor, we call Franklin Moore to the stand."

The door opened, and Franklin strode into the courtroom, head held high with an aura of confidence.

"Are you gainfully employed now, and if so, where?" asked David.

"Yes, I now work at the US Agency for International Development. But I worked at the EPA for four years, from 1990 to 1994."

"While you were at the EPA, did you receive any promotions?"

"No, sir," Franklin said, "I did not."

The words rolled across his lips. The air of confidence was giving way to another emotion. "If I might add, sir, I didn't receive a promotion until I left EPA and started working at the US Agency for International Development." Franklin looked deep in thought, like he was reliving a part of his past that was best forgotten. "As I remember it," he said, "a gentleman named Paul Cough received a promotion that I thought I was entitled to."

"What race is Mr. Cough?"

My parents, Majestice Thompson
Coleman and Samuel Coleman Jr.,
circa 1950.
Author's collection

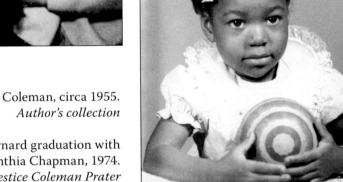

(right) Marsha Coleman, circa 1955.
Author's collection

(below) At my Barnard graduation with
friend Cynthia Chapman, 1974.
Majestice Coleman Prater

(right) MIT professor Willard Johnson, speaking at a United Nations conference on desertification and deserts that I organized at Howard University, Washington, DC., circa 1986.
Marsha Coleman-Adebayo

(below) I couldn't reconcile being in Ghana while confined to a classroom.
Author's collection

Segun Adebayo in the Nigerian Air Force, circa 1980, after graduation from MIT. *Author's collection*

(right) Aunt Ruth, Segun, and Mom in Detroit, January 19, 1981, the day after Segun and I married. Segun shows off his wedding ring. *Author's collection*

(below) Segun and me at our wedding, with best lady Remi Aluko, in Santa Barbara, California, 1982. *Bolaji Aluko*

(above) Mom, me,
Mama, Segun,
Olusina, and a family
friend, with Segun's
father, Augustus
Adebayo, in Nigeria,
circa 1989.
Author's collection

(right) In Ethiopia
for the UN, with
a field manager
at a fuelwood
plantation, 1987.
Author's collection

On my UN assignment in Ethiopia. The "good" mother who approached me with her child was never far from my thoughts. *Author's collection*

First Lady Hillary Clinton during a photo session and briefing for the delegation to the Beijing Women's Conference, 1995. *Author's collection*

A vanadium worker disabled by side effects of vanadium poisoning. The names of the vanadium victims are being withheld due to legal considerations. *Marsha Coleman-Adebayo*

A vanadium worker who was disabled by side effects of vanadium poisoning and abandoned by the mining company. *Marsha Coleman-Adebayo*

After I was removed as executive secretary of the Gore-Mbeki Commission I visited vanadium victims. We called this woman the "Cloak Lady." Her husband had recently died. She mounted her silent protest by wearing a black lace cloak during our photo session—the same one that she wore during her husband's funeral.
Marsha Coleman-Adebayo

(above) Me, Jacob Ngakane, comrade Violet, and Dr. Joanne Godley during our independent inspection of the Vametco vanadium mine in 1998.
Author's collection

(right) Former vanadium worker Benedict Sabone outside his home in Brits, South Africa.
Marsha Coleman-Adebayo

Jacob Ngakane, Congress of South African Trade Unions (COASTU) representative. He endured torture during the apartheid regime. He reported the vanadium tragedy in Brits, South Africa, to the Gore-Mbeki Commission.
Author's collection

The late Sis Bessie Mdoda in South Africa. "If her smile could not pierce their hearts what chance did we have?" *Marsha Coleman-Adebayo*

Students of the Ncedwe Community Center run by Sis Bessie Mdoda, circa 1996. EPA had promised to provide funding to convert Ncedwe to an environmental training center. *Marsha Coleman-Adebayo*

EPA administrator Carol Browner and I testified at the congressional hearing "Intolerance at EPA: Harming Science-Harming People." *Courtesy of Kevin Rice by permission of family*

Congressman Sensenbrenner in 2001, announcing his intent to reintroduce the No FEAR Act on the first day of the next session of Congress. Left to right: Dwight Welch, Anita Nickens, Segun Adebayo, me, Selwyn Cox, and Leroy Warren. *Norris McDonald*

No FEAR Coalition members—Dwight Welch, Selwyn Cox, Anita Nickens, Blair Hayes, Leroy Warren, and me (back to the camera)—with federal employee supporters celebrating the unanimous passage of the No FEAR Act by the House of Representatives on October 2, 2001, with Congressman Sensenbrenner, who joined in singing "We Shall Overcome." *Author's collection*

The Freedom Bus Ride to Capitol Hill with Norris McDonald of African American Environmentalist Association (AAEA) and hundreds of federal employees to the office of Senator Joseph Lieberman. *Dwight Welch*

Sharpton and Lieberman in Senate Hart Building during the Freedom Bus Ride. The No FEAR Act was successfully brought before Lieberman's committee one week later and the full Senate the following week. *Associated Press*

White House photo of the signing of the No FEAR Act. Standing with the president, from left to right, are Rep. Connie Morrella, R-MD; Sen. Thad Cochran, R-MS (obscured); Rep. Sheila Jackson Lee D-TX; Rep. Jim Sensenbrenner, R-WI; Dr. Marsha Coleman-Adebayo; Sen. John Warner, R-VA; Attorney General John Ashcroft (partially hidden); in foreground Cari Dominguez, chair of the EEOC; Rawle King, national legislative director and president of the Region XI Council, Blacks in Government; in background Leroy Warren, chair of NAACP Federal Sector Task Force; and right, Dr. Ruby Reese Moone, SCLC. *AP/White House, Paul Morse*

So many brave federal employees did not live to see the signing of the No FEAR Act. I was overcome with emotion as the president signed the law. *White House photo*

At the Good Housekeeping Woman of the Year Award ceremony (left to right): Joyce Megginson, me, Senator Elizabeth Dole, and Janet Howard. *Segun Adebayo*

No FEAR Coalition members and class agents (left to right: Tanya Ward Jordan, Joyce E. Megginson, and Janet Howard) testify during a No FEAR tribunal during Whistleblower Week in Washington (W3) about widespread discrimination within the US Department of Commerce. *Norris McDonald*

Jon Grand at W3 describing the brutal retaliation he endured at EPA after testifying in the case of Coleman-Adebayo v Carol Browner. *Norris McDonald*

Congresswoman Sheila Jackson Lee discussing civil rights abuses inside the federal government with radio host Joe Madison during the 2007 No FEAR W3 tribunal. Jackson Lee was an original sponsor of the bill, and Madison provided support to federal employees on his daily radio show. *Norris McDonald*

An annual May meeting of whistleblowers at W3 was convened in Washington by the No FEAR Institute to commemorate the signing of the No FEAR Act. *Victor Holt*

A documentary film crew provided by Danny Glover captures interviews I conducted in South Africa along with faculty and students from Barnard and Smith Colleges, in 2006. *Author's collection*

The Barnard College delegation to South Africa in 2006. Left to right, back row: Our park ranger guide, Hayley Holness, Professor Timothy Halpin-Healy, Alexandria Wright, Kendra Tappin, Tyler Halpin-Healy, Professor Diane Dittrick. First row: me, Folasade Adebayo, Alexandra Severino. *Author's collection*

Me and Noam Chomsky in Cambridge in 2009. *Glenn Ketterle*

With Danny Glover for a Washington Post article announcing a film on the No FEAR struggle. *Nessa Wilkerson*

March for the No FEAR Act. Rev. Al Sharpton joins No FEAR Coalition leaders to march on Senator Joseph Lieberman's office. US Marshal Matthew Fogg, Norris McDonald, Blair Hayes, and I are standing next to Shapton.

"White American." Franklin's tone of voice was rich with defiance even while he maintained his composure. David asked Franklin if he had witnessed the name-calling I had testified about. "In fact," Franklin replied, "we were both called 'honorary white men' at a staff meeting."

I looked at the jury. They were spellbound, their body language unmistakable.

"Did you say anything to Mr. Sielen about it?"

"I explained to him why I was offended—I told him that for a black American who spent time in the southern portion of Africa and came and went in South Africa, that it was an insult to be referred to as an honorary white man."

I was hoping David would point out the insulting and degrading practice during the apartheid regime of requiring all foreign people of color to have "Honorary White" stamped on their passports when traveling to "whites-only" areas of South Africa.

David, sensing Franklin's tension, followed with a question on Franklin's "role in the Gore-Mbeki Commission."

"I was the staff person who supported the USAID principals in the Binational Commission, primarily for the Environment Committee. I worked with Kathy Washburn, Marsha Adebayo, and Ken Thomas. That was until EPA removed Dr. Adebayo around the beginning of 1997."

"Had you ever heard any negative comments about Marsha from OIA management?"

"One of those in the [group of] Bill Nitze, Alan Hecht, Alan Sielen, [said] that they felt there was a problem with Marsha's work because she was too close to the South African people."

"Why didn't you consider that a criticism?"

"I think the only way you can do development work is to be close to the people for whom the development is to benefit," replied Franklin. Some of the jurors were nodding their heads in agreement.

Franklin testified about the trip that I organized to the township of Alexandra. He told the jury that under his leadership, USAID had been prepared to provide funds to assist this desperately poor area. He described the trip as a way of educating Bill Nitze and other colleagues about the conditions in South Africa's townships.

He added that the township tour had been so successful that the vice president's office had recommended that USAID or EPA organize a tour for Vice President Gore in order to emphasize American support to clean up areas like Alexandra. He added that removing me from the program had altered those plans. Franklin had waited years to discuss the countless instances of those dire conditions going unaddressed.

David asked him if he recalled the party in South Africa that Tami Sokutu had invited the American delegation to attend.

"Mr. Nitze asked me two questions. What would people be wearing at the party? And he asked me how people would talk at the party." Franklin was becoming agitated. "I asked him what he meant by how would people talk at the party. He said to me, 'Will they be speaking good English? Because in my dealings with the world there is a correlation between the ability to speak proper English and the ability to be hospitable and provide good circumstances for your guests.'"

Shapiro asked him how he had responded to Bill Nitze's question. "I was incensed," Franklin said, squirming a little in his seat. Franklin's grandmother had recently died, and he was still grieving. "I told him he should realize that as a black American, one of my grandmothers had a third-grade education." His voice began to falter, but he struggled through it, the words sounding like coughs.

"She is the woman who taught me more about hospitality in my life than anyone I know," Franklin managed to say before having to pause and collect himself. "And that I was truly insulted by anyone, particularly an American coming from our culture, who could turn to someone and say that they believe there was a relationship between the ability to speak proper English and to be hospitable to friends and guests."

Franklin's eyes blazed. "So I was *very* incensed."

David was watching the jurors as Franklin's emotions swung between near-weeping and rage. Several jurors were showing discomfort; the women's faces knotted sympathetically. Shapiro knew he had scored heavily and was looking for more. He asked Franklin to describe how Nitze had characterized South African liberation hero Peter Mokaba to Ambassador Bill Richardson at that same party. "Bill Nitze leaned forward to Bill Richardson and said, 'He's one of the young lions of the country—you know—necklacing.'" Franklin informed the jury what necklacing was.

"Did you have knowledge as to whether Mokaba was involved in necklacing?"

"Yes, I did. I reacted to that because, while Peter Mokaba is a young lion and had a number of famous speeches that were aimed at white

South Africans during the struggle, Peter Mokaba was never known as someone who—"

Wyneva Johnson had been squirming in her seat during this line of questioning and leapt to her feet. "Objection, Your Honor! He's not answering the question. He's giving a speech about Peter Mokaba!"

Judge Kollar-Kotelly sat motionless on the bench. "Objection overruled. Mr. Moore is entitled to give his reaction. Continue, Mr. Moore."

"I was outraged," Franklin said. "I said to refer to necklacing is to accuse someone of murder and that I thought it was outrageous that one would refer to Peter Mokaba as a murderer because he was a political activist." Franklin was visibly upset.

"To your knowledge, was Peter Mokaba a murderer during freedom fight time?"

"No. Nitze said that the reason he had made the statement was to give Bill Richardson a flavor of who Peter Mokaba was and what his politics were. I thought accusing someone of being a murderer was not a proper way to give a flavor of who they are and what they believe." Franklin's words dripped with contempt, letting the word flavor linger in the air.

"Was there ever an agreement to do the technology program that Mr. Kasman was on by the Gore-Mbeki Commission?"

Franklin said he believed Mark Kasman had taken a couple trips related to ETI. "It was the desire of Bill Nitze, who was the EPA principal seniormost person, that environmental technology become a part of the US side of the package. But no, sir, I don't believe it made it out of box one."

The jurors seemed puzzled about the ETI and its relevance to the case. I was convinced that this line of questioning was another Shapiro setup in which he was laying the groundwork for evidence that would become clear later. David moved on to another question concerning Franklin's opinion of whether my work in South Africa had been effective.

"One example of her effectiveness was her ability to put together a project that at some level within the US government, among senior political affairs, can provide a photo op. I mean that's a little harsh, but that's the reality of the business. And there was consideration on the vice president's staff that Vice President Gore would go to see Alexandra Township. The South Africans were extremely pleased with her work."

David, looking directly at the jury, asked Franklin if "EPA was effective in its work in the Gore-Mbeki Commission" after my removal. "No, sir," Franklin said sadly. "On the criteria that I have used for effective, no."

David was finished. Wyneva lifted herself slowly from her desk, tissue in hand, with Franklin as her mark. She approached Franklin gingerly. He had carried himself well and seemed likable with the jurors.

"Now, you did not participate in the discussions with Dr. Coleman-Adebayo's supervisors with regard to her work on Gore-Mbeki did you, as they evaluated her work?"

"No, I did not."

"And you were not familiar at that time, between 1995 and 1996, with all aspects of Dr. Coleman-Adebayo's work, were you?"

"No."

In two questions Wyneva had elicited that Franklin was not aware of how my supervisors had rated my work in South Africa. She paused and looked down at her notes before asking the next question. "Now, Mr. Mokaba is known for the comment 'one bullet, one settler,' is that correct, Mr. Moore?"

"'One bullet, one settler,' yes."

Wyneva returned to her seat. There was no telling if she had successfully resurrected the specter of fear that Nitze had tried to cast over Ambassador Richardson regarding Mokaba. In reality, the quote "one bullet, one settler" had never been attributed to Peter Mokaba.

||||||||||||

David called Mark Kasman. Mark and I had started work at EPA OIA on the same day. We didn't work in the same division, but Mark was someone who would come over to my area of the office to chat with Inga Barnett or another office assistant, Linda Brent. Before our interaction with the Gore-Mbeki Commission, I would have described Mark as the boy next door. He was pleasant and inoffensive. But David's suspicions about Mark still hung in the air.

When Deputy Minister Holomisa and other Mandela representatives had raised objections about the Environmental Training Institute on the basis that it was not humanitarian but rather a disingenuous way to undercut South Africa's fragile environmental industry, they were assured by EPA that the ETI was not an American private sector initiative. But in one 1995 document titled "EPA's International Programs: Serving US Environmental, Economic, Foreign Policy, and National Security Interests" the ETI is described as an "important vehicle for enlisting the private sector on behalf of the environment."

Mark Kasman approached the witness stand.

"You have never traveled to South Africa previously?"

"I have not."

"Did you consider yourself an expert on South Africa at the time that you were appointed to be the point person by Alan Sielen?"

"No," Kasman said, in a disarmingly open admission. Kasman said his rank in the office did not permit him to hold discussions with senior OIA managers, like Sielen, Hecht, or Nitze.

"Did you report to Sielen in your position as point person?"

"Well, I'm not that high up, so I report to a lot of people. So in this case, for this work, I would report on a day-to-day basis to the director for the Office of Bilateral Affairs, Pat Koshel."

Mark Kasman had been sitting in the staff meeting when Alan Sielen called Franklin and me honorary whites. We'd had numerous discussions about how humiliating this incident was. Both Franklin and I considered Mark a friend and colleague.

"Did you ever hear Mr. Sielen make an insensitive racist remark?"

"I heard him make an insensitive remark—but I don't think there was an intent of racial—"

David cut him off. "I'm not asking you to interpret. I'm asking you was it racially biased?"

"Racially biased? I think that depends how you—if we're looking at it in the context I would say, no." David looked over his shoulder at me, mouthing "no racial bias" with an I-told-you-so look on his face.

"I see. Can you tell us what you heard him say?"

Kasman testified that at a meeting Sielen talked about going to the same school as Jackie Robinson and therefore having an understanding of some of the same issues as Robinson.

"What about that was ignorant?"

"I thought that it's difficult for a middle-class white man to truly understand all of the issues that an African American man, especially one who would be such a leader and broke such barriers as Jackie Robinson was, so I thought that was not an appropriate statement."

"And insensitive?"

"Yes."

"Did you ever hear any other racially insensitive or, as you would call it, 'ignorant' remarks by Mr. Sielen on racial grounds?"

"There is one other statement that I don't know that I would label it that way. . . . There was a series of meetings on diversity and hiring and that sort of thing. And there were people sitting in the room. The way I remember it is that Dr. Coleman-Adebayo had entered the room, and at that point it was said, something of the nature of, 'Marsha could be made an honorary white man.' And that's the extent of what I remember."

"Who said it?"

"Mr. Sielen."

"Did you consider that an ignorant remark?"

"Not especially."

"An insensitive remark?"

"Maybe, yes."

"Did you say something to Mr. Sielen about it?"

"No."

"This 'honorary white man' comment, how did that strike you? Did you talk with him about that, Sielen?"

"No."

"Why not?"

"It was hard to approach a boss about something stupid." Mark was giving all the right answers. I took a quick look at the jury, and number 3 was nodding in agreement. The others were clearly following his testimony and seemed to be with him.

"At the time Sielen made this remark, the one that you heard— 'honorary white man'—to Marsha Coleman-Adebayo, she was the point person for the South Africa program, wasn't she?"

"That's right."

||||||||||||

Wyneva approached the podium, papers trailing her. Her voice was full and confident but not annoyingly so. She focused on Kasman in the same way that a government bureaucrat might hone in on saving the last penny of taxpayers' money—dispassionate and thorough. She shuffled her papers, looking for a specific question on an unknown page. She finally found it. "When you say that the project was informally adopted by the staff, what did you mean by that?"

"Well, what happened is that immediately following the meeting, Mr. Joubert, Tinus Joubert—Dr. Coleman-Adebayo's counterpart as the primary coordinator for the South African side like she was for EPA— Mr. Joubert caught me immediately following the presentation and said, 'Mark, I have a much better understanding of this project now,' and that 'we see how this can work out and will be contacting you about this in the next weeks to start moving forward on them.'"

Wyneva Johnson looked like she had hit pay dirt. "No further questions. Thank you."

I looked at the jury. Had they heard what Kasman had just said? He was admitting that he had been involved in back-channel discussions with senior Afrikaner bureaucrats. He never mentioned one conversation with Mandela's representatives. Were we to believe that someone who had just testified in regard to his status in the office that he was "not that high up" would independently back-channel a discussion with elite, old-guard Afrikaner South Africans without a direct order?

Shapiro engaged Mark on redirect examination. Wyneva had opened the door on the back-channel discussions between the US government and Afrikaner operatives. Mark made no effort to conceal his role as a conduit for back door negotiations with Afrikaner insiders for the US government. This gave Shapiro his way in to challenge the schoolboy innocence that Kasman had presented.

Shapiro got right to the point.

"By the way," David said, "this Tinus Joubert, I think you said . . ."

"Tinus Joubert."

"He was from the South Africa side?"

"That's right."

"He was an Afrikaner, wasn't he? A settler, a white settler? A white South African?"

"Yes."

"And who, in July 1996 during that conference, was the deputy minister for Environment and Tourism in South Africa?"

"I don't recall, at that time, if Bantu Holomisa was still in or not."

"What about Mr. Mokaba?"

"I believe so."

"Nothing further." David returned to the table and busied himself with notes in his briefcase. He turned his face slightly so I shielded him from the jury.

"That hurt." David closed his briefcase and spoke under his breath without looking at me. "I hope you don't have any more friends like him."

Kasman had come across as the all-American boy who had found Sielen's remarks crude but not necessarily racist. He had left the impression that I was misinterpreting signals at my job. But if I was misinterpreting signals from inside the EPA, then the American public, indeed, the South African public, was also under the false impression that US foreign policy was supporting the newly elected government of Nelson Mandela, all while representatives of the US president and vice president opened up back-channel discussions with Afrikaner forces within South Africa.

IIIIIIIIIIIIIIII

Deputy Minister Bantu Holomisa had been dismissed from his position only a few weeks after playing a vital role in championing the concerns of black South Africans during the transition process. Further, he had strongly opposed the USETI program. After Holomisa's removal, the new deputy minister, Peter Mokaba, had been deliberately kept in the dark. This virtually guaranteed that the EPA could manipulate a course for South Africa that was aligned with US corporate interests, working with the same Afrikaner and other white operatives who had terrorized black South Africans during apartheid and who still oversaw vanadium mines.

Kasman testified that he was asked to replace me and become the point person for the BNC in late December 1996 by Alan Sielen, who was then the deputy assistant administrator. He testified that from 1997 to 1998 he had shared the South Africa responsibility with colleagues John Armstead and Francesca Di Cosmo, in EPA's Philadelphia office. According to his testimony, Kasman was asked by Sielen to assume my position approximately two weeks before my dismissal. After my removal, the decision makers for American policy toward South Africa no longer had to contend with anyone questioning their environmental assumptions or their competency with respect to the country's cultural and political nuances. Among the remaining staff responsible for implementing the BNC mandate, there were none with any general experience in dealing with South Africa or, as Franklin Moore pointed out, with an affinity toward indigenous South Africans. After our testimonies, I was heartened to see what I perceived as sympathy in the jurors' faces. More important, I was encouraged that, despite David's warning, the plight of vanadium workers and EPA's decision not to conduct an independent investigation of the poisoning had become an issue of the trial.

llllllllllll

Kathryn Washburn was among my closest colleagues on the Gore-Mbeki Commission. She was the director of the Department of the Interior's Office of International Affairs and represented Secretary Bruce Babbitt on all foreign matters. Vice President Gore's office had asked her to coordinate the Environment and Conservation Committee. Through daily briefs and conversations I had found Kathy to be staunch in her commitment to environmental protection as well as social justice. Francesca Di Cosmo and John Armstead were hand picked by Bill Nitze and Mark Kasman to assist them with South Africa after I was removed from the commission. Consequently, Francesca, John, and Mark formed the new South Africa team and worked closely with Kathryn.

David was looking forward to his direct with Kathryn. Wyneva, David asserted, knew that a strong testimony from Kathryn could signal trouble. Joanne Hogan crossed on behalf of the agency.

"I want to draw your attention to the mid-1990s and ask you if your job brought you in contact with the vice president's office and how that came to be," David began.

Kathryn replied, "Vice President Gore formed the Binational Commission with the vice president of South Africa, and this established government-to-government relations for the first time. We had not been dealing with their government during the apartheid period. So Gore asked five cabinet secretaries from the US to join him on this commission."

Kathryn's nervousness had gone. She had assumed a stately, dignified, and precise manner that could easily have been mistaken as officious by those who did not know her. "My boss, Secretary Bruce Babbitt, the head of the Department of the Interior, was in charge of one of the five committees which dealt with the environment."

"Which agency of the US government was the most active in terms of projects on the ground in South Africa during this period of time on the environment committee?"

"EPA."

"How did that come about?"

"Marsha had the energy and the interest, and she was very motivated to get some results. Under Marsha's leadership, EPA started out on a very friendly basis. She organized study tours for South Africans, and when you spend twenty-four hours together a day, she developed a good personal rapport with them."

"Do you know if the South Africans requested any of the people from the US specifically to come over there and work more closely with them, between Gore-Mbeki official biannual meetings?"

"I happened to get a copy of a letter addressed to Bill Nitze that they had sent to Secretary Babbitt requesting that Dr. Coleman-Adebayo go when the new deputy minister took over that department," Kathy said, indicating that Peter Mokaba had requested that I travel to South Africa to brief him.

"Were there other letters regarding Dr. Coleman-Adebayo, and from whom?"

Ken Thomas had also written to Bill Nitze, complimenting my work with South Africa. His letter said that since I had started working with the committee, things had gotten better: "Things had gotten off the ground, things were moving forward. We were getting progress. And I think it was in comparison to many of our other committees where we just hadn't been able to get that much going. . . . At that time, the EPA committee was the most active of any of our committees."

"Could you tell us if you know a Francesca Di Cosmo and who she is?"

"Well, she's now the person that I coordinate with through the EPA committee—she works in Philadelphia. Francesca and John Armstead were asked to play leading roles when they were brought on by Mark Kasman and Bill Nitze, after they removed Marsha from the South Africa program."

"How did she impress you?"

"She—she did not impress me! I commented at the time that I thought she was speaking down to the South Africans. I thought she was very undiplomatic. She was speaking down to them, like she was talking to children. And a lot of Americans have a tendency to say what we are doing is the only right way to do things."

"Can you tell us what race Ms. Di Cosmo is?" David looked at the jury.

"She's white."

"You mentioned the '96 Gore-Mbeki Commission biannual meeting. Do you recall a program called ETI and who made the presentation?"

"Yes, Mark Kasman made the presentation."

"Was ETI—the technical thing he was proposing—was that adopted by the Gore-Mbeki Environmental Committee?"

"I know that—no, it wasn't."

"Why not?"

"Well, the South Africans spoke to me after the EPA meeting and said that they were concerned—they wanted me to talk to Secretary Babbitt and—"

Joanne Hogan, jumped to her feet. "I object. This is all hearsay."

David sat down, satisfied with his direct examination.

The South Africans had tried to reach out to Secretary Babbitt through Kathy Washburn. She had been their only remaining hope. But the train had left the station, and US private sector interests—not the newly empowered South African people—drove the process. With the plea to Secretary Babbitt deep-sixed, ETI was free to move unfettered by conscientious oversight in South Africa.

Joanne Hogan strode to the podium wearing a dark blue suit that could have come with her class ring. She was thin, of medium height, with a drawn, serious face that seemed impervious to empathy.

"Ms. Washburn, you testified regarding two letters on your direct examination: one by Mr. Babbitt and one by Mr. Thomas. How did you receive copies of those letters?"

"The letter from—I think the letter that he showed us was from Deputy Minister Mokaba from South Africa and that—and that was sent to the department, and I got it from our executive secretary, the normal way I would get copies of letters that are sent to Secretary Babbitt. The other letter, the copy of the letter from Ken Thomas, was faxed to me by Ken from South Africa."

"Do you know any of the other assignments that were given to Marsha Coleman-Adebayo during the 1995–1996 time period?"

"Besides South Africa? No."

"Do you know the specific assignments that were given to her by her supervisors with respect to the South African program?"

"No." Kathy took a deep breath. Hogan had settled in on a line of questioning that made Kathy feel uncomfortable. She adjusted her body in the hard chair, but I also saw in her eyes that Hogan had stirred up the Kathy I knew in South Africa, the Kathy I had seen after she had encountered the death camp of a township.

Hogan continued with her questions. "And you're not aware of whether or not she completed her work in a timely manner; isn't that correct?"

Kathy took her time with the answer to this question. Perhaps she did not know the entire range of assignments at EPA, but she could authoritatively answer this question. "The assignments that I gave her, she did."

Hogan, perhaps remembering the oldest adage of oral examination—never ask a witness a question that you don't know the answer to—decided to end her line of questioning there.

Shapiro signaled that he would like to redirect and approached Kathy, confident and with a slight smile. "Ms. Washburn, did any of her supervisors ever complain to you about her work?"

She looked first at David and then the jury and slowly said, "No."

"Thank you, Ms. Washburn. You may take your seat."

‖‖‖‖‖‖‖‖‖‖

"We are in big trouble," David said, as he fumbled with the door to his office, finally kicking it as a way to hold it open for my entry. "If we have another witness like Kasman, we're not going to win this case. It's as simple as that."

David threw his briefcase onto his desk.

"Kasman came off like the boy next door—no dog in this fight." David affected a singsong voice. "He's just trying to do his job!"

I didn't know whether to laugh or throw up but watched David for my cue.

"You have any more friends like Mark Kasman?"

I called Mike Bland again when I got home.

"David is the most lovable madman I've ever met, Mike. Every word, every gesture, every raised eyebrow in court is a choreographed event. He missed his Shakespearean calling. But even he can't do a thing against the likes of Mark Kasman."

"Mark Kasman? He was just in Chicago the other day badmouthing you."

"What? Mike, you can't be serious!"

"I didn't hear it, per se, Marsha, but believe me, the agency's buzzing about the homegirl who's dared to take on Browner. Everyone's talking about it. I have a colleague named Jon Grand who told me he heard Kasman calling you the Rosa Parks of EPA. And he didn't mean it as a compliment."

"Can you put me in touch with this man, Jon Grand? Do you think he'd be willing to testify at my trial, Mike?"

"I'll put it to you this way, Marsha: if there is anyone in the agency who would come to your defense, Jon would. He's as straight up a guy as I've ever known. Hang on. Let me get him on the line."

I sat biting my nails while Mike got Jon Grand. Rosa Parks of EPA. I was so angry I was shaking.

"Hello, Marsha? I've got Jon Grand on the line."

"Hi, Jon."

"Hello, Marsha. Sorry to meet you this way, but I'm honored anyway."

"Thank you, Jon. Can you tell me what you heard?"

"Yes. There was and has been much conversation, watercooler conversation, about your case. I was in my office with Mark Kasman, and we were trying to schedule something for this week, actually. This was about two weeks ago. And Mark said he'd be in his office because everyone was going to be around because of a case that was going on with the EPA's Rosa Parks."

I asked Jon if Mark had been complimenting me by comparing me to Rosa Parks.

"Oh, no. Mark was complaining about you, that you're a black woman who does not know her place and that the whole office was going to suffer because you had decided to pursue a lawsuit. His comments were dismissive and racist."

"Jon, I know you don't know me, but I really need to have you come to Washington, DC, and repeat what you just told me in front of the jury."

Jon said three of the sweetest words I've ever heard before or since. "I'll be there."

Another miracle. I called David, and he quickly called Jon to schedule a date for his testimony.

Day Three

"Waxmonsky is on his way overseas. They're trying to get him out of town until your trial is over. I think he's in Canada, but he's gotta get his passport at home before he can leave the country. So if you're going to get him, it's gotta be when he comes home to get his passport."

"Thanks," I said to the whisperer, and hung up. I was half dressed, throwing my clothes on, and hunting up my Bible. "Segun! We've got a shot at Waxmonsky!"

"Hello, David? Get your process server ready—Waxmonsky is coming in tonight. We also need a date for Jon Grand. . . . Yeah, let's catch up in court."

"Segun! Have you seen my Bible?" I always put my Bible in the same place every day after we returned from the courthouse, but it was nowhere to be found. Finally, in total frustration, Segun handed me a small, green New Testament the size of a deck of cards.

"Marsh, large or small, it's the same word of God. We're going to be late. Let's go."

\|\|\|\|\|\|\|\|\|\|\|

Ken Thomas had been my primary contact in the US Mission in South Africa. I had spoken with Ken nearly every day during the time we worked together on the Gore-Mbeki Commission for over a year. It was Ken who had counseled me to be careful and start keeping a written record. When I first described the treatment I was receiving to Ken, his reaction was swift and immediate.

"Waxmonsky isn't catching all this flak," Ken had said. "He travels to Russia all the time without anyone pulling him back. You're definitely getting treated differently than Waxmonsky."

Ken was from the Midwest and had traveled throughout the world. He was a longtime friend of Bill Nitze's and came from the same country-club stock. But that was where the similarities ended. As good as

Mark Kasman had been on the stand, he had impeached himself by naming Ken Thomas as one of the people who had criticized my work in South Africa.

"Mr. Shapiro, please call your first witness."

"Mr. Kenneth Thomas." The procedure was becoming familiar.

"Good afternoon, Mr. Thomas. Are you gainfully employed?"

Ken settled into the witness chair. If not comfortable, he was clearly confident. "Yes, I'm a Foreign Service officer with the Department of State. I serve as the deputy counselor in the economic section of the US Mission to the United Nations."

"What was your job in South Africa?"

"From August 1995 to August 1997, I was the environment counselor and liaison for Vice President Gore's office, for the Gore-Mbeki Commission in Pretoria, South Africa. I was the overall coordinator for the Gore-Mbeki Commission. My permanent offices were in Pretoria, but I also was assigned temporary duty in Durban and Cape Town."

David lost no time in getting to the heart of Ken's testimony.

"Who was the staff person for OIA to the Gore-Mbeki?"

"Marsha Coleman-Adebayo."

"Can you tell us if you observed the work of Marsha Coleman-Adebayo interacting with the South Africans?"

"Yes, I did."

"How did she do?"

"I felt—I was perfectly pleased. The new government, Mr. Mandela's government, very much wanted the US to provide greater assistance in what we call brown issues, meaning wastewater and toxic releases, things that gave people diseases. This was a priority for them, and that was one of the reasons that EPA got more involved."

"How did Dr. Coleman-Adebayo do at this work?"

"In the beginning, most of our contact was over the phone, because she was in Washington and I was in Pretoria, and with the time difference, you have to schedule unusual phone sessions because of the six- to seven-hour time difference. So most of the work was done in what I called a triangular method, which is, she would call me for advice and information. She would then interact directly with the South African government officials that were in her portfolio. Then they would contact me or I would contact her because I was really there to try to facilitate the direct interaction between our expert agency and their expert agency."

Then David asked, "On the environment committee, in terms of the actual projects on the ground in 1996, which agency of the US, which partner in the US team, had the most going?"

"By having Marsha assigned to the environment committee—the EPA. I was quite clear with Bill that I and the South Africans wanted Marsha to work on the committee full-time."

"Did anyone ever contact you from the South African side and request Marsha Coleman-Adebayo's presence in South Africa?"

"Yes, I received inquiries from two quarters. One from the provincial level, which was then the new province, the Eastern Cape, and from a staff assistant to Peter Mokaba's office while he was the deputy minister, specifically asking if Marsha could spend more time or come out."

"Do you recall seeing Nitze in South Africa?"

"Yes, on two occasions."

"We do need a break," Judge Kollar-Kotelly said, interrupting Ken's testimony. "You can step down, sir."

"No, Your Honor," Ken twisted sideways to address the judge. "I would prefer to remain seated during the break."

Judge Kollar-Kotelly, teasing out whether Ken was challenging her authority, told Ken that he didn't have to stay seated. But Ken, being a lawyer and a government employee, was well versed in the playbook and was not going to let the government use any of its techniques on him. He knew his testimony could be compromised. He did not speak to anyone or move. Ken remained in the witness stand throughout the break for nearly an hour.

The message Ken sent was not lost on Wyneva and the government.

IIIIIIIIIIII

"Do you remember Nitze calling the EPA—in your office?" David asked when the trial resumed.

"Bill and I," Ken said, "had met that day with, among others, Dr. Cameron, and Francois Hanekom, who I now remember was the deputy director general. Bill had also met with Bantu Holomisa, and I think he had a social function with Holomisa that day or that night. Bill and I came back to my office to discuss the purpose of the trip, which was—OK, where do we go from here? . . .The issue was raised of whether or not the US could detail an EPA official to work at the Ministry of Environment. So Bill and

I went back and discussed what we had learned, and Bill agreed that he fully now understood the nature of the problem and that in fact it would be wise to try and make an arrangement to have somebody from the US work in the ministry. He said he was going to call or check with his office."

"Before he called, did Marsha Coleman-Adebayo's name come up?"

"Yes, so I was pleased that Bill agreed with me that we needed to do this, and I said, 'I assume that you will send Marsha Coleman-Adebayo.' And Bill said, 'Well, that's under discussion. That is a possibility.' He then asked if he could use my phone."

"Tell us about the side of the conversation that you heard."

Joanne Hogan jumped to her feet. "Objection! Hearsay!" The judge ruled that Ken could only testify to what he heard and said.

"He was talking to someone named Alan," Ken said calmly. "He called Marsha's name a couple of times."

"Did you have further conversations with him about Marsha when he hung up?"

"Yes, after he got done with the call, he said, 'Well, there's a lot of issues here. We've got some personnel issues in Washington. I'm going to have to go back and consult about this, and I don't think we will be in a position to respond to the South African side while I'm here, other than to say that we're positive on the idea that someone come down and that we will get back to them as soon as we can.'"

In government employment parlance, when Nitze used the phrase "personnel issues," he was referring to the fact that I had filed an employment complaint against the agency.

"Did you send him a letter or memo?"

"Yes, I sent him a memo that it would be very helpful if Marsha could be assigned to this full-time because she had been doing the work."

"How did you think she was doing?"

"I always found Marsha, from the very first phone call, to be very bright. And she's very enthusiastic and was always willing to stay late, and she tended to get in early, and that way we had the maximum time to be on the phone because of the seven-hour time difference."

"In 1996, how did she get on?"

"Her relationship was excellent—was the subject of conversation. That is, she had the best connection of any US government official to Bantu Holomisa, and he thought very highly of her, and he told me so."

"How was her relationship with the South Africans?"

"That's complicated. It depends on which group of South Africans you're discussing." Ken gathered his thoughts before continuing. "In 1995, the Ministry of Environment was highly reflective of the prior apartheid regime, was almost exclusively white, and in South Africa, more importantly, it wasn't just white, it was Afrikaners. At the highest levels," Ken explained, "there was a political understanding of the reality and that the future was the future and the past was done. . . . There was tremendous resistance from the leftover Afrikaner bureaucrats."

"Resistance to what?" asked David.

"Resistance to the new regime, resistance to the Mandela government, resistance to the whole concept that their world had been turned upside down."

Turning to the jury, Ken continued, "So now I can answer your question." A few jurors almost smiled.

"In the beginning, Marsha's relationship with that second- or third-level bureaucracy was difficult, and they frequently would call me and try to politely ask if I couldn't please get someone else that they could work with? And they wouldn't say—anything bad, but it was very clear to me—"

"Objection!" Joanne Hogan called out. David waved his hand. The judge did not have to rule on the objection.

"Mr. Thomas, without going into the discussions of what other people told you, what was your impression of how Dr. Coleman-Adebayo got on with the South Africans?"

"At the time that she first started working on the matter, given the staffing patterns I described, I think she was having some difficulty in implementing what we wanted implemented with the ministry."

"Those people that you mentioned before, what race are they?"

Ken turned again, looking directly into the faces of the jurors. "They were all white Afrikaners."

"I have nothing further, Your Honor."

⁞⁞⁞⁞⁞⁞⁞⁞⁞⁞⁞⁞

For Joanne Hogan's cross of Ken, the government had called in reinforcements—another attorney sat at the desk, and additional attorneys were seated in the audience, taking copious notes. Hogan seethed her way through the cross-examination, as though anger were some magic elixir.

"Mr. Thomas, you were not directly involved with all of the assignments that Marsha Coleman-Adebayo did on the Gore-Mbeki project, were you?"

"I was in South Africa."

"Are you aware of all of the assignments that she was given with respect to that by her supervisors?"

"I am only aware of those projects that touched on South Africa, in South Africa, if you see what I mean."

"Are you aware of all of the specifics that her supervisors gave her, her specific assignments with respect to the Gore-Mbeki Commission?"

"No."

"And you didn't have any discussions with her supervisors over what you thought of her work—isn't that correct?"

"No. I discussed the projects we were working on and how she was implementing them, both with Pat Koshel and Bill Nitze. I wouldn't say extensively, but I had discussions with them."

Hogan had finished. As soon as Ken Thomas stepped down from the witness stand, Wyneva Johnson rushed to the microphone and announced in her Southern-laced drawl, like it was an emergency, "The plaintiff has a Bible on top of the Federal Rules on her table!"

Wyneva's eyes were wide as if the book were a turd, lying there on the table.

"I'm not making any comment on her faith or her religion, but I do think that's inappropriate right in front of the jury to have that."

The judge looked to David for an answer. "Is there a particular reason to have the Bible in court as part of the—"

"Your Honor, I want you to see this," David said, quickly holding it up at eye level. "It's just her personal Bible was sitting on the table. She's been reading when the jury is not here."

David turned, looking at Wyneva with utter contempt.

"I'm just asking," said Judge Kollar-Kotelly. "It's a very small, little book, I would point out for the record."

"Marsha takes comfort in it," David said, affecting innocence. "That's the purpose of it, yes."

"I have no problem with her having it," Judge Kollar-Kotelly said. "Can we just not have it sitting prominently?"

Kollar-Kotelly looked at Wyneva. "Is there anything else?"

"No, Your Honor," said a subdued Johnson.

I looked at Segun, astounded. The Lord was in the midst of this. I saw meaning in my earlier frustration at not finding the large Bible I usually brought to court. If I had found it, the government may have moved for a mistrial, claiming I was attempting to influence the jury. I bowed my head and said a prayer. "Lord, thank you for turning my sorrow into joy. Amen."

ıııııııııııı

Right from our first meeting in South Africa, Brad Brown and I had been friends. Our love of Africa and our commitment to finding a way to reverse the course of centuries of exploitation and abuse of indigenous people had cemented the bond. Brad's New England brogue would have pegged him as a highbrow blue blood from Harvard, but if you stopped there you would have missed the depth of the man, his expansive embrace of life, and the courage he showed in the face of others to which the appellation "blue blood" more than applied.

"Are you gainfully employed, Dr. Brown?" asked David. Brad said he was a director and scientist at the National Oceanic and Atmospheric Administration's fisheries research laboratory with expertise in fisheries.

"Do you know William Nitze, and how do you know him?"

"I know Nitze. I know him through his being the lead person for EPA during the Environment Committee meetings. I had made our report on our work in this area, which at that time was singled out for praise by the South African leadership at the Environment Committee meeting, recommending that we work with historically black colleges and universities both in South Africa and the United States. Following the breaking of that meeting, Mr. Nitze came and said, something to the effect, 'I wish you all hadn't gone and done that because now we're going to have to work with those schools and those people.'"

Joanne Hogan quickly took to the podium to cross Brad once David had finished questioning him.

"You don't know the specific assignments that Marsha Coleman-Adebayo was given by her supervisors in 1995 or 1996, do you?" This one question embodied the government's strategy of trying to establish that only EPA managers were qualified to discuss my performance.

Brad replied, "I was certainly privy to directions in that. I know some of the general praise that was given to her—in terms of what was said in a general sense in meetings and discussions with Nitze, in terms of her assignments, in terms of being responsible for it—"

"Dr. Brown, my question was, you don't."

"Your Honor, she interrupted him," Shapiro objected.

"He gets to finish his answer," the judge ruled.

"I know in a broad general sense relative to . . . that because he made statements . . . in praise of her and her responsibilities for putting various programs together at the meeting. But beyond that, no, I don't. I have never seen her performance plan. I am only aware of the praise she was given for her work in the meetings in public by Mr. Nitze."

"Thank you." Hogan concluded her questioning.

|||||||||||||||

Afterward, I returned to Shapiro's office with him. He leaned back in his chair and exhaled slowly, puffing his cheeks. Shapiro didn't like it when things were not going well, and things were not going well.

"Kasman is still going to testify for the defense," David said. "My sense is that it's not going to be pretty." He drummed the desktop. "We still have the government's chief witness against you. There are bound to be more surprises."

I was glad it was Friday and there would be no more days in court that week. David huffed and puffed some more before we agreed to meet in the morning and review the case. David was in the convoluted zone of legal strategizing that cut him off from the rest of humanity. He was nearly muttering to himself when I started to leave.

"And Marsha?" David called to me as I neared the door. I turned and met the mean stare he had fixed on me. "Lose the big Bible. Wyneva is looking for anything to drive the last nail in our coffin."

Saturday

"What the hell took you so long?" David called out to us as soon as he heard the door open. David had roused us before seven o'clock. He was already on the case and had been wondering where we were.

Before we could sit down, he barked, "Look, I'm not going pussyfoot with you. We took some hits this week, and I'm not sure how many more Mark Kasmans we can take and still survive."

David was seated in his swivel-back executive chair. Piles of files and manila folders bearing my name were scattered on his desk. He had a worried look on his face from digging.

"We have to turn this situation around, or we're going down." David spun his chair around to check something on his computer. "First of all, Marsha, I don't know how you're going to do this, but you are going to track Gary Waxmonsky down or we have no comparator. You need to call everyone you know. Don't leave a stone unturned—we need his testimony!

"Second, what is Mark going to testify about this week—do you have any clue?"

What could I tell him that he didn't know? There were so many unknowns. As Segun and I left the office, I realized that David had never made eye contact with us.

When I returned home, I spent hours on the phone talking to anyone who might help us locate Waxmonsky.

Sunday

Segun and I had started attending Macedonia Baptist Church soon after Sade's birth. The church was part of the historic trail of African Americans in Montgomery County, Maryland, where the city of Bethesda is located. Slave cabins could still be found within walking distance of mansions. The church sat atop a hill overlooking the main thoroughfare of Bethesda on River Road. Through taxes and political maneuvers, African Americans had been run out of Bethesda in the earliest days of gentrification. The church remained a prominent totem of the black population that had built a farming community in this area.

Macedonia, a small church with a huge heart, gave me comfort that Sunday. On a good day, we might have had seventy people worshiping there. Segun became a deacon and years later was called to the pastorate. Pastor Sterling King Jr. had come to my trial in support. His wife, Dr. Rosalyn King, one of the first black women in the nation to receive a doctorate in pharmacology, called me regularly to assure us of our being in her prayers. The congregation knew I was finally having my day in court. Winks and nods of support showered me during the service, but my soul was not at peace. After Deaconess Betty Genies welcomed our visitors, I rose:

"Rev. King and my fellow brothers and sisters, I am now in court fighting for my civil and human rights. I could not remain silent about the acts of contempt for human life that I witnessed at EPA. Now my family has been dragged through the mud. Ecclesiastes 9:11 says, 'The race is not given to the swift or the battle to the strong.' I am clinging to these words, and I ask you to keep me in your prayers."

Sister Mae King's voice captured the power of ancestral yearnings. She invoked huddled enslaved Africans warming themselves under cover of night around the fire of a plantation prayer meeting. She turned slightly from her second-row pew, leaned her head back, and sang:

Why should I feel discouraged?
Why should the shadows come?
Why should my heart be lonely and long for heaven and home?

Sister Iris Washburn turned and stood up. Like the sound of the Atlantic Ocean hitting the rocks of her native Jamaica, she changed the tempo to reflect a Caribbean flavor, a uniquely Jamaican beat:

When Jesus is my portion
My constant friend is He.
His eye is on the sparrow and I know he watches me.

⁕

I'm back in Detroit and feel my grandfather's warmth and love as I sit at our dining room table. Daddy is writing his sermon. My feet barely reach the floor.

"Marsha?"

"Yes, Daddy?"

"What do you think about this title for my sermon? 'Let Not Your Heart Be Troubled'?"

Betrayal Is Best Served Cold

Day Four

David Shapiro was storming across the plaza behind the statue of General Meade in front of the courthouse, holding his cell phone to his ear with one hand and gesturing with his other hand in between adjusting the strap to his briefcase. I couldn't tell if he was frustrated, angry, ecstatic, or all three. When he saw Segun and me approaching, he snapped his phone shut and waved us over.

"We got him!" He was smiling broadly. "One of your moles called me after ten last night."

"David, who?"

"Waxmonsky! They were going to sneak him in last night and then slip him out to Russia in the morning. He was only going to be in town overnight." David shook Segun's hand with a broad smile. "He wouldn't even have come into town, except he had to get his passport. But for that, we never would have gotten him."

"That's fantastic, David!"

He held the door open for us, almost yelling as we stepped inside the stone halls of the courthouse.

"And get this—I get a call about an hour ago from the process server who had just gotten a call from Waxmonsky who was saying he was going to bill the server a hundred and fifty bucks to have someone come

238

and clean up all the cigarette butts and M&M wrappers he left in the bushes on the side of the house. The server says, 'Hey, it was after midnight by the time the guy got home. I had to stay awake somehow!'"

"So he served the papers?"

David laughed. "Walked right out of the bushes. He said cigarette butts and candy wrappers weren't the only thing they'd have to clean up, from the look on the Waxmonsky's face. I told him I didn't care what he charged as long as he showed up in court today. He's our second-to-last witness."

"Have you talked with him?" I wanted to know what we might expect.

"No, it doesn't matter. If he's hostile, I'll take him apart with the record. He doesn't stand a chance." As Segun and I made our way through the metal detectors, David headed briskly toward the courtroom. He was dialing a number on his cell when he disappeared around a corner.

||||||||||||||

"What grade are you?" David asked Waxmonsky, who was now securely ensconced in the witness chair.

"GS-15."

David was making the point that Waxmonsky was a higher grade than I was, although we were performing the same job.

"In terms of the point person for the Gore-Chernomyrdin Commission, who was that?"

"That would be me." Dr. Waxmonsky was an unassuming man who, except for his height, was close to nondescript. He had an open quality to his face that gave him believability.

"Gore-Mbeki was a vice presidential initiative in the same sense that Gore-Chernomyrdin was, correct?"

Waxmonsky agreed.

"You were the point person for EPA environmental committee work on Gore-Chernomyrdin, and Dr. Coleman-Adebayo was the point person for the Gore-Mbeki South Africa program, correct?"

Again, Waxmonsky agreed.

"Mr. Waxmonsky, do you recall being a member of a team doing the Gore-Chernomyrdin work as part of a team at OIA?"

"No, sir. I was essentially an independent operation. As executive secretary of the Gore Russia program, I did not have a lot of routine contact with colleagues in my office."

David was startled by this answer. Was he hearing that Waxmonsky had not been required to be a part of a team, when I had been removed and vilified for not being a team player? David tasted blood in the water.

"Well, wasn't there a group of people in EPA who were a team for Gore-Chernomyrdin after 1995?"

"No, sir, not. The team structure, as I recall, was introduced in late '95, and we all had the option of participating in one or more of these teams. I opted not to, and I had the support of my management, as I recall."

"I'm sorry, I didn't catch . . ."

"And I did have the support of my management in that preference not to be involved in what I conceived to be an artificial construct."

"Teams?" David asked with as much incredulity as he could muster. "You were anti-team?" He belabored the point. "Were you ever criticized by OIA management for not being a team player?"

"Not in my hearing, certainly, no."

"And during the entire time that you were doing Gore-Chernomyrdin, who up until, say, 1997, who was your supervisor? Who signed your performance appraisal?"

"That would have been Pat Koshel."

David looked over at me. His eyes were lit up, trying to suppress a smile. Two people—one white, one black—treated diametrically differently by the same supervisor. This was the textbook definition of discrimination. I looked at Segun. He nodded.

"What were your performance ratings from 1995 onward?"

"All outstanding."

"And can you tell us in that first year that you had Gore-Chernomyrdin, 1994, how many trips did you make to Russia?"

"My records suggest that I made six."

Again, David was highlighting the difference in how Pat Koshel and Nitze had treated me and how they had treated Waxmonsky. I had not been allowed to travel, even when the head of South Africa's Environment Department requested my participation in writing.

"In 1996, how many times did you go to Russia?"

"Four times."

David finished his questioning, came back to the table, and sat down. As he pulled up his chair, he tapped his fingers on a folder.

"Manna from heaven," David said.

Agency council Joanne Hogan recognized the government had just taken several unexpected hits from Waxmonsky's testimony. Perhaps musing about the wisdom of bringing Gary back from Canada, she started her cross.

"Good afternoon, Dr. Waxmonsky. Could you briefly describe to the jury what the Freedom Support Act is?"

Waxmonsky summarized the act and said that his travel was derived from the legislation.

"Objection, Your Honor," David said, rising to his feet. "This is irrelevant."

The judge allowed some flexibility. In the end, Gary noted that he was not aware if there was a similar act with South Africa. Joanne glanced at Wyneva for help.

"I have nothing further," Hogan said.

David saw no need to redirect. He made a deferential nod to the jury and rose to his feet.

"Your Honor, at this point, I rest."

IIIIIIIIIIII

It would have been sweet if at such a moment we were all whisked away to Barbados to recuperate for a week; but in the real world we were treated instead to the words "We now move to the defense case," uttered by Judge Kollar-Kotelly.

As Wyneva readied herself, a comment David had made early in the process crept into me: "I can't tell you who it will be, Marsha, but I would bet my practice that one of the key witnesses for the defense will be a black woman."

One of David's strengths was his prior experience as an AUSA, where he had learned all of their tricks.

"But who, David? Who?" I had insisted.

"I have no idea, Marsha, but I know it's coming—and I know you'll be astonished when she shows her true colors."

I drove myself to distraction trying to discover who that could possibly be. There were so many women of color. There were so many who might see this trial as an opportunity to score big points with the agency by testifying against me. But who?

A person of color turned traitor was not without bountiful historical examples. Throughout slavery, some blacks, notoriously and despicably, had taken refuge in one of the only outlets they had: betrayal. But the prospect of a phantom traitor made me crazy. After convincing myself on different occasions that each and every woman of color in my office was the one, I decided the best thing would be to try to focus on those things over which I had some control, if only to spare myself the torment.

Then one night I worked after hours at the agency because of a log-jammed workload. I was trying to put a mark in the pile of tasks that had backed up on me, and I thought I was the only one in the Environmental Justice office. I was in a cubicle, filing some papers away into a cabinet.

"No. I like Marsha. I really do. I don't have anything against her. I feel badly about the way she's being treated. But a girl's gotta do what a girl's gotta do. I need to get to California."

My skin lifted everywhere. It was her. I began to shake. I could not believe it. She had been my mentor and I thought she had been my friend. I was torn between wanting to go pull her hair out and slipping out of the office without her knowing I had discovered her. I decided to slip out undiscovered.

||||||||||||

"Please raise your right hand and state your full name for the record."

"My name is Clarice Elaine Gaylord."

Wyneva Johnson asked if she was currently employed.

"Now I work for the EPA in our Region IX office, which is in San Francisco."

Johnson asked if Gaylord knew me and if she had supervised me.

"Yes, for six months she did a detail in my office."

Clarice testified that I had approached her about working in the Office of Environmental Justice. She had worked with me on the Beijing women's project, and I had found her helpful and instructive. She had approved the request because she needed a staffer with good writing skills to edit an annual report on Environmental Justice. However, when asked about my writing, she asserted that often my writing was "too militant" and that "we needed to have the tone toned down a little to make it less threatening, less aggressive. . . . In some cases some of our readers complained," she said, "that the language was very flowery and very intellectual."

She stated that the agency writers have to aim for an eighth-grade readership and that I was not happy dumbing down our message to that level.

The knife was just beginning to cut.

There had been a National Environmental Justice Advisory Council meeting in Baltimore in 1996, when the NGOs I had been working with as part of the study tours had proposed moving the South Africa program out of the Office of International Affairs and into the Office of Environmental Justice. This was in response to the reticence NEJAC had encountered within OIA toward investigating vanadium poisoning. NEJAC hoped that if the South Africa program could be moved to the Office of Environmental Justice, there might be a chance to save lives.

Dr. Gaylord testified that during the NEJAC meeting she met me in front of the door to the committee room. I told her, she said, that there would be a resolution to move the South Africa program from OIA to her office and that I would move with the program. Shifting from one side to another in her seat, she relayed how upset she had become because NEJAC had never engaged in program or staff issues and no one had discussed this resolution with her. Gaylord went on to say that Alan Sielen had asked her to take me on after the six-month detail period ended, adding that she had declined because she knew that I was looking for a promotion.

Wyneva had gotten what she wanted from her black woman.

There were times in the trial when David was in complete control, when every facial expression, every posture, was communicated to the jury by design. His oratory style, his diction, his tone of voice: pitch perfect. And then there were other times when David would go silent and still. I don't know if I've ever experienced more profound quiet than when David was quiet. When Dr. Gaylord was testifying, David for the first time seemed tentative. Here was the black woman, who for all appearances had no ax to grind with me, who had just said I was difficult and aggressive and needed to be toned down.

As he approached Clarice for his cross-examination, David seemed lost. He looked at Dr. Gaylord.

"What was actually passed or recommended by NEJAC to the administrator with regard to South Africa, the administrator would then send down to the various EPA program offices?"

"Yes, for action."

David placed a document on the monitor that displayed pieces of evidence for the judge and jury to see.

"I wonder if you could look at Plaintiff Exhibit 26. By the way, who is Lily Lee?"

David established that Lily was a special assistant to Browner on NEJAC issues and then asked Clarice to look at a NEJAC report on South Africa.

"Have you ever seen this document?"

After reviewing the document, Clarice said she had not.

"Is there anything in this document about NEJAC recommending the transfer of the South Africa program to your office?"

Not in that memo, Clarice stated.

Shapiro turned to her performance evaluations of me, noting that there were five rating levels in the federal system—outstanding, exceeds expectation, satisfactory, less than satisfactory, and failure—and that Gaylord had given me outstanding ratings consistently until the time of the NEJAC meeting. Clarice said the rating dropped with my performance. But David saw the rating drop as a ploy straight out of the playbook.

The exchange became furious.

"This is the annual report that Marsha Coleman-Adebayo produced for you, isn't it?"

"Well, no. I understand from my staff they had to send it out to a contractor to finish, and I did a lot of writing myself because I know what I wanted in here."

"I wonder if you could turn to the cover page. Read it to us, please."

Gaylord read, "'Text edited by Marsha Coleman-Adebayo.'"

"Anyone else given credit for editing the entire document?"

"No," Gaylord said defiantly, "because I never put my name on anything."

"I wonder if you could take a look. Publish this to the jury—this is the standard form. You gave her an outstanding on this, didn't you?"

Clarice took a deep breath, rolled her eyes, and looked up. "Mm-hmm. I'm sorry, yes."

"Please read your comments to the jury."

Clarice lowered her voice, seeming to have difficulty reading.

"It says, 'Work with Office of Environmental Justice, our office, and other EPA staff to marshal document through the approval process and to ensure completion of the report.'"

David demanded, "And can you tell us, having given her an 'outstanding,' can you read to the jury what your handwritten comments are on performance highlights?"

Again Clarice shifted in her chair, looking increasingly uncomfortable.

"OK. 'Marsha worked diligently to get the annual report through the agency's approval process. She worked side by side with the Office of Enforcement and Compliance Assurance's editor and negotiated word and language changes. Using her past editorial experiences and connection, the report is generally cleared for printing.'"

David was getting his mojo back. He put another document on the screen.

"Had you had a newsletter before?"

"No."

"So Marsha Coleman-Adebayo had to invent the newsletter, didn't she?"

"Yes."

"Can you read the comments that you made describing this performance?"

"'Many of the articles for the *Monitor* were basically ghostwritten by Marsha. This was difficult because most of the subject matter was unfamiliar to her. She showed a high level of dedication and commitment to delivering the issues. Received several compliments on the readability and format of the issues.'"

David had the jury's attention. Gaylord's assertiveness dwindled. Finally, David asked her if I ghosted her contribution to the Environmental Justice report and the *Monitor* newsletter.

Clarice faced the jury with eyes downcast. "Yes."

David turned his back on Clarice and looked directly into the eyes of the jurors. "Thank you, Your Honor," David said, walking away from Clarice.

Not once since walking into the courtroom had Clarice even looked in my direction. Where she had begun defiant and proud, as she left the witness stand, Clarice seemed belittled in her own eyes. I had the feeling it would be a long, hard flight back to her new home in California.

IIIIIIIIIIII

Wyneva Johnson called Mark Kasman to the witness stand. His first appearance had hurt us, and we still hadn't recovered from it. Kasman was the only witness David feared. As Kasman approached the witness stand, David looked at me.

"Did I mention Jon Grand called me last night?"

I looked at David.

He continued, "He can't make it. Father's eightieth birthday. Sorry."

"No!"

David nodded. "But there's a bell I want to ring from this guy's first testimony—about back channels with his white Afrikaner buddies. We've got to hurt him somehow, but without Jon Grand . . ."

Wyneva's voice overlaid David's. "Now did there come a time when you were in your assignment at the EPA that you began working on some projects in Africa?" She paused. "What projects did you work on?"

"I worked on technology cooperation projects in South Africa, specifically with partner organizations, the US Environmental Training Institute and the National Association of Development Agencies."

"What was the purpose of the projects?"

"The purpose of these projects was to provide technical and management solutions, based on the American experience, to address South Africa's environmental challenges."

"Did you have the occasion to work with Marsha Coleman-Adebayo during that, in 1996?" Wyneva asked him to describe the interaction.

"Dr. Coleman-Adebayo was the coordinator, and I was the subject matter expert on technology. It was a peer relationship, but she was the lead. It became a bit difficult over time, working together."

David leaned back in his chair and said under his breath, "His gloves are about to come off. Brace yourself."

"Why was it difficult?" Wyneva asked.

"First of all," Mark said, "the technology cooperation programs were being misrepresented sometimes as a technology export program, which was a barrier that was difficult to overcome, because the purpose of this was to address the environmental problems, not to export environmental goods and services. As it went on, there were a lot of times where there were missed meetings, where Dr. Coleman-Adebayo did not show up for meetings, not just inside the agency, but with people who had come from outside of the agency to attend these meetings, and that was an embarrassment. Sometimes meetings were also cancelled at the last minute. There was also a sense—a feeling—a disappointment that relevant information needed to implement these programs was not being shared, and that was a strong frustration too."

"Did you have any concerns about Dr. Coleman-Adebayo's approach to inclusiveness of the employees at EPA?"

"Yes, I did," said Kasman. "But the real thing that concerned me the most was when I approached Dr. Coleman-Adebayo about my concerns about how difficult it was to implement the activities I was working on, and she had met some of the partners that we were working with, she told me that—something—the nature I didn't quite get: 'You don't quite get it, Mark. I only want African Americans or people of color working in South Africa.' That she 'didn't want white people working in the field in South Africa.' And that was a real concern to me. . . . My reaction was that this was wrong, that we use whoever has the best expertise, and especially in a multicultural society and working with a society that's trying to become a multicultural society, that it was important to send the best people regardless of race."

By this time David was taking prodigious notes, writing like a California seismograph. The jury was with Kasman on every word. Body language is difficult to get right, but the jurors sat upright, leaning forward, their breathing shallow. I had no idea how David would counter Mark's slash-and-burn testimony.

"Now, did there come a time when you were asked to play a more active role in the South Africa project?" Wyneva continued. "And what were you asked to do?"

"I was asked to work on South Africa, December 1996. I was asked to temporarily become the point person for South African activities."

I nearly jumped from my seat, having just heard for the first time that Kasman had been asked to take over my responsibilities a full month before Sielen had removed me. But Mark remained relaxed and authoritative, saying that he was "to work with the government of South

Africa representatives to get the program off the ground, to see where the US expertise would be helpful to the South Africa request for assistance from the US."

"Now, once you took over that responsibility, did you learn that there were criticisms of Dr. Coleman-Adebayo's work?"

"Unfortunately, there was a barrage of criticism again," Kasman sighed. "They came from the South African government, the US Agency for International Development in South Africa. They came from the US Embassy in South Africa. They came from other working group managers on the same committee that we were in under the Gore-Mbeki structure."

David's apprehension was playing out. I could hear his breathing quicken. I found myself holding my breath.

"Would you identify those persons by name and race?"

"From USAID the person would be Russell Hawkins. From the Department of Environment and Tourism in South Africa, that would be Sidney Gerber, who is a white Caucasian, and Tinus Joubert, who is also white. From the embassy, it was Ken Thomas, who is white. From the other working group, one person was Jacqueline Rousseau, an African American."

Ken Thomas was one of my strongest supporters. Perhaps Wyneva had failed to brief Kasman that Thomas had just testified on my behalf.

"Did you ever hear Nitze say that he did not want any work done by EPA with historically black colleges?"

"No. In fact, it was encouraged when it was proposed, and we did it. . . . It was encouraged by everyone up the line of the chain of command in my management, which would be Pat Koshel—Ms. Pat Koshel—Mr. Alan Sielen, Dr. Alan Hecht, and Mr. Bill Nitze."

And finally, Wyneva asked, "What did you bring to the South Africa program?" Mark looked directly into the eyes of the jurors.

"I think, first of all, I brought a can-do, results-oriented energy, but very strong analytical skills for program management and for program implementation as well as the ability to distill great amounts of information into relevant briefings for our partner organizations and also for our management or decision makers, both at EPA and South Africa. Also the ability to work with others and to share credit and build an ownership over a joint activity."

"Was there anything that you assumed responsibility for in 1997 that had not been completed by Dr. Coleman-Adebayo?"

"Well, in '97 it was as if everything was left hanging."

I was worried. Mark had acquitted himself above any of our expectations, although he seemed to have lifted many of his answers from a Miss America contest. Shapiro, however, had seen and heard these answers before. The government's all-out assault was in full force.

David looked at the jury as if to say, Can you believe this guy? He strolled to the podium, and from the moment he opened his mouth, the gloves were off.

"Mr. Kasman, it is true, is it not, that you took over the South Africa program as the principal program officer about the same time you were given a GS-15 promotion?"

"I was asked to take it over before I was given the promotion," Kasman objected, adding, "Yes, I was awarded that, but it was simply close timing."

"Close timing." David's voice was stern and rapid. "You recall your deposition, sir?"

"Yes, I do," Mark said.

"And you were under oath then?"

"Yes, I was."

"I took it in my office, didn't I, about a year ago?"

"Yes, you did."

"You were asked the following questions and gave the following answers:

"Question: 'So it was at that point you got a promotion to GS-15 in early 1997?'

"Answer: 'In January. I was on travel when I got the call for the job offer. The panel didn't happen, but the interviews and everything happened in December.'

"Question: 'It was really at the time that you were taking over South Africa?'

"Answer: 'It was—it was in the same time that I got that dropped in my lap, yes.'"

Looking up from the transcript, David peered over his glasses and asked pointedly, "So it was at that point you got a promotion to GS-15 in early 1997?"

Kasman hesitated but had to answer.

"It was—it was in the same time that the South African project dropped in my lap, yes."

"So you gave a truthful answer here?"

"I gave a truthful answer in both."

Shapiro asked who, back in 1996 and '97, had made the final decision to promote someone. "I would guess on that it would have been Mr. Nitze."

"And who was it that had to approve you being given the South African assignment to be his top staffer on South Africa?"

"Mr. Nitze."

"Now, in 1996, in July, you did go to the Gore-Mbeki Biannual meeting in Washington, correct?"

"That's correct."

"You were the pitchman for ETI to the [South African members of] environmental committee, correct?"

"That's correct."

"And you pitched it to the Gore-Mbeki binational meeting?"

"That's right."

David continued, "And it didn't get approved in that meeting, correct?"

"Correct."

David looked at the jury to see if they were connecting the dots. "It didn't get approved at that biannual meeting [when] you made the pitch?"

"The official approval was at the February '97 meeting."

Kasman had just said he was the pitchman. But for the first time it occurred to me as I watched him testify that he was also the front man for the continued partnership between the Afrikaners and American businesses.

"In fact," David continued, one of the things "that helped a lot was the main person in the environmental portion of the government of South Africa changed right after the meeting, isn't that right? Mr. Mokaba took over for Mr. Holomisa?"

"I don't know what that had to do with it, frankly," Kasman said.

"You wouldn't know?" David had caught Kasman completely off guard with his question linking Holomisa's dismissal to US plans to launch ETI.

"No. I'm saying—I'm saying—that I don't think the change in personnel had anything to do with this specific project."

David didn't buy it and pressed Kasman. "But that was the project that you were connected to, ETI, in terms of South Africa at that point, mid-1996?"

Kasman's testimony struck me like a thunderclap, confirming the November 19, 1996, memo he had sent to Bill Nitze. Bantu Holomisa and I had stood in the way of the BNC's hidden agenda to continue the same cozy relationship with the old-guard apartheid elites under the guise of the ETI's environmental green flag. My removal and the elimination of Bantu Holomisa—whether Bantu's dismissal was with US complicity or happenstance, we'll never know—represented a seismic shift in the dynamics between OIA and the new South African government. Bundled with keeping Peter Mokaba in the dark after he replaced Bantu Holomisa, the problems surrounding the ETI Trojan horse should have quickly fallen away. Even without benefit of the full briefing he was entitled to, Peter Mokaba's instincts, experience, and awareness of the immediate needs of the South African people made him suspicious of the OIA's agenda for ETI. That explained the need for covert backroom deals with Afrikaners.

With Kasman's revelation I was acutely aware of David's admonishment that the jury would be watching any body language and the more of an even keel I could keep, the better.

"You would agree that the South Africans who you mentioned, that you heard criticism of Marsha Coleman-Adebayo, were the Afrikaner South Africans, correct?"

"They were the white—white South Africans."

"But not just whites—they were Afrikaner. They weren't just English speaking?"

Mark conceded the point.

"How many times had you dealt with South African leadership, governmental or community-based leadership, before January of 1997, other than your pitch in 1996?"

"Well, in addition to the pitch, there were other side meetings at that time, but that would have been it."

"Nothing further?"

"Nothing other than July '96."

What Kasman had said was equivalent to throwing gasoline in my face. While in 1996 I was being bent over backward for trying to help newly liberated people in the mines and in the townships, consistent with the goals of the Gore-Mbeki Commission, Kasman was carrying on business as usual with the very Afrikaners who had created, maintained, and were still maneuvering to repackage the old realities of white-skin privilege within the trappings of a new South Africa. Mandela had just been released from prison after twenty-seven years of torture. Biko was dead. Chris Hani was dead. Thousands had died in South Africa, and the blood was still flowing. We had the reports of vanadium poisoning. Yet the United States was carrying on business with their Afrikaner cohorts who still controlled economic power despite the political change. The masses of people, however, who had risen up to throw off a white supremacist government that had adopted the swastika as its emblem, were still being betrayed.

For the first time, I realized that I had been their unwitting instrument. Were it not for David's counseling me to avoid displays of emotion in front of the jury, I might have screamed.

"And prior to then, had you ever traveled to South Africa?"

"No."

"Thank you. Nothing further, Your Honor."

"Redirect," said Judge Kollar-Kotelly. David started to walk back to the plaintiff's table but stopped suddenly, looking over his shoulder at Mark.

"I'm sorry. I do have one more question." David paused before asking, "You are white, aren't you?"

Mark looked dazed, but it was the answer that would underscore David's cross: "I am white."

David Shapiro sat down at the table next to me and took a sip of water. He was calm and attentive. He could have been a ventriloquist. With the glass on his lips, he said loud enough for me to hear him, "Take that, you son of a bitch."

David put the glass down on the table and listened to Wyneva's cross. When Kasman stepped away from the witness stand, David leaned back in his chair and stretched.

"That really hurt. I landed some punches, but he kicked our ass. We've got to find a way to discredit this guy or we're done. That really hurt."

"Marsh, what are you doing?" It was Segun's voice.

"Honey, I'm buried in documents. Nitze is testifying tomorrow, and I know that, lodged somewhere deep in one of these documents, there's a smoking gun."

I didn't hear him approaching where I had spread out all of my notes and papers, but I sensed a presence, good and gracious.

"Come, Marsh, take a break. You won't be disappointed."

"Sorry, Segun. No can do. In fact, I doubt whether I'll be able to sleep tonight. Give me a rain check. I won't be so crazy tomorrow."

Segun persisted, bumping his hip against my shoulder. This was unlike him. He never insisted.

I didn't try to hide my irritation. "OK, OK, what do you want to show me?"

"Close your eyes," he said, taking my hands.

I followed, but I couldn't relax. I felt like I was leaning back on water skis. Then a coolness came under my toes. And a soft, violet tinge shaded my closed eyes.

"Segun. What do I smell?"

"Do you like it?"

"Yes."

"Then you can open your eyes."

The hallway to our bath was lush with rose petals and flickering tea lights. "Segun, you . . . ?"

He swirled me around in midsentence, pointing up at our shadows. We chuckled as they danced on the ceiling.

The bath was alive with tea lights and bubbles, creating sounds that only we could hear. Calming. Soothing. My body nestled in votive flames. Segun massaged my hair, neck, shoulders, and back.

I woke to our deep breathing between familiar sheets.

23

Discrimination or Disappointment?

Day Five

Nitze had in some ways seemed an aloof figure to me, but never more so than when he strode toward the witness stand that day among common people who held the weight of judgment in their laps.

"Good morning, sir," said Wyneva. She was particularly perky.

"Good morning."

Nitze's resume included: president, Alliance to Save Energy; deputy assistant secretary of state for environment, health, and natural resources; fourteen years as a lawyer working for Mobil Oil Corporation, first in New York and later in Japan; and, at the time of the trial, assistant administrator at the Office of International Activities, United States Environmental Protection Agency, and board of directors, Aspen Institute. Mr. Nitze had graduated from Harvard College in 1964, spent two years at Oxford, and then attended Harvard Law School. During a two-month period in the summer of 1975, he had been the acting general manager, Mobil Zaire, and general counsel, Mobil in Japan. In the late 1980s, he had worked in Nigeria for Mobil on oil exploration and production.

In a refrain he would repeat throughout his testimony, William Nitze said, "I represent the administrator, and I also represent the president of the United States, who appointed me to this position. And in a sense, I also represent the Congress and the American people."

I hoped that the jurors were catching the breeze from the revolving door connecting stints in public service to private corporations that Nitze had just described.

"Did you have any particular objectives with regard to South Africa?"

"Yes," Nitze said, "there was a legacy of inadequate infrastructure, inadequate resources to deal with many pollution problems, particularly . . . problems of waste, not just at the municipal level, but from the mining industry, from the power industry, from many industrial activities where pollution was directly affecting thousands, if not millions, of people and was not properly managed and controlled."

This was a significant statement coming from Nitze—and telling. The first instance he mentioned beyond the municipal level was the mining industry. Vanadium mining had been the focus of my concern and communications throughout my short tenure as the executive secretary. Vanadium mining had been the focus of much of the efforts of the study tours. And I was convinced vanadium mining was behind my dismissal. It surprised me that Nitze would mention the mining industry at all, given the pushback the agency had mounted against my advocacy for the miners and other victims in Brits. I had thought that the government would go to some lengths to avoid the topic.

Nitze continued. "You have a case of a country which was just emerging from a very traumatic and difficult period of its history under the apartheid regime. Nelson Mandela had performed really a miracle. And Nelson Mandela did it. Now because of that—"

Shapiro rose. "Your Honor, I think we stretched far afield. The question was, what's Gore-Mbeki?"

"But there's a reason here," Nitze said before the judge could rule. "President Clinton felt that the United States, which had been through a somewhat similar experience, with slavery, the Reconstruction period, all of our unhappy history of race relations, could help South Africa in a more intensive way accomplish the goals of its transition."

"Mr. Nitze, have you traveled to Africa before?"

"Yes, my first trip to Africa was between my freshman and sophomore years at college. I had a roommate, John Slocum, whose father was working at the American Embassy in Egypt, in Cairo, and because of that connection, my roommate and I decided that this would be a good time to visit Africa, starting with Egypt, learn something about the continent, spend some time with Jerry's [*sic*] family, and then return for our sophomore years. It's interesting that we did not have—"

"Your Honor, again," Shapiro rose, "we are getting a lecture. When did you first go to Africa? was the question."

Nitze was no novice. His roots, his heirs, his education, travel, interests, indeed his pedigree lent themselves to extensive networks in government and industry, contacts that included indigenous chiefs, secretaries of state, lawmakers, and lawyers for the extractive industries.

Wyneva continued. "Now, as the assistant administrator, do you have any specific policy objectives with regard to South Africa?"

"Yes. We want to help South Africa build capacity so the communities in South Africa at all levels, the new provincial government, municipalities, small towns, have the ability to reduce the pollution which is affecting the health of their families and which is affecting their environment."

"Now, Mr. Nitze, when you began your service as the assistant administrator for OIA, did you have any particular expectation of employees?"

"Yes . . . Dr. Coleman-Adebayo was supposed to communicate our mission, our objectives, the content of our programs, and basically what was going on in our relationship both within the United States and within South Africa."

Wyneva asked about our luncheon meeting on the boat when he had offered me the South Africa program.

Nitze said, "As I remember it, Marsha Coleman-Adebayo had some initial reluctance to undertake this new assignment, although she had expressed interest in working on Africa, and she certainly demonstrated an interest in working on human rights issues, justice issues, things of that nature. But after our discussion I think I convinced her, and she accepted, that this particular assignment would fit very well with both the agency's needs and her particular interests, which were very much focused on what I'll call social justice and community issues, which were an important component of our work in South Africa.

"For example, and to her credit, Marsha Coleman-Adebayo organized a visit to a township in Johannesburg called Alexandra, where we got an on-the-ground feel for what the situation is in poor urban communities, at least in Johannesburg. . . .

"She required a great deal of help in terms of making sure that we had the budget; that the right rooms were available at the right time, that we had coffee and doughnuts available."

Judge Kollar-Kotelly looked incredulous.

"Do you recall having a conversation when you were in Africa with Mr. Mokaba?" Wyneva asked. "Did you ever make any comments to Secretary Richardson and use the term *necklacing*?"

"Secretary Richardson had just assumed his duties as secretary of energy," Nitze recalled, "and it was clear that Mr. Mokaba not only had responsibility on the pollution issues that I was working on but also was heading the South Africa effort to deal with climate change. Mr. Moore was also present during the conversation. I mentioned Mr. Mokaba's role as a militant leader in the ANC, and that's when I made the reference to necklacing. Mr. Moore corrected me, and I accepted the correction."

"Did you mean to offend Mr. Mokaba?"

"No, absolutely not," he insisted. "I had a good relationship with Mr. Mokaba. We had good discussions about various aspects of our program at that meeting."

Wyneva asked if there were any responsibilities regarding technology or the Environmental Training Institute that were assigned, and did "Marsha Coleman-Adebayo agree with that?"

"She was not terribly enthusiastic about this part of our work," Nitze said, adding, "Now in fairness, initially some of the senior officials at the South African ministry were concerned that this particular idea was an export promotion project for the US and they didn't want a project that was just designed to push US exports. . . . Our job was to convince them that this was not primarily an export promotion project but a capacity-building project that would help them."

In a particularly revealing statement, Nitze laid it out baldly. "Frankly, as the spring wore on now in 1996, I felt that Dr. Coleman-Adebayo was not very enthusiastic or supportive about this project. She kept indicating that the South Africans had objections to it, but what we really needed is not to have repeated to us that the South Africans had concerns—we knew that. We needed help in overcoming those concerns and making this part of our work a success."

They didn't care what the South Africans wanted. They needed someone to ram the program through. That's what Mark Kasman had been for.

"Did you have any observations at that time as to whether Marsha Coleman-Adebayo was a team player or not with regard to the South Africa program?"

Nitze's response was quick. "Yes, but not well enough. . . . If she had thought up an idea—particularly if it was an idea focused on her area of interest, which was community activism, human rights, that agenda—she would be genuinely enthusiastic and supportive, although she would very much want to run the show on her own and not necessarily consult with her colleagues . . . and, frankly, did not work with other people, such as the people in our technology office in a teamlike way." According to Nitze, it was at this stage that he began to have real concerns about my support of ETI led by Mr. Kasman and whether I would work with EPA teams in Philadelphia.

"What group, if any, was chosen to handle funding for South Africa? And please tell us about a meeting with US community groups."

"I chose a group led by John Daniels. We had a meeting at EPA headquarters that I felt was very critical of EPA and specifically of myself, since I was the lead EPA official. They criticized me for not getting the grant money out to South Africa and more importantly not moving our environmental programs forward as rapidly as they could have been moved. What disturbed me is I got the feeling at that meeting, in fact, I believe it happened—that Marsha Coleman-Adebayo, instead of supporting me and instead of generally supporting the idea that the agency was doing its best and that we were trying to respond to the needs of the South Africans—I got the feeling that she was on the side of the Environmental Justice participants who were critical of me."

"Was Mr. Daniels subsequently given the—awarded the grant?"

"He was given a noncompetitive sole source grant of $250,000."

"Did Marsha Coleman-Adebayo object to Mr. Daniels' selection?"

"Yes, she did. She objected that I had made that decision without sufficient consultation with all of the environmental justice representatives around the table. Earlier that year, as I've mentioned, we had decided that we needed to formalize a team arrangement and that I needed the help of one of my senior managers, and I selected Mr. Sielen . . . because one area where I was not confident of Marsha Coleman-Adebayo's performance was in engendering the kind of teamwork and cooperation within EPA and between EPA and other parts of the government. . . . Things reached a stage where, frankly, I thought she was, to put it in a phrase, being defiant."

Teamwork. Cooperation. Defiant. It struck me how sanitized the language was when it was used in the context of a federal court proceeding. At the agency, management's preferred word for "defiant" was *uppity*. "Don't make waves" they sanitized to *teamwork* and *cooperation*.

"Now, you indicated that after the meeting you felt that her tone was defiant."

"Shortly after she received a short memorandum indicating that her performance was unsatisfactory," Nitze said. "This whole development was certainly part of the rationale for that 'unsatisfactory' indication."

This comment was straight out of the playbook. I received an "unsatisfactory" memo because he thought I was defiant.

"Did you ever make a statement that you felt a person's ability to speak English or a certain language affected their ability to be a host or their basic character?"

"No. I believe that speaking English well is important, but someone having a good heart, a good character, being a hospitable person, does not depend on their ability to speak the English language well."

"Have you made any comment that said that you did not have any interest in working with historically black colleges?"

"No—and the proof is in the pudding. We have worked with them. Just this last May, Mr. Kasman organized a visit of environmental justice groups from South Africa to the United States. . . . There were four historically black colleges that participated in that event."

"Thank you. No further questions, Your Honor."

Judge Kollar-Kotelly invited David to proceed with the cross.

"Have you noticed that some of the jurors are trying not to barf from this arrogant SOB?" David said after leaning over to me. Before standing up, he added, with singsong Southern accent, "Some days—I just love my job."

David walked to the podium, carrying his notes. He didn't look at Nitze. He wasn't impressed with Nitze, his heritage, or his pedigree. He wanted to show he was fed up with all this privileged drivel and was about to cut through the pretense. His questions were borderline demands.

"Who was the executive secretary for Gore-Russia, and what was his race?"

"Gary Waxmonsky. White."

"What was his position?"

"His principal role as executive secretary was to staff me and my work on the Gore-Chernomyrdin Commission. He also had others related to work in Russia. But, yes, that was his principal task, to staff me."

David challenged Nitze on how many times Gary had traveled to Russia.

"If I told you that he went six times in '94, five times in '95, and four times in '96, would you disagree with those numbers?"

"No," Nitze said, "because that was the original rhythm."

"It is true, is it not, that for the year and a half that Marsha Coleman-Adebayo was the executive secretary for Gore-Mbeki, she went to South Africa—was allowed to go to South Africa—just once? Isn't that right?"

"Her travel was not approved because we didn't feel it was necessary to achieve the objectives of the program."

"She was sought in South Africa. The South Africans wanted her to come, and the US Embassy sided with them and asked you to let her come. Isn't that right?"

"Not precisely. Mr. Thomas, the science and technology officer at the embassy, when he was aware that we were planning the community grants program, felt that he did not have the time to do that work himself, and he wanted help, and he would have been happy to have somebody, and in particular, Marsha Coleman-Adebayo, come out and help him," Nitze explained. "I did not feel, and the other members of the office did not feel, that such a detail would be appropriate or necessary for the program. I do remember a letter specifically asking for Marsha Coleman-Adebayo from Mr. Mokaba."

Shapiro pressed Nitze to remember if Brad Brown had been present at one of the earlier meetings of the commission and whether Nitze had challenged Brown about using traditionally black universities in South Africa.

"Don't you remember saying to him, 'I'm sorry you said that because now we're going to have to use those universities?'"

"I do not recall making such a remark to him."

"Weren't you with Brad Brown in South Africa, in a park with Franklin Moore and Marsha Coleman-Adebayo, and you talked about having to speak English and how well one speaks English in your opinion is how well one conducts oneself, how hospitable one is?"

"I don't remember making that remark."

"You deny it, don't you?"

"I say I don't recall making that remark. I've already addressed that one on direct."

David was making Nitze uneasy. "You do deny it, don't you? I did hear right, when you were testifying on direct, that you deny having made that remark?"

"I said I don't recall it."

Judge Kollar-Kotelly intervened. "Well, does that mean that it's your best memory that you didn't make it?"

"My best memory is I did not make it." Nitze was looking down and speaking softly.

"I wonder," David began, "this trip to South Africa in November, I think we've already said you went alone."

"Well, I think what you're referring to is that I combined that trip with a visit with my family to South Africa over the Thanksgiving vacation. But in terms of my professional duties, yes, I went alone."

"You were told by Marsha Coleman-Adebayo that, unfortunately, the new deputy minister, Mr. Mokaba, would not be present, correct?"

"I was told that he was out of the country. And, although he was my co-equal, he was not the person that I really needed to work with in order to nail down the details of these programs. It was important to sit down with the staff at the ministry and make sure that we had the mechanisms in place to get the community grants program going and to get our technical assistance work underway."

This was a bold-faced lie that contravened all diplomatic protocol.

"The staff of the ministry was Dr. Cameron, right?"

"I met with at least three. I met with Dr. Cameron and several others."

"All white."

"Well, yes, three white officials." Nitze's face was flushed. He looked toward Wyneva Johnson.

"Dr. Coleman-Adebayo urged you to put your trip off so you could meet with Mr. Mokaba, the person who was at your level, correct?"

"Yes, but we needed to get this community grants program moving forward. We had a commitment to the South Africans. We were already being criticized for not getting the program into place. We were going to have a commission meeting the following February, and it was important before the end of the year, before the Christmas holidays, to get these things worked out, and I did."

For people outside of the government, Nitze's disingenuousness might have gone unnoticed. Assistant administrators are hand wavers; they never work out the details—they delegate the details to their staff. It would appear that there was a different motive for Nitze's trip than what he would have had the jury believe.

"It is true that the person at your level, Mr. Mokaba, wanted specifically Marsha Coleman-Adebayo to meet with him?"

"I remember a letter asking for Marsha Coleman-Adebayo to go to South Africa. I don't remember it in the context of working out the matters I've just described."

David stepped back, almost facing the jury.

"Your Honor, perhaps we can look at the plaintiff's 36 in evidence." Jurors started to adjust in their seats; they were familiar with David's setup. "This is a letter to you, from the deputy minister of environmental affairs and tourism, P.R. Mokaba, MP, isn't it?"

"It is."

"And in this letter, which is dated October 7, he specifically writes to ask for Marsha Coleman-Adebayo to come to South Africa to continue her work started with the people that had been on the study tour, correct?"

"Yes."

"The team concept in South Africa did not really begin until after you decided that you didn't want Marsha Coleman-Adebayo there any longer, isn't that right?"

"No," Nitze insisted, "we required all of the people involved in this effort to work together and support each other's work from the very beginning."

I studied the jury for any indication of their recognizing that Nitze had just contradicted Gary Waxmonsky's insistence that he had never been required to be a part of a team and had received outstanding ratings every year.

David returned to the subject of Nitze's Thanksgiving trip. "And this is more than a month before you went to South Africa alone in November of '96 over the Thanksgiving holiday, isn't that right?"

"That's correct."

"How long were you gone?"

"As I remember it, the total length of my trip was about a week, maybe a little more."

"And your family met you when you went through a game park in South Africa, is that right?"

"That's right. We spent about three or four days together after my official meetings."

David performed between Nitze and the jury, using his eyebrows, shoulders, mouth, posture, and demeanor—engaging Nitze with the jury as his audience, their heads going back and forth between the two. He looked at Nitze with utter contempt.

"And the government paid your way there and back, correct?"

"The government paid for my plane flight, that's correct, not for any of my expenses on personal travel."

"Isn't it a fact that the South Africans, the new South Africans, were interested in pollution control and public health, and that's the focus that Marsha Coleman-Adebayo brought to it and changed the whole focus of this committee to brown issues, which is where the new Mandela group in South Africa wanted to go? Isn't that right?"

"Yes, and that is precisely the mission of the US Environmental Protection Agency—that's why I asked her to staff me in that effort."

Nitze proved to be a skilled and shrewd witness. He considered his lofty waxing about planet Earth sufficient to obscure the reality of the retaliation I had faced and the plight of vanadium miners.

I was emotionally spent after Nitze's testimony. I thought his shoulders were slightly bent when he left the witness stand. David's cross might have been the first time that William Albert Nitze had ever been held to account for the consequences of his position on everyday people, a rare incident in an otherwise pristine life in which his place, name, and pedigree had always been enough. A wave of his hand could mean life and death for people he couldn't even see, like the ones who surrounded him when he was ankle deep in the raw sewage that overflowed the townships he hadn't bothered revisiting or the orphans he hadn't inquired about during his Thanksgiving vacation to South Africa. For all his insistence that he had gone to get things done, he had yet to send a team of doctors to investigate the vanadium poisoning of the miners in Brits.

||||||||||||

Wyneva readied herself for another examination, leaning over and comparing notes with the two other female attorneys, and called Alan Hecht. She didn't waste time.

"Did you ever make a comment to Mr. Sielen that Marsha Coleman-Adebayo was uppity?"

"No. I don't recall ever making that comment, and I certainly wouldn't use it. It's just not a word that I would use." This was the same formula Nitze had used—it wasn't something they would say.

"Do you recall an occasion where there was a request by a South African official in the government that Marsha Coleman-Adebayo come to Africa?"

"It didn't leave much of an impression on me," Hecht said. "It didn't have a big impression on me."

The deputy secretary from another country's environmental ministry wrote to EPA, and it didn't make a big impression. "Ask him if the deputy minister from France would have impressed him," I whispered to David.

Alan looked deflated when Shapiro began his cross. It appeared Wyneva had anticipated David going after Hecht about the "uppity" remark, but that point had already been established by several other witnesses, despite Hecht's denial. David had other plans.

"Now, you recall, don't you, Dr. Hecht, having a session with Marsha Coleman-Adebayo where you screamed at her? You called her in specifically to raise your voice to her?"

"Yes."

Ms. Johnson rose to object. "Your Honor, beyond the basis!"

"Well, I'm assuming that there's some issue that will be tied up. Continue."

"I recall an incident in which I yelled at her, yes."

David fixed his eyes on Hecht. "You banged on the table?" David pantomimed hitting the table with his fist. The jury sat frozen in their seats.

"That, I'm not certain about," Hecht said, suddenly aware of his own size and shifting his weight in his seat. David's voice rose, demonstrating a man's yelling.

"It was just the two of you in the office, wasn't it?" David demanded. "Yes."

"You called her in specifically to raise your voice to her." "Yes, I did!"

I watched the women jurors, who, to a person, sat back stiffly. Two of them looked at me with furrowed brows, near bursting into tears. Before that incident, I had never experienced being assaulted by a man. Whether these women ever had been or not, they conveyed a sense of their wanting to hold me, protect me, of feeling for themselves the humiliation of being pinned unexpectedly inside a closed office by a much larger, much stronger man, his spit and sweat flying as he bellowed in their faces. Once again I felt the shame that had kept me from calling the police that day, as if it were me who were guilty.

Again I felt the fear that senior managers at OIA instilled with yelling, name calling, and physical threats during meetings. I looked back at the women in the jury and tried not to cry, remembering being hysterical when I called Segun, babbling, and him telling me to come home.

As Hecht left the witness stand, he seemed naked. His face was red and tight. He had to wait for the clerk who had a folder for the judge. Hecht stood briefly with his hands crossed in front of himself like they were cuffed, then put one in his pants pocket, removing it again and looking down as he walked quickly out of the courtroom.

||||||||||||

If that wasn't bad enough, I still had to sit through the testimony of another supervisor, Alan Sielen.

"We—Mr. Nitze is appointed by President Clinton. He represents President Clinton and Vice President Gore." We had heard this phrasing before.

"We," Sielen continued, "had certain objectives that we were trying to pursue in South Africa, and it became very clear after a while that Marsha Coleman-Adebayo just wasn't supporting what the president and Vice President Gore wanted to accomplish there. And it was really hurting us. It was hurting the office."

"Did there come a time when you had a conversation with her with regard to her continued leadership on the project?"

"Well, in January 1997, I sat down with her and had a one-on-one meeting and had to tell her that she was being removed from the South Africa program."

"And what did you tell her?"

"We had a very strong commitment to the people of South Africa, and that she—I was disappointed and Mr. Nitze was disappointed that—she wasn't behind it. She wasn't supporting what we were trying to accomplish. And it was—it was hurting this administration. It was hurting EPA. Most important, I think it was hurting the people of South Africa that we were trying to help."

"Did you make any comments to her that she was too close to the South African community or to Afro-Americans in your discussion with her?"

"No. No." Sielen's double negative spoke for itself in view of the direct testimony the jury had already heard. But Sielen would not be so adamant when asked if he had ever referred to me as an honorary white man.

"I don't know—I don't know whether or not I did. I don't remember ever saying anything like that."

Even with prodding from the bench as to whether or not it was his best recollection that he did not, Mr. Sielen never denied saying it.

||||||||||||

Wyneva's examination of my immediate supervisor, Pat Koshel, started with a series of queries about her background.

"Please tell the court something about your work history."

"Before working at EPA, I spent ten years at the US Agency for International Development."

When Wyneva asked if Pat had worked for any other government agency prior to joining the EPA, I nearly fell on the floor upon hearing her answer. Pat hesitated, fidgety, looking around.

"Yes. When I first graduated from college, I went to work for the Central Intelligence Agency."

When I had worked on the Hill, there was a common expression: Once in the CIA, always in the CIA. In many ways, this made perfect sense; the pieces of the puzzle were falling into place.

When I had first told Pat about my concerns about vanadium workers, she had tried to dissuade me. "Why don't you spend some time and decorate your new office," she had suggested. Before her CIA revelation, I had never been able to understand why telling her that people were dying in South Africa had prompted a Martha Stewart moment. But it is not without significance that the CIA lists vanadium as a strategic mineral;

it seems plausible that the vanadium workers found themselves caught between the pestle of profit and the mortar of US strategic interests.

"There was a request," she testified, "to help deal with the vanadium issues." She explained that "EPA people in the Philadelphia office had spent a couple of years reviewing documents for an interministerial group. So, I think we followed up or had plans to follow up on almost all of the commitments. . . . We were asked in late '96 to actually send someone to South Africa to review these documents, which covered human health. . . . And the government of South Africa in fact paid for someone from the Philadelphia office to go. It turns out that he was a veterinarian."

David seemed unusually morose during the cross of Pat Koshel. David was eyeing the jury, recalling what they had heard during Waxmonsky's testimony.

"You would criticize anyone who wasn't a good team player. That would be a normal criticism that you would have as a supervisor?"

"Yes." David allowed the jury to watch Pat stew in her answer before he moved on to South Africa.

"Ms. Koshel, you would agree, would you not, that Mr. Waxmonsky traveled all the time to Russia and that Marsha was not allowed to travel?"

No, Koshel replied, she would not agree to that. "Gary traveled more during . . . that period than Marsha Coleman-Adebayo." She added, "Marsha had a number of responsibilities to do in the office that we felt were more important than travel to South Africa."

"Now, Mr. Nitze went to South Africa in November during this very same time frame alone, correct?"

"That is correct. I believe at that time, Mr. Holomisa was not in the government. He had been fired." Pat testified that she was not aware that Mokaba (who had replaced Holomisa) was not in the country at the time. She shifted in her seat while wiping perspiration from her forehead.

"Mr. Nitze went to South Africa alone in November 1996 to do precisely what, madam?"

"He went because nothing was happening under the program, and he wanted to make sure that some things got back on track, so that we could have on-the-ground activities take place that following couple of months."

Shapiro looked at the jury with a smirk—eyebrows high. "Madam, didn't he go on a family vacation to meet his family and get the government to pay his way over?"

"He went—he went to deal with the program, sir."

"Madam, did you know he was going on a family vacation and getting the government to pay his way over?"

"He was going—"

Before Pat could finish, David started in again. "Did you know that he went—"

"Objection, Your Honor!" shouted Wyneva.

"I asked a specific question, Your Honor!" David shouted back. He continued, "Did you know he was attending a family vacation in South Africa over the Thanksgiving recess, school recess, when he went?"

"He had planned this to go and do work in South Africa. I think because of the timing he was joined by his family." The courtroom was quiet. Even David could not believe what he had just heard her admit. Koshel, who had insisted earlier that Nitze had gone to South Africa to get the program "back on track" had confirmed that Nitze had planned a family vacation to the game parks to coincide with the holiday.

David stood and stared at Koshel. His silence allowed the jurors to connect the dots.

"Now, you knew prior to removing Marsha Coleman-Adebayo from the South Africa program that she had filed an EEO complaint, a complaint of discrimination, isn't that right?"

"Sir, I did not remove Marsha Coleman-Adebayo from the South Africa program."

"You had a hand in it, didn't you?"

"I was consulted—but it was not a decision—it was a decision by the senior management."

"You recommended it?"

"No!"

‖‖‖‖‖‖‖‖‖‖‖

"Marsha, Segun," David started. It was after court, around 6:00 P.M., and we were debriefing in David Shapiro's office on I Street.

"I always try to play it straight with my clients. I took your case on contingency, so I also have some skin in the game. Pat Koshel and the

Alans were really of no consequence. But Kasman and Gaylord really hurt us. I'm not sure we can recover in time to win this case. I'm going to spend the evening working on my closing—hoping that I can pull this out of the air—but it doesn't look good."

Out of the corner of my eye I could see Segun's legs bouncing under the desk.

"We had some great witnesses," David said. "We gave it our best shot. Whatever happens, you need to be able to make peace with yourselves. Most people never get to this point—a jury trial—it's very rare!"

David continued on about our noble justice system, but I tuned out the ending of his speech. My heart was sick. I needed to go home and rest. Segun tried to cheer me and get my mind off the only thing that I could think about—losing. Mercifully, it was soon time to go to bed and try to rest before another day in court. I knelt to pray and thank God for another day, but the words seemed as hollow as whatever words I might have to use to tell my mother I had lost. All night, through uneasy sleep, I could find no words at all to tell Sina and Sade.

||||||||||||

"Hello, Marsha?"

I had no idea who it was. I had fallen asleep on my knees. Someone was on the phone, but I didn't recognize the voice.

"Sorry for waking you up, Marsha. I'm an early bird, and I thought I would call you before going into the office."

"I'm sorry, but who's calling? I don't recognize your voice."

"Sorry, it's Jon Grand. I just returned from my father's birthday celebration and thought I would call and get the news on your trial. I was sorry to disappoint you."

"Jon, you won't believe this, but today is the last day of the trial. It isn't going so well."

I was waking up in a hurry.

"I hate to ask you this, but . . ." My voice became frail. "I know that you don't know me, Jon," I said, "but could you take the first plane out of Chicago and come and testify about what you heard Mark Kasman say about me?"

"I'm on my way!"

"What did you say?" I heard myself ask.

"I'm on my way," Jon said. "I believe there's a 9:00 A.M. plane from Chicago O'Hare that I can make."

I closed my eyes—oh, how great you are, Lord. "Thank you, Jon. My husband is telling me that he will pick you up at the airport. By the way—what do you look like?"

The phone rang once. "Who the hell is this?" David barked.

"David, it's Marsha. Sorry for calling so early, but Jon Grand called this morning! He's on a plane headed for Washington, DC! David, I am so excited—we have a chance to pull the covers off Mark."

"What time is he landing?"

"About two hours from now."

"I need to call the court and Wyneva—got to go." I was about to hang up. "Oh! By the way, Marsha, did I mention that these cases are like roller coasters?" He laughed. "Damn! We're back in the game!"

Jon Grand was on the plane from Chicago to Washington. Segun was on his way to National Airport with a sign for Jon to know him by. David was calling Judge Kollar-Kotelly to tell her that a witness had stepped forward to impeach the testimony of Mark Kasman. O'Hare is famous for its delays. My prayer: Lord—please—not today!

Day Six

David used every legal maneuver he knew to buy time. The court was not aware that Jon was in a different state and that we were awaiting his arrival. During my rebuttal testimony, Segun walked into the court-room and signaled thumbs up—Jon was sequestered in the witness room. David took a deep breath.

"May it please the court, my witness, Jon Grand has arrived," David said.

Jon walked through the doors, and I saw him for the first time. If a human being could look like an angel, Jon was my angel. He quickly glanced at me out of the edge of his eye, but he focused on the seat he was about to occupy.

"Could you state your full name, sir?"

"Jon Thomas Grand."

"Mr. Grand, where do you live?"

"Chicago, Illinois."

"Where are you gainfully employed, what is your position, and for how long, sir?"

"I'm with Region V of the US Environmental Protection Agency for the past thirteen years. I am the director of the Office of International Activities. "

"And can you tell us if in your duties you come into contact with the OIA at headquarters?"

"Yes, I do."

"I want to draw your attention to a gentleman by the name of Mark Kasman. Can you tell us how you know him?"

"I've dealt with Mr. Kasman for, oh, probably nine years professionally."

"I want to call your attention to the last time you dealt with Mr. Kasman. Can you tell us when that was, and the subject matter?"

"Yes. That was on July 27, 2000, I believe. It was a Thursday. There was a group of officials from Egypt who had come to the US and specifically requested a visit to Region V to look at some environmental software that we had been developing. Mr. Kasman was their contact here in the US, and he sent a note to me asking if they could come and then accompany them to the region. He said that he would be in the office—everybody would be around—because of a case that was going on involving EPA's 'Rosa Parks,' as he called it."

David cocked his head and squinted. "He said what?"

Jon started to repeat his answer. "It was a case, an EPA—"

"Objection, Your Honor!" shouted Wyneva.

"He said it once," Judge Kollar-Kotelly stated. "You don't have to have it twice."

Shapiro looked at the judge in bewilderment. "I just want to make sure who said what. Tell me exact—"

But Judge Kollar-Kotelly cut David off. "He has said it. He said specifically who said it."

"What did you say in response to that?" David offered.

"I didn't say anything."

"Can you tell us how he said it?"

"Objection, Your Honor!" Understanding the high stakes of this moment, Wyneva Johnson was on her feet again.

"No. I think that I'll allow that," Judge Kollar-Kotelly ruled.

Jon took his time with this answer.

"It was not laudatory," he said finally. "It seemed dismissive."

"Sir, do you know Marsha Coleman-Adebayo?"

"Actually, I don't. We've talked on the phone, and I believe we may have met once or twice in OIA, just passing, but I really don't know her personally."

Wyneva was quick on her feet. Moments before she approached Jon to question him, she huddled with her cocounsels.

"Counsel asked you about your contacts with Mr. Kasman and what capacity you do work with him. What was the nature of the contacts you had with him?"

"It's been sort of on a needs basis. He had put together, for example, an extensive informational package. We explored the possibility of doing some additional work in Indonesia . . . where he had program responsibilities."

"No further questions, Your Honor."

Wyneva Johnson had to bring Mark Kasman back to refute Jon Grand's allegations that Mark had made the "Rosa Parks of the EPA" statement. Where a day earlier it had seemed time was standing still, since Jon's early call, it was moving at warp speed. The jury seemed surprised to see Mark again—no doubt, Mark was surprised as well.

⸽⸽⸽⸽⸽⸽⸽⸽⸽⸽⸽

"Mr. Kasman," Wyneva was cautious, "did you have the occasion to take a trip to Chicago in the past month, and did you have the occasion to meet with Mr. Jon Grand?"

"Yes, I did."

"And what was the reason for your meeting with him?"

"Mr. Grand is the regional international coordinator. We have an international coordinator in each of our regional offices, so he was hosting our visit in Chicago at the EPA region."

"Did you have any conversation with him about your availability in connection with the delegation?"

"Yes, I did."

"What was that conversation?"

"Mr. Grand asked me about what was keeping me busy, would I be available in the next coming weeks, and I told him that I would not be available."

"In response to your comment that you would not be available, what, if anything, did Mr. Grand say?"

"Well, I had said that I would not be available because I would be on call to testify in a case, and Mr. Grand asked me if it was the Coleman-Adebayo case."

"And what was your response to that?"

"'Yes.'"

"Did you say anything else in response to his question?"

"Yes, I remarked that I was frustrated that there was going to be a period of two weeks that I was going to be on call and not be able to work, given all the other responsibilities and all the other work that was happening right now."

"In your conversation with Mr. Grand, did you reference or refer to any famous civil rights leader?"

"No."

"Did you make any reference to Rosa Parks in your conversation with him?"

"No, I did not." Wyneva thanked Kasman. She had an annoyed expression on her face as she looked at the jury while walking to her seat.

Shapiro, buoyed by Jon's testimony, realized the outcome of the trial hung in the balance. As far as David was concerned, Mark had just lied under oath, and David was going to reveal that. David's face was steely. He rose and took to the podium, collecting himself before he iced Kasman.

"You told Mr. Grand that you would be unavailable for two weeks because of this case?"

"That's right."

"And so somebody had told you that this case was going to be two weeks long at that time?"

"What I was told is that we didn't know the exact length, but we had to be on call for that length of time."

"You were at your office yesterday, correct?"

"Well, for the last two weeks I've been mostly in the witness room, but yesterday, yes, I was in my office."

"So what you told Mr. Grand, then, was that you would be available because you wouldn't be out of town, isn't that right?"

"No. That's not right."

Shapiro looked toward the jury, his cheeks sucked in, and then turned back to Mark.

"Mr. Kasman, you've had dealings with Mr. Grand right along, haven't you?"

"Objection, Your Honor!" Johnson was on her feet. Judge Kollar-Kotelly allowed the question.

"You've had dealings with Mr. Grand for the last few years, haven't you?"

"Oh, yes."

"Pleasant dealings?"

"Professional dealings."

"You know him to be an honest fellow. I mean, when he makes representations to you in the line of business and so forth, you've never known him to misrepresent things, have you?"

"Well, yes, I have."

"Oh." David raised his eyebrows, tilting his head back. "Many things?"

"Occasional things."

"I see," David said. "But you never misrepresent things to him?"

"Not—" Kasman stumbled. "No," he said.

"Didn't you mention Rosa Parks—when you said you called—you referred to Marsha Coleman-Adebayo as 'EPA's own Rosa Parks,' didn't you?"

"Mr. Shapiro," Kasman said, "I did not say that."

David did an almost pantomimed physical response to Kasman's denial, as if he were recoiling from the shock in slow motion. Then he squinted and fixed Kasman in a direct stare that ended with his turning toward the jury, his eyebrows raised in disbelief.

"No further questions." David walked back to our table, shaking his head ever so slightly, and sat down.

"Gotcha, pretty boy," he said under his breath as he pulled in his chair. David turned to me deliberately and whispered in my ear, "Not exactly the kind of guy you'd want living next door." He leaned back in his seat, looking at Kasman, still shaking his head.

Johnson quickly returned to the podium.

"Mr. Kasman, what did you mean by [saying] you have known Mr. Grand to misrepresent things?"

"In one of his positions," Kasman said, "he was representing the EPA in our embassy in Copenhagen and was doing the staff work there for our—I guess you would call it bilateral relationships with the European Environment Agency, which is located in Copenhagen. He promised to send us briefing materials that never came through. That's an example."

With that, the defense rested.

||||||||||||

After a brief recess, Judge Kollar-Kotelly turned to the jury.

"Members of the jury, we have resolved everything, and we are ready to proceed with the closing arguments."

David was up first.

"Well, it's been some time since I got to address you directly. You may recall that in the opening statements we said that this time would come. What happened to Marsha Coleman-Adebayo? Well, it seems clear that she was doing just fine. She was working at a GS-14 level, wasn't getting any higher—but she was just fine. Nobody was thinking bad of her. They weren't promoting her until she got it in her head to seek what other, what whites—what white men got."

David began a long accounting of the record, asserting that there was ample evidence—serious evidence—that he wanted the jury to consider in the privacy of the jury room: the UN Women's Conference in Beijing; laudatory letters from the First Lady, from Carol Browner, from Madeleine Albright—even Nitze's recognition; a very successful Oakland Conference, where Carol Browner herself singled me out for recognition—but no promotion.

"Not a single document was produced by the government that was critical of her performance—only testimony that, 'Well, you know, she didn't really do it, we did it. It wasn't really her.' No documents to that effect. No documents. 'She was late with assignments. We had to pick up the slack for her.' Where are the documents? Where is the paper trail? You will have to decide whether that really happened that way or it's just a justification being offered to you now. We don't see a document critical of Dr. Coleman-Adebayo until December 13, 1996, when she's on her way out."

David's voice said, Try to be reasonable—come on. You heard the testimony.

Shapiro continued, "Two great programs, national significance, vice presidential-level arrangements. Gore-Chernomyrdin with Russia.

Gore-Mbeki with South Africa. Two very important countries to us. Vice presidential level. The person in charge of Gore-Chernomyrdin, Gary Waxmonsky—not involved in this at all—came on, testified, has no ax to grind. Massive travel. Does his job. Doesn't have to play on a team. Doesn't like teams. Everybody knows it. Yet he's not held to that standard. Outstanding ratings. He fills the job at the 15 level."

He paused a moment to emphasize the importance of the comparator.

"Gore-Mbeki, Marsha Coleman-Adebayo, GS-14. Does a great job, still GS-14. Got to travel to South Africa—once—for the official Gore-Mbeki meeting at the very beginning of her time being the executive director for EPA's Gore-Mbeki program. They don't want to even say that that was her title—but it says so in the official documents. It's very clear in promotion how there's disparate treatment here. Disparate between black women, blacks, women, whites, and males. It's like somebody turned on a light and all the cockroaches scattered."

Shapiro paused over his notes. It was like he was meditating. When he resumed, his voice was softer and more alluring.

"There were heroes here that testified. Heroes. But of all the heroes, there's Inga Barnett. The woman is not in the professional category. She's working her way up, but she told you what it was like under Mr. Cough. Inga Barnett, who told you that Mr. Cough took away her $750 annual award, to give it to a white guy, a GS-14, who was making over $100,000 a year."

David turned from the podium and wholly faced the jury, collecting himself.

"We trust in this country's jury system. You bring to the evidence, collectively and individually, a common sense, and because you weren't involved you don't come choosing sides. The claims here have been clearly delineated. The evidence was also clearly delineated. Marsha Coleman-Adebayo expects only justice here and expects a clear review of all that you've seen and heard and will get a chance to review, both individually and collectively. She asks only that you give her justice by your award. Thank you."

"Ms. Johnson, closing. Why don't you go forward."

"Good morning, Ladies and Gentlemen. At the beginning of this trial you took an oath that you could be fair. You also agreed that you would listen to all the evidence, and at the conclusion of all the evidence you would make a decision. Now, what the judge instructed you was that as a juror you were to make a decision without sympathy or favor. Does it mean you make a decision based on the evidence, not based on what the person's skin color or race or sex is? That you make a decision based on whether they go to church or not, whether they read the Bible or not? But you make your decision based on the evidence."

This was a new Wyneva Johnson. Her posture, tenor, confidence, and likability were quite different from the disheveled, almost bumbling Wyneva of the preceding days.

"You heard Dr. Clarice Gaylord. You saw that she's African American. She told you she's a PhD. She told you that she gave Dr. Coleman-Adebayo an 'exceeds expectation' because that's what she deserved. And when Dr. Coleman-Adebayo complained about it and went to her deputy, she said, 'Don't you dare change that rating.'"

Johnson's eyes were ablaze as she hung Clarice's declaration in the air. The jurors heard.

"Now," Wyneva continued more calmly, "what is Dr. Gaylord's intention to discriminate against her? She's African American. She's female. What evidence was there that she intended to discriminate against Dr. Coleman-Adebayo because of her race, her sex, or her color?"

This new persona was most effective. Several jurors adjusted themselves in their chairs.

"Mr. Nitze says it was his decision, Ladies and Gentlemen, that Coleman-Adebayo be given the chance to be the program leader for South Africa. Who was the person that gave her that opportunity? What was his race? Was he African American, white? Or what was his sex, what's the gender here? A white male here, the same person who Coleman-Adebayo says discriminated against her, gave her an opportunity to be the program person in South Africa. Why did he say he did that? He said that he—while he has some concerns—he believed that she brought certain talents and skills to that job, so he offered her the opportunity to do that.

"What you heard was he said at the beginning, her work on Gore-Mbeki was fine. But then you hear Mr. Nitze say that they were concerned about the logistical work. So, is that discrimination? Is that discrimination when she's praised?"

Again Wyneva paused at the import of the words, her brow furrowed.

"Then you hear from Mr. Nitze that, and the evidence counsel introduced about letters from the South African community that said that they wanted Coleman-Adebayo to come to South Africa, well, whose decision is that to make, Ladies and Gentlemen, in terms of the government to government? Whose decision is it to make that a staff person is to go to a specific country? The government submits to you, and the testimony has been, that that was Mr. Nitze's decision to make. Wasn't that his role to make and not that of Dr. Coleman-Adebayo? So what does Mr. Nitze tell you? He tells you that there came a point in time when he lost confidence in her. He said he lost confidence in Coleman-Adebayo.

"Moreover, Ladies and Gentlemen, the government's evidence has been that with regard to Marsha Coleman-Adebayo, here is a person who was obviously disappointed. Dr. Clarice Gaylord told you she was disappointed, but that is not discrimination. And what the challenge is, and the statute says, that an employer should not discriminate against somebody because of their race or sex or color, but it does not say 'disappointment' in there. And that's what we submit has happened here."

Johnson prowled back and forth behind this idea before continuing. She was confident.

"An employee who is well paid, who is accomplished, who is being praised, who has lost no money, no benefits, has received a promotion, is disappointed that she didn't get an 'outstanding.' The evidence in this case that you've heard from the witnesses, that you will see in the documents, that you are seeing from the documents, indicate that a high-level employee with outstanding educational credentials, a person who was accomplished, was disappointed—not discriminated against."

Wyneva locked eyes with the jurors, nodding, and then thanked them and walked back to her table.

"Thank you," said Judge Kollar-Kotelly. "Mr. Shapiro, rebuttal."

"Thank you." David held his fist to his lips in thought.

"The government says there's no evidence of discrimination. The government says there's no evidence of retaliation. The government says there's no evidence of a failure to reasonably accommodate. You have to ask yourself whether this is so, or if it's just the government doesn't have any explanation for the evidence that there is."

David looked at me with a concerned smile that he carried over to the jury.

"You may recall that all throughout the trial every time you came in or went out, everybody in the well of the court stood. It's a tradition because, you see, you're the judges of the facts. The judge is going to tell you that. You're the exclusive judges of the facts. That's why we have juries. No Senate confirmation necessary for the job. All we ask is that you don't—that you don't unlawfully discriminate."

David held up his finger for emphasis.

"We want you to be discriminating. We want you to look carefully." He lowered his hand. "Senate confirmation confers a lot of power—but it doesn't confer the right to discriminate. You have to ask yourself whether discrimination and retaliation was done here."

David pointed toward me.

"She was driven out of OIA." David stood for a moment pointing. The evidence supporting that, he said, "comes from black people and white people, from disinterested people, and the main question that you must ask yourself is: Who do you believe—the paper trail—or the lack of paper trail? People who have no interest in the outcome of this case, who take risk in some cases to testify—or people who are justifying their own actions?"

He squinted with his eyebrows raised, nodding as he took the jurors in individually.

"Thank you, Your Honor."

Waiting

Everything has limits.

Given enough stress—from heat, pain, worry, cold—the body shuts itself down. But time has no limits. And time is serious. And time adds up. And time is like the distance between a bullet and flesh. And then it is over.

It's the waiting.

So the third day was like the first day was like the fourth day was like the day the Lord rested. Even God takes a day off.

The light in David Shapiro's office had a way of turning everything into everything else after a while, turning faces into portraits into people passing on the street.

With time, a room becomes a chair where Mother lies beyond a pair of swinging doors, dying in fluorescence. It becomes the day I turned inside her at my father's disappearance, becoming time and weight and eternity.

So there was no way for David to know that his questions opened more questions. As there was no way for me to know that Jacob opened wounds and before they had healed they would take Bantu Holomisa. And when he was gone they would come for me.

There was no way to know that the fingers curled around the stems of happy glasses, lifting wine to the end of apartheid, were the same fingers, infected with greed, that had punched names into keyboards that set hurt in motion, and that words we all heard were only spoken. There was no way to know that a man named Jon, out of a sense of right, would take a flight from Chicago to repair a wrong.

When this all began there was no way to know the man, Segun, would be all of the man I most needed.

There was no way to know what it would mean when a small white paper passed from one hand to another and the jury was in.

The Verdict

"David Shapiro here."

I could tell by the sound of David's voice that he was talking to the clerk at the courthouse.

"Yes. Yes. We're on our way." He hung up and yelled to me. "Marsha! Get your bags! The jury's in."

I quickly called Segun to ask him to meet me at the courthouse. I couldn't imagine the reading of the verdict without him. "This is Segun Adebayo. Please leave your name and number at the beep."

How I hate voice messages. "Segun, the jury has come in. Please make your way to the courthouse."

For the past four days, news media trucks with satellite dishes and reporters had been milling around the courthouse. I had wondered what issue was so important that film crews and media were camped out.

David and I arrived at the courthouse within fifteen minutes. We took our seats at the plaintiff's table. I tried to call Segun again. I thought I would absolutely burst—exhausted, excited, terrified, giddy, nervous, all at once. The clerk came in to tell us that the jurors had taken a walk and would be back in a few minutes. My breathing was shallow, and my hands were clammy. I began to hyperventilate. Miscellaneous people started trickling into the courtroom. Where was Segun? I looked around. It seemed that half of the courtroom was full, and I didn't recognize a single person. I reached over to David and asked him who all of these people coming into the court were.

He snickered, "These are all the Department of Justice attorneys and staff who have been working against you for the past five years."

It was shocking.

At that moment, I noticed a chair at the end of the plaintiff's table that I'm sure had been there the entire length of the trial, but it seemed different today. I felt energy beyond detection.

Lillian? Are you here? My heart reached for this spirit. I turned to David to ask him if he saw or felt this same energy.

"All rise. The court is now in session."

I turned in the direction of this spirit. Lillian, this is for you!

Judge Kollar-Kotelly took her seat. "It is my understanding that we have a verdict in this case. I would ask that there be no outburst when the verdict is read. Bailiff, please bring the jury in."

This morning time moved so slowly. Five minutes seemed like forever. Now everything raced. I looked around. No Segun. The jury entered the room. I looked at the three women who sat directly in front of me. They all had slight smiles on their faces, but somehow there was a light that could only be seen when I closed my eyes. At the same time, I noticed that the foreman, the only white man on the jury, had tilted his head ever so slightly toward Wyneva.

Judge Kollar-Kotelly asked the foreman to hand over the verdict sheet to the bailiff. The judge opened the envelope. Her voice rose from the other side of time.

"In the matter of *Marsha Coleman-Adebayo v. Carol M. Browner*, we find for the plaintiff on the basis of race and color discrimination.

"In the matter of *Marsha Coleman-Adebayo v. Carol M. Browner*, we find for the plaintiff on the basis of sexual discrimination.

"In the matter of *Marsha Coleman-Adebayo v. Carol M. Browner*, we find for the plaintiff on the basis of a racially and sexually hostile work environment."

I started crying and hugging David. I was crying so loudly that I barely heard the last finding.

"We find for the defense on the basis of handicap discrimination."

I looked at David. "Kachen kachang," he said.

"What is 'kachen kachang'?" I said through my tears.

"Money, my dear. Money."

Ah, David.

I looked over at Wyneva's table. She and her colleagues were shaking their heads and starting to pack up their folders and books.

I mouthed what was in my heart to the jury: thank you.

Segun walked into the courtroom, minutes after the jury verdict. He sat in his usual seat. He didn't know why I was crying, if these were tears of joy or heartbreak. I turned to him and mouthed, We won! He closed his eyes and folded his hands in prayer. I saw tears roll down his face. We had won.

After the judge dismissed the jury "with the thanks of the people of the District of Columbia for your service," David's associate came and handed him a note. "Marsha, you need to dry your eyes and put some lipstick on. The press is outside, and they would like an interview."

"Aren't you coming?" I asked David.

"Nope, I don't do the press thing. My stage is in the courtroom."

I was on my way to the ladies room to clean up my face. I thought Segun was going to hug me. Instead, he said, "Turn around."

"Why?"

"Stop asking so many questions! Just turn around."

I felt the cool tickle of a light chain on my neck. "So that's where you were! Out shopping for jewelry when I was calling!"

Segun hung a delicate gold necklace with a cross pendant around my neck.

"Happy Birthday, Marsh!"

I had forgotten it was my birthday.

All of the major networks were there.

What a difference a jury verdict makes—one minute I was a pariah, the next a phenom. There were reports of the victory on the local channels. When the news made its way to EPA, laughter, applause, and joy burst through the gray halls.

I started my statement to the press by thanking Segun and my family for their vigilance and support. I thanked my God for giving me the power and courage to wage the battle. I hoped, I said, that my victory would send an unequivocal message about the importance of fighting corruption within the federal government and resisting intimidation. And for the first time I spoke openly about vanadium victims in Brits, South Africa.

"Why do you think a woman administrator, Carol Browner, would have put you through this?" "Isn't she sympathetic to discrimination?"

"What does it mean that you've won this victory?" "Will other federal employees now feel free to speak out about corruption?" "What are your next steps?"

I called upon Congress to hold hearings to investigate what had happened to me and others; it was time for a thorough investigation of the crimes in Brits, South Africa, and the abuse within the federal government.

A familiar face was standing slightly off to the side of the media. I recognized her face but couldn't remember her name.

"Hi, Marsha. Congratulations! My name is Beth Sokul. I'm the senior counsel on the House Committee on Science. My boss, Chairman F. James Sensenbrenner, would like to meet you."

She started to walk away, but, thinking better of it, she turned her head slightly with a mischievous smile. "Did EPA really give you 120 days to name every toxin in the human body?"

Can You Hear Me?

"'I was called "uppity," an "honorary white man," and a host of other derogatory names, as well as being denied promotions,' she said yesterday. 'There is a culture of intimidation and intolerance at the EPA.' Can you believe it, Segun?"

I was reading him the story in the *Washington Post* with the headline, "EPA ordered to pay $600,000 in bias suit: woman alleged racial, gender discrimination at agency's highest levels."

"'Marsha Lynne Coleman-Adebayo, 47, was sent from the agency's Office of International Activities and into a domestic position in 1997 after years of what she said was racial and sexual harassment. Coleman-Adebayo, a senior official and African affairs specialist, won the suit after a two-week trial and nearly three days of deliberations in U.S. District Court.'"[1]

It was beginning to set in. I usually read the *Post* about what was happening in other people's lives.

I said, "After all that, Segun, listen to what the agency had to say about the finding against me. 'The suit named EPA administrator Carol M. Browner as the defendant. The EPA released a statement that indicated that the agency may appeal the verdict.' And this is the part that really gets my goat: 'We're disappointed, but this is obviously a mixed decision,' the statement read. 'The agency defended itself vigorously against these charges. We will be reviewing further options available to us along with the U.S. Attorney's Office.'"

I put the paper down and looked at Segun.

"After four years, after my personally pleading to her directly, after letters from my attorney imploring her to avoid this, and now—even after a verdict against her—she still can't see past her own nose and career to realize that people are suffering at EPA and possibly dying in South Africa."

So this would be the facelift racism presented to the twenty-first century. There might not be anyone standing in the doorway at OIA to block my return to work after the victory in the courts; no one would make inflammatory comments to an obliging press. Instead there would be the studied, direct-sounding language of the sort that gets generated from think tanks, announcements boasting statistical improvements, a catalogue of positions filled, and the disbelief that anyone could make such claims in this day and age. Given the resources available to the agency, given the voice of the jury, given the fact that the judge had allowed the highest award by statute to stand, one might have expected a degree of contrition from Browner. Instead, here was the defiant EPA administrator along with Attorney General Janet Reno—both beneficiaries of the courage displayed by demonstrators at Selma, Birmingham, and the Petus Bridge blood bath—two Southern white women vowing to focus the power of the US government and continue the fight against me. The more things change, the more they stay the same.

Had Browner any curiosity in discovering who among her senior managers had been implicated in the illegal practices, there were twelve volumes of sworn court transcripts naming names and dates. Had there been any consideration that perhaps racial discrimination and retaliation were flourishing inside the agency and adversely affecting the lives of the employees, Browner could have listened to the charges, honored the findings, and set an example by calling out all those implicated in discrimination and retaliation. She could have sent a loud message throughout the agency by firing the guilty. Instead, she announced her disappointment with the verdict and mulled her options. Everything looked worse in black and white. If this *Post* article was any indication, the plight of the vanadium victims wasn't even being mulled.

After my verdict and fully armed with a jury mandate from common people, Browner had a golden opportunity to take a stand and announce that enough was enough. She could have declared, It may always have been this way in the past, but this is my administration, and I will not have it. It was the perfect teachable moment if ever there was one.

But since the jury verdict was not to her satisfaction, she hired two law firms, Covington and Burling, and Holland and Knight, to provide the real verdict, the best whitewash that taxpayer money could buy. Nothing but the best for her "good people." She would later testify under oath about EPA employees, "They are good people. Good people." Having PR wonks from the priciest law firms in Washington conduct a "study" of whether retaliation and discrimination existed in EPA was how the Browner administration reacted to the verdict.

On January 19, 2001, Carol Browner issued a memorandum to all EPA employees titled, "Report on Diversity and Fairness in the EPA Workplace." This was a follow-up to a memo Browner had written the previous September after the Freedom Plaza demonstration. "Thousands of staff members participated in listening sessions around the agency," and "a highly respected Wash., DC firm" would:

> undertake an independent review of the Office of International Activities (OIA) at EPA. This review follows a jury verdict by the US District Court for the District of Columbia in August that found that an EPA employee in OIA had been discriminated against based on race, color and gender. The judge recently issued a final ruling in favor of the employee on claims of discrimination and hostile work environment.[2]

While Browner went to great lengths to distribute the Holland and Knight report electronically for all to see, the same thoroughness was not lavished on a rebuttal of the report that was prepared by the president of National Treasury Employees Union (NTEU) Chapter 280, Dwight Welch:

> In the Appendix (page A-2) of the Holland and Knight Report (HKR), they report that the Administrator claims to be "completely blindsided by the Adebayo case." A truer description would be that Ms. Browner had ignored Dr. Adebayo, the Unions, and other critics of the discrimination problem at EPA.[3]

Browner also announced the creation of a new Office of Fairness and Opportunity that would operate under her supervision. The obvious solution was to fire those implicated by the verdict. Instead, Browner sought PR cover for herself, at taxpayer expense, under the guise of proactive concern for fairness and opportunity.

⸻

There was deep thumping through the speaker.

"Can you hear me?"

Leroy Warren tapped on the microphone we had set up directly across from EPA headquarters on Pennsylvania Avenue in Freedom Plaza, the speakers facing the building directly under Administrator Browner's window. An array of federal workers held signs: END RACISM AT EPA; WHISTLEBLOWERS ARE NOT CRIMINALS; BROWNER MUST GO; INVESTIGATE VANADIUM POISONING; and END DISCRIMINATION AT EPA.

The NAACP along with EPA unions and civil rights groups had decided to organize a demonstration in celebration of my court victory as well as to send a message to Carol Browner and Vice President Gore that abuse would no longer be tolerated inside of EPA. Warren had written numerous letters to Vice President Gore, asking him to rein in Browner. He never received a response. Browner had served as Gore's Senate chief of staff, and it was common knowledge that his political clout had been behind her selection as EPA administrator.

"If the press is ready, we will begin."

A friend had made professional posters and printed leaflets announcing the demonstration. Ten years later I still dare not name this friend or even that friend's gender because retaliation inside the federal government has no statute of limitations. This was mid-August, a time of year so notorious in Washington, DC, for its heat and choking humidity that Congress goes home and the president goes on vacation to escape the withering temperatures. Still, my sign-maker friend met me at a prearranged location dressed in a long trench coat, wearing dark sunglasses and gloves, petrified of being identified and fingered. I imagined the administrator across the street, eying our assemblage like a lineup, her long, accusing finger pointing: That one, the one standing to the left, the woman in the brown dress . . . You know what? They're all guilty—except for the man with the sign on the right. He's our guy. He's down there taking names.

The NAACP was eager to endorse the successful outcome of the trial. Leroy, as chairman of the NAACP Federal Sector Task Force and a member of its national board of directors, was leading the demonstration, which the Environmental Protection Agency Victims Against Racism and Discrimination (EPAVARD) had organized. What better place than in Freedom Plaza, right in front of EPA headquarters? One by one, we stood at the podium and stated the case.

"The jury has now stamped the word *guilty* on the doors of the management of the OIA and EPA. Guilty for practicing racism. Guilty for practicing sexism. Guilty for creating a hostile work environment," I said. "EPA is the house that [Vice President] Gore built—he should clean it up! We call upon Congress to convene hearings on civil rights violations. . . . The jury verdict has no teeth unless the agency holds these people accountable and dismisses them immediately from federal service.

"In closing, Ms. Browner, instead of curling up in a fetal position, you should accept the responsibility, dump the human rights violators, and create a culture here at EPA that's inclusive, that has justice at its center and equity at its core."

Anita Nickens had been standing behind me and at a slight angle. While Leroy introduced her, I noticed that Anita was trembling. I had not known her long, having met her at an EPAVARD meeting. Anita's was another story that had been brought to Browner's attention but ignored. Anita had hand delivered a letter about it to Browner's office.

At the first National Tribal Environmental Council on Indian lands, in Cherokee, North Carolina, Ms. Anita Nickens, a mother of two and a highly decorated EPA employee, was the new, upwardly mobile appointee assigned to work with a nonsupervisory GS-14 on the conference.

"I was the point of contact for the participants attending the conference from the agency." Her voice and hands were shaking so much I was afraid she would come apart.

During the conference, Anita had received a call from her female manager, requesting that she return to the lodge where she and five white female EPA employees were staying. The supervisor's direct order was that upon her return to the lodge, she was to clean the toilet Administrator Carol Browner would use.

"I told the manager I would not do it," she continued, but, fearing retaliation for not following orders, she did it, reasoning she would file a complaint on her return to Washington.

When she returned to the lodge, she cleaned the bathroom, hauling away garbage, including beer cans and wine bottles, and cleaning the toilet.

With her voice breaking and hands trembling, Anita struggled to continue.

"Later that evening, just before the closing ceremony, the manager told several conference attendees that I had cleaned the toilet for the administrator 'because the bitch could not use the toilet behind someone else.'"

Nickens slipped out of the rear door at the conference, she said, "because I did not want anyone to see my face. I was so embarrassed and blamed myself for giving in to my manager's request that I felt like a scorned woman. I locked myself in the room and cried."[4]

Linda Plummer was next. Linda was an attractive woman, bright and well spoken, a former federal employee who simply had not been able to tolerate the environment inside the government. She was outspoken and a known political quantity in Washington, DC, holding the position of president of the Montgomery County NAACP. Her presence at the rally sent a strong signal to both Browner and official Washington that the jury verdict would not be ignored.

EPA attorney Steve Spiegel spoke about anti-Semitism in the agency. Dwight Welch told stories of people he represented as president of the NTEU and how many had been forced to resign or were fired as a result of blowing the whistle. Selwyn Cox, cofounder of EPAVARD, called for the initiation of a class action suit against the EPA. LaShanda Halloway, an attorney, discussed her demise once the agency realized that she would not remain silent in the face of corrupt practices. Rawle King, president of Blacks in Government, spoke on behalf of thousands of federal employees suffering under the weight of discrimination and retaliation for speaking out against illegal behavior. Dana Hawkins flew in from Atlanta, Georgia, to represent her coworkers in the South. Ron Harris, a union leader at EPA Chicago, relayed the stories of dozens of employees fired after refusing to carry out illegal orders. Theresa Fleming-Blue told her moving story of becoming ill because of the stress at the EPA.

The rally ended with Rev. Sterling King, my pastor, giving the benediction. I later found out that EPA employees from North Carolina, Pennsylvania, and Texas had flown to Washington in hopes of speaking at the rally. The next morning, the *Washington Post*'s federal page featured a photo of Nickens and me embracing at the demonstration, with Leroy Warren looking on. The article's headline read, "RAMPANT BIAS AT EPA IS ALLEGED."[5]

|||||||||||||

I wrote a *New York Times* editorial titled, "Toward a Fair Federal Workplace" that not only discussed the conditions inside the federal government but also detailed the plight of vanadium workers.[6] Newspapers around the country featured articles on the singular victory that had eluded so many. The attention David Shapiro had predicted was materializing. Calls came in from *Good Housekeeping*, who named me their woman of the year[7]; during the award ceremony, actor Danny Glover appeared on video, congratulating me on my victory and announcing he would produce a movie about my experience; the National Treasury Employees Union's *Inside the Fishbowl*, a newsletter for EPA union employees edited by Dwight Welch, sent monthly shockwaves throughout the agency[8]; *Government Executive* magazine published over thirty articles on our burgeoning movement; and prominent Washington, DC, radio host Joe Madison asked me for a series of interviews. His audience was primarily federal employees. The conditions inside the EPA were finally being publicly discussed.

And then I received one call that stood out. It was midmorning when my office phone rang. "This is Dr. Coleman-Adebayo."

The silence was somehow stuttered. I couldn't tell what I was hearing until I realized that the person was crying.

"Are you all right?" I asked.

"I'm sorry, Dr. Adebayo. I just had to call and tell you what you have done for me." The woman's voice was weak as she spoke between bursts of blowing her nose. "I had written my resignation letter last night before I went to bed. I sat in my kitchen this morning, looking at my children, wondering how I was going to take care of them without a job, but I just couldn't take any more. Then the Lord told me to turn on my television, and there you were, talking about how the government discriminates—and you beat them. I could not believe my eyes. And I said to myself, if she can do it—I can do it. I took my resignation letter and tore it up."

She was laughing and crying and snuffling her nose.

"I just wanted to say thank you. If you can do it, I can do it."

Behind Closed Doors: The Browner-NAACP Meeting

"Marsha, she—I mean, Carol Browner—called the NAACP, and it seems that she wants to talk."

It took me a minute to recognize the gravelly baritone of Leroy Warren.

"Leroy, what are you talking about? In about two weeks we testify before Congress." I was convinced Leroy had confused a request from Browner with something else. That Browner would have contacted the NAACP didn't make sense.

"It seems that she would like to meet with us before the congressional hearings. Maybe she's nervous about what I will say, or maybe she wants the NAACP to pressure you to shut up. I don't know. To be honest," Leroy continued, "Browner didn't really want you to be a part of the meeting, but I told Hilary Shelton that I didn't play that way. If you were not invited to the meeting, I wasn't going."

Hilary Shelton was director of the NAACP Washington bureau and senior vice president for advocacy and policy. But among Washington insiders, titles were only one way to describe people, and Hilary was a Washington insider's insider. Tall and handsome, Hilary is considered the face of the NAACP in legislative circles and has been part of Washington's political royalty for decades.

High-profile representation at the meeting was a strong indication that the NAACP understood the historic significance of my court victory. It assigned its chief legislative and political insider to handle the situation. Shelton had worked with the last four presidents. His gatekeeper fingerprints were affixed to most, if not all, important pieces of civil rights legislation. Not unimportantly, he was the son-in-law of Ambassador Andrew Young, an heir to the Martin Luther King Jr. legacy. That alone made Hilary's presence significant. Add to this the widely held belief that the NAACP was a division of the Democratic Party, and the incentive for Browner's seeking African American allies was clear. Knowing that Republicans were about to publicly grill her as to why a jury—and OSHA—had condemned EPA's hostile culture, Browner needed some cover, and she needed it fast.

The people who filed into the room before her would almost have seemed comical if the effects of their positions in power had not been so devastating to those beneath them. Browner's deputy chief of staff, Ray Spears, was a slight man who seemed uncomfortable in his own skin. He kept twisting his neck from side to side—the type of stereotypic mannerisms that have become comic relief in mafioso impressions. Spears sat at the table, neither looking at the NAACP representatives nor engaging me in any way. He had a faraway stare, eyes animated as marbles—glassy, with no light looking out. Rafael DeLeon, an Afro-Latino protege of Spears took his seat after acknowledging his role model.

Next came Ann Goode, the woman who had recruited me into the EPA. I had met Ann, it seemed, ages ago, when we had both marched as antiapartheid demonstrators outside of the South African Embassy. She walked in, greeting my NAACP compatriots and me.

"How are your children, Marsha?" I couldn't believe Ann was greeting me as if nothing had happened. In her role as director of the Office of Civil Rights, she could have stopped the madness at any time before the trial.

"My children are fine," I said with sarcasm, "considering that they have been dragged through the mud for the past four years." God! I thought. She is still trying to act as though she has some connection to the "little people" inside the agency!

She seemed surprised that I did not chirp a perfunctory "fine." As our eyes met for an instant, I tried to reconcile this person with the woman I had thought I knew from the marches.

Two or three more of Browner's lieutenants marched into the room and sat stone-faced at the table.

Ira Patterson, who preferred to be called simply "Patterson," was Leroy Warren's right-hand man. He walked in and sat on our side of the table. A little later, as Carol Browner entered, everyone rose, offering her their hands. Leroy Warren bent toward me. "You should stand up," he whispered. "Browner is in the room."

I looked up at Leroy. How many times had I tried to get her to look at the tragedies occurring inside her own agency? How many letters had she ignored about the deaths of vanadium victims?

"I have no intention of standing for a person I do not respect."

Carol made her way to where I was sitting and offered her hand to me. "Dr. Coleman-Adebayo."

"Administrator Browner."

We had never addressed each other using formal titles before—it had always been "Carol" or "Marsha."

The lines had been drawn.

||||||||||||

Browner started the meeting by discussing the upcoming October 4 congressional hearing and acknowledging that she had heard there were problems at the agency. She never looked at me. After holding forth for half an hour on how much she admired Dr. King, a somewhat less inspired reprise of her Martin Luther King Day speech, Leroy and Patterson became agitated.

"Ms. Browner, we have sat here for almost twenty minutes now, and you have not mentioned that Dr. Coleman-Adebayo recently won her case against you and your agency on the grounds of race and sex discrimination and a racially and sexually hostile work environment."

A hush fell over the room.

Leroy continued. "I personally wrote to you on numerous occasions, asking you to meet with me, and you couldn't find the time. You knew that there was a problem with your agency. So I find your last-minute conversion unbelievable."

Patterson picked up where Leroy had left off.

"Ms. Browner, we have sat here for nearly a half an hour, and you have not mentioned one time what you intend to do to correct this situation." He looked around for emphasis. He was mad as hell. "Do we have the word *fools* written on our foreheads?"

Browner's face tightened. She started taking deep breaths and looking toward her African American staffers.

"We are aware of Dr. Coleman-Adebayo's court case," said Ann Goode. "As director of the Office of Civil Rights, I am working hard to correct this situation."

"Oh, tell that to someone else!" Leroy shouted. "I stopped by your office before coming to this meeting. You were supposed to prominently display the Coleman-Adebayo court case on your bulletin board so that EPA employees would be informed about the court's decision on discrimination, Ms. Goode. I couldn't find it. Could you tell me where it is displayed?"

"Well, Mr. Warren," Ann stumbled. She looked down, embarrassed to be called on the carpet in front of Browner. "It's not up yet, but—"

"Again, I say, save it," Leroy fumed. "Nothing has happened since the court ruled to show us that you or any of your house brothers and sisters are taking the court ruling seriously!"

Patterson looked directly at Browner. "I know you called us here because the Democratic Party believes that it controls the NAACP. No one controls me or Leroy."

Browner asked Ray Spears to offer some ideas. Spears continued along the same line as Ann Goode, arguing that the environment at EPA was not as bad as the court decision indicated. Nevertheless, he stressed, the agency was committed to trying to improve the working conditions for minorities and women.

Leroy and Patterson sat looking at Spears, waiting for him to finish. Leroy took the lead.

"Ms. Browner, I know you're from the South, so you must know that on the plantation, you have two kinds of black folks: the house folks, the blacks who worked in the kitchens and their job was to serve the master; and the field folks, who were catching hell every day and were trying to run away. We have sat here and listened to two of your house Negroes—and we are fed up! Nothing that you or your house Negroes have said has convinced us that you're serious about doing anything to address the serious racism and sexism you have here at EPA." Leroy sat back and shook his head. "Now I'm convinced that *you're* the problem."

Hilary tried to salvage the meeting. "I'm sure Ms. Browner will try her best to come up with something to alleviate this situation," he said, looking at Leroy. "But Carol," he added turning to Browner, "we need to see something, and we need to see it soon."

I leaned forward. "Administrator Browner, everyone here who is sitting on your side of the room played a role in the discrimination and retaliation I experienced. Everyone you have brought to the table is guilty of perpetuating a system of dehumanizing oppression at the EPA that has not allowed people to do their jobs if they disagree with their supervisors or you. This agency is run like an eighteenth-century plantation, with black overseers and white managers—whose job is to break anyone who is not compliant. How can a scientific agency operate like this?

"There are people in South Africa who are dying from the effects of vanadium exposure! All I wanted was to do my job and bring this to the attention of the agency. You refused to speak to me, and when my attorney, NAACP, and others tried to intervene, they were shut down. The only thing they received was a form letter saying that you would not meet with us.

"I agree with my NAACP colleagues. Nothing is being achieved by this closed-door meeting. If my court victory is to be translated into meaningful change, the only way that will come about is through appealing to the people of this country to pressure Congress to hold you and your managers accountable for the corruption at this agency."

Ms. Browner looked down and said, "Well, I suppose we will meet at the hearing."

Leroy, Patterson, Hilary, and I looked at one another, nodding our agreement.

The meeting was over.

Congressional Hearings: Intolerance at EPA

The [NAACP] Task Force . . . will conduct Protest Demonstrations at EPA, to show our Strong displeasure with Ms. Browner's disgraceful racist regime. . . . We desperately ask for your personal intervention.
　　　　　—Letter to Vice President Al Gore from Leroy Warren Jr.

It is dark, and I don't want this to be happening. Some pull, like an undertow, is sweeping me away from where I want to be, snuggled and warm under a layer of down. I am aware of my arm lifting and moving, but it is so much better over here. I drift back toward where I was. A day without weather. My back pressed against Segun. Yes. Again my arm is moving, this time my hand finding a cold, solid object. There is a rattling sound. What? What do you want?

—Marsha? Marsha!

This is my mother, but it is not my mother's voice.

—Marsha, get up!

I look at the clock. "Hello? Who is this?"

"Marsha, its Theresa Fleming-Blue. Are you up?" Theresa said in her deep, throaty voice, tinged with southern rhythm and the authority that comes from years in the pulpit of a Baptist church.

"Theresa, it's six o'clock! What . . . why are you calling me at six o'clock in the morning?"

"This is the day the Lord has made, Marsha. This is the day we've all been waiting for."

Segun is a light sleeper and usually cannot get back to sleep once he is roused by phone calls or any interruption. I understood that Theresa must have had an urgent need to talk to me to be calling so early, but how could I avoid waking up Segun? My hushed voice was beginning to have an effect. Segun drew a deep breath and moaned.

"Theresa," I whispered into the phone. "I have to use another phone so I don't wake up Segun. Hang on, I'll be right back."

I eased out of bed and out of the room and at first thought to use the phone in the kitchen, but Sade's room was close enough to be too close, and Sina's room was adjacent to that. So I found myself scurrying down the stairs to the basement office, fumbling with my bathrobe tie as I wiped the sleep from my eyes.

"Theresa? OK, I just picked up the basement phone. Let me go back upstairs and hang up the phone next to my bed so I don't wake up Segun, OK?"

As I climbed the stairs I began to realize what day it was, and I was suddenly wide awake despite having spent half the night poring over my statement for whatever small irregularities the legal beagles at the agency could sniff out and use to dismiss the whole thing. That thought in itself got my breathing hurried, to say nothing of the stairs I was climbing. I slipped back into the bedroom and placed one end of the receiver into the cradle first, lowering the other end as I bit my lip and watched to see if it would wake my husband. He had stayed up with me late the previous night in what had become a tag team of finding something wrong with the document, pointing it out, panicking, working out a solution together, and then handing it back to the other to wait for the next Achilles's heel to jump out of the pages. Finally, he had given up, realizing that the only useful purpose we were serving was ensuring that we'd both wake up tired in the morning.

"Marsh," he had said, "you can torture yourself for as long as you like, but I fear these endless revisions are only going to make the finished product worse." He had turned to start toward our bedroom and then stopped, lowering his head and turning it to one side as if thinking. Then he had come back and held me, kissing me on the cheek.

"I won't try to convince you to come to bed, sweetheart," he had said. "But you have done all you can do."

"I know, sweetie, I know." I had kissed him back and felt relieved to relax into his powerful grip, to reach my arms around him as tightly as I could, as I held the statement next to our faces as if to shield us from a bright light.

"Thank you, sweetie, for everything you do." I had squeezed him, closing my eyes. "Go to bed. I won't be long."

Now he was so still he seemed not to be breathing, and I had to fight the urge to climb in beside him and sleep for three days. I slipped back out of the room and bounced quickly down the stairs where I could talk in a normal voice for the first time.

"Theresa? Are you there?" I was out of breath. "OK, now what are you talking about? Why are you calling me?"

"Because you're testifying today, Marsha. And we're all going to be there with you. We've all been praying and fasting, asking Jesus to watch over you. Food has not touched these lips in two days, Marsha. Two days so Jesus will know that I'm clean, that I'm right in his ways, and that I'm worthy of his name."

"But the hearing isn't until eleven o'clock!"

"That's why I'm calling you now, Marsha. I'm calling you to the Lord Jesus. Marsha, let's pray. Let's pray that the Lord will be with you today. Will you get on your knees with me now? Do that with me, Marsha. Will you get on your knees and pray Jesus to be with you, and in being with you he will be with all of us who will be standing beside you today? Pray with me, Marsha. Pray with me."

When I hung up the phone, it was still only 6:17. "Jesus!"

I had set the alarm for 6:30 thinking that would give me ample time to review my statement, call my attorney, shower, and get into battle mode. A lot of people were putting their hope and confidence in me. And while I knew they were suffering, and I had seen the conditions where they worked, I was not sure I could articulate my own experience and pain. As I mounted the stairs, the day began to stretch before me like a long corridor in a building I had never before seen.

As I entered the kitchen I could see the doorways to the rooms where Sade and Sina were sleeping. I would make them toast and pour them juice that would be waiting for them in clear, sparkling glasses. I would make Segun his favorite eggs. But right then I had a hollow no food could satisfy. I almost felt sick. So, while there was much to do, children to wash and feed and dress, and the hour I had set to get up and get started was almost there, still, I entered our bedroom filled with the heavy breathing of my husband and the smell of a man asleep. And that was what I wanted. I slid into the bed like water, pulling myself close to his warmth, to his skin. We sidled together like one who pulls on a coat and is still getting used to it then nestled together and lay still.

Segun, lax and heavy on the other side of sleep. Me, leaving Theresa's words in the space outside this room, finding the smell of a man's shoulders and neck, this man who was with me even when I would have thought he'd have turned away, this man who had stayed and helped and encouraged. The tingle of his hair against my nose, the warmth of his skin, the rise and fall of his deep breathing, was all there was at that moment.

iiiiiiiiiiii

The ride to the Rayburn House Office Building was like the ride to anything with everything at stake—thirty-five minutes of lights that would not stay green, traffic that would not unsnarl, and morons who drove like they had gotten their licenses out of bubble gum machines. After whisking Sade to Bannockburn Elementary School, Sina, Segun, and I were caught in the time warp between where we really wanted and needed to be—and this. I made some gesture toward interest in Sina's well-being in the backseat but realized that Pac-Man was consuming him from inside a little device that made annoying, repetitive noises.

So I fell back once more into the minutiae of the words on the pages I had been poring over for days. Segun maneuvered the car through the traffic like some disembodied priest, holding forth on the weight of the moment.

"Sina, these are the forces, the very same forces, that thought they could break Dr. King," Segun continued, refusing to concede that Pac-Man would win the attention battle. "These are the powers Gandhi fought in South Africa and then in India. You must always remember this."

Now conceding that Pac-Man had won the battle between man and son, Segun drew on a technique that had worked for thousands of years in traditional societies. He called Sina by his entire name for emphasis and to signal that he would not be defeated by the little green monsters in a child's toy.

"Olusina," he said, with manly emphasis and resonance. His voice indicated there would now be consequences for not listening. "You must always remember what your mother did on this day. Whether her message is received with gratitude or scorn, whether it leads to victory or defeat." He looked in the mirror at our son. "And one day this burden may fall to you."

Finally we found a parking spot several blocks beyond ideal and began thrusting the things we needed together in bunches that we hung over our shoulders and forearms. Sina frantically tried to gobble the last of the blue meanies as he got out of the car.

The three of us walked briskly toward Rayburn. I reached to take Sina's hand, and he took mine, knowing he had no choice. I looked at my watch, realized there was still plenty of time, and slackened the pace.

For the first time I was aware of the beautiful weather, the cool, sharp autumn air, and the clean shadows the sun cast on buildings and below trees. There was something close to music in the center of me, which slowed everything. This moment, trivial as it seemed, was what it would take. This was the place. This, the eternal. I resolved to let the events that were about to unfold come.

It was a short ride from the basement to the floor where the Science Committee room was, but the elevator's lift was like the force that had been carrying the process along apart from me. The small cubicle being lifted in the bowels of Rayburn carried the last refuge we would have before the very public spectacle of the hearing room. I was entering a place that seemed without sound—or where sound happened somewhere apart from me, our footsteps almost clattering away from where we were going.

ıııııııııııı

"Do you think Carol Browner will ride up in an elevator or on her broom?"

"Sina!" I protested, but I had to laugh. Before I could say anything more, the doors slid open to the hall on the first floor. Almost simultaneously the elevator next to us opened, and Carol Browner and her entourage burst forward, Browner first, followed by Ray Spears, Rafael

DeLeon, Romulo Diaz, Dr. Timothy Fields, and a trail of faithful agency lawyers. I stopped dead still as if hit by a blast, taking Segun's arm.

"Let's wait. Let them get down the hall. I don't want to walk in together."

Browner's group moved like a motorcade, very tight, crisp, official, the sound of her heels striking the marble floor like a woodpecker, her bobbed hair bouncing above her straight back and shoulders. She acknowledged no one in the hall, as if leading her own parade, all eyes to the front. As they swept away from us, I relaxed my grip on Segun's arm and turned toward Sina. "That's her."

Sina had already figured this out. "Why do they act so mean?" His face wrinkled in disgust.

I squeezed his fingers in mine and gave him a slight smile. "Come on. We can go now."

We started down the hall, and it was surprising how many people there were, waiting in a line that stretched down both walls, two abreast. Rayburn is an enormous structure, the walls very long, but the lines stretched to the end of the corridor, disappearing around the corner. Most in line were African Americans and other people of color, union members, environmentalists, and progressive whites. Many were women. As we walked along I began to realize I knew some of them and gave a few a nod or a smile. Most, however, I had never seen before.

"Go get 'em, Marsha!" someone called out to my left.

"You go, girl!"

I tried to suppress a smile, as it was a bit embarrassing.

"God bless you, Marsha!" sounded through the hall. Then someone started to clap. And then others. And still more, until it built into applause. I could feel my throat tightening, my eyes welling with tears.

Sina leaned toward me and spoke in a low voice. "Who are all these people, Mom? Do you know them all?"

I smiled at him and shook my head. "No, Sina. I know some of them"—I looked back toward the lines—"but these are the people it's all about."

Some of those gathered stepped forward as we passed and touched me on the arm or shoulder. Some said nothing but offered knowing nods of encouragement. Others added a personal touch: "I love you, Marsha," or "God bless you." Still others handed me small pieces of paper they had folded carefully and pressed them into my hand. "Tell them my story, Marsha. I've been waiting for this for years." This continued all the way to the Science Committee room, where reporters and cameras and video crews had already assembled. The flashes started popping immediately. The video cameramen squinted behind their eyepieces like snipers.

Browner's crew had assembled itself to the side of the witness table and was huddled together like a team around the coach, taking last-minute instructions. Browner's face was taut, her head moving emphatically as she talked, the veins in her neck bulging. We both went to some length to avoid eye contact as I approached the witness table. I realized, as her team broke the huddle and took their seats beside her at the table and behind it, that considerable thought had gone into her stage management of this event.

Timothy Fields, an African American who was highly placed in the EPA as the assistant administrator for Superfund sites, sat to Browner's right. He was fair skinned, with a kindly, open-faced, avuncular nice-guy bearing, the man you'd want to sit next to at a baseball game.

Directly behind her sat Ray Spears, deputy chief of staff. He was the consummate go-to guy when management needed to silence a whistle-blower, "troublemaker," or employee who refused to look the other way. He could run with a Democrat or a Republican. It wasn't in his constitution to ask questions. To his right was Ann Goode, the director of the Office of Civil Rights. Ann and Ray had both attended the closed-door meeting earlier with Browner and the NAACP.

In the next row back was Rafael DeLeon, director of the Office of Human Resources, a brown-skinned Afro-Latino man. He was adept at blending in with the background and nodding yes to whatever the official line was. Rafael liked to recall that he hailed from New York, from an immigrant, working-class background. He had learned the rules of the agency and knew that in the absence of a merit system, promotions and advancement were earned on the bureaucratic battlefield.

And then there was Carol Browner, headstrong, confident, who had scoffed at all pleas for assistance; ignored those coming from community groups; committed significant agency resources to attorneys, court fees, man-hours, and energy; and now found herself called on the carpet by a House oversight committee. It was doubtful that she or any in her entourage had ever doubted the agency would prevail in court. And why would they? The government always prevailed in court, considering the obscenely disproportionate resources at its disposal as compared to those of the average employee.

IIIIIIIIIIIIII

The previous afternoon I had received a phone call from EPA. Someone was whispering into the phone. "Administrator Browner is compiling a large chart that she's going to present tomorrow showing how great things are for us here at EPA—be prepared—I have to hang up now."

"Wait!" I called into the phone. "What is your name, and what is going to be on the chart?"

Silence. Then, "I'm sorry, I can't tell you anymore. I've already said more than I should. Good luck. I have to go now."

IIIIIIIIIIIIII

Two people were testifying with me: Leroy Warren, with whom I'd worked closely, and Ron Harris, whom I really didn't know. Ron was the chief union steward for the American Federation of Government Employees. Leroy was retired from federal service and had rallied the troops on more than one occasion once we had decided it was time to take the message into the streets.

Leroy had written several letters on my behalf directly to Ms. Browner, asking to meet with her to avoid open confrontation. He had proved himself a wily strategist.

"She doesn't even acknowledge my letters," he had said in exasperation after three letters he had sent directly to Browner vanished into the EPA black hole. "At least this way," he said with a grin, looking around the hearing room, "we'll know for certain that she's getting our message verbatim."

In the front of the room the committee members began coming in with their staffs, exchanging pleasantries. Most of them seemed relaxed—they knew they were on display and on camera. Maybe they were a little too relaxed, a little too glad to see their colleagues. It was a practiced routine, and some were better at it than others. Chairman F. James Sensenbrenner was not at home in this performance. He looked serious, somewhat out of breath, and almost puffed as he made his way to his seat, carrying a heavy bundle of papers and notebooks. This was only my second time seeing many of the members; the first time had been over a year before when the Science Committee had convened a bipartisan hearing to listen to witnesses' allegations of discrimination and retaliation at the agency.

For the most part, they were strangers to me, although I had met on several occasions with the chairman's office and once with Sensenbrenner himself. When we had last spoken he had told me, "You come back when you've got something. I'm not going to take on the other party's president and his EPA administrator based on the complaints of one lonely policy analyst—or even the testimony of a bunch of folks from the EPA. It'll be he said, she said, and I'm not going to get laughed out of town on that with you. If you come back with a verdict in your favor, that's different. That's no longer allegations anymore—that's findings. You come back to me with a jury's finding, and I'll go to the wall with you."

True to his word, with the verdict the chairman had put the wheels in motion for today's hearing. By Washington standards it had moved at light speed.

Sensenbrenner had been livid when he heard that EPA, in another act of retaliation, had tasked me with naming every toxin in the human body and had assigned a deadline for completing this of 120 days. Sensenbrenner knew the playbook as well as anyone. This was a simple case of an agency out of control, American public be damned. If they had to be placed at risk to retaliate against one "uppity" woman, so be it. It was no accident that the hearing was labeled "Intolerance at EPA: Harming People, Harming Science?"[2]

I also knew Rep. Connie Morella, the Republican representing my district. Connie had been supportive, writing letters to Browner that had gone unanswered. But more than Congresswoman Morella, Sensenbrenner's chief of staff, Beth Sokul, was the catalyst for whatever occurred between the chairman and me. Sensenbrenner was a conservative Republican with very deep pockets via the family fortune from Kimberly-Clark. While Sensenbrenner's politics couldn't have been further removed from mine, Beth and I hadn't defined our relationship by what was different about us but rather by what we had in common: husbands, children, and the demands of professional careers at odds with both.

Today Beth came in wearing a neck brace from having fallen and broken a vertebra. She moved with the frozen posture of a figurine, having to turn her entire body to look to either side. In the crush of preparation for the hearing I had forgotten she was hurt, and it surprised me to see her moving this way. But even with the unnatural restriction, she hadn't lost an ounce of her toughness, her command of the situation. She noticed me as her body swept her vision over the room from the elevated members' platform, and smiled. On top of everything else, Beth was four months pregnant.

And then there was Congresswoman Sheila Jackson Lee. A full-throated liberal, Jackson Lee had come of age in the 1960s when she had worked with the Southern Christian Leadership Conference as another Walter Fauntroy prodigy, joining him in the bare-knuckled turbulence of the Deep South. She had a deep, powerful voice like the woman who held her seat in the same district, and whom Jackson Lee still considered her role model, Barbara Jordan.

Jackson Lee walked through the doors at the back of the members' platform with an intense, charismatic aura. She didn't bother with pleasantries but went straight to her seat, followed by her harried staffer who sat down behind her and looked out at the room through his thick glasses.

A whole lot of untitled folks were also in the room, people you'd never find gracing the cover of a magazine or featured as a guest on *60 Minutes*. Scores of them were EPA and other government workers, who had taken the day off to be in the room when an oppressive part of their lives was finally revealed openly to the world. This was the first time in a very long time, indeed—if it had ever happened before at all—that a subordinate officer at a federal agency was testifying under oath against the administrator seated beside her.

Toward the back of the room sat Norris McDonald, the president of the African American Environmentalist Association. Norris was a conservative and in just about every aspect of his philosophy disagreed with me, save one—human rights. Through the years of this ordeal, Norris had been unyielding in his support; he had organized an environmental watershed trip for the Gore-Mbeki South African study tour. Norris strained to see over the shoulders of those in front of him, trying to get a clear sight line to the front of the proceedings.

Attorneys Steve and David Kohn, directors of the National Whistleblowers Center in Georgetown, were seated next to Norris. They represented the legal team that defended whistleblowers against abuses in the agency.

Members of my church family were in attendance too: Pastor and Dr. King, Minister Edna Young, Minister Charlie Davis, and other members of the congregation. Standing room only. And then I noticed another very major influence in my being there today. Seated directly behind me was David Shapiro. To overlook David would be to miss the bulldog sitting discreetly on the back porch.

As the chairman was about to gavel the hearing to order, I noticed the one person whose presence was perhaps the symbol of the effort we'd waged against the agency in general and Administrator Browner in particular: Anita Nickens. Our eyes met, and she raised her eyebrows knowingly. Anita was on public record because of the statement she had read in Freedom Plaza.

⑊⑊⑊⑊⑊⑊⑊

Chairman Sensenbrenner gaveled the hearing into session. Immediately, Congresswoman Eddie Bernice Johnson, a Democrat from Texas and a member of the Congressional Black Caucus, raised a point of order.

"In this venue, Mr. Chairman, I do not see the sincerity of this committee. Instead I see a political stunt."

We didn't expect the administrator to have a party loyalist on the committee. And although I had been tipped off to expect the agency's graphic-laden presentation, this objection came completely out of left field.

Chairman Sensenbrenner, clearly annoyed by the suggestion that he was unfair and the characterization of the hearing as a political stunt, pointed out that he was in possession of a memorandum from the agency's legal counsel pertaining to employee privacy rights that claimed it would "be impossible for the agency to discuss the harassment claims in an open session of the Congress." He said that, in effect, "the only way we would be able to get the EPA to make that type of a response would be for the committee to order the public out of the room and members of the press out of the room."

My heart stopped.

"We have not had a closed hearing since I have been the chairman, and I do not want this to be the first closed meeting of my chairmanship."

Applause broke out behind me throughout the room. Sensenbrenner had made his stand. After the chairman had dispatched the argument and as he was readying himself to continue, another Democrat, Lynn Rivers of Michigan, raised a parliamentary inquiry, knocking the chairman off his stride. "I am not willing to infringe on the rights of some individuals in order to vindicate the rights of others," she argued.

I had spent enough time on the Hill to know that this kind of procedural grandstanding was the way the game was played, but it surprised even me to see the Democrats putting party before principle this way. This was, after all, the party of FDR, Adlai Stevenson, the Kennedys. This entire hearing would not have happened but for LBJ's 1964 Civil Rights Act, the underpinning of my victory in the courts. Still, a sacred cow is a sacred cow, and Rivers clanged away on her cowbell in case the reporters had missed Eddie Bernice Johnson's more subtle cue.

While the chair and Rep. Rivers wrangled back and forth, I took the time to review my statement, especially the part I had written the previous night after being tipped off that Browner had put together an impressive dog-and-pony show. Congresswoman Johnson was trying to get this entire proceeding cancelled or moved behind closed doors. She must have known there was no way the chairman was going to let that happen, but she had some bell ringing of her own to do. In many ways this was theater, especially for the Democrats who had no gavels to slam. They were taking time and making objections and hoping that their friends in the press would pick up their cues.

Another Democrat chimed in, but this time it was Sheila Jackson Lee. The fair and dainty white woman from Michigan in the navy blue, dotted Swiss dress didn't stand a chance, not with the chairman, and certainly not against the commanding presence, booming voice, and precise articulation of the congresswoman from Texas.

"Mr. Chairman, first of all, there is a lot of hurt in this room." Jackson Lee was calm, her tone conciliatory but firm. "There are no members," she continued, "who you are seeing here today who would not rise to the occasion to stand against mistreatment of employees based on the issue of race. So we want the light to shine on this question."

Jackson Lee was deviating from the lead of her Democratic colleagues, who were trying to protect their party's president. The congresswoman's voice and pace continued calmly and confidently, despite the risk she was taking by going off message. She concluded, saying of discrimination, "I've lived it, I see it, I feel it. The pain is very deep, and I don't want this to be a frivolous hearing where you leave here feeling empty and unsure whether we are sincere."

A quiet murmur of approval came over the audience, as a Democrat had finally placed principle over party loyalty.

ıııııııııııı

The chairman announced that the administrator had taken the unusual move of requesting that she make her opening statement last. Usually, in deference to the most senior person, the administrator testifies first. So the agency knew, without knowing exactly what we were going to be saying, that whatever we testified to would be damaging and difficult to overcome in the court of public opinion. They already had in their possession ample evidence of my testimony from the court transcript in my case; Leroy Warren's letters, though not replied to, had given them a pretty accurate blueprint of his statement; Ron Harris had represented scores of people, each one of whom had filed formal complaints with the agency. In saving Browner's opening statement for last, their plan seemed to be to unring the bells the three of us would be ringing.

After hearing the chairman's words—"Dr. Coleman-Adebayo, why don't you go first?"—I launched into my prepared statement.

"Why have we come to Congress? In 1963, Dr. Martin Luther King Jr. had that question posed to him as he sat in a Birmingham, Alabama, jail cell. He replied that he was in Birmingham because injustice was in Birmingham. Mr. Chairman, we are here today because injustice is at EPA.

"On August 18 of this year, a jury of the US district court in Washington found the EPA and this administrator violated Title VII of the US Civil Rights Act. The jury found the agency guilty of racism, sexism, color discrimination, and creating a hostile work environment. Until my jury verdict, press, and C-SPAN coverage of the announcement of this hearing, the administration only paid lip service to the concerns of civil rights abuses in the agency."

I testified that despite my work experience and education, "the OIA made it consistently clear that I was an intruder in their world; I could participate in high level staff meetings, I was told, only because my colleagues regarded me as an honorary white man."

I also had to make a preemptive move against the sophisticated presentation my anonymous source had warned me about. We had all seen how effective graphics were when used to make a point. I was afraid that if Browner were allowed to wow everyone present with her polished, just-so gimmicks, the reality of the agency's hostile work environment and Browner's role in it would be lost.

"I understand that Ms. Browner is going to present a number of statistics, so let me offer in advance of that: her reliance on statistics to try to offset the jury's verdict and other charges of discrimination completely misses the point. Numbers are used out of context to erase the human face of the problem. And once the problem is dehumanized, discrimination can flourish. By claiming that discrimination, based on numbers, is not a problem, Browner gives permission for it to continue.

"Josef Stalin had noted in an offhand quip about his genocide, 'One man's murder is a tragedy. A million murdered is a statistic.'"

I restated my opening question. "Why have we come to Congress? Because the agency and the executive branch have refused to police themselves and address those injustices. Therefore, Congress must take steps to ensure that prohibited personnel practices are not tolerated and that disciplinary action, including firing, is taken against all managers who violate the civil rights of employees. Secondly, we ask Congress to conduct a review of the Office of General Counsel and the Office of Civil Rights. We need a community oversight for it. Third, Congress should order a review of all terminations or firings, with the goal of reinstating employees who were fired by discriminating managers. Finally, discriminators must be held financially liable for their misdeeds, not US taxpayers."

I ended my statement by saying, "Mr. Chairman, my story and Anita Nickens's story are but two of hundreds of stories which represent the new face of discrimination in the twenty-first century. How else might one explain the fact that African Americans make up 18 percent of EPA's workforce but represent 57 percent of those fired by the agency. . . . Those numbers suggest a well thought-out and executed policy of discrimination."

Despite David Shapiro's last-minute advice to me against raising the vanadium issue, I had decided that I could not forfeit this unique opportunity to present the case of vanadium miners to Congress, the press, and the American people.

"In another example of gross insensitivity, South Africa requested EPA's assistance on behalf of a community which had been poisoned by vanadium mining. When I attempted to perform my job, I was officially reprimanded, refused travel requests, and removed from the position." As I spoke David Shapiro kicked the legs of my chair.

The chairman moved quickly to Ron Harris. I sat back and gathered myself as Ron began to speak. Ron presented data from his work as a union representative. He brought the statistics to life with vivid stories of careers destroyed and health problems triggered by unrelenting retaliation. He called upon Congress to act swiftly to address a dire situation.

As Ron spoke, the adrenalin rush I'd felt from being under oath, before Congress, and on camera began to subside. I felt satisfied that I had done what I had come to do. I had called out the agency and Administrator Browner. I had spoken of the horrors experienced by hundreds of agency employees. And I had blown the whistle on the crimes that were still being inflicted upon a poor community in South Africa with the knowledge of Carol Browner and the White House.

Leroy Warren began his statement next. "Discrimination at EPA is real, it's painful, and it's pervasive. There is no accountability. The EEO program is in shambles." Warren's testimony continued, "There seems to be a situation at EPA where if you complain or ask questions about what is wrong, you're basically facing a death sentence as far as upward mobility and promotions."

Leroy's raspy voice and southern phrasing carried through the room. "You have a job, but you have no future at EPA." His timing and tenor were superb. "Thurgood Marshall and Martin Luther King Jr. would have been ex-employees if they had been working at EPA today."

"Mr. Warren, may I interrupt?"

Sensenbrenner looked disoriented, trying to find the origin of the voice.

"Mr. Chairman, down here. It's Rep. Kevin Brady of Texas." The congressman continued, "Both during Mr. Warren's testimony, Mr. Harris and Dr. Coleman's testimony, our administrator has continued to make faces during their testimony. It is distracting and very disrespectful. I would ask the chair to direct her to just professionally listen to these people's statements and concerns."

"Mr. Chairman, please!" Browner objected, keeping her index finger raised at the end of her long forearm, elbow resting on the table. She pointedly glared at the chairman as he spoke.

"We're all adults here. We all have to be held accountable for what we do or what we don't do." Sensenbrenner seemed almost to enjoy saying this. "And everybody else can be the judge of that." He asked Mr. Warren to continue.

The further he got into his statement, the livelier he became.

"We tried to talk to the administrator. She knew as early as April that there was a problem, because we had a meeting in the library. We said some things there. It went back to her. I deliberately said some things to see how many leaks we would have. It leaked like a sieve, because the spies were there." And then, with an insult directed at the African American members of Browner's team, Leroy alluded to the blacks who had worked inside the "big house" during slavery and opposed those enslaved in the fields, who were instigating revolts against their enslavers. "The house brothers and sisters carried the message back."

Leroy's voice had steadily been getting louder. Someone stepped in from the side and hit the switch on his microphone, whether to turn it on or off was not clear. His voice resonated in the room either way.

"I sent a letter to the administration in May. Nobody responded. That's the situation we're in. We want this problem solved. We're not asking for quotas. We're not asking for you to give us something. We have people who are highly qualified, they're competitive, and they can do the job if they're given the chance. When you go to court, win a decision, and then nobody's punished"—he pointed to me—"Who has been punished for calling this woman an honorary white man? Does she look like she's white?" Leroy was hot. "Where are the procedures for prohibited personnel practices? I don't care how we got to America; we're all here. We have got to live together. You could take your dog to EPA, and if you treated your dog the way they treat some of the black people, you'd be in jail for treating a dog like that. But if you treat black people like that, you're rewarded, promoted, and move forward."

Having witnessed the murmurings of her employees from the back of the room when Leroy Warren said, "It is not the most qualified who get rewarded but the most accommodationist," Carol Browner readied herself to begin her testimony. But first Chairman Sensenbrenner asked her "for your personal assurances that there will be no retaliatory action taken against the two EPA employees who are testifying here today."

"Mr. Chairman, let me begin by saying there will be no action against the people who have chosen to come here today. This is an incredibly important issue to me and to my colleagues at the EPA." Her tone was good, her posture slightly forward, engaged. "And I thank you for holding a hearing."

There was a slight buzz in the room; it was common knowledge that Congressman Sensenbrenner had threatened to subpoena Browner if she refused to appear voluntarily.

"I do," she reiterated, "because it is important." There was anger in her forceful leaning forward with the words "I do." It registered in her face and her voice. As she continued, her pacing slowed and became more controlled.

"Now I want to bring to the committee's attention what we have done, what we are continuing to do, and what we will do," she said, "because building an EPA that is fair, equitable, and supportive of all at EPA is one that I take very, very seriously. And I have taken seriously since day one. . . . We will not, we do not tolerate discrimination, whether it be race, gender, religion, age, disability, or sexual preference."

Browner pointed out that the Clinton administration had adhered to its deep beliefs that "the federal workforce would and should look like America" and that her concerns did not only apply just to those who took their families to national parks on vacation but to all people, including "those children who still can't breathe in the inner cities and are still being affected by lead poisoning."

She had done a good job setting up the argument. It was now time for the charts.

"Now, I do think taking a moment to review [hiring and promotions at EPA] is important to the work of this committee," she said. After conceding that it was not the be-all and end-all, she asserted, "It is certainly an important component." With four-color graphics, Browner launched into an array of statistics showing that the number of minorities in the SES, "has more than tripled. More. Than. Tripled. For women at that level it has increased 50 percent."

By this point the contrition was out the window. We were now entering the offensive phase of the strategy. The posture, the tone of voice, had changed, and Browner's hands, which she had kept to her sides when she began her statement, were now sticking the air in front of her, her finger pointed at the committee to dot her exclamation points.

"And let me tell you something," Browner said, fully in charge. "That. Didn't. Just. Happen." Her pointed finger came down to the desk and back to eye level with each word. "That happened because I said it was going to happen. And my managers"—she sliced that finger across her body a foot above the table—"worked to make it happen."

The hand came down on the table. This was classic Browner: reality was what she said it was.

"And I want to say something about those minorities who have been hired and promoted." The voice softened again. "They are good people, Mr. Chairman. They are committed people. They are good people."

Returning to her contrite tone for a moment, the administrator reiterated that even though the agency had taken such strides to hire and promote these "good people," those actions still were not "adequate to the challenge that we face as a society, as a government, and as an individual agency, to ensure fairness and equality for all. It is a piece of a complicated, ongoing effort."

"Ms. Browner," a weary-voiced Sensenbrenner interrupted, "I've been real generous with the time, more so with you than with the other three witnesses. You've been going on for about ten minutes now. Can you wrap it up in a minute or two so the committee members can ask questions?"

Her voice was calm and soothing, her pace relaxed, slow. "We've made a lot of progress in this country; we've made a lot of progress in this administration. But the challenge of a fair and equal workplace is an ongoing challenge."

She ended with a flourish, quickening and raising her voice, leaning forward into the words. "And then we need to ask ourselves again: what else do we need to do? That is what we're doing at the Environmental Protection Agency."

In a truly virtuoso performance, Browner had said not one word about the jury's findings. Not one word about those in her direct chain of command who were implicated in those findings. Not one word in acknowledgement of the hostile work environment she had administered and helped create.

Chairman Sensenbrenner led the round of questioning, directing his first inquiry toward the three witnesses to discrimination and retaliation in the agency. He cited the case of Dr. Rosemarie Russo, an EPA scientist "who just won a Department of Labor–OSHA case against the agency for retaliation." The agency was found to have retaliated "because the agency used Dr. Russo's deposition testimony from a whistleblower case and [the referendum he] authored . . . that questioned EPA science." Sensenbrenner made a point of noting the origin of the charge. "According to OSHA—not Dr. Russo—EPA retaliated by removing her from the Athens, Georgia, lab she ran for sixteen years and moving her to a job in Washington, DC." Sensenbrenner asked if that had been our experience.

Before I addressed the issue of Dr. Russo, I said, "Behind me sit some of the bravest people I have ever met in my entire life. We at EPA live within a culture of intimidation and harassment. And so I would also like for Ms. Browner to give us a guarantee that my colleagues who sit behind me today will also not be retaliated against for participating in this hearing."

"We will need their names so that that administrative leave is given." A murmur spread through the room like a lion had just walked through the door. This was followed by nervous laughter. I heard someone behind me say, "Right, like I'm going to sign something that says I was here today."

Browner was quick on her feet and turned what could have been a very embarrassing moment into a display of magnanimity. "If they're uncomfortable giving us their names, we're happy to provide a mechanism where they'll feel comfortable." She went on to say she wanted to go further because of how important the hearings were. "[We] want to reach out and make that happen."

Addressing Browner directly, Rep. Jerry Costello gave the administrator the opportunity to respond to my allegations. "You've heard Dr. Coleman-Adebayo talk about a decade of racial and retaliatory abuse. You've heard her testify that she wrote you a letter in 1997 concerning that discrimination and received no response. She has indicated to this committee under oath that she believes that up until now, until there was a verdict in her case, and until this committee scheduled this hearing, the agency has given nothing but lip service to these complaints. I want to give you an opportunity to respond to that."

The congressman also asked Browner to describe the numbers of annual complaints. "If you could respond to the lip service versus what action you have taken and the fact that apparently you did not respond to a 1997 letter."

"This is not—" Browner started after a pause. She spoke with her elbow on the table, cheek resting on her fist. "The issue of equality and fairness in the workplace is not an issue that I just came to. Absolutely. Positively. Not. We would not have achieved the kind of growth in our minority representation in our senior ranks if I simply made this an issue three, four, five weeks ago. We would not have diversity action plans that were finalized in 1997 if I simply made this an issue several weeks ago. . . . It's not a problem that's going to be solved, society hasn't solved the problem either, but I certainly think that we have a demonstrated record, we have demonstrated commitment, and we're going to continue to do everything we possibly can to create a fair workplace."

In my mind I could see the transcript of this hearing and imagined what it would look like were it limited to what Browner had said about Costello's query and what an adversarial exchange between them might be like:

REP. COSTELLO: If you could respond to the lip service versus what action you have taken and the fact that apparently you did not respond to a 1997 letter.

ADMIN. BROWNER:

REP. COSTELLO: You didn't say a word about the charges of discrimination.

ADMIN. BROWNER:

REP. COSTELLO: And the charges of racism? Sexism?

ADMIN. BROWNER:

REP. COSTELLO: The jury found that you helped create a hostile work environment. Could you address that?

ADMIN. BROWNER:

REP. COSTELLO: Ms. Browner, I am holding in my hand a letter dated March 3, 1997, sent to US EPA administrator Carol Browner by Dr. Coleman-Adebayo's attorney. The letter says, in full, quote

"Honorable Carol M. Browner: I am legal counsel to Dr. Marsha Coleman-Adebayo. As you have doubtless heard, Dr. Coleman-Adebayo has filed two administrative complaints against the EPA. She sincerely believes that you do not fully know the extent of the abuse she has taken from the Office of International Activities Managers, and that you are likewise unaware that she has been stripped of her responsibilities as Executive Secretary for the Gore Mbeki Commission, in part, because of her refusal to misrepresent to you, the Vice President's office, the Office of the Interior, or to representatives of Non-Governmental Organizations, that EPA was taking steps to fulfill commitments made during the Gore-Mbeki talks last July, when in fact, OIA was doing little or nothing to fulfill these obligations. . . .

OIA officials, with your knowledge made a major shift in South Africa policy and disregarded obligations undertaken at the July of '96 Gore-Mbeki meeting. Throughout this period, Dr. Adebayo made repeated requests to travel to South Africa to carry out her program manager responsibilities, every request was summarily denied. Eventually the South Africans became so frustrated that the Deputy Minister of Environmental Affairs himself wrote to Administrator [*sic*] Nitze, with a copy to you, asking that Dr. Adebayo be sent to South Africa to brief him on all aspects of the EPA program. This request was likewise denied. Thereafter she was summarily removed as South African Program Officer. . . .

She has even seen memoranda sent to your office containing factual inaccuracies. . . . You likewise have the opportunity to put a stop to the rogue behavior of these OIA managers, before they can further harm the reputation of the agency. Dr. Adebayo and I would be willing to meet with you at an appropriate time for the purpose of discussing and hopefully resolving these complaints."

Unquote.

Administrator Browner, would you please respond to this?

ADMIN. BROWNER: On the advice of counsel I reserve the rights afforded me under the Fifth Amendment of the Constitution to refuse to answer that question on the grounds that it might incriminate me or those I am associated with.

I seethed at the way the procedural format of this hearing and the timidity of the members was allowing Browner to run on and on with whatever she wanted to say without addressing the questions. She was adroit in consuming the allotted time in answering the first question posed to her so that there would be no follow-up that could pin her down. Unfortunately, like most veteran political operatives, Browner had been well schooled in avoiding questions and using misleading statistics.

||||||||||||||

Months earlier—well before the trial, even—there had been a rash of stories by Dwight Welch published in *Inside the Fishbowl*, the EPA National Treasury Employees Union's newsletter. These stories had been highly critical of Browner, expressing a deep undercurrent of frustration among workers of color and the progressive white community at EPA that was reminiscent of the preriot conditions in 1960s Detroit.

Carol Browner's reaction then was the prototype for her presentation on the day of the hearing. She had called a town hall meeting with the stated purpose of clearing the air through honest discussion. The tickets to the meeting were scarce and selectively distributed. As in the hearing, honest discussion had been confined to carefully managed statistics, with the director of the Office of Civil Rights, Ann Goode, monopolizing the first hour of the meeting with an offering of superlatives about the agency before opening up the floor to questions. Even then, staff people had controlled the microphones and screened malcontents from the process. I had arranged for the first questioner to hand the mic directly to me when she finished.

"Ms. Browner, you are running EPA like a twenty-first-century plantation!" I had blurted out before the staffer could gain control of the mic. Near pandemonium had broken out as the pent-up frustration vented in the room.

Realizing their ruse had failed, Browner and her minions quickly adjourned the meeting. But the energy and anger in the room had convinced me that we could channel our passions constructively, and I had posted another meeting for people interested in organizing a group to support our efforts. The meeting was very well attended, and EPA Victims Against Racial Discrimination (EPAVARD) was born. EPAVARD represented the first time the agency had ever faced a concerted effort at fighting back within the organization.

The monopolizing of the hearing on this day was a carbon copy of the town hall meeting that had happened so long ago. Mercifully, there would be a scheduled vote, and Chairman Sensenbrenner gaveled the meeting into recess. Segun and Sina came to me. Segun kissed me on the cheek.

"You did very well, sweetheart. I am proud of you." I squeezed his hand. "Very proud of you." Sina kissed me too, without the usual accompanying teenage embarrassment. He was not aware of how much that meant to me.

"I have to find somewhere to collect myself," I told Segun. "I have to be alone."

"Of course. Sina, come with me."

Sina kissed my cheek again. I left them both and made my way out of the hearing room.

‖‖‖‖‖‖‖‖‖

My face was hot and everything was closing in as I headed down the hall to a restroom. There were so many things racing across my mind it was like I'd just rolled down a long hill inside a barrel—except I wasn't dizzy, my thoughts were. Browner had managed to control the pace and the subject of the hearing. She was very good: her appearance, her comportment. But for her tendency to get a little too full of herself and an occasional flash of haughtiness, she had to be satisfied with the way the day was going. I walked into the women's room. Thankfully, there was no one else in there, so I could let out my frustration: "Jesus Christ! The woman was just convicted of violating my civil rights, and they're treating her like she's Mary Poppins!"

I ran cold water on my hands and then dipped my face into them, moving my head slowly to let the water lap over my eyelids, my forehead, my cheeks and chin. I patted my face dry and placed the damp towel on the back of my neck, then on my throat and under my chin, keeping my eyes closed while letting my anger subside.

"That is much better," I said out loud. "Much better. Never fight mad." If no one else took it to Browner after the recess, I would. There would be plenty of opportunities, as at least another six members would direct questions my way. Two could play this game. Ask me a question and that would be the end of your five minutes, every sixty seconds of every minute of it. That was the strategy now. I knew I might get animated, but it wouldn't be with anger. I knew that becoming angry would mean I was in a power struggle, and there was no way to win a power struggle in there.

The hallway was buzzing with well-wishers encouraging me: "We love you, Marsha," and "Don't let up, you've got her on the ropes!"

After the break Eddie Bernice Johnson threw Browner a softball like a blown kiss. "What do you hope to get from this hearing?"

There it was, the moment Carol Browner had been waiting for since she had ordered damage control into full operation. Speaking with her elbow propped on the table, her long fingers holding the side of her face, she was relaxed, confident, respectful.

"First of all, let me tell you what I'd like to get from this hearing—and I think we are getting it, Mr. Chairman—which is the support of all members of Congress as we move forward with affirmative action at the EPA. We are committed to this. It is difficult; it's challenging. I think that is true for the entire government. But I really, really want to leave here knowing you, Mr. Chairman, and all members of this committee share my commitment to affirmative action." Fold up the chairs, boys— our work is done here.

But then it was my turn.

"I don't think there's anyone at this table that disagrees with that," I began. "I'm a recipient of affirmative action programs despite all the universities and degrees that I have, but certainly I wouldn't have had those opportunities had affirmative action not been in place when it was time for me to go to school." I could see Mr. Diaz out of the corner of my eye, his head down, jotting notes, nodding approvingly. "You are absolutely right. We are reaching out to everyone possible—to please help us—because we are in a lot of pain."

Diaz stopped writing and looked up.

"We have people who are sick because of the racism and sexism at EPA. . . . We have a very serious problem at EPA. And when I tell you that all of us in our own ways are dying a little bit every day, because we go into these horribly stressful environments, Monday through Friday, from eight o'clock in the morning until six o'clock at night. We have supervisors who are monitoring the quote-unquote time and attendance issue. We have supervisors in which there is nothing you do that is right. And after a while you begin to even question yourself in terms of what's wrong with me? And we had to organize ourselves into the EPA victims organization, so that we could support ourselves and so that when we saw each other going down and becoming ill, we could support each other. We are all dying a little bit every day, and this is a plea of help from people who are literally dying.

"Now, we are committed to the environment. We are committed to protecting our communities. But this agency is run like a twenty-first-century plantation. And this has to stop. And this is why we've taken this incredible effort here and come before you. And to really beg, both the Democrats and the Republicans, to please help us.

"As I said in my statement earlier, there was really very little attention to the issues we discussed until the jury verdict, until it appeared in the *Washington Post*, until it appeared on C-SPAN, and this hearing was announced. The NAACP, I believe, wrote three letters to Ms. Browner. They did not even receive the courtesy of a response. Not even an acknowledgement that they had received the letter. I wrote her a letter in 1997 because I had worked with Ms. Browner on a project, and I truly believed that if she knew that someone she had worked with was being called names, was undergoing the most horrible harassment that you can imagine, at least from a person-to-person level, she would have done something.

"As you read the letter, it said, my attorney starts off by saying, 'I'm writing this letter against my better judgment because my client really believes that you are unaware of the situation at EPA and that if you were aware you would do something to stop it.' I received a form letter in 1997. Not even from Ms. Browner—from her deputy. That is our experience. When we cry out, we get these little form letters. And then we're treated to these diversity action plans, when we're all supposed to sit around and sing 'We Are the World.' But we are dying here. And that is the reason we're at this hearing."

"The gentlewoman's time has expired."

They hadn't seen that coming. The change in the room was palpable. Eddie Bernice Johnson looked like she had just swallowed a toad. I had gone into the women's room floundering, angry, lost. I had cooled my hands and face. And I had also said a prayer: "We have come too far and suffered too long, Lord. The voice of truth is being drowned out by crows. Please help me find the words to break through."

Rommie Diaz wasn't nodding approval anymore. They had overestimated their position. Their timing wasn't so impeccable. They had been thinking, Game over, but there was a long way to go.

And then it was Jackson Lee's turn. Having deep roots in the civil rights movement herself, she has been more responsive to the idea of investigating retaliation and other civil rights issues through the committee than anyone.

She stated her position, that the hearing was vitally important and a signal of the issues we had to confront "federal government-wide. I am looking at very serious people who have experienced very troubling incidents in their lives. . . . If we do not ferret out the actors who are part of the problem, we may have a hearing in the next session, the next session after it, and the next session after it. If the lights go out on the Congressional session of the 106th Congress, I will leave here knowing that the ills that have been presented in this Congress today or this hearing will at least be addressed until we are able to return for legislative action."

That was the operative phrase of the whole spectacle: legislative action. Without it, the likes of the people who were gathered to my right, attesting to their virtues and the panacea of affirmative action, would be able to continue their intimidation of the federal workplace with impunity.

"Dr. Coleman-Adebayo," Jackson Lee continued, "could you tell me, this term 'honorary white man,' someone articulated that to you, as I understand it. Where is that person at this point?"

"He is in the same position—well, actually, he has been promoted since I was called honorary white man. I was in the Office of International Activities. At that point he was my boss, he was the director for the Multilateral Unit of OIA. He is now the deputy assistant administrator for the Office of International Activities."

The idea of that was so ludicrous I couldn't help smiling while I said it.

"And if you ask me where any of these people are who called me these names, they're either still in their same positions or they've been promoted. That is the general rule at EPA. And until people are either fired or severely disciplined for violating prohibited personnel practices, which is, in fact, a duty Ms. Browner could carry out today—if she wanted to—these people will continue to stay in those positions and call people like me, and like you, and other people who look like us, names."

"Administrator Browner," Jackson Lee said, "let me thank you for looking us in the eye and realizing that we have to confront this. You have widespread jurisdiction. But let me get down to the real focal point as we close this hearing. Tell me how come we cannot ferret out—and I understand the laws of civil service—but ferret out these individuals. . . . Can you tell me something that you can do right now to ferret out these bad actors?"

Browner's confidence was shaken. Her words were not as quick and easy in response to this question. She stammered about "looking very carefully at the cases that have been filed, the cases that have been dispensed with, problem."

She groped for an answer and after rambling, not very convincingly, fell back into the script: "I have personally looked at the numbers. And it raises for me some very real questions."

The chair then recognized Rep. Nethercutt of Washington State.

"Mr. Harris, I just want to ask you, sir, if you feel at any time that you have been subjected to any demeaning treatment by the EPA in connection with your work?"

"Yes, on several occasions, but in all honesty it did not start out that way." Harris was cautious as he continued. "I do believe you would be pertaining to my driving. They needed a driver for Ms. Browner. He asked me to do it to help the agency. I told him, 'No problem.' I did not mind it. After meeting Ms. Browner, I further did not mind it. My opinion of her, she was very respectful toward me, and I in turn respected her. I felt it demeaning when it was then made a part of my job, by the agency, which I didn't feel was right. As I protested, they then put it in another black male's job, and a white male's. The white male was never even asked to drive Ms. Browner around, only myself and the other minority."

He cringed as he added, "At that point, I did feel the Driving Miss Daisy syndrome. But I don't want to reflect that towards Ms. Browner. She really was respectful toward me. This is the agency in Chicago that I'm referring to. If I were asked to drive Ms. Browner around tomorrow, I would not mind doing it."

Browner was given an opportunity to respond.

"I like Ron Harris." Her cool demeanor was gone, replaced with seething anger. "I look forward to going to Chicago so that Mr. Harris can drive me." Her cadence was slow. "In fact I just said to Mr. Harris, because I may be in Chicago in the next week or so, 'Maybe I'll see you.' The last time I was in Chicago, I didn't see Mr. Harris. I don't know why. I don't make these decisions. I'm not in any way involved in these decisions. I do enjoy getting to spend time with my colleagues. Mr. Harris and I have visited about his family; we have visited about what he does to enjoy himself. I know Mr. Harris is a good man. And I have really enjoyed my time with him." There she put her foot down.

"If Mr. Harris was ever asked, on my behalf, with my name, it was without my knowledge." Her long index finger stabbed the air; she was clearly upset.

"I will confirm that," Ron agreed. "That's why I specifically stated that it was the agency and not Ms. Browner."

Harris's Driving Miss Daisy remark had opened a hole in the agency's defense. I look forward to Ron driving me? I thought. I was shocked when he reached across my body and extended his hand to Carol Browner.

South Carolina's Mark Sanford decided to bite into this bone.

"I think it begs the larger question, and I mean this respectfully," the congressman said. "I grew up down south, and down south there were plantations, there were full employments, and there were a lot of minorities working on the plantations. But the issue was: did they get to think while they were there, not did we have a bunch of them. So the question that is the nexus of this whole debate—not are there so many more minorities—but have they been free to think as human beings, as talented individuals, while they're at the EPA? That's the core question, not a bigger blue chart.

"So I'll direct my question to Dr. Coleman-Adebayo: has this progression to push people into a certain box, regardless of whether there is more of them or fewer of them, hampered the conduct or use of good science? That's the critical question. Have people been free to go wherever science might take them, as opposed to where EPA might want them to go, based on the science they want to hear?"

"I certainly felt very stifled in terms of my work in Africa," I replied. "I felt that I was not free to raise the kinds of issues that were the environmental issues in South Africa, because of the particular position of the people who were heading up the office. And so a lot of the name calling that you have read in my testimony are by the same managers that were given the responsibility for leading our South Africa effort. So when you have an assistant administrator calling an African leader a necklacer or a murderer, that's a particular way of thinking about South Africans or about this particular leader. And so what kind of policy do you really expect from that kind of person? . . . It's important to say that when we do not fire or discipline these people when they have violated prohibited personnel practices, we continue to get this type of recycled racism in the agency. And that's what we have going on now.

"Diversity and racism are two different things. . . . On the plantation there were a lot of different people. It didn't mean that black folks were in charge. And we have a very small voice at the agency, although she's bringing in a lot more people. People learn the rules pretty quickly. If you speak out, you don't stay at the agency very long. This is a civil rights, human rights issue."

"The gentleman's time has expired, and the gentleman from Michigan, Mr. Nick Smith, is recognized."

Looking directly at the administrator, the congressman asked her, "Do you believe that Dr. Coleman-Adebayo was treated fairly by the agency?"

After beginning her reply inaudibly, Administrator Browner responded, "I am troubled by what I have heard and by an initial review of the transcript. The judge has not issued an order yet. The jury has made their findings. There has not been an order. I want to be very, very clear about this. I am deeply troubled by what is in the transcript."

"Is that a no? You don't believe she was fairly treated by the agency?"

"I do not believe, based on the transcript, what I have seen of the transcript, she was treated by her colleagues with the respect any employee deserves. With the respect that any employee deserves." Then turning to me, Browner said, "I'm sorry—it's rubbish."

Ms. Browner's mic had been intermittent throughout the hearing, and I could not get mine turned on before I asked her if she was going to fire any managers. Unfortunately, neither her apology nor my question could be heard widely in the room. When at last I got the mic turned on, I attempted to repeat my question.

The congressman wanted to use his time and moved on. He continued to question Browner.

"The judge in the case issued an order on liability in the case, is that correct?"

"No. As I understand it, the jury has heard the testimony," Browner responded. "Very troubling, deeply discerning," she added, and then, correcting herself, "deeply troubling to me. They have issued their finding. The judge has not issued an order. I want to say something. We will, absolutely, when we get the judge's order, we will comply. Absolutely."

"So you won't appeal?"

"You know what? I wish I got to make these decisions, but unfortunately, I got a Justice Department."

"My guess is you've got a lot of influence in that decision."

"And let me tell you what I'm going to say. I don't want it appealed. I cannot tell you what the Justice Department will say."

Despite this assertion, Browner had not sent a letter to the DOJ asking for the department not to appeal; rather she had hired two pricey law firms to refute the verdict in my case.

Mr. Smith yielded his remaining time to Mark Sanford, who said, "This discussion is indicative of the problem, which is, 'Well, Justice Department may do something.' It was interesting during the discussion with Mr. Harris, earlier, Ms. Browner, you said, 'I don't make the decision, I had no knowledge of' whether or not he's going to be hired as, basically, the boy driver in Chicago."

"Mr. Chairman!" Browner protested.

"The floor belongs to the gentleman from South Carolina."

"I think that the question is," Sanford continued, "ultimately it goes back to Truman, or whomever it was: 'The buck stops here.' If there is discrimination in this organization, then ultimately, rather than saying, 'I'm sorry this happened out in Chicago,' somebody ultimately has to take responsibility and to say, 'This cannot stand, it's got to change, and these are the ways it's going to change.' As opposed to, 'We had some nice conversations in the car, and I'm sorry the white guy didn't have to drive, but this guy did.' That just seems kinda weird."

Browner attempted to protest, but her mic was off.

"You will have an opportunity, Administrator Browner, to answer the question." Sensenbrenner's tone was firm. "This chair has been fair at this hearing. The chair will be fair until the end of the hearing. Being fair means stopping people from interrupting other people who have been recognized. The gentleman from South Carolina."

Sanford directed his question to Leroy Warren. "From your viewpoint, do you think that the EPA senior management fully recognizes or acknowledges the degree to which discrimination may or may not exist within EPA?"

"I don't think they fully comprehend the scope of the problem across the board. The administrator might, but somewhere there's a cutoff where she's not getting information, or she's not acting on it. Which one of the two, I don't know. But let's take the most egregious case we've had. An employee forced to clean somebody's bathroom. And that employer is walking around free."

Warren was calm and dispassionate.

"This is America. This is not some Soviet prison camp. The mere fact that these things have not been dealt with sends a signal to the world that you can treat black women any way you want to. I have sisters, I have nieces, and I have white and black friends and Hispanics and Asians. I don't believe nobody should be mistreated. My answer to you clearly is: By their actions they're not responsive. And there is a certain amount of denial if you listen to what has happened here today."

"The gentleman's time has expired. Ms. Browner, would you like to respond to the comments that the gentleman from South Carolina made?"

Browner was visibly shaken and on the verge of tears. She was as vulnerable as I had ever seen her, hands interlocked, with her chin hidden behind them.

Sensenbrenner announced it was time to close the hearing. "Ms. Browner, I said I would give you the chance. You may have it."

"Thank you, Mr. Chairman, and thank you to every member of this committee for reaffirming a commitment to affirmative action."

Her voice had softened. Her face was tight. The confidence she had displayed at the beginning of the second session was gone. In the last hour she had made a trip to a place called vulnerability, a place every subordinate knew—particularly minority subordinates, who felt it acutely twenty-four hours a day under her tenure—but that Browner herself had never experienced as the administrator. She was struggling to come partway back. She held on to the words she had planned to close with, as if to prevent falling apart.

"I would never suggest that a white woman, coming of age when I did, could have experienced what a person of color could have experienced.

But like Dr. Coleman-Adebayo, I went to law school under affirmative action. I would not be sitting here but for affirmative action. This hearing has been, at times"—she paused, but without the showmanship of her earlier, staged performance—"disturbing to me.

"Mr. Sanford, perhaps you didn't intend it. I'm going to assume you didn't intend it. You created an appearance that somehow or another, I think the phrase was, I wanted the black guy to drive me." Her voice faltered. "That is deeply offensive to me."

This was different. She was off the script.

Sensenbrenner began to move to his final statement.

"Mr. Chairman, if I might," Carol Browner interjected.

Browner's recuperative powers were borderline miraculous. Were this not something akin to kabuki theater, one might have expected the administrator to come to her senses and fire everyone seated behind her. Instead, she went into a rehash of all the charts and statistics, ending with, "We're going to continue in the closing days of this administration to do every single thing in our power to build on our record. But you cannot ignore our record."

There are records—and then there are records. The record Browner was referencing was a statistical smoke screen rising from internal damage control. The record she had been called on the carpet for was the criminal record of the agency's abuses—which she had just spent the day trying to avoid discussing. This was a chastened Carol Browner. It was hard to imagine the hearing had gone the way she had thought it would.

"It is now time to close this hearing," Sensenbrenner said before going on to thank the witnesses, the representatives from the EPA, and the employees and members of the public for taking the time to listen and participate.

"I have a request of you, Ms. Browner," Sensenbrenner continued. "Spend your personal time between now and January 20 cleaning up this mess so that the new president, and whomever he appoints as EPA administrator, does not get a can of garbage to start out the new administration."

In the last four hours I had seen with my own eyes a black man from Chicago offer comfort to a woman he knew to be a facilitator of grievous acts. I had seen a white man from South Carolina upbraid a white woman from Florida for her treatment of blacks. And I had witnessed that same woman fall from the heights of arrogance and invincibility, after minute exposure to a tiny spore that didn't even approximate the poison she had tolerated, enabled, ignored, and served daily to my colleagues and friends. Yet even that much was enough to break through the husk that power had put between itself and its victims.

I prayed that would be enough.

On my first day back at EPA after the hearing, I stepped out of my office at midmorning and walked down the hall and out of my area. It was like I was stepping out of my body. As I walked I heard my own voice echoing from further down the hallway. I instinctively walked toward the source, one of many monitors that are used to communicate messages to the workforce. C-SPAN's coverage of the hearing was being broadcast throughout the agency. Whether it was a sign of conciliation from Browner or another instance of insurrection, I had no way of knowing. A large group of employees was gathered below the monitor, watching like brokers watch the numbers on Wall Street. I could tell from their comments that this was a friendly group. They were so engrossed in the footage that no one noticed my approach.

"Whoooo-weee! You tell 'em, sister!"

"Who is that? Anybody know her?

"I've never seen her before, but I'm gonna look her up and go shake her hand."

"It's about time someone called them on this stuff."

This was a very different reception from the dominant reaction in my own group. I was able to stand among them in silence for a few minutes and watch their reactions to the video. It was obviously the first time any of them had seen it. I had viewed it at home a couple times, but only with Segun and some friends, who were all sympathetic. This was the first time I could observe the reaction of EPA colleagues who didn't know me from a can of paint. I was struck by how mesmerized they all were. It was like they were witnessing a lunar eclipse or something miraculous. When it got to the point where I testified that the agency was run like a twenty-first-century plantation, the group broke out into laughter, jubilation, and applause.

"There it is!"

"Man, that woman's crazy! You know they gonna put the word out on her!"

An African American woman about my own age chimed in her agreement. "I've been waiting a long time to see this." She turned toward me to give me a high five. She stopped and looked at my image on the monitor and then looked back at me, pointing at my image.

"Is that you?"

I smiled. "That's me," I said, laughing.

"Lord, have mercy!" She hugged me like I was the twin sister she hadn't seen since birth. "I'm going to hug you now while I have the chance. You won't be here long enough for me to ever do this again."

||||||||||||||

If there was any question about a change of heart or move toward humility for Carol Browner from having to experience the disinfecting light of a day before the Science Committee, Browner put it to rest the next morning during an interview with the *Early Show* on CBS.

"Perhaps people behaved poorly," Browner punted. "Perhaps they had ulterior motives. It's the political season."

Today I'm Gray

I wish I could say I know what is bothering me, but I can't. What I can say is that it has been bothering me for a while now and I am just beginning to realize it. I thought I would have been fired by now, but that isn't it. After the Congressional hearing I thought very briefly that there was a chance the agency mafiosi would come to their senses, but they haven't. And that isn't it. There is always the easy mark on my mother for bugging me about something or another, but no. It isn't even Segun. I don't even know what I should go to bed thinking about so I can work it out in my sleep. I am utterly and miserably baffled.

Well, sort of. Since the hearing there has been a weird devolution back to some sense of normalcy, whatever that might be. Ever since coming to EPA, normal has been eighteen-hour workdays, eating Chinese food with my baby daughter on the floor next to me in the office late at night, flights to every nook and cranny of the earth, one notable flight on Air Force Two, a month in China, midnight phone calls to Africa because of the time difference, death threats and all the rest of it from the anonymous EPA callers—so I can't imagine why in the world I would be experiencing a certain ennui.

The truth is, I'll have to slow down somehow and use a big bath towel to wipe off the grease that has accumulated all over my body from life in the supersonic lane. Just sit somewhere tranquil and wipe away, starting with my hair and working my way down my body until I've gotten rid of every last hint of it between my toes.

True, grease has its uses. It's what keeps the gears of the machinery moving. And grease is what it takes to keep the gears from grinding you to pieces. That's why when you ask a political person a question—whoops!—they slip it like it's a wet bar

Journey to No FEAR

The legislation could not have been passed without the sheer pain and the sheer agony of so many employees who came forward to mention that their lives were made almost in the form of a nightmare because they chose to stand up.

—*Representative Sheila Jackson Lee*

No grassroots political struggle has ever prevailed operating under a white flag. In democracy, if the people want to influence governmental authority—which has gotten so cozy with corporate lobbies and their dizzying resources—the people must organize and force the politicians to intervene. I knew that with a court victory I could no longer be dismissed as an uppity agitator. This is not to say that the government would not continue to paint me as the next Malcolm in a pantsuit, but they could no longer portray the story as irrelevant. Everyday Americans had just weighed in. Media was running with the story, and the elephant was loose. If we wanted to put the story's momentum toward any meaningful reform, the time to move was upon us.

This is where my political science background, Congressional Black Caucus Foundation experience of mobilizing constituencies, and knowledge of lots of people at various levels and departments on the Hill would prove invaluable. The NAACP and SCLC, representing

of soap. Slippery as she goes! See someone approaching whom you may have a bone with? Slip into an adjoining office and let them pass. Got a little something for the folks back home? Slip it into the rider the president can't possibly veto. It's a slippery place, Washington. Greased with money, power, and cunning. But none of these are going to help me out of this funk. Hand me the bath towel. I've had enough of grease.

If I really wipe it all off, the amenities come off with it: the paycheck, the travel, the access to the express lane past all the gatekeepers between me and the people who make the decisions, access that is gained by my simply saying, "This is Dr. Coleman-Adebayo from OIA." But by far the most worrisome is losing the ability to provide for my children the opportunities and lifestyle my mother could never even have dreamed of. Kiss all of that good-bye. Why, you could fit all the people who have ever known that kind of grease in US history into a single 747 and still have a few empty seats in coach. That's why it's so difficult to let go, and so few who have tasted it ever do. But this thing has been gnawing on my face. I know it. Yet when I look in the mirror today I don't see any evidence. These are my eyes. This is my nose. These, the same lips. I still look pretty good, considering. I wish I could say that I feel like absolute shit. But that's the problem: I don't. If I did, I'd have to do something to take action against it. Maybe I just have to keep winnowing away.

I had thought that by virtue of hard work and applied brainpower I'd have been embraced by those in power. Hard work and excellence had always paid off before. They got me through the Ivy League. It turned out I could be at home within America's elite institutions as much as I was at home at a Black Panthers children's breakfast program in Detroit. Or just as marginalized. I've been riding the laser-thin beam between them without realizing it had sawed me in two. But don't think of it as one-half white, one black. No. Think of it as someone who is sawed in two, with a healthy aversion to gray.

And there it is. Today, I am gray.

28

A Call to History

"Hello, Marsha? This is Beth Sokul."

She didn't have to identify that sultry voice. When I'd first met Beth, it had surprised me that someone with her outward appearance of conservatism could have such a seductive and passionate voice. The more I got to know her and see her brilliant and savvy mind in action, the more it seemed the only voice she could possibly have been given.

"Do you have a few minutes to talk?"

I was in my office ruminating anyway. "Of course, Beth. What is it?"

I was actually surprised to hear her voice again so soon after the hearing. Whatever that day might have put in motion, if anything, would still be months away. The likelier reality was that Sensenbrenner had had his way with Carol Browner and would savor the fact of her humiliation as a small part of his other, more pressing concerns.

"How are you, Marsha?"

"Honestly? It's a little weird, Beth. If I thought I was isolated before the hearing, let me tell you . . ."

"I bet." Beth had not called this time to listen to my complaints. "Listen, Sensenbrenner wants to introduce legislation as the result of your testimony."

I nearly dropped the phone. I was too stunned to say anything, especially since the last time Beth and I had spoken, she had told me legislation was a long shot. "Maybe 5 percent of all hearings ever result in proposed legislation," Beth had said. "So don't get your hopes up. There's only a small possibility that Congress might act."

"I was instructed to call Sheila Jackson Lee," Beth continued. "She is going to cosponsor the bill. We are talking with her office to see what form the legislation will take. We're drafting the language right now."

"That's fantastic! Oh my God! Thank you so much, Beth! And thank Chairman Sensenbrenner! You have no idea how gratifying this is. It's like someone has thrown me a lifeline!"

"Now, Marsha, tell me what you think about this: All through your testimony you kept using the word *fear*. 'We work in an atmosphere of fear.' 'Fear and intimidation.' What do you think of the 'No FEAR Act'? Our staff came up with that. The Notification of Federal Employees Anti-discrimination and Retaliation Act. No FEAR."

"Are you kidding? I love it! Beth, this is a gift from God! You have no idea."

"No FEAR, Marsha. We're going to see this thing through. This legislation would be the first civil rights and whistleblower law of the twenty-first century."

By then I had forgotten what I had wanted to complain about earlier.

I was so happy I stood up and danced a jig beside my desk, stifling the "Yahoo!" that would get me fired for unlawful exuberance. The Congress of the United States of America was taking my side of the two stories they heard that day in Room 2320 of Rayburn. Now, as a nation, we would consider condemnation of the policies of the Browner administration. There were a hundred people to call: Segun, the group, my friends, family. We would have to organize, comb through Congress to see where our friends—and enemies—were. There were so many things that would have to get done. I was reeling from excitement, satisfaction, and disbelief. But most of this, I suddenly realized, was just more grease. It was how you got things done in this town.

I began with Segun. I called him, and we danced together over the phone to the accompanying music of the thought of legislation. I called my mother, and we rejoiced. I called Theresa Fleming-Blue. "What did I tell you, Marsha? Didn't I tell you the Lord would see you through? Didn't I tell you we were fasting for this day?" And she was so right. This was what I needed. Segun, Mom, my friends, and trust in the Lord. The rest was grease. In the small, bright, cramped, and improbable sanctuary of my office inside the EPA, I closed down inside this inner sanctum that has been with me all along and offered my thanks.

millions of untapped assets, could help with mobilization. I kept these as talking points when I followed up with Beth Sokul about meeting with Chairman Sensenbrenner, even though Beth needed no additional prodding.

Beth invited me into the congressman's office and said, "You will need a political base to fight for this bill."

Beth was disarming, straightforward, and kind. Her two young sons were in the office, playing with an erector set, engaged in the loud negotiations that occur between siblings. This was not the buttoned-down corporate atmosphere I'd expected from a Republican congressman. Beth listened to what I'd gone through at EPA, responding as I might expect a friend to, first thoughtful, then outraged.

"The chairman has watched your case closely and has been appalled by what he's learned. He has instructed me to make No FEAR my highest priority. Here's my cell number. Here's my home phone. You can call me any time of day or night. He will help you in this fight."

As I tucked her business card into my purse, Beth looked at me and smiled. "Looks like you and I are going to be attached at the hip for as long as this takes."

IIIIIIIIIII

Dr. Ruby Reese Moone and I met to discuss creating an organization based on the model of EPAVARD to lead the fight to pass the No FEAR Act. Sis. Moone was the wife of the late Dr. James Moone, a friend and close confidant of Dr. King, and was the president of the Maryland/DC Chapter of the Southern Christian Leadership Conference. There were others we could enlist from all across the country.

We began organizing, drawing from the federal workers who had supported me during the trial: Janet Howard, Joyce Megginson, and Tanya Ward Jordan from the Department of Commerce, who were plaintiffs in a class action discrimination complaint; Altheria Myers at the Department of Agriculture; Dr. Bill Ellis from the Library of Congress; Michael Bland and Jon Grand from EPA's Chicago office; Dennis Young, Woody Hatcher, and Quinton Lynch from the Corporation for National and Community Service; Matthew Fogg of the US Marshals Service; Pat Lawson from EPA headquarters; and many others, all targets of discrimination. The more we organized, the more word got around, and the more we heard from federal workers. This was not limited to EPA but was government-wide.

Another man, Blair Hayes, had come to one of our meetings several months earlier and confided to me later that the meeting could have been a Tupperware party. A giant of a man physically, Blair worked at the Department of Health and Human Services and had been embroiled in a long string of complaints and lawsuits because he refused to give in and look the other way in the face of racism and corruption. He had already won three lawsuits against the government under the skillful guidance of David Shapiro.

"And I'll tell you something else, Marsha. When I first came to your meetings and heard you and a lot of other ladies sitting around and talking about taking on the federal government—I thought you were crazy. Here you were planning on taking on the most powerful machinery on the face of the earth with your bare hands! But after I listened for a while, and especially after I heard you speak, I decided, 'There's no way you're fighting this fight without me!'"

These people had become circumspect from having been abused by their agencies. Beth Sokul kept her promise to help us find a base from which to fight. She arranged a meeting between our group and Stephen Kohn, president of the National Whistleblowers Center. Stephen and Michael Kohn were Washington's premier whistleblower attorneys. Their partner, David K. Colapinto, had joined them to form the National Whistleblowers Center, in Washington, DC. Steve immediately agreed to allow us to use their conference facilities and all necessary equipment. We were on our way.

We brought in Leroy Warren, Selwyn Cox, and Dwight Welch. From the beginning, I argued that the coalition had to utilize the tactic of in-your-face activism. "Otherwise," I argued, "the coalition will be marginalized and ignored."

For over a year the No FEAR coalition used every tactic imaginable aggressively fighting to get HR 5516 passed in the 106th Congress, with two powerful allies, Republican Sensenbrenner on the right and Democratic congresswoman Sheila Jackson Lee on the left, with both offices fully mobilized. The No FEAR Coalition was at the center of the lobbying efforts, with a small group of courageous allies and friends. For many of us, this was not our first rodeo. We wrote letters, organized fax

campaigns, visited hundreds of congressional offices, forged partnerships with various national organizations interested in workplace issues,
spoke at conferences, networked with churches nationwide, attended a
conference at Harvard organized by a student named Macani Toungara, and worked phone banks. There were many ups and downs, drawbacks and setbacks, but there was no stopping us.

The first House hearing in consideration of the No FEAR Act was
held before the Science Committee, still chaired by Sensenbrenner, who
gaveled it through. Shortly thereafter came the election of 2000, with
the Republicans retaining control of the House and Sensenbrenner in
a position of seniority. Upon taking on chairmanship of the Judiciary
Committee, he called another meeting to reintroduce the No FEAR Act
in the 107th Congress, and it became HR 169. Sensenbrenner gaveled
it through this committee also, in early January. Beth Sokul called me
after the committee meeting.

"We have a date for the vote, Marsha. Mark it on your calendar. The
bill will be going to the floor September 11, 2001."

<hr />

The day before anything important is the Day of the Gremlin. I've
planned weddings, faced publication deadlines, been so buttoned down
I was buttoned up to my neck. But I have yet to see the job in which,
when the last day arrives, everyone's done enough, and the deadline
gremlins do not abound. It could be the cake, the printer, the accommodations, or likely all of these, but I knew going in—the day before the
vote was going to be hell.

The No FEAR Act would be going to the floor the next day, and for
many of us, this was not our first brush with the fickle pre-vote tally
maelstrom that could toss and heave in many directions at once. Much
of what could sink the bill (or any bill) lay in what couldn't be seen in
the water—the bottomless maw of a subcommittee, a rules nicety, any
of the endless ways the opposition could deliver the coup de grace to a
bill that looked like it was sailing toward a waiting president. Having
worked on Capitol Hill navigating a bill through chop, I was well aware
of the crosscurrents and undertows. But this was different. This wasn't
some other people's precious cargo—this was our lives. This was my
life. Everything was on the line.

"We have to do this, Marsha," Segun had insisted time and again in response to my wanting to quit. "This is larger than you now. This is the first time anyone has gotten this far. They will have to change something now, win or lose."

"But what if something blindsides the vote tomorrow? The truth is," I summed up to Segun, "the fate of this vote could depend on whether some unknown lobbyist could have gotten to the right chair, the right chief of staff, or was waiting with some procedural challenge, if need be. What then? Would it have been worth it all then?"

So many plans had gone awry, it being impossible to predict the latest tactic by those federal bosses and their managers who were allied to stop our movement. We represented the potential to free federal employees, when confronted with corruption or discrimination, to speak out without fear. I clung to Segun's words that day, through all the anticipation, the incessant meetings, the last-minute phone calls to members of Congress and with our allies.

We believed that if we could pass the No FEAR Act, federal employees who had filed formal complaints against supervisors they alleged were involved in waste, fraud, or abuse would then have the full weight of law supporting their efforts to protect the public. Federal employees who exposed financial corruption were looking forward to the vindication that would come with Congress passing the bill. This bill would free them to save precious taxpayer dollars. For victims of racial and sexual discrimination, the looming vote represented the day when their race or gender would no longer limit their potential. There were echoes of the Year of Freedom.

Last-minute opposition was anticipated from foes of the bill; that made it more important than ever that supporters rally together. We continued our discussions all day, whether huddled in the halls of Dirksen Senate Office Building or hovering around conference calls with Beth Sokul. Leroy Warren, the NAACP, union leaders including Dwight Welch, other members of the NTEU rank and file, and legions of courageous fighters from the No FEAR Coalition—who simply didn't know how to quit—were all on it. The day consumed the National Whistleblowers Center, our electric hub, where bodies moved in different directions or in concert or even treaded water—in total disbelief that the next day Congress might finally pass the No FEAR Act.

Calls, e-mails, texts, faxes, rumors, and requests for clarification all poured in from believers and nonbelievers alike. "How do you know we won't be sabotaged again?" "Is this a cruel joke—is Congress playing us?" I could only listen—there were no guarantees. The hills had been more numerous than the valleys. We had met more enemies than friends—our numbers were few but daring, people who felt that by principle or destiny, we were deeply intertwined. This close to the ratification, we could not fail.

We spent ten hours that day calling 435 congressional offices—and then surveyed one another to divine whether the members had said anything that should convince us they would vote for the No FEAR Act. We kept a tally of each call. By noon, the tally seemed improbable—we hadn't found a single office that had indicated it would vote against the bill. We called Congresswoman Sheila Jackson Lee's office to see if they had better intelligence than we had on the vote. We were told that the congresswoman was working all of the members, the various caucuses, the Black Caucus, the Caucus for Women's Issues.

Late in the day we also received some very good news. The Republican majority leader, Tom DeLay, in support of Congressman Sensenbrenner, had rallied the Republican majority. Congresswoman Jackson Lee rallying the left, and Sensenbrenner, the right, had made a formidable team. But would it be enough? We continued to call allies and congressional offices until there wasn't a single member's office open on Capitol Hill.

In the rush to tie off loose ends and ensure that nothing could go wrong, all of us had gotten so consumed that we nearly forgot to order the pizza we'd decided this late in the day was the easiest way to celebrate the impending passage of No FEAR. Mark Harrison, the congressional liaison for the United Methodist Church, had offered to serve as our host. The faith-based community was fully engaged. We were less than twenty-four hours from being able to speak openly without fear— to tell the world when danger was near without certainty of retaliation, job loss, or threats to our livelihoods, our minds, or our lives. We all sat around a table, tired, hungry, and spent. At the end of a frenetic day, we all forgot the weight for a moment. We were only a group of friends eating pizza.

It was night when I finally left the Capitol district for the drive home to Maryland. I had been running so long, had been trying to keep things moving forward so hard, had looked at the mountain of things that remained to be done so intently and for so long, that when suddenly there was nothing more I could do, it was like some invisible force reached inside my body and released the knot that had been holding it all together. I felt something close to catatonic, emotionally and spiritually spent. Tomorrow would usher in a new era, one that many before us had championed in their own way.

If my case exposed injustice in the American workplace, then No FEAR represented a law that could protect the less powerful from the uberpowerful—this, because the growing experience for all Americans had become unequal access to equal standing and unequal representation under the law, with, in this corner, the Department of Justice and, in that corner, Joe and Joanne Q.

That was the challenge No FEAR was placing before the House. How were we, as a people, going to protect federal workers from known patterns of criminality within our own government? It was a question that took over a year to formulate, organize, implement, and modify as it was sniffed and poked and prodded—by those who own our elected representatives—for any scent of threat to the status quo, the most concerned being the union that represents federal managers. But with enough grassroots effort and an intense campaign to get letters, e-mails, and bodies in front of representatives, even the money-drippers could be neutralized. Having done all of this, our activist troops were exhausted.

There is a melancholy that accompanies any job well done, when all that the struggle has required—the sacrifice, the concentrated energy, the trust in friends who are carrying their share of the load—embraces us and we encounter a power larger than us all. As I drove home, my thoughts turned to all the people who had offered their hands and reached for the torch. It was a satisfying moment. We had, in our own small way, carried it to the next station.

‖‖‖‖‖‖‖‖‖‖

It was a sparkling-clear September day, one of those rare days in Washington when it feels like anything is possible. It was about seventy degrees. The Capitol dome was inscribed on a crisp, blue sky, with no trace of Washington's unbearable humidity. Approaching the United States Capitol, I felt confident. If you've ever tried to find legal parking anywhere near the Capitol, you know how frustrating that can be. But on that day, some allies in Congress had made things easier by providing special parking privileges near the Capitol building. A little thing, but it made me feel powerful.

It was also a beautiful day politically. In a city where black people and white people—Democrats and Republicans—live separate lives, ignoring and talking past one another, Congress had come together and was about to pass the first civil rights and whistleblower law of the twenty-first century. I was so pleased and proud to have Dr. Ruby Reese Moone with me. After her husband's death, Sis. Moone took on much of his work. She had been a big part of the Poor People's Campaign in Washington in 1968. About five feet tall, with long black hair and a deep southern drawl, she was the chaplain at the University of Maryland, and I adored her. I called her Sis. Moone out of respect for her status in the civil rights movement—a surprisingly feisty warrior for her outward appearance.

Sis. Moone had driven her car to my house around 8:00 A.M. I had been on the phone with coalition partners past midnight with last-minute plans. Congresswoman Connie Morella of Maryland had arranged to provide the tickets to the House of Representatives gallery where the voting would take place. All the way to Capitol Hill we relished examining the similarities and differences between passing the 1964 Civil Rights Act and No FEAR. Sis. Moone's advice and guidance had been indispensable to our strategy.

"God," she said, "has allowed me to live to see two civil rights laws passed into existence."

She reflected on her late husband. "How proud he would have been to see 'the next generation' carrying on the struggle." She laughed. "I can't believe anyone ever questioned that we would pass this law."

I laughed too, adding, "But we found common ground. We made the American political system work." In victory, enemies seem naive.

Congressman Sensenbrenner's arrangements for us to park in front of the Capitol were both a gesture of respect and recognition that I would have a considerable amount of literature, posters, and other memorabilia with me that morning. Two long, hard years of work were about to culminate. I was so happy that I couldn't concentrate on what the woman standing beside my car was telling me about a bomb at the World Trade Center when I pulled into the special parking area.

"I'm sorry, excuse me?"

"I need to check your car. The World Trade Center was bombed again this morning."

The female guard told me that she had to search my car and trunk.

I turned to Sis. Moone. "Maybe the Capitol is on alert, because this is the anniversary of the first Trade Center bombing."

Overhearing me, the guard said, "It's not because of an anniversary. About an hour ago a plane flew into the World Trade Center."

"What does that mean?"

"I don't know," she said. "The Capitol is on alert, and all cars have to be checked."

We spotted our group, standing in front of the Capitol and talking about the bombing in New York. No one had any additional information. The air was heavy with fear and anxiety. I called Beth Sokul to find out more—if anyone had the latest information, Beth did. As soon as she heard my voice, Beth said, "Marsha, where are you?"

"I'm standing with our group in front of the Capitol. What the heck is going on in New York?"

Her speech was racing and anxious but delivered in a low, tenuous voice. "We're monitoring the situation. It doesn't look good. It looks like the planes were intentionally flown into the World Trade Center. This could be an act of terrorism."

I couldn't wrap my mind around planes being intentionally flown into the World Trade Center . . . a second attack at the same site—it seemed surreal.

"Sit tight," Beth said, "I'll get more information and call you back."

Sis. Moone and I didn't know what to think or do. It started looking like all of our plans were in jeopardy. Beth called me a few minutes later and told me that we should start moving to the gallery section of the Capitol where the House votes took place. She explained, "Congressman Sensenbrenner is in the underground train on his way to the Capitol to introduce the bill."

Later Beth called back and said, "Most likely the Capitol will be shut down after this vote. There's a possibility that the Capitol could also be under attack."

The North Tower of the World Trade Center had been hit at about quarter of nine in the morning, and, within minutes, news of the attack had reached Congress. When the South Tower of the World Trade

Center was hit just after nine, we opined that this was no accident. I informed our group that we should get in line, that the congressman was on his way.

As we started moving toward the Capitol steps, a large plane flew over the building—so low that I could see the symbols on its belly. We all looked up because of the roar of the engine. Someone remarked, "I thought the Capitol was a no-fly zone." The plane circled, taking some outer route.

I called Beth again for reassurance and comfort. She said, "The vote is on." We needed to get into the gallery as quickly as possible.

Within minutes, we heard a loud explosion from the direction of the Pentagon. I wasn't sure what had happened, but I felt deep in my gut that the low-flying plane I'd just seen was not being navigated by some poor pilot who'd lost his bearings.

Norris McDonald ran over to me. "Marsha, I'm a single father. This morning the World Trade Center was bombed—now the Pentagon. I'm out of here. I think we're standing on ground zero." Norris took off.

We were standing on the side of the Capitol and could see the Pentagon belching black and gray smoke. I called Beth again and told her that smoke was coming from the direction of the Pentagon. Then a guard screamed out from the top of the Capitol steps, "Run for your lives! The Capitol is under attack!"

Somebody in the crowd yelled, "The Capitol is under attack!" And then hundreds of people started shrieking and running down the Capitol steps.

People were losing their footing. Faces blurred past. People dropped their purses and pocketbooks and briefcases in a mad scramble, and other people tripped over the jettisoned personal items littering the ground. Within milliseconds, hundreds, perhaps thousands of people started streaming from the Capitol, men and women, shouting and pushing, bunny hopping down the short steps. People were tumbling down the Capitol steps like feathers, tripping over one another, eyes bulging, with only one thought in mind: How do I get out of here?

Where was Sis. Moone? I remembered that before the rush, she had been standing next to me. I couldn't see anyone I knew. I yelled out her name but got no response. I was being jostled by the crowd and by a sense of survival. I saw Leroy Warren. He was on the ground with blood gushing from his head. He had fallen or fallen victim to the mob rushing for safety. Janet and Tanya were trying to stop the bleeding while Joyce and Altheria were exhorting him and others to flee.

But where was safety?

I finally caught a glimpse of Sis. Moone standing by herself next to a tree. She was bent over, holding her chest. Her breathing was labored. I ran over to her. "Sis. Moone, this is not the time to have a heart attack. We have to run!"

She looked up and gave me a slight smile as if to say, I've seen war before. "OK, let's go."

She was sixty-two years old, and she'd just run down a long staircase in a panic. Obviously, she needed a rest. But we were all going to die, we thought, if we didn't get out of there. I dragged her by the hand and pulled her down the street, quickly. Where is the safety? Where are we going?

It's a good distance from the Capitol to the congressional administrative buildings. We passed the Rayburn Building. These buildings no longer represented the seat of US power—they were simply targets that we had to get as far away from as possible. Congressional staffers and visitors were fleeing. There were screams and yells—people calling out names. Friends and coworkers. Loved ones. Nothing made sense. What's happening? Who is after us? Why?

Beth Sokul had told me, "We're going to pass the bill first—and then recess," just before the phone lines died. What's happened to Beth? Where is she? Is she in this stream of bodies fleeing Rayburn? The world was crumbling beneath our feet. Will this be over in minutes? Hours? Ever?

‖‖‖‖‖‖‖‖

Beth, I later found out, had dropped the phone when the evacuation order was given. She, like her colleagues, ran to the nearest exit in hopes of surviving what they thought would be another bombing. She made her way down the corridor. People were shouting and pushing and trying to get an advantage. She finally arrived at the steps. Congressional staffers, like their counterparts at the Capitol, were running for their lives.

Halfway down the stairs, with hundreds of people pushing and shoving behind her, she remembered that she had left her No FEAR folder on her desk. Beth elbowed her way back up the stairs away from safety. She

found her way back through deserted corridors that only minutes earlier had been filled with alert staffers attending constituents. Now, with
everyone gone, the clamor outside filled the long stone halls with the
sounds that fear makes. She reached her desk and looked around—she
was alone. Once she found her folder, she was gripped anew with fear,
realizing that coming back might turn out to be her last act on earth.
She picked up her phone.

"Stan, pick up the phone," Beth said as the number rang. She got the
recording. I'm sorry, we're not home. If you want to speak to Beth or
Stan, please leave a message.

She waited for the beep. "Stan, pick up the phone . . . please!" Then
quickly, "Stan, Rayburn is being evacuated. They blew up the World
Trade Center this morning and"—her voice cracking—"I think the
Capitol is next. If I don't make it, I love you!" Tears rolled down her face.
"Please tell my boys that I love them."

This woman, a white, middle-class professional, who had so little in
common with me in her cultural background, had scratched and clawed
her way against all the panicked people fleeing—to get to that folder. She
had come to believe so strongly in the No FEAR bill that in her heart
and by her actions, she was ready to give her life for it. And Congressman Sensenbrenner said repeatedly in the days and weeks following, "I
almost died for this bill." He had gotten stuck in the tunnel beneath the
Capitol as the terrorists took aim at Washington.

I tried to call Segun on my cell phone to let him know that I was
fine and that I had survived the evacuation. Sis. Moone and I found a
small cafe open on Pennsylvania Avenue. It became a sanctuary—congressional staff members and folks from all walks of life were huddled
together in total disbelief. I prayed that Segun would be able to pick up
our children and that the school would not release them to anyone but
him. The thought that my children were vulnerable nearly drove me
mad. I was frantic, desperate. I considered removing my dress shoes
and running, but to where? I went outside for fresh air. Soldiers were
posted on the tops of buildings with guns in hand. Military vehicles
were moving to their posts. Within hours, Washington, DC, was a militarized zone.

||||||||||||

Whistleblower protection in that first, queer daze after the attacks seemed insignificant to most Americans, but to us it was ironic. We knew instinctively that some unknown federal workers could have warned—or more than likely did try to warn—America about those very attacks. In fact, on September 13, 2001, two days after the disaster, Dwight Welch in his capacity as both an EPA biologist and union leader wrote to EPA administrator Christine Whitman warning her about human exposure to chemicals combusted as a result of the attacks on the Pentagon and the World Trade Center.

> As I drove by the Pentagon on Wednesday, I noted the building was still burning! This old building is loaded with toxins such as asbestos, PCBs, and materials which upon burning could create even more toxic combustion products. . . . The decision to encourage nonessential Pentagon employees to report to work not only compromised employee health and safety and showed a lack of compassion for the grieving. . . . On my way to work today, I heard a radio broadcast which indicated that the EPA said that smoke coming from the Pentagon and the WTC [World Trade Center] was not all that hazardous. I hope this was an error on the part of the broadcaster. I would like to see that data upon which this pronouncement was made.[1]

Dwight's warning, as well as other whistleblowers, would be ignored. Firefighters, first responders, and volunteers were exposed to toxic substances. Dwight never received the courtesy of a response to his memo.

Considering that whistleblowers, such as Dwight and Siebel Edmonds, continued to sound the alarm, it took some getting used to when the congressional and media reaction to our raising the topic of No FEAR legislation was greeted with questions about our relevance after 9/11. If you weren't about 9/11, you didn't exist for either Congress or the news. But we existed among ourselves, and we were not going to be brushed aside any more than was F. James Sensenbrenner, who called to say he was serious about No FEAR legislation and was going to see it through. Sadly, the next few years would find whistleblowers in the forefront of telling truth to power when intelligence officers revealed that the government had known a lot more about the impending 9/11 disaster than the Bush administration had led the country to believe.

The House vote was rescheduled within a week of Sensenbrenner's call, for October 3, 2001. Scores of federal workers were sitting in the ornate gallery of the US House of Representatives. To many of the nervous, fidgety, battle-weary, and post-9/11 traumatized federal workers, this was the day that we had dreamt about, fought for, and perhaps even secretly thought we would never see. Win or lose, this was our day.

Congressman Sensenbrenner took to the podium, with Beth Sokul seated behind him. "Mr. President, it is my honor to introduce the first civil rights law of the twenty-first century—No FEAR. The law is being introduced because of the outrageous abuse that is taking place in the federal government and its impact on national and international policy."

The wild swings in emotion that had washed over all of us in the last month had redefined exhaustion for me. After the push to get the vote right before the attacks, we had all been nearly giddy approaching the Capitol the first time around. The anguish that had unfolded with the deadly attacks had knocked down a part of all of us.

Congresswoman Sheila Jackson Lee took the podium.

"Mr. President, I rise to cosponsor the first civil rights act of the twenty-first century—No FEAR. . . .

"Federal government workers have fought long and hard. Many have lost their families, their jobs—everything they hold dear—to see this day." The congresswoman's voice was deep and powerful. "If we could place a human face on this law, it would be the face of Dr. Marsha Coleman-Adebayo. She has been a tireless fighter and leader."

I felt the hands of coalition members patting me on the shoulder. One of them spoke softly to me from behind. "How does it feel to have the entire Congress condemn the way EPA treated you?"

Segun squeezed my hand.

The vote was called. The illumination of the names of the 435 members was near blinding, the feeling otherworldly. Members representing every community in the United States spilled onto the floor of the Capitol. They were laughing and horse trading votes. Sensenbrenner, Sokul, and Jackson Lee looked up into the gallery; their eyes were asking: Do you see what is happening? The moment was here. Our eyes communicated back: Are you sure you have the votes to pass this law?

In the gallery we were federal government workers, we were family, we were friends, and we instinctively all locked arms. One member of our group leaned over the back of my chair.

"What's the magic number?"

"218."

We were dead silent before the numbers began to appear in the yea and nay columns posted on the wall above the podium. We were prepared for a fight. We had all tasted victory and defeat before, but none of that seemed as laden as the outcome today. Fifty votes went into the yea column, then one hundred.

150.

Someone said, "My God! We are looking at a unanimous vote for No FEAR!"

Two hundred yeas. We looked at one another—what was happening?

210.

218!

"My God!" I whispered loudly to Segun, "We just passed a law!"

Sensenbrenner, Beth, and Jackson Lee looked up to the gallery, giving us the thumbs-up. We were still waiting for the hammer to hit with the votes in the nay category, but the yeas kept piling up: 300 . . . 350 . . . 400 . . . 420. No FEAR had passed the House of Representatives! We all jumped up and started hugging and kissing. Some were crying.

It is a rare moment most will never see when history greets victory with a kiss.

Beth Sokul met us as we filed out of the gallery. She was reserved but overjoyed. We all took turns hugging her. Beth is in our blood forever now.

"We need to see the chairman," I told her. "We need to savor this moment together."

Beth called him on his cell phone. Segun and most workers had to leave before the core of our group followed Beth down the long hall that was filling with laughter and its echoes. The chairman was sitting behind his desk. He stood up when we arrived.

"Mr. Chairman," I said, "today we have made Martin Luther King and all the civil rights martyrs proud. We have just passed a law without money or resources. What we had was our faith in Almighty God and a passion for justice. Under your leadership, and Congresswoman Jackson Lee's, the US Congress has carried out its historic mission to fight for people who cannot fight for themselves. Today, the Congress was truly the people's house. And we thank you, and Beth, for all of your commitment and hard work.

"I would like to celebrate this moment in the way that Dr. King taught us, by singing 'We Shall Overcome.' Do you know the words?"

I had never understood the words to this song before that moment.

We crossed our hands, in the traditional style, and sang with all our hearts. Young Republican staffers, hearing unfamiliar sounds coming from the chairman's office ran in as if Congressman Sensenbrenner had been taken hostage, but stopped—first embarrassed and then delighted—when they found Sensenbrenner absorbed in the singing.

As we started to file out of the office, thanking Beth and the chairman for the vote, Blair Hayes stopped to shake hands with him.

"The way you look, and the party that you represent, and the state you come from," Blair said, "I never would have picked you as someone who would have supported someone who looks like me."

Sensenbrenner laughed. As I turned to leave, the congressman pulled me aside. "Marsha, you had me and Jackson Lee on this side of Congress. The Senate is going to be a completely different ball of wax."

Riding the indescribable high from the vote, I told Sensenbrenner, "After the year and a half it took to win this vote—we're ready for anything."

Al Sharpton:
The X Factor

Beth called very soon after that to say that Republican senator John Warner would sponsor on the Senate side. If we already had a Republican sponsor and the Democrats were the civil rights party, I thought, how hard could it be?

Ah, Candide. It soon became clear that in the Senate the Democrats had circled the wagons around their president and were not about to go to the mat for civil rights abuses that happened during his administration. OK, we reasoned, in this we're faced with another challenge. We started canvassing the Senate side looking for allies among the Democrats but getting utterly nowhere. Federal workers who were supporting the No FEAR Act were getting knocked around right and left when their agencies identified them. There were more than a few huffing and puffing sessions where No FEAR coalition members vented frustration at being stonewalled by the Democrats. We contacted every Democrat in the Senate, the liberal lions including Ted Kennedy, Robert Byrd, and Pat Leahy. None of the members would meet with us personally. They had no time for us in their schedules. Those offices that did grant meetings did so perfunctorily.

I had read every book I could find on the civil rights movement for guidance on getting the No FEAR Act passed, and we did everything by the rules. The coalition had faxed letters, marched in front of offices— all the traditional things that were supposed to have an impact on Congress—to no avail. We were becoming perplexed and frustrated.

of soap. Slippery as she goes! See someone approaching whom you may have a bone with? Slip into an adjoining office and let them pass. Got a little something for the folks back home? Slip it into the rider the president can't possibly veto. It's a slippery place, Washington. Greased with money, power, and cunning. But none of these are going to help me out of this funk. Hand me the bath towel. I've had enough of grease.

If I really wipe it all off, the amenities come off with it: the paycheck, the travel, the access to the express lane past all the gatekeepers between me and the people who make the decisions, access that is gained by my simply saying, "This is Dr. Coleman-Adebayo from OIA." But by far the most worrisome is losing the ability to provide for my children the opportunities and lifestyle my mother could never even have dreamed of. Kiss all of that good-bye. Why, you could fit all the people who have ever known that kind of grease in US history into a single 747 and still have a few empty seats in coach. That's why it's so difficult to let go, and so few who have tasted it ever do. But this thing has been gnawing on my face. I know it. Yet when I look in the mirror today I don't see any evidence. These are my eyes. This is my nose. These, the same lips. I still look pretty good, considering. I wish I could say that I feel like absolute shit. But that's the problem: I don't. If I did, I'd have to do something to take action against it. Maybe I just have to keep winnowing away.

I had thought that by virtue of hard work and applied brainpower I'd have been embraced by those in power. Hard work and excellence had always paid off before. They got me through the Ivy League. It turned out I could be at home within America's elite institutions as much as I was at home at a Black Panthers children's breakfast program in Detroit. Or just as marginalized. I've been riding the laser-thin beam between them without realizing it had sawed me in two. But don't think of it as one-half white, one black. No. Think of it as someone who is sawed in two, with a healthy aversion to gray.

And there it is. Today, I am gray.

A Call to History

"Hello, Marsha? This is Beth Sokul."

She didn't have to identify that sultry voice. When I'd first met Beth, it had surprised me that someone with her outward appearance of conservatism could have such a seductive and passionate voice. The more I got to know her and see her brilliant and savvy mind in action, the more it seemed the only voice she could possibly have been given.

"Do you have a few minutes to talk?"

I was in my office ruminating anyway. "Of course, Beth. What is it?"

I was actually surprised to hear her voice again so soon after the hearing. Whatever that day might have put in motion, if anything, would still be months away. The likelier reality was that Sensenbrenner had had his way with Carol Browner and would savor the fact of her humiliation as a small part of his other, more pressing concerns.

"How are you, Marsha?"

"Honestly? It's a little weird, Beth. If I thought I was isolated before the hearing, let me tell you . . ."

"I bet." Beth had not called this time to listen to my complaints. "Listen, Sensenbrenner wants to introduce legislation as the result of your testimony."

I nearly dropped the phone. I was too stunned to say anything, especially since the last time Beth and I had spoken, she had told me legislation was a long shot. "Maybe 5 percent of all hearings ever result in proposed legislation," Beth had said. "So don't get your hopes up. There's only a small possibility that Congress might act."

"I was instructed to call Sheila Jackson Lee," Beth continued. "She is going to cosponsor the bill. We are talking with her office to see what form the legislation will take. We're drafting the language right now."

"That's fantastic! Oh my God! Thank you so much, Beth! And thank Chairman Sensenbrenner! You have no idea how gratifying this is. It's like someone has thrown me a lifeline!"

"Now, Marsha, tell me what you think about this: All through your testimony you kept using the word *fear*. 'We work in an atmosphere of fear.' 'Fear and intimidation.' What do you think of the 'No FEAR Act'? Our staff came up with that. The Notification of Federal Employees Anti-discrimination and Retaliation Act. No FEAR."

"Are you kidding? I love it! Beth, this is a gift from God! You have no idea."

"No FEAR, Marsha. We're going to see this thing through. This legislation would be the first civil rights and whistleblower law of the twenty-first century."

By then I had forgotten what I had wanted to complain about earlier.

I was so happy I stood up and danced a jig beside my desk, stifling the "Yahoo!" that would get me fired for unlawful exuberance. The Congress of the United States of America was taking my side of the two stories they heard that day in Room 2320 of Rayburn. Now, as a nation, we would consider condemnation of the policies of the Browner administration. There were a hundred people to call: Segun, the group, my friends, family. We would have to organize, comb through Congress to see where our friends—and enemies—were. There were so many things that would have to get done. I was reeling from excitement, satisfaction, and disbelief. But most of this, I suddenly realized, was just more grease. It was how you got things done in this town.

I began with Segun. I called him, and we danced together over the phone to the accompanying music of the thought of legislation. I called my mother, and we rejoiced. I called Theresa Fleming-Blue. "What did I tell you, Marsha? Didn't I tell you the Lord would see you through? Didn't I tell you we were fasting for this day?" And she was so right. This was what I needed. Segun, Mom, my friends, and trust in the Lord. The rest was grease. In the small, bright, cramped, and improbable sanctuary of my office inside the EPA, I closed down inside this inner sanctum that has been with me all along and offered my thanks.

Journey to No FEAR

The legislation could not have been passed without the sheer pain and the sheer agony of so many employees who came forward to mention that their lives were made almost in the form of a nightmare because they chose to stand up.

—Representative Sheila Jackson Lee

No grassroots political struggle has ever prevailed operating under a white flag. In democracy, if the people want to influence governmental authority—which has gotten so cozy with corporate lobbies and their dizzying resources—the people must organize and force the politicians to intervene. I knew that with a court victory I could no longer be dismissed as an uppity agitator. This is not to say that the government would not continue to paint me as the next Malcolm in a pantsuit, but they could no longer portray the story as irrelevant. Everyday Americans had just weighed in. Media was running with the story, and the elephant was loose. If we wanted to put the story's momentum toward any meaningful reform, the time to move was upon us.

This is where my political science background, Congressional Black Caucus Foundation experience of mobilizing constituencies, and knowledge of lots of people at various levels and departments on the Hill would prove invaluable. The NAACP and SCLC, representing

millions of untapped assets, could help with mobilization. I kept these as talking points when I followed up with Beth Sokul about meeting with Chairman Sensenbrenner, even though Beth needed no additional prodding.

Beth invited me into the congressman's office and said, "You will need a political base to fight for this bill."

Beth was disarming, straightforward, and kind. Her two young sons were in the office, playing with an erector set, engaged in the loud negotiations that occur between siblings. This was not the buttoned-down corporate atmosphere I'd expected from a Republican congressman. Beth listened to what I'd gone through at EPA, responding as I might expect a friend to, first thoughtful, then outraged.

"The chairman has watched your case closely and has been appalled by what he's learned. He has instructed me to make No FEAR my highest priority. Here's my cell number. Here's my home phone. You can call me any time of day or night. He will help you in this fight."

As I tucked her business card into my purse, Beth looked at me and smiled. "Looks like you and I are going to be attached at the hip for as long as this takes."

||||||||||||

Dr. Ruby Reese Moone and I met to discuss creating an organization based on the model of EPAVARD to lead the fight to pass the No FEAR Act. Sis. Moone was the wife of the late Dr. James Moone, a friend and close confidant of Dr. King, and was the president of the Maryland/DC Chapter of the Southern Christian Leadership Conference. There were others we could enlist from all across the country.

We began organizing, drawing from the federal workers who had supported me during the trial: Janet Howard, Joyce Megginson, and Tanya Ward Jordan from the Department of Commerce, who were plaintiffs in a class action discrimination complaint; Altheria Myers at the Department of Agriculture; Dr. Bill Ellis from the Library of Congress; Michael Bland and Jon Grand from EPA's Chicago office; Dennis Young, Woody Hatcher, and Quinton Lynch from the Corporation for National and Community Service; Matthew Fogg of the US Marshals Service; Pat Lawson from EPA headquarters; and many others,

all targets of discrimination. The more we organized, the more word got around, and the more we heard from federal workers. This was not limited to EPA but was government-wide.

Another man, Blair Hayes, had come to one of our meetings several months earlier and confided to me later that the meeting could have been a Tupperware party. A giant of a man physically, Blair worked at the Department of Health and Human Services and had been embroiled in a long string of complaints and lawsuits because he refused to give in and look the other way in the face of racism and corruption. He had already won three lawsuits against the government under the skillful guidance of David Shapiro.

"And I'll tell you something else, Marsha. When I first came to your meetings and heard you and a lot of other ladies sitting around and talking about taking on the federal government—I thought you were crazy. Here you were planning on taking on the most powerful machinery on the face of the earth with your bare hands! But after I listened for a while, and especially after I heard you speak, I decided, 'There's no way you're fighting this fight without me!'"

These people had become circumspect from having been abused by their agencies. Beth Sokul kept her promise to help us find a base from which to fight. She arranged a meeting between our group and Stephen Kohn, president of the National Whistleblowers Center. Stephen and Michael Kohn were Washington's premier whistleblower attorneys. Their partner, David K. Colapinto, had joined them to form the National Whistleblowers Center, in Washington, DC. Steve immediately agreed to allow us to use their conference facilities and all necessary equipment. We were on our way.

We brought in Leroy Warren, Selwyn Cox, and Dwight Welch. From the beginning, I argued that the coalition had to utilize the tactic of in-your-face activism. "Otherwise," I argued, "the coalition will be marginalized and ignored."

For over a year the No FEAR coalition used every tactic imaginable aggressively fighting to get HR 5516 passed in the 106th Congress, with two powerful allies, Republican Sensenbrenner on the right and Democratic congresswoman Sheila Jackson Lee on the left, with both offices fully mobilized. The No FEAR Coalition was at the center of the lobbying efforts, with a small group of courageous allies and friends. For many of us, this was not our first rodeo. We wrote letters, organized fax

campaigns, visited hundreds of congressional offices, forged partnerships with various national organizations interested in workplace issues, spoke at conferences, networked with churches nationwide, attended a conference at Harvard organized by a student named Macani Toungara, and worked phone banks. There were many ups and downs, drawbacks and setbacks, but there was no stopping us.

The first House hearing in consideration of the No FEAR Act was held before the Science Committee, still chaired by Sensenbrenner, who gaveled it through. Shortly thereafter came the election of 2000, with the Republicans retaining control of the House and Sensenbrenner in a position of seniority. Upon taking on chairmanship of the Judiciary Committee, he called another meeting to reintroduce the No FEAR Act in the 107th Congress, and it became HR 169. Sensenbrenner gaveled it through this committee also, in early January. Beth Sokul called me after the committee meeting.

"We have a date for the vote, Marsha. Mark it on your calendar. The bill will be going to the floor September 11, 2001."

ıııııııııııı

The day before anything important is the Day of the Gremlin. I've planned weddings, faced publication deadlines, been so buttoned down I was buttoned up to my neck. But I have yet to see the job in which, when the last day arrives, everyone's done enough, and the deadline gremlins do not abound. It could be the cake, the printer, the accommodations, or likely all of these, but I knew going in—the day before the vote was going to be hell.

The No FEAR Act would be going to the floor the next day, and for many of us, this was not our first brush with the fickle pre-vote tally maelstrom that could toss and heave in many directions at once. Much of what could sink the bill (or any bill) lay in what couldn't be seen in the water—the bottomless maw of a subcommittee, a rules nicety, any of the endless ways the opposition could deliver the coup de grace to a bill that looked like it was sailing toward a waiting president. Having worked on Capitol Hill navigating a bill through chop, I was well aware of the crosscurrents and undertows. But this was different. This wasn't some other people's precious cargo—this was our lives. This was my life. Everything was on the line.

"We have to do this, Marsha," Segun had insisted time and again in response to my wanting to quit. "This is larger than you now. This is the first time anyone has gotten this far. They will have to change something now, win or lose."

"But what if something blindsides the vote tomorrow? The truth is," I summed up to Segun, "the fate of this vote could depend on whether some unknown lobbyist could have gotten to the right chair, the right chief of staff, or was waiting with some procedural challenge, if need be. What then? Would it have been worth it all then?"

So many plans had gone awry, it being impossible to predict the latest tactic by those federal bosses and their managers who were allied to stop our movement. We represented the potential to free federal employees, when confronted with corruption or discrimination, to speak out without fear. I clung to Segun's words that day, through all the anticipation, the incessant meetings, the last-minute phone calls to members of Congress and with our allies.

We believed that if we could pass the No FEAR Act, federal employees who had filed formal complaints against supervisors they alleged were involved in waste, fraud, or abuse would then have the full weight of law supporting their efforts to protect the public. Federal employees who exposed financial corruption were looking forward to the vindication that would come with Congress passing the bill. This bill would free them to save precious taxpayer dollars. For victims of racial and sexual discrimination, the looming vote represented the day when their race or gender would no longer limit their potential. There were echoes of the Year of Freedom.

Last-minute opposition was anticipated from foes of the bill; that made it more important than ever that supporters rally together. We continued our discussions all day, whether huddled in the halls of Dirksen Senate Office Building or hovering around conference calls with Beth Sokul. Leroy Warren, the NAACP, union leaders including Dwight Welch, other members of the NTEU rank and file, and legions of courageous fighters from the No FEAR Coalition—who simply didn't know how to quit—were all on it. The day consumed the National Whistleblowers Center, our electric hub, where bodies moved in different directions or in concert or even treaded water—in total disbelief that the next day Congress might finally pass the No FEAR Act.

Calls, e-mails, texts, faxes, rumors, and requests for clarification all poured in from believers and nonbelievers alike. "How do you know we won't be sabotaged again?" "Is this a cruel joke—is Congress playing us?" I could only listen—there were no guarantees. The hills had been more numerous than the valleys. We had met more enemies than friends—our numbers were few but daring, people who felt that by principle or destiny, we were deeply intertwined. This close to the ratification, we could not fail.

We spent ten hours that day calling 435 congressional offices—and then surveyed one another to divine whether the members had said anything that should convince us they would vote for the No FEAR Act. We kept a tally of each call. By noon, the tally seemed improbable—we hadn't found a single office that had indicated it would vote against the bill. We called Congresswoman Sheila Jackson Lee's office to see if they had better intelligence than we had on the vote. We were told that the congresswoman was working all of the members, the various caucuses, the Black Caucus, the Caucus for Women's Issues.

Late in the day we also received some very good news. The Republican majority leader, Tom DeLay, in support of Congressman Sensenbrenner, had rallied the Republican majority. Congresswoman Jackson Lee rallying the left, and Sensenbrenner, the right, had made a formidable team. But would it be enough? We continued to call allies and congressional offices until there wasn't a single member's office open on Capitol Hill.

In the rush to tie off loose ends and ensure that nothing could go wrong, all of us had gotten so consumed that we nearly forgot to order the pizza we'd decided this late in the day was the easiest way to celebrate the impending passage of No FEAR. Mark Harrison, the congressional liaison for the United Methodist Church, had offered to serve as our host. The faith-based community was fully engaged. We were less than twenty-four hours from being able to speak openly without fear— to tell the world when danger was near without certainty of retaliation, job loss, or threats to our livelihoods, our minds, or our lives. We all sat around a table, tired, hungry, and spent. At the end of a frenetic day, we all forgot the weight for a moment. We were only a group of friends eating pizza.

It was night when I finally left the Capitol district for the drive home to Maryland. I had been running so long, had been trying to keep

things moving forward so hard, had looked at the mountain of things that remained to be done so intently and for so long, that when suddenly there was nothing more I could do, it was like some invisible force reached inside my body and released the knot that had been holding it all together. I felt something close to catatonic, emotionally and spiritually spent. Tomorrow would usher in a new era, one that many before us had championed in their own way.

If my case exposed injustice in the American workplace, then No FEAR represented a law that could protect the less powerful from the uberpowerful—this, because the growing experience for all Americans had become unequal access to equal standing and unequal representation under the law, with, in this corner, the Department of Justice and, in that corner, Joe and Joanne Q.

That was the challenge No FEAR was placing before the House. How were we, as a people, going to protect federal workers from known patterns of criminality within our own government? It was a question that took over a year to formulate, organize, implement, and modify as it was sniffed and poked and prodded—by those who own our elected representatives—for any scent of threat to the status quo, the most concerned being the union that represents federal managers. But with enough grassroots effort and an intense campaign to get letters, e-mails, and bodies in front of representatives, even the money-drippers could be neutralized. Having done all of this, our activist troops were exhausted.

There is a melancholy that accompanies any job well done, when all that the struggle has required—the sacrifice, the concentrated energy, the trust in friends who are carrying their share of the load—embraces us and we encounter a power larger than us all. As I drove home, my thoughts turned to all the people who had offered their hands and reached for the torch. It was a satisfying moment. We had, in our own small way, carried it to the next station.

ııııııııııı

It was a sparkling-clear September day, one of those rare days in Washington when it feels like anything is possible. It was about seventy degrees. The Capitol dome was inscribed on a crisp, blue sky, with no trace of Washington's unbearable humidity. Approaching the United States Capitol, I felt confident. If you've ever tried to find legal parking

anywhere near the Capitol, you know how frustrating that can be. But on that day, some allies in Congress had made things easier by providing special parking privileges near the Capitol building. A little thing, but it made me feel powerful.

It was also a beautiful day politically. In a city where black people and white people—Democrats and Republicans—live separate lives, ignoring and talking past one another, Congress had come together and was about to pass the first civil rights and whistleblower law of the twenty-first century. I was so pleased and proud to have Dr. Ruby Reese Moone with me. After her husband's death, Sis. Moone took on much of his work. She had been a big part of the Poor People's Campaign in Washington in 1968. About five feet tall, with long black hair and a deep southern drawl, she was the chaplain at the University of Maryland, and I adored her. I called her Sis. Moone out of respect for her status in the civil rights movement—a surprisingly feisty warrior for her outward appearance.

Sis. Moone had driven her car to my house around 8:00 A.M. I had been on the phone with coalition partners past midnight with last-minute plans. Congresswoman Connie Morella of Maryland had arranged to provide the tickets to the House of Representatives gallery where the voting would take place. All the way to Capitol Hill we relished examining the similarities and differences between passing the 1964 Civil Rights Act and No FEAR. Sis. Moone's advice and guidance had been indispensable to our strategy.

"God," she said, "has allowed me to live to see two civil rights laws passed into existence."

She reflected on her late husband. "How proud he would have been to see 'the next generation' carrying on the struggle." She laughed. "I can't believe anyone ever questioned that we would pass this law."

I laughed too, adding, "But we found common ground. We made the American political system work." In victory, enemies seem naive.

Congressman Sensenbrenner's arrangements for us to park in front of the Capitol were both a gesture of respect and recognition that I would have a considerable amount of literature, posters, and other memorabilia with me that morning. Two long, hard years of work were about to culminate. I was so happy that I couldn't concentrate on what the woman standing beside my car was telling me about a bomb at the World Trade Center when I pulled into the special parking area.

"I'm sorry, excuse me?"

"I need to check your car. The World Trade Center was bombed again this morning."

The female guard told me that she had to search my car and trunk.

I turned to Sis. Moone. "Maybe the Capitol is on alert, because this is the anniversary of the first Trade Center bombing."

Overhearing me, the guard said, "It's not because of an anniversary. About an hour ago a plane flew into the World Trade Center."

"What does that mean?"

"I don't know," she said. "The Capitol is on alert, and all cars have to be checked."

We spotted our group, standing in front of the Capitol and talking about the bombing in New York. No one had any additional information. The air was heavy with fear and anxiety. I called Beth Sokul to find out more—if anyone had the latest information, Beth did. As soon as she heard my voice, Beth said, "Marsha, where are you?"

"I'm standing with our group in front of the Capitol. What the heck is going on in New York?"

Her speech was racing and anxious but delivered in a low, tenuous voice. "We're monitoring the situation. It doesn't look good. It looks like the planes were intentionally flown into the World Trade Center. This could be an act of terrorism."

I couldn't wrap my mind around planes being intentionally flown into the World Trade Center . . . a second attack at the same site—it seemed surreal.

"Sit tight," Beth said, "I'll get more information and call you back."

Sis. Moone and I didn't know what to think or do. It started looking like all of our plans were in jeopardy. Beth called me a few minutes later and told me that we should start moving to the gallery section of the Capitol where the House votes took place. She explained, "Congressman Sensenbrenner is in the underground train on his way to the Capitol to introduce the bill."

Later Beth called back and said, "Most likely the Capitol will be shut down after this vote. There's a possibility that the Capitol could also be under attack."

The North Tower of the World Trade Center had been hit at about quarter of nine in the morning, and, within minutes, news of the attack had reached Congress. When the South Tower of the World Trade

Center was hit just after nine, we opined that this was no accident. I informed our group that we should get in line, that the congressman was on his way.

As we started moving toward the Capitol steps, a large plane flew over the building—so low that I could see the symbols on its belly. We all looked up because of the roar of the engine. Someone remarked, "I thought the Capitol was a no-fly zone." The plane circled, taking some outer route.

I called Beth again for reassurance and comfort. She said, "The vote is on." We needed to get into the gallery as quickly as possible.

Within minutes, we heard a loud explosion from the direction of the Pentagon. I wasn't sure what had happened, but I felt deep in my gut that the low-flying plane I'd just seen was not being navigated by some poor pilot who'd lost his bearings.

Norris McDonald ran over to me. "Marsha, I'm a single father. This morning the World Trade Center was bombed—now the Pentagon. I'm out of here. I think we're standing on ground zero." Norris took off.

We were standing on the side of the Capitol and could see the Pentagon belching black and gray smoke. I called Beth again and told her that smoke was coming from the direction of the Pentagon. Then a guard screamed out from the top of the Capitol steps, "Run for your lives! The Capitol is under attack!"

Somebody in the crowd yelled, "The Capitol is under attack!" And then hundreds of people started shrieking and running down the Capitol steps.

People were losing their footing. Faces blurred past. People dropped their purses and pocketbooks and briefcases in a mad scramble, and other people tripped over the jettisoned personal items littering the ground. Within milliseconds, hundreds, perhaps thousands of people started streaming from the Capitol, men and women, shouting and pushing, bunny hopping down the short steps. People were tumbling down the Capitol steps like feathers, tripping over one another, eyes bulging, with only one thought in mind: How do I get out of here?

Where was Sis. Moone? I remembered that before the rush, she had been standing next to me. I couldn't see anyone I knew. I yelled out her name but got no response. I was being jostled by the crowd and by a sense of survival. I saw Leroy Warren. He was on the ground with blood gushing from his head. He had fallen or fallen victim to the mob

rushing for safety. Janet and Tanya were trying to stop the bleeding while Joyce and Altheria were exhorting him and others to flee.

But where was safety?

I finally caught a glimpse of Sis. Moone standing by herself next to a tree. She was bent over, holding her chest. Her breathing was labored. I ran over to her. "Sis. Moone, this is not the time to have a heart attack. We have to run!"

She looked up and gave me a slight smile as if to say, I've seen war before. "OK, let's go."

She was sixty-two years old, and she'd just run down a long staircase in a panic. Obviously, she needed a rest. But we were all going to die, we thought, if we didn't get out of there. I dragged her by the hand and pulled her down the street, quickly. Where is the safety? Where are we going?

It's a good distance from the Capitol to the congressional administrative buildings. We passed the Rayburn Building. These buildings no longer represented the seat of US power—they were simply targets that we had to get as far away from as possible. Congressional staffers and visitors were fleeing. There were screams and yells—people calling out names. Friends and coworkers. Loved ones. Nothing made sense. What's happening? Who is after us? Why?

Beth Sokul had told me, "We're going to pass the bill first—and then recess," just before the phone lines died. What's happened to Beth? Where is she? Is she in this stream of bodies fleeing Rayburn? The world was crumbling beneath our feet. Will this be over in minutes? Hours? Ever?

‖‖‖‖‖‖‖‖‖

Beth, I later found out, had dropped the phone when the evacuation order was given. She, like her colleagues, ran to the nearest exit in hopes of surviving what they thought would be another bombing. She made her way down the corridor. People were shouting and pushing and trying to get an advantage. She finally arrived at the steps. Congressional staffers, like their counterparts at the Capitol, were running for their lives.

Halfway down the stairs, with hundreds of people pushing and shoving behind her, she remembered that she had left her No FEAR folder on her desk. Beth elbowed her way back up the stairs away from safety. She

found her way back through deserted corridors that only minutes earlier had been filled with alert staffers attending constituents. Now, with everyone gone, the clamor outside filled the long stone halls with the sounds that fear makes. She reached her desk and looked around—she was alone. Once she found her folder, she was gripped anew with fear, realizing that coming back might turn out to be her last act on earth. She picked up her phone.

"Stan, pick up the phone," Beth said as the number rang. She got the recording. I'm sorry, we're not home. If you want to speak to Beth or Stan, please leave a message.

She waited for the beep. "Stan, pick up the phone . . . please!" Then quickly, "Stan, Rayburn is being evacuated. They blew up the World Trade Center this morning and"—her voice cracking—"I think the Capitol is next. If I don't make it, I love you!" Tears rolled down her face. "Please tell my boys that I love them."

This woman, a white, middle-class professional, who had so little in common with me in her cultural background, had scratched and clawed her way against all the panicked people fleeing—to get to that folder. She had come to believe so strongly in the No FEAR bill that in her heart and by her actions, she was ready to give her life for it. And Congressman Sensenbrenner said repeatedly in the days and weeks following, "I almost died for this bill." He had gotten stuck in the tunnel beneath the Capitol as the terrorists took aim at Washington.

I tried to call Segun on my cell phone to let him know that I was fine and that I had survived the evacuation. Sis. Moone and I found a small cafe open on Pennsylvania Avenue. It became a sanctuary—congressional staff members and folks from all walks of life were huddled together in total disbelief. I prayed that Segun would be able to pick up our children and that the school would not release them to anyone but him. The thought that my children were vulnerable nearly drove me mad. I was frantic, desperate. I considered removing my dress shoes and running, but to where? I went outside for fresh air. Soldiers were posted on the tops of buildings with guns in hand. Military vehicles were moving to their posts. Within hours, Washington, DC, was a militarized zone.

|||||||||||||

Whistleblower protection in that first, queer daze after the attacks seemed insignificant to most Americans, but to us it was ironic. We knew instinctively that some unknown federal workers could have warned—or more than likely did try to warn—America about those very attacks. In fact, on September 13, 2001, two days after the disaster, Dwight Welch in his capacity as both an EPA biologist and union leader wrote to EPA administrator Christine Whitman warning her about human exposure to chemicals combusted as a result of the attacks on the Pentagon and the World Trade Center.

> As I drove by the Pentagon on Wednesday, I noted the building was still burning! This old building is loaded with toxins such as asbestos, PCBs, and materials which upon burning could create even more toxic combustion products. . . . The decision to encourage nonessential Pentagon employees to report to work not only compromised employee health and safety and showed a lack of compassion for the grieving. . . . On my way to work today, I heard a radio broadcast which indicated that the EPA said that smoke coming from the Pentagon and the WTC [World Trade Center] was not all that hazardous. I hope this was an error on the part of the broadcaster. I would like to see that data upon which this pronouncement was made.[1]

Dwight's warning, as well as other whistleblowers, would be ignored. Firefighters, first responders, and volunteers were exposed to toxic substances. Dwight never received the courtesy of a response to his memo.

Considering that whistleblowers, such as Dwight and Siebel Edmonds, continued to sound the alarm, it took some getting used to when the congressional and media reaction to our raising the topic of No FEAR legislation was greeted with questions about our relevance after 9/11. If you weren't about 9/11, you didn't exist for either Congress or the news. But we existed among ourselves, and we were not going to be brushed aside any more than was F. James Sensenbrenner, who called to say he was serious about No FEAR legislation and was going to see it through. Sadly, the next few years would find whistleblowers in the forefront of telling truth to power when intelligence officers revealed that the government had known a lot more about the impending 9/11 disaster than the Bush administration had led the country to believe.

The House vote was rescheduled within a week of Sensenbrenner's call, for October 3, 2001. Scores of federal workers were sitting in the ornate gallery of the US House of Representatives. To many of the nervous, fidgety, battle-weary, and post-9/11 traumatized federal workers, this was the day that we had dreamt about, fought for, and perhaps even secretly thought we would never see. Win or lose, this was our day.

Congressman Sensenbrenner took to the podium, with Beth Sokul seated behind him. "Mr. President, it is my honor to introduce the first civil rights law of the twenty-first century—No FEAR. The law is being introduced because of the outrageous abuse that is taking place in the federal government and its impact on national and international policy."

The wild swings in emotion that had washed over all of us in the last month had redefined exhaustion for me. After the push to get the vote right before the attacks, we had all been nearly giddy approaching the Capitol the first time around. The anguish that had unfolded with the deadly attacks had knocked down a part of all of us.

Congresswoman Sheila Jackson Lee took the podium.

"Mr. President, I rise to cosponsor the first civil rights act of the twenty-first century—No FEAR. . . .

"Federal government workers have fought long and hard. Many have lost their families, their jobs—everything they hold dear—to see this day." The congresswoman's voice was deep and powerful. "If we could place a human face on this law, it would be the face of Dr. Marsha Coleman-Adebayo. She has been a tireless fighter and leader."

I felt the hands of coalition members patting me on the shoulder. One of them spoke softly to me from behind. "How does it feel to have the entire Congress condemn the way EPA treated you?"

Segun squeezed my hand.

The vote was called. The illumination of the names of the 435 members was near blinding, the feeling otherworldly. Members representing every community in the United States spilled onto the floor of the Capitol. They were laughing and horse trading votes. Sensenbrenner, Sokul, and Jackson Lee looked up into the gallery; their eyes were asking: Do you see what is happening? The moment was here. Our eyes communicated back: Are you sure you have the votes to pass this law?

In the gallery we were federal government workers, we were family, we were friends, and we instinctively all locked arms. One member of our group leaned over the back of my chair.

"What's the magic number?"

"218."

We were dead silent before the numbers began to appear in the yea and nay columns posted on the wall above the podium. We were prepared for a fight. We had all tasted victory and defeat before, but none of that seemed as laden as the outcome today. Fifty votes went into the yea column, then one hundred.

150.

Someone said, "My God! We are looking at a unanimous vote for No FEAR!"

Two hundred yeas. We looked at one another—what was happening?

210.

218!

"My God!" I whispered loudly to Segun, "We just passed a law!"

Sensenbrenner, Beth, and Jackson Lee looked up to the gallery, giving us the thumbs-up. We were still waiting for the hammer to hit with the votes in the nay category, but the yeas kept piling up: 300 . . . 350 . . . 400 . . . 420. No FEAR had passed the House of Representatives! We all jumped up and started hugging and kissing. Some were crying.

It is a rare moment most will never see when history greets victory with a kiss.

Beth Sokul met us as we filed out of the gallery. She was reserved but overjoyed. We all took turns hugging her. Beth is in our blood forever now.

"We need to see the chairman," I told her. "We need to savor this moment together."

Beth called him on his cell phone. Segun and most workers had to leave before the core of our group followed Beth down the long hall that was filling with laughter and its echoes. The chairman was sitting behind his desk. He stood up when we arrived.

"Mr. Chairman," I said, "today we have made Martin Luther King and all the civil rights martyrs proud. We have just passed a law without money or resources. What we had was our faith in Almighty God and a passion for justice. Under your leadership, and Congresswoman Jackson Lee's, the US Congress has carried out its historic mission to fight for people who cannot fight for themselves. Today, the Congress was truly the people's house. And we thank you, and Beth, for all of your commitment and hard work.

"I would like to celebrate this moment in the way that Dr. King taught us, by singing 'We Shall Overcome.' Do you know the words?"

I had never understood the words to this song before that moment.

We crossed our hands, in the traditional style, and sang with all our hearts. Young Republican staffers, hearing unfamiliar sounds coming from the chairman's office ran in as if Congressman Sensenbrenner had been taken hostage, but stopped—first embarrassed and then delighted—when they found Sensenbrenner absorbed in the singing.

As we started to file out of the office, thanking Beth and the chairman for the vote, Blair Hayes stopped to shake hands with him.

"The way you look, and the party that you represent, and the state you come from," Blair said, "I never would have picked you as someone who would have supported someone who looks like me."

Sensenbrenner laughed. As I turned to leave, the congressman pulled me aside. "Marsha, you had me and Jackson Lee on this side of Congress. The Senate is going to be a completely different ball of wax."

Riding the indescribable high from the vote, I told Sensenbrenner, "After the year and a half it took to win this vote—we're ready for anything."

Al Sharpton:
The X Factor

Beth called very soon after that to say that Republican senator John Warner would sponsor on the Senate side. If we already had a Republican sponsor and the Democrats were the civil rights party, I thought, how hard could it be?

Ah, Candide. It soon became clear that in the Senate the Democrats had circled the wagons around their president and were not about to go to the mat for civil rights abuses that happened during his administration. OK, we reasoned, in this we're faced with another challenge. We started canvassing the Senate side looking for allies among the Democrats but getting utterly nowhere. Federal workers who were supporting the No FEAR Act were getting knocked around right and left when their agencies identified them. There were more than a few huffing and puffing sessions where No FEAR coalition members vented frustration at being stonewalled by the Democrats. We contacted every Democrat in the Senate, the liberal lions including Ted Kennedy, Robert Byrd, and Pat Leahy. None of the members would meet with us personally. They had no time for us in their schedules. Those offices that did grant meetings did so perfunctorily.

I had read every book I could find on the civil rights movement for guidance on getting the No FEAR Act passed, and we did everything by the rules. The coalition had faxed letters, marched in front of offices— all the traditional things that were supposed to have an impact on Congress—to no avail. We were becoming perplexed and frustrated.

"This is the party of Adlai Stevenson? FDR? The Kennedys? Man!" Blair was tapping his foot. An emergency meeting had been called to discuss the status of the No FEAR act.

"Nothing. Not one of them is willing to break ranks," said Leroy Warren. "I'll tell you where this will live or die, and that's in Governmental Affairs." The Governmental Affairs Committee was Joe Lieberman. "We've gotta get Lieberman on board, or it's over," Leroy said. "You ask me? It's over."

"Excuse me, gentlemen? You'll have to forgive my voice. I was involved in an accident recently and broke my neck." I wasn't sure at first who was talking. The voice I fixed to Pat Lawson was deep and powerful. This voice was high and raspy like she had laryngitis. "I come from a sharecropper family. Do you know what that means?"

Her injured voice made the words so much stronger.

"I come from a place where your enemies kill you with their bare hands."

She continued, "I mentioned my accident. When I called my supervisor and told him that I was in the hospital"—Pat began to laugh—"you won't believe what I'm about to tell you: the agency actually sent a letter to the intensive care unit notifying me that I was AWOL because I had not filled out papers for sick leave! That's the kind of tactic we're up against. Those are the kinds of thugs we're dealing with. They'd kill you on Christmas Eve and leave you wrapped in ribbons under the tree. I don't think the United States Senate is going to stop us."

Blair Hayes had already won a few fights in the courts. He sat listening and then added, "I've been wrestling this monster for over ten years now. I've spent so much time in court that I'm considering buying life insurance for my lawsuit. I've seen them pull every dirty trick in the book—but didn't any of it stop me. We haven't begun to fight."

Blair was wound tight. When he listened, his eyebrows were raised, the words building up inside made him writhe in his seat. He couldn't even conceive of being turned back.

"Suffering, resilience, passion, and never giving up." Walter Fauntroy's tenor voice was soft. His sharp eyes were looking back to the days when his friends and fellow warriors—Martin, Ralph—took the first emphatic steps of defiance, anticipating dogs, clubs, and worse to be unleashed in the morning. His fingers were laced, his elbows on the table.

"Andy Young, a close confidant of Dr. King, told me a story that has always encouraged me. In Birmingham, Alabama, Andy and Ralph Abernathy were leading a demonstration. They could hear the whining and barking as the sheriffs brought in the dogs. The fire hoses were in the ready position to separate the flesh from the demonstrators. " Fauntroy's face lit as he looked at each of us around the table. "But first the police chief allowed the demonstrators to kneel and pray. Right there in the middle of the road, they hit their knees. Abernathy, in the southern tradition of repeating cadence, got so full of the Spirit his prayers were almost like singing. Abernathy could pray! He prayed for so long in this singing style that the dogs started to lie down and go to sleep. The people, realizing that they were facing imminent destruction, started to moan and cry out to the Lord. After Abernathy finished praying, the police commanded the dogs to attack, to destroy the demonstrators, but the dogs had been lulled to complacency—it was a miracle that no one was hurt!

"The power of this story is that the Lord will make a way, somehow—but you must first step out on faith, and it must be a faith without fear!"

Rev. Fauntroy looked at each of us with a nod and a smile. "It's always darkest just before dawn, but perfect love cast out all fear."

"But weren't you afraid?" Tanya asked. There were so many people who had come before us, who cast long, iconic shadows, with saint-like certitude. Yet here was a man who had written speeches for Dr. King, who had locked arms with others and walked into the churning combine of terrorism and state sponsored violence in the segregated Deep South.

"Afraid?" He looked at the rest of the group as if insulted.

"We were petrified!"

Fauntroy burst into laughter and turned back toward Tanya, taking her hands between both of his.

"But seriously, Tanya, what is there to fear if you haven't established the right to exist? Everyone in this room is afraid. That's a given. What we do in spite of fear defines us.

"The soul that on Jesus has leaned for repose,

"I will not I will not desert to his foes;

"That soul, though all hell would endeavor to shake,

"I'll never, no, never, no, never forsake."

Rev. Fauntroy had a presence that filled his surroundings whether politically or tactically, whether before an audience, a congregation, a

small group, or one on one. Into his sixties he still moved with athleticism, still worked eighteen-hour days, still traveled the country and world imbued with the dream. The confidence and strength of the elders was with us.

"Martin used to say, 'Darkness cannot put out darkness; only light can do that. Hatred cannot put out hatred; only love can do that. We must match our enemy's capacity to inflict suffering with our own ability to endure it.' So really, with our faith in God—we had nothing to fear." Fauntroy's face became taunt almost tearful. "The last time I spoke with Martin, he knew that he was a marked man. He called me before he boarded the plane to Memphis. He had taken on the US government, and he realized that threats to his life were not only coming from fringe southern elements but from the heights of respectable power. But he wasn't fearful. The last thing he told me was: 'Walter, if they get me, tell them that before the smoke clears,'" Fauntroy took a moment to gather himself and release the pain with a deep exhalation, "'my soul will be shouting in glory.'" Rev. Fauntroy offered this prayer-like story to everyone in the room. "This is the legacy that Martin left all of you in the No FEAR Coalition. Draw upon his courage," Fauntroy exhorted us. "The spirit that marched in the face of murderous racists that released water, from water canons so powerful that women, men, and children tumbled through the air as through they were paper airplanes and stripped off the bark of trees is the power that will allow you to confront your enemies with moral authority." As if measuring each individual's response to his words, he looked around the table. Tanya, Joyce, and Janet were wiping tears away, Blair was lightly tapping the table with his fist, Matthew's eyes were closed as if in meditation, and Woody and Quinton sat reverently. Fauntroy continued, "Is life worth living without justice, dignity, peace?

"One of the reasons I decided to get involved with the No FEAR Coalition was that I saw in everyone here the same spirit that Martin, Andy, and so many others possessed. We were able to accomplish miracles because of our faith in God!"

Everyone in that room had been personally inspired by the courage and benevolence of Dr. King and Rev. Fauntroy. Collectively, we had tapped into their reservoir of grace.

Later Fauntroy took me aside and told me, "Always watch, during any campaign, for the X factor—something completely unexpected that can turn the tide. The dogs fell asleep. That was the X factor. Hitler never imagined that the Russian winter would have been the X factor that led to his defeat at Stalingrad. Napoleon's army starved to death on its way to Moscow after the Russian army burned all of their crops."

His wry smile and keen eyes flashed.

"George Washington was finished in New York. Cornwallis had him outmanned and pinned down. The war was over in the morning. But with sunrise came a fog so thick the British couldn't strike. And Washington's army slipped across the Hudson and escaped. There is always an X factor, Marsha, and there will be one for No FEAR. You have to recognize it—and seize it."

We had about four weeks to get No FEAR passed by the Senate before the process would end and we would have to start the cycle all over again from scratch with a new session of Congress—another vote in the House and then one in the Senate. This portended great risk. We might have passed the vote unanimously in the House that time, but, though our stars seemed aligned, Congress was fickle. We met with Senator Warner, fully aware of the stakes.

John Warner had just turned seventy-five and was still a handsome man, the bones carved into his deeply hollowed cheeks. Virginia has never known a more charming man. Warner was a moderate Republican and keen on No FEAR.

"I have dedicated staff and resources to the passage of this bill. Unlike the House, your lack of resources will weigh heavier against you here. The opposition is well oiled, efficient, determined. Even without opposition per se, the interests with resources get the grease. It is by no means clear which way this will go."

There was seriousness about Warner and a sincerity that was easy to trust.

"But you have my personal assurance," he added with the cadence of a Virginian gentleman, "that I will do everything I can to see this bill through."

We knew Warner was friends with Joe Lieberman and asked him if he could help us with Governmental Affairs.

"I've got your back on the Republican side," he told us. "Senator Lieberman is going to have to be brought around by the Democrats."

Why not make a direct appeal to Lieberman? It seemed the logical place to start. Warner's endorsement got us a meeting with Lieberman's chief of staff, Michael Alexander. During our first meeting Michael had been cool to the idea of No FEAR. We had to convince him of its relevance. But it is difficult to gain a meeting with senators generally, and it becomes only more difficult as one ascends the ranks to senior members and committee chairs.

Lieberman chaired the Governmental Affairs Committee, was the past vice-presidential nominee of his party, and had been in the Senate for thirteen years. As a legitimate heir apparent, Joe Lieberman had designs on the White House in 2004. With all of this, his political standing was among the select few, and Michael Alexander guarded Lieberman's schedule penuriously.

Then one day I happened to be looking through the Library of Congress, Thomas section, when I noticed that Senator Russ Feingold had sponsored No FEAR in the Senate. No hullabaloo, no bombast. He was not going to devote staff or time to it, I was told when I called his office to thank him. But: "You have a Democratic sponsor now. This should get you appointments."

"I don't see the relevance," Michael Alexander said in response to our request for a meeting with Lieberman. "The senator is deep into the process of developing an Afghan strategy, the Enron debacle is eating up his time and energy, and there isn't the slightest chance of your bill rising to the significance of those issues. I'll be happy to present your case to the senator, but I would not get my hopes up too high if I were you."

"What do you say in response to the door being slammed like that?" I asked Rev. Fauntroy.

Fauntroy curved his index finger across his upper lip, holding his thumb under his chin. "He's the chairman of the Governmental Affairs Committee. It sounds to me like the chairman would like you to pay him a visit there."

Rev. Fauntroy's insights always brought a smile to the faces of our fiery coalition.

|||||||||||||

"You all are going to have to take a seat. You can't stay against the wall."

We knew the Capitol police would not allow us to stay where we were, lining the perimeter of the hearing room, since we all held 8½-by-11-inch signs with our laser-printed message for Senator Lieberman before us at belt level: PASS NO FEAR SENATE BILL 201.

We decided going in that none of us would get arrested, so when the police asked us to find a seat we went along with the program. OK, OK. No problem. And then one by one we got back up over the course of the next hour and took our stations along the wall, playing cat and mouse with security.

Senators are nothing if not skilled at maintaining their cool in tense situations, or ignoring them. Joe Lieberman kept it together very well, but a few furtive glances toward the back of the room betrayed his consternation. At one point he beckoned Michael Alexander to his side. Michael bent at the waist by the chairman, and then they both looked at us while Michael spoke into Lieberman's ear.

"We got him," Blair said to me softly. "You see that? We got him."

Blair was right. After the committee meeting someone from Lieberman's office called Leroy Warren asking, "Can't you control your people?"

Leroy told him no, he couldn't, because "they aren't my people—they're No FEAR."

Michael Alexander called me at home that night. "What's up with you guys? What's the point of trying to embarrass the chairman?"

"We need to meet with Senator Lieberman."

"I told you what the senator's schedule and priorities are."

"Then maybe we need to spend more time with the chairman."

We were at the point in the conversation when the next one to speak would lose. Alexander held out impressively, but I wasn't budging.

"All right, Marsha. What are you doing next Wednesday? Why don't you come in and talk to us again."

"Praise the Lord!" Rev. Fauntroy yelled, clapping and laughing. "I was lost, but now I'm found! Blind, but now I see! Old Joe Lieberman is a wise man indeed! It took us months of slapping LBJ around before he came to his senses."

"Thank you so much, Rev. Fauntroy!" I said. "You were absolutely right. Lieberman was so rattled by all the Negroes in his meeting that he didn't even break for lunch! Then as soon as it was over, he ran out the back door!"

"Hee hee hee! I'd have liked to have been there to play checkers on his coattails!" Fauntroy yelled. "That's the way it is, Marsha. These guys get all full of themselves and how important they are."

He quickly turned serious. "He who slides shall slide again. Good, good. This is how it works. Joe wants to be president. But presidents have to appeal to everybody. Joe Lieberman has no idea how much he needs us." The reverend laughed again. "

Blair and I arrived to a meeting in progress when we got to Michael Alexander's office on Wednesday. Michael was already into a conversation with Hilary Shelton, the Director of the Washington Bureau of the NAACP, who had been in the closed door meeting with Browner.

"Hello, Marsha," Michael said. "Please."

Hilary needed no introduction. NAACP was a major supporter of the Gore-Lieberman ticket. Hilary only stayed briefly and then excused himself for another commitment. This did not sit well with Blair Hayes, who wanted the NAACP to sit in on the entire meeting.

After Hilary left, Michael Alexander got right to the point. "All right. What do you people want?"

"Well, first of all, Michael, thank you for giving us your time. I worked with the Congressional Black Caucus Foundation on the Hill for years, so I have a real appreciation for the role of staff. If it weren't for people like you, very little would get done.

"But I also know the limitations of staff, and that there are times when the people need face time with the members to make the necessary personal connections that will garner the members' full enthusiasm."

"I've already told you, Marsha. I'm the one you will be dealing with. The senator has priorities, commitments, responsibilities. He doesn't need any more on his plate."

Blair Hayes wore suits tailored to fit the body he took to the gym religiously. Michael Alexander could have been Blair's alter ego—five foot eleven with bureaucratic airs. Blair fixed his gaze on Michael and asked, "Why do you disrespect us?" The whole room buzzed.

Michael returned the glare. "The senator assigned me to take care of this. I'm going to take care of it. If you are going to meet with anyone, you will meet with me. It's as simple as that."

"Tell me something, Michael," I interjected. "Have you ever sued the United States government? Have you ever done that and won? You have no idea what you are dealing with here. Have you ever been threatened with rape? Has anyone ever threatened to kill you?

"Every one of us on this side of the table has endured those kinds of tactics, Michael, those kinds of indignities. And let me tell you what that does. It galvanizes people. You have no idea who you're dealing with here. We're literally fighting for our lives. Now, we're offering to meet with the senator behind closed doors. That would be our preference. Or we can meet with him in public. You have a choice between which of the two it will be. But we will meet with Senator Lieberman."

Blair slipped out of the office before me as I put my things together and Alexander walked out the door. I could hear Blair in the hallway bellowing. Staff people who heard Blair stepped into the hallway to see what was happening.

"Who the hell does he think he is, disrespecting us that way? He treated us like we were nobody!" Blair was addressing the building, pacing back and forth. There were four or five staffers watching him. I could see Michael Alexander beyond Blair, walking away, when he suddenly turned around and walked back toward Blair.

"What's going on here?" Alexander demanded.

Blair's eyes were ablaze. He pointed a finger at Michael.

"We'll see you again. We will see you again. And the next time, it will be under different circumstances. The next time, it will be on our terms."

There are times when listening is all one can do. I listened as Blair thundered through black steel mountains that reached to fifty-one feet in the Hart Building's ninety-foot-tall, sky-lit atrium, his voice echoing in the aluminum clouds over Alexander Calder's mobile-stabile sculpture. But, for all of his fury, Blair was a man of peace.

I knew there was an annual NAACP Federal Sector Employment Conference scheduled for that week. We would find enthusiasm there for pressuring Lieberman. No FEAR Coalition members could sit around a table with federal colleagues and develop a strategy. I waited for the storm that was Blair to subside before mentioning it.

⁞⁞⁞⁞⁞⁞⁞⁞⁞⁞⁞

Despite what I had told Blair about the enthusiasm we'd find at the conference, tactical differences between the NAACP Federal Sector Task Force and the No FEAR coalition still nearly kept me from attending the meeting. As I looked over the agenda my instincts seem confirmed: the No FEAR bill hadn't made the list—the task force felt it had no chance of passage.

I was talking with Hilary Shelton, determined to find a way to partner with the task force to apply pressure on Senator Lieberman, when the doors at the back of the room swung open and all the heads turned as a wave of excitement swept the room. In walked a team of huge body-guards, photographers, and staffers who preceded and flanked the man in the center of it all, the Reverend Al Sharpton.

Al Sharpton meant media coverage; he meant organization and con-stituencies; and most important, Al Sharpton represented what I had been waiting for: the X factor. I never would have thought to contact him independently, but there he was—and I just knew he was it. I stood between Janet and Joyce like we were middle schoolers at a dance, try-ing to muster the nerve to approach Sharpton and struggling to fig-ure out what to say when I did. Sharpton worked his way in among the people he knew, shaking hands, nodding, pointing to others who were some distance away, and then excused himself while he answered his cell phone, stepping away to talk.

This was my chance. Without saying anything to the others, I walked directly in front of Rev. Sharpton.

"Hello, Rev. Sharpton. My name is Marsha Coleman-Adebayo, and I would—"

"Can't you see I'm on the phone?"

I scurried back to Janet and Joyce, hoping they hadn't witnessed what I had just done.

"What did he say? What did he say?"

"He thinks I'm an imbecile."

"What?"

"I just made a complete fool of myself. I'm leaving."

"No! What do you mean? You can't leave!"

"I'm not leaving, but I should. What an idiot!"

Sharpton's body language said he was about to hang up. Without hesitation, I walked right back to him. "I'm sorry, Rev. Sharpton, I apolo-gize for interrupting you earlier."

He was annoyed as only a New Yorker can be, looking at me with his eyebrows raised as if to say, Yeah?

"My name is Marsha Coleman-Adebayo. I recently won a civil rights lawsuit against the EPA." I gave him the background and the abridged version. "We passed the No FEAR bill in the House with a unanimous vote. This is the first civil rights legislation of the twenty-first century, but I can't get to first base with Senator Lieberman. We have less than a month to get it out of the Governmental Affairs Committee, or it will die with this session of Congress. I would really appreciate any help you might be able to provide."

Sharpton's expression relaxed. "Can you come to New York next week?"

"Of course."

He reached into his lapel pocket, producing a business card and a pen with which he wrote on the back of the card. "This is my office; the number on the back is my personal assistant. Call and make an appointment for Tuesday and tell Adrienne that I told you to call."

It was as simple as that.

Three days later I was briefing the No FEAR Coalition on the outcome of the New York trip.

"He's on board. He says he thinks it's a travesty for this to be blocked by Lieberman, who will be courting the black community in two years. He'll join our protests."

There was general excitement in the room with that news, but Selwyn offered a particularly notable insight. "You know what?" Selwyn said. "We need a Freedom Ride, just like the sixties."

"That's brilliant." Rev. Fauntroy beamed, high praise from a man who had been pivotal in the civil rights movement of the sixties and had led the Selma, Alabama, demonstrations. "We need to tie it to the history of what has happened before. A Freedom Ride to Capitol Hill, with hundreds of people from all over America saying, Enough is enough."

"We can put signs and posters, and . . ." Suddenly the room was abuzz with excitement.

While I was all for it, I also had concerns.

"This is all well and good—I love the idea—but isn't it going to take a lot of money for buses?" I hate it when I'm the one to throw cold water on genuine enthusiasm, but a real pall settled on the room. We all looked from face to face at the others present, with no one offering any suggestions.

Then Woodrow Hatcher, a federal employee from the Corporation for National and Community Service, walked directly up to me like he was going to give me a big hug and pressed a ball of bills into my hand. "Maybe this could help to pay for leaflets and ink."

Blair had his checkbook out. "This will rent a podium."

Pat Lawson chimed in, "Marsha, I will rent a bus, and I will hire a driver."

"My church has a bus. I'll talk to my pastor," said Quinton Lynch.

"My church has a bus too," offered Rev. Fauntroy.

Then Joyce Megginson said, "My husband owns a bus company. We will get you as many buses and drivers as you need."

By the meeting's end, we had money for fliers, posters, drivers, and buses. Rev. Sharpton wrote to Lieberman requesting a meeting. Unlike the hundreds of letters the No FEAR Coalition had written to Lieberman that had been ignored, the most significant thing about Sharpton's letter was that the day before the Freedom Ride, Lieberman's office called us to say that the senator would meet with us. The only thing left was logistics.

And hypothermia. The day of the Freedom Ride, March 3, dawned a deep purple on the horizon with red-orange glowing below it as though the edge of the earth were smoldering. The white of the Capitol building shone against a deep blue, pristine sky as the morning advanced in a clean, cold winter's grip. Single-digit temperatures in Washington are rare reminders for those of us from northern climes of the sting of cold that characterizes winter in the northern states. I joked with Rev. Sharpton that he could take the frigid temperatures with him when he went back to New York.

"All the more reason to light a fire under Senator Lieberman," Sharpton quipped.

We knew in the days leading up to the Freedom Ride that we would need permits. The security clampdown on the Capitol after the attacks had seen Washington transformed from a city fairly open to public demonstrations to one where squads of heavily armed guards right out of *The Terminator* were now visibly stationed everywhere around Capitol Hill. We had firm commitments from enough participants to fill six buses, and the eight buses we were planning for would represent a logistical nightmare for traffic, security, and whatever hopes Lieberman still held for our disappearance.

Clarence Day was a man familiar with the obstacles designedly placed in the way of any such demonstrative enterprise, having worked in public security for his entire career. Mr. Day knew all of the regulations; and more important than that, he knew all of the people in charge of their enforcement. We knew that eight busloads of angry federal employees disembarking on the Capitol might be more than the government could take, so we had to ensure that our Freedom Buses would make it from Freedom Plaza to the Capitol without tying up the entire traffic flow in the District and that they would be allowed access to the Capitol when we arrived. Mr. Day negotiated with the Capitol police and got the necessary concessions including permits to reroute traffic. Had it occurred to any of us, we would have been wise to apply for a "stop arctic air mass permit" as well.

It was so cold at Freedom Plaza that everyone stood huddled close together like a herd of Mongolian yaks. Speakers took to the microphone, fumbling through their speeches with gloves on, their voices trembling from the shivers.

"The same people that feel Americans should fight for freedom try to silence the Americans who work for the federal government," Sharpton cried, the words leaving his lips with accompanying white clouds that looked like smoke. "We didn't get beat down thirty-seven years ago by sticks and nightclubs to be beat down now by memorandums."

Chairman Sensenbrenner sent a message that Sis. Moone read as the president of the SCLC. "The federal government must be the role model for civil rights, not for civil discrimination. Justice demands action by the Senate."

Blair Hayes spoke as another victor in the courts. "Senator Lieberman, let my people go. You don't want to pass No FEAR," Blair boomed, "because it would give a victory to this Republican president. When is the right time to do right? Right now!"

"I've seen dogs, fire hoses, clubs, and hangman's knots," yelled Dick Gregory. "But didn't none of them scare me half as much as the gentlemen in suits who make the laws of this country, who can smile and offer reassurances while they stab us all in the back."

"I know Joe Lieberman," Rev. Fauntroy smiled. "And I know he's no fool. If he wants all of y'all to vote for him come 2004, he's going to have to pay for our hamburger today."

Joe Madison, the host of *The Black Eagle*, a popular Washington-based radio show, bellowed, "What are you going to do about it? Block the first civil rights law of the twenty-first century?" Madison had gone on hunger strikes to protest apartheid and was a veteran of the civil rights struggle in the South.

He looked straight ahead, challenging both the federal employees on the plaza and those looking out the EPA windows: "What are you going to do about it? Well today, these No FEAR folks have decided to take the fight to Joe Lieberman. They are not sitting around complaining—they are about to board freedom buses and place their bodies on the line."

The buses filled rapidly. They were warm, but more than this there was a sense of purpose in our boarding. The cold was invigorating in the way it symbolized our standing somewhere unfamiliar, harsh, but within tolerance, another unpleasant thing bringing us together. The link with history and the first Freedom Ride that had required the accompaniment of military escorts led to our singing the old songs of resistance and solidarity. "Oh Freedom" and "Ain't Gonna Let Nobody Turn Me Roun'" once again filled the space inside buses with federal workers who had seen what the 1964 Civil Rights Act had done for human rights in the American workplace.

"I came from a sharecropper family," said Renee Berry, an employee at the United States Patent and Trademark Office. "I am the first one in my family to hold a professional degree. I have a JD from Georgetown, a master's in chemistry, and a second master's in business. It seems the only thing my color has done is make me invisible. We are not considered for promotions. I have been in litigation with the agency for so long I'm considering adding a room to my house for my claim. I am now working in a childcare facility."

One after another the stories came.

A white unionist stood to say, "I'm fifty-nine years old and was fired because I refused to remain silent when I witnessed sweetheart deals between contractors and the government. I have health issues but no income, no health insurance."

This same scenario played out serendipitously inside every bus on the way to the Hill. By the time we reached Hart, we were fired up. It was on. But Al Sharpton didn't want everyone to clamor up to Lieberman's office. He wanted to go alone, escorted by a few key No FEAR coalition members. I objected, knowing how much these workers had risked coming out today and feeling how much it would mean to them to be in or near the center of the confrontation. But Sharpton insisted.

"We don't have to drive the buses inside the building. Lieberman knows how many buses we have here today. We don't need a mob—we need a meeting. We will come back and brief them on the outcome when we're done."

We marched to the Hart Senate Office Building chanting, "No justice, no peace! No fear!" Our people stayed on the first floor of Hart, singing civil rights songs. Sis. Moone, Al Sharpton, and I started up toward Lieberman's office. I heard voices and footsteps behind us and looked back to see that Blair Hayes, federal marshal whistleblower Matthew Fogg, and Dwight Welch were coming also. This was the next time that Blair Hayes had warned Michael Alexander about. There would be no denying Blair Hayes admittance.

As soon as we opened the senator's door, flashbulbs started popping. The press was in full attendance in Lieberman's office. This was largely due to a story that had appeared the day before in *Roll Call*, a daily that was distributed to every member's office and all media outlets. The heat was on. Lieberman had to know there was no way to spin this. The office assistant said the senator was waiting to see us and escorted us to a conference room where Michael Alexander and the senator were waiting. Lieberman stood up and greeted us, but during the introductions the press started knocking on the door. They wanted shots of Lieberman and Sharpton.

"Why don't we let them in so they can meet their deadlines," Lieberman suggested. "We can talk afterwards."

When the photographers and reporters had cleared the room, Rev. Sharpton spoke first. "I didn't come here to embarrass you, Senator," Sharpton began. "I came to stand with federal workers who are being systematically discriminated against and have already been vindicated by two branches of the government—in the House, with the unanimous passage of a No FEAR resolution, and in the courts, with a jury finding in *Coleman-Adebayo v. Browner*. I'm here to stand with Dr. Moone, whose late husband worked shoulder to shoulder with Dr. King in the earliest days of the SCLC, and I stand with the No FEAR Coalition and its founder. Marsha can take it from here."

"Mr. Chairman, I would have preferred never to have come here like this. But after letters, phone calls, faxes, and most recently meetings that led nowhere beyond Michael Alexander, the impending deadline to pass No FEAR Act out of your committee and the hope it represents to millions of federal workers left us no choice."

"We have had a very hectic schedule in Washington since nine-eleven," Lieberman said.

"No, Senator," I said. "The House took time during our national grief to convene and voted 420 to zero to pass No FEAR legislation. This bill has been languishing in the Senate Governmental Affairs Committee for one year. We have made repeated requests to your office. We are now down to the last few weeks in this session to get this legislation passed, or we will have to start all over again. This is simply unacceptable."

Lieberman turned to Michael Alexander. "When is the earliest possible date that we could convene the Governmental Affairs Committee?"

"I think next week," Alexander replied, just as free and easy as if he hadn't noticed Blair Hayes fixing him in a scowl like Smokin' Joe Frazier.

"Then let's schedule a committee meeting," Lieberman said. Turning to me, he promised, "I'll get it out of the committee and onto the floor."

A year and a half of organizing and letter writing, phone calls, and demonstrations, and when this diminutive man from Connecticut who would be president snapped his fingers—voila.

We returned to the atrium with everyone, federal workers, reporters, photographers, converging on Rev. Sharpton.

"We expressed our concern with the slowness, and he assured us that he is going to move this bill to a markup by the Easter recess period," Sharpton said.

This is what people power means. If all of those government workers had not shown up, the fate of the No FEAR Act would have been left to the mercilessness of the gatekeeper.

"This was a very successful political action," I added. "I'm hopeful that Senator Lieberman will keep his word. But if not, we will board other freedom buses and come back to visit him!"

A March 25, 2002, *JET* magazine article with pictures of Senator Joe Lieberman and Al Sharpton led off with the headline, "MAJOR CIVIL RIGHTS BATTLE ERUPTING ON CAPITOL HILL OVER FEDERAL EMPLOYEES 'NO FEAR ACT,'" accompanied by pictures of Dick Gregory, Rev. Walter Fauntroy, Joe Madison, and Rev. Al Sharpton speaking to employees at the demonstration before boarding the freedom buses.

> Protesting the continuing discrimination in federal government against minorities and women, an aggressive coalition assembled in the nation's capital to launch a spring drive. . . . The No FEAR Act has been languishing in the Senate Governmental Affairs Committee since March of 2001. The House passed by a 420–0 margin.[1]

Within one week, we were back inside the committee room. No FEAR was the second agenda item. The room was full again and eerily still. Most committee members showed. With little fanfare, Lieberman went about the business of taking the extraordinary measure of having the committee approve the bill and send it directly to the floor for a vote. Start to finish, it took all of thirty minutes.

ıllıllıllıllı

It was one of those days in Washington that could leave you numb, a long day at work where everything was Mardi Gras. The agency I had prevailed against was in full-court retaliatory mode. My colleagues didn't know whether they should clap or jump out the window when they saw me approaching. The days left in the congressional session were growing thin. John Warner's office had called about a week earlier to say that in about two weeks No FEAR would be coming to a vote. And then midweek he called again to say the vote was pending.

"It's coming up soon, but I can't say when," he said on the day of the vote. "Instead of you waiting around for four hours in the gallery, why don't you wait until I call you when it's going to the floor for a vote." I went to a meeting of the coalition after work where we decided we had done everything we could do. The hurry-up-and-wait game was killing us.

When I got home, Sade said, "Mommy, everyone has been calling. Everyone." My messages were full and flashing. I only made it through the third one.

"Hello, Dr. Coleman-Adebayo, this is Senator John Warner here about 8:30 tonight from the well of the Senate. I am calling to inform you that the United States Senate has just passed the first civil rights law of this century. Congratulations, young lady, you deserve a lot of credit. We put a statement in the *Congressional Record*. Well done, madam— you've made history! Good night."

I didn't know whether to laugh or cry, so I did both, Sade and I screaming, hugging, and jumping in the kitchen. There was a flurry of phone calls. First I called my mother, and then tracked down Segun and members of the No FEAR Coalition. After the excitement had died down, there was something I needed to say to Sade.

"Thank you, sweetheart, for being so understanding. I know all of this may not make much sense to you right now. But we have just passed a law that I believe will make a difference in your life and other children like you. It is my prayer that you will never experience what I have lived through. I cannot begin to tell you how much I love you and Sina."

I couldn't hold back the tears.

After the Senate vote, the bill went to the conference committee to reconcile the two versions between the House and Senate. I'm happiest when I can worry about things, so I was in worry heaven imagining devils and details and derailments. But Beth called and said we had passed it out of committee.

"We got a date for the president to sign," she added. I paused for a second, thinking there had to be some snag in those words.

"Congratulations, Marsha," Beth said after a bit, when my usual flurry of questions failed to materialize. "Start making a list of guests you'd like to invite to the May 15 signing."

That was the easy part. Mom, Segun, Sade, Sina, Blair, Rev. Fauntroy, Tanya, Janet, Joyce, Matthew, Dwight, Leroy, Sis. Moone, Altheria, Patricia, Woody, Quinton, Bro. Dennis, Rev. King . . . I had over a hundred names in no time. I saw my whole family tree and circle of friends watching from the gallery as a conservative Republican president of all people signed the law that continued the struggle for civil rights and whistleblower protection into the new millennium.

But George W. Bush had other designs. He didn't want anyone from the public.

Immediately I organized a protest-letters campaign. "Who does this guy think he is, the president of the United States?" Even I had to laugh at my own absurdity sometimes.

In the end, after much protest, he gave us ten slots.

‖‖‖‖‖‖‖‖‖‖‖

On May 15, 2002, Sis. Moone and I were sitting in the anteroom to the Oval Office with personal letters to all of the government officials thanking them for their support. Attorney General John Ashcroft walked in for the signing. This was my first face-to-face meeting with the man who ran the Justice Department. It had teams of lawyers who had worked against me in my trial and who were at that very moment working against other federal workers just like me. I should have restrained myself, but I could not suppress confronting him.

"It was my lawsuit that inspired this law," I said to Ashcroft. "There is a cancer inside your department. At this point your Justice Department goes after people like me and tries to destroy them. I need to know that you will stop this and that you can personalize this."

Ashcroft uttered some benign words about being pleased to attend the signing ceremony when the door opened and President Bush welcomed us into the Oval Office. Senator Warner introduced me.

"This is Dr. Marsha Coleman-Adebayo. She won a civil rights case she brought against the EPA in 2000. It was her lawsuit that inspired this legislation."

"It's an honor to meet you. Sorry we couldn't accommodate more people, but there just wasn't a way to do it with my schedule today."

The president took us in where we all stood awkwardly while the protocol officer arranged us behind the president's desk for the signing, placing Leroy Warren and me at the far right. John Warner saw this and took me by the arm, saying, "Marsha, you're my date for this program." He brought me directly behind the president, where I stood between him and Congressman Sensenbrenner.[2]

The president opened a blue envelope with the presidential seal that lay on his desk. Standing directly behind Mr. Bush, I could see the language of the bill and started reading about a social scientist who had experienced discrimination at the EPA. It might have been the blue folder. I started having flashbacks. Lillian Pleasant. Sis. Bessie. And then the strangest sense that someone was crying. I was thinking, Who on earth is crying?, when my knees went out. Congressman Sensenbrenner put his arm around me.

"She's been through a lot, Mr. President," Sheila Jackson Lee said as the president turned around and stood up. President Bush took me in his arms, and I wept, trying to stifle my sobs, his hand patting me on my shoulder. I noticed I was getting makeup on him and started to draw back.

"No, no. You stay here as long as you need," he said.

I realized he hadn't finished signing. "I can cry later, Mr. President. Could you please finish signing?"

Everyone laughed. "She's an activist, sir," said Jackson Lee.

And then it was over. The president of the United States had affixed his signature to the No FEAR Act, and we were ushered out of the Oval Office. Outside, after exchanging thanks and congratulations with those assembled, Congresswoman Sheila Jackson Lee took Sis. Moone and me by the hands and led us to a podium where reporters were gathered in the Rose Garden.

"We have just witnessed the president of the United States signing the first civil rights whistleblower law of the twenty-first century," Jackson Lee began, going on to say that the law represented the culmination of efforts that had begun a long time before any of those assembled were born.

"What does it mean?" a reporter asked.

"It means that federal workers now have a chance they did not have before. It means that federal managers are now on notice that discrimination and retaliation against their employees is no longer par for the course. It means that federal workers now have the full force of the law behind them when they report waste, fraud, and abuse."

After I addressed the press, the three of us found ourselves walking away through the Rose Garden together, the tall arching windows of the Oval Office as our backdrop when Sis. Moone stopped.

"You know, if he were still alive, Dr. King would not have missed this signing today. This carries on his work. In '64 it was a Democratic president who signed the Civil Rights Act. Today it was a Republican president. I wish my husband had lived to see this."

Jackson Lee studied her, knowing Sis. Moone had been a friend of Dr. King's and that they had been soldiers in the struggle.

"Dr. Moone, I know this must be a bittersweet moment for you, and I know you have put a lifetime into the struggle. But today is not about who signed this law, it's about the people who demanded it. George Bush has never done a thing for civil rights. He couldn't care less about civil rights. He signed this law today because you, the SCLC, Marsha, and all of the No FEAR Coalition members—meaning everyday people, federal workers, unions—came together and made him sign this legislation. That's the significance of this day. Today represents another step along the way. But in the case of the larger goals of No FEAR, of protecting whistleblowers, of bringing those who retaliate against them to justice, today is just the first step." On June 10, *JET* magazine announced what we had witnessed in the oval office: "EPA Worker's Battle Against Bias Sparked Recent Signing of Century's First Rights Bill."[3]

I realized that the true test lay not in the ratification that day of the No FEAR Act but in what the reaction would be of common people to the continued manifestations of subtle apartheid within the American federal government itself. The entrenched sanctions this American apartheid unleashed behind closed doors on its own employees—and behind the immaculate facade of monuments to freedom and justice that it presents to the outside world—was the dark revelation of my trial. The real test would begin in earnest after the media apparatus had been disassembled and cleared away, after No FEAR's allotted fifteen minutes of fame had become old news. The real test would come if countless, anonymous Americans continued to be subjected to entrenched bureaucratic tyranny. The real test would come when enough of us insisted on honoring our own worth.

Vanadium

*Multi-megawatt vanadium redux fuel cells for mass storage [is]
one of the coolest things I've said out loud.*
                    —President Barack Obama to business leaders

There is one central underground stream that meanders invisible
through this story. It is the source and the mouth. Without it, there is
no story. With it, the narrative could not be otherwise. It's vanadium
poisoning. Reports of vanadium miners who had died, were dying, and
would soon be dead haunt every page of this book and every event it
describes. Yet it is an underground stream, and is likely to remain so,
because to know something requires that we do something, and vanadium, like the goddess of its name, is so alluring and so destructive that
most prefer not to know. That heart-sickening reality is what has kept
most Americans, indeed, most inhabitants of planet Earth ignorant of
the subject.

After over a decade of having vanadium poisoning lying like a naked
corpse on our dining room table and giving commands, demanding
that I report the story, demanding that I go to trial, demanding that
I mention vanadium poisoning in sworn testimony before Congress,
demanding that a law get passed, still the corpse lies there wondering
what it will take. I have written to the last chapter in the book, and her
story still remains untold.

This chapter covers roughly a decade in a period we might mistakenly identify as the pivotal years in my life. While it is true that these years have been pivotal for me, my case is but a piece in the much larger story. This chapter is an exposé of the underground stream beneath the visible tributaries—from complaints against EPA to the signing of the No FEAR Act—that reveal the stream has been there all along. Like everything else in this book, it begins and ends with the miners themselves.

꜀꜀꜀꜀꜀꜀꜀꜀꜀꜀꜀

It was the kind of evening the reality of apartheid had been able to hide behind for so long in South Africa: balmy with an easy breeze. The moderate temperature, low humidity, and endless stars made this place seem idyllic. None of the young women from Barnard College had yet seen the townships. They were still getting their legs after the long flight from New York and adjusting to the time difference. The four young women were Alexandria Wright, a philosophy major; Hayley Holness, studying political science; Alexandra Severino, a chemistry major; and Kendra Tappin, a student of American history. These women were younger incarnations of my dear Barnard sisters Cynthia, Beatrice, Thorny, and Sylvia. We were also joined by two professors, Diane Dittrick and Tim Halpin-Healy, from the environmental sciences and physics departments.[1] My daughter Sade and Tim's son, Tyler, accompanied the group. None of them had seen Brits, that acrid little place that had the feel of any working class town thrown up to support the industrial manufacture of products that would make other people in other countries and places more comfortable.

"This was years before independence," Jacob began calmly. At first not everyone was paying attention to him. I wasn't even sure whom he was talking to, because Jacob in some strange way seemed to be addressing the night itself. His voice was both soft and distinct, and as he continued it gripped everyone who had come to this open balcony for an informal meeting to get acquainted with the others who would be taking part in the mission to Brits. One by one they would hear the rolling *r*'s and the clear melody of Jacob's voice and stop what they were saying in midsentence, turning their head to listen.

"They had gathered at the union steward's house, which I can assure you is much smaller than even this ledge we are now gathered on, and much less ornate."

The group was with him now, settling in, listening.

"But the breeze, even there among a group of miners still covered with grit and film from a day in hell, was just as welcome and refreshing as it is here. And there were just as many stars, although they were not so easy to see inside the box of that windowless house.

"It is dry in Mothotlung Township. The dryness made worse by the fact of it being in the Afrikaner stronghold of Bothuswana. The men sitting on the furniture were large, their muscles compact from hard work, and their sheer mass tested the legs of his father's couch that had been his sister's couch and was now Henry's, the shop steward. Others were seated around a table, some with their heads resting on elbows, others sitting backward on the chairs they had pulled away from the table to be closer to the center of the group. 'Comrades, we have to do something,' Henry said to them. 'We are dying. One by one, we are dying. And for what? To enrich the Americans?'

"Johan challenged this immediately. 'Are you asking us to strike? To risk our jobs?' 'I'm asking you to fight for your lives,' Henry said. 'But what good is life if we don't have jobs? Are we going to eat dirt?' Johan barked. I could see that the group seemed to concur, as they nodded and looked at one another.

"'What are you eating now?' Henry fired back. He could see this hurt them as some dropped their eyes to their laps. Garrison was standing by himself in the corner. Henry walked over to him. 'Garrison, open your mouth.' Garrison looked insulted. 'Please,' Henry asked gently. When Garrison opened his mouth, his tongue was bluish green.[3] It could be seen even in the poor light, just as you can see it here by my telling you, except none of the miners showed your surprise. They had all seen it themselves. Turning from Garrison, they were all looking down. Henry could feel their shame.

"He went to another worker. 'When was the last time you didn't piss or shit blood?' The worker studied his feet. 'Nkomo,' Henry said, turning where the other sat at the table. 'Can you still blink your eyes and pull out blood? Let's see!' Nkomo winced, and I swear to you that a trickle of blood rolled down his cheek."

A collective *Eeuuw*! went up from among the girls. Jacob milked that image before he continued.

"'Comrades! How long can we tolerate this situation?'"

It wasn't clear if Jacob was quoting himself or addressing this to the group of Americans.

"'My wife will leave me if I don't bring in money,' Johan said. 'I have children.' 'Seriously, comrades,' Henry said back to all of them, 'when was the last time you were able to meet your wife's needs? We all know *power* is the first thing that dies when you start work at Vametco.'"

Jacob lowered his voice. "This is a very private thing. It is not easy to say it in front of you now, and it was not easy to say it to the men. But they all knew it was true."

"Excuse me, Mr. Ngakane." It was Alexandra Severino, the soft-spoken junior from the Bronx. "I'm sorry to interrupt you, but I need to be clear. Are you saying vanadium makes miners impotent?"

"Yes!" His eyes were wide, the veins bulging in his neck. "Every single one of them fears the humiliation of that. And do you know what they said? They said, 'The doctors treated us with milk—that's all we need.' That's what they said! The company doctors told them that milk could prevent vanadium poisoning.

"'Comrades! Wake up! Milk does not protect you from the vanadium!' This was the very essence of the problem. Some workers murmured agreement, some of them rejection, but it was easier for them to argue about milk than to face their own impotence.

"Mswade's voice broke above the bickering. 'I will take my chances with the vanadium.' He stood up to leave, but Henry knew the first place Mswade would stop before he went home was at the company to tell them of the meeting.

"'Comrades, I beg you. We must stand together,' Henry implored them in Setswana, '*Kutlwano ke matla, matla go batho.*' It means, Unity is strength. This brought the group back to Henry, and Mswade returned to his seat. 'Can we agree to a strike tomorrow?' 'What are our demands?' they wanted to know. Garrison made the strongest point. 'We need more money. Why should the Afrikaners and Americans become rich—while we die like dogs?'

"'Comrades!' Henry said, barely containing himself. 'We must be prepared for how the company will react to our strike. They will send in their dogs. They will send in their goons and tanks. They will have guns. We must be prepared to fight for our lives and our families!'"

Jacob was on his feet as Henry must have been that night. For the first time Jacob seemed to remember where he was. His body relaxed as he looked around at us and smiled.

"It was not that different for Martin Luther King and Walter Fauntroy and others the night before Selma. They knew what they were facing. We, none of us gathered here on this balcony under these stars, would have met each other and shared our experiences if they had been afraid to stand up for their lives, their dignity, and for every one of us on this ledge here tonight."

‖‖‖‖‖‖‖‖

It was nearly ten years after I first learned about vanadium that this group from Barnard College listened intently as Jacob Ngakane retold the story of the night before the miners first went on strike at Union Carbide's Vametco vanadium mine.[1] When I was removed from my South Africa assignment, I had first found the shock of the dismissal paralyzing. But now, with a newly enacted law in hand, I started to look for solutions that weren't driven by governmental policy. Barnard's reputation for challenging the status quo, particularly within the tradition of Zora Neale Hurston, June Jordan, Margaret Mead, and Dorothy Height, was what got me thinking.

"This is an absolute outrage!" Vivian Taylor had said, after I briefed her on Brits. Dr. Taylor was associate dean of the college and close to the president of the college. "Let me call some people and see what we can do."

I told Dean Taylor that what I really wanted to do was assemble a team of professionals and students that could accompany me to South Africa on the kind of fact-finding mission the agency had stonewalled. "Let's put some of these magnificent young minds to work on this and see where the science leads."

Vivian Taylor was passionate about providing Barnard women with leadership roles. The vanadium issue provided a perfect opportunity for Barnard women to be on the cutting edge of science and provide leadership in a human rights struggle. She knew that the Mellon Mays

Undergraduate Fellowship program (MMUF) was interested in research that transformed the lives of disadvantaged people. I believed she could be a potent ally in marshaling the resources we would need to implement a mission to South Africa.

Among the people Vivian Taylor had contacted was Barnard president Judith Shapiro. Shapiro knew all too well the consequences when those who should have done something did nothing. She relied on trusted colleagues and the senior leadership within the college with similar passions: Dean Dorothy Denburg, professor Rosalind Rosenberg, Provost Elizabeth Boylan, and Dean of Studies Karen Blank. They realized that Barnard women were encouraged to provide not only national leadership but global vision. The Shapiro, Taylor, Denburg, and Rosenberg team was unstoppable, and Barnard women were about to make history and set precedence for all women's colleges to follow. Within weeks, Dean Taylor had found support for the project through the MMUF and GE programs. The itinerary was worked out in minute detail in order to ensure the safety of the young women. The interviews of vanadium victims would be conducted at a conference on vanadium with a visit to the township.

I had been invited to speak at Smith College, outside Boston, as a whistleblower during this period. My court victory had given me the gravitas that David Shapiro had predicted. I was making public appearances representing the No FEAR Coalition as well as continuing to work on a full time basis at the agency. I would take annual leave to perform my No FEAR activities, always starting my speeches with a disclaimer informing the audience that I was not representing the EPA but rather a coalition of courageous federal employees determined to make it safe to warn the public when danger was present. Smith had invited me to speak on the issue of women and whistleblowers. Both interest and incredulity were expressed at Smith, with many people saying they could not believe that the United States government had crushed dissent within its ranks. Several faculty members approached me after my talk and expressed interest in having Smith join Barnard in the South Africa fact-finding mission.

This and Barnard's reactions were the responses I had expected from the White House and EPA when I had raised the subject of vanadium poisoning. The combined resources of these two colleges couldn't approach the budgetary latitude and manpower of the US government, yet even with the modest resources we could scrape together, the team we assembled was impressive.

As I savored how delicious it was to hear Jacob Ngakane retell his story to a new generation of young Americans, it did not take long to see that this was no ordinary selection of young college women. They each possessed talents that seemed far in advance of their age.

Alexandra Severino had all the smarts you might expect from a New Yorker. She was quick on her feet, cute as a button, but also a marshmallow. She reminded me in some way of what a young Sis. Bessie must have been like. Hayley Holness, tall and slender, was confident and in control. I enjoyed Hayley's company. She was a good listener. She was brilliant, with a kind and open disposition. Alexandria was sweet, beautiful, and intellectually pensive; she had a winning smile. Kendra was fiercely independent and had looks that would make a model cringe. She enjoyed an exacting intellect that masked a deeper mystery.

Our plan was to gather as much information as possible in the short time we had—four days with the Barnard team. And for a week prior to that I would interview as many miners as I could, capturing them on tape with a film crew provided by actor and longtime activist Danny Glover.

||||||||||||||

When all participating parties had arrived, including a large contingent from Smith College, we would convene at a conference center outside the city limits of Brits, with representatives of the local Brits government, and conduct a roundtable with miners available to provide testimony of their experience in the mining industry. Heeten Kalan, my ally during the NEJAC confrontation with Bill Nitze, would attend. Jacob Ngakane had also invited a South African civil rights attorney, Richard Spoor, to join us.

We hoped that this roundtable would give us the blueprint for the rest of our inquiries, providing background on the mining process, details on who the key community members were, and information about what practices the mining industry was deploying in response to the growing resistance they were getting from the organizing miners. It would be a busy week that culminated with a report presented by the members of the Barnard research team before the acting mayor of Brits.

Essentially, we put together another study tour modeled after the two EPA tours, minus the hidden agendas and political posturing.

On some deep level I owed it to Sade to bring her with me. I cannot explain this. It was not because I had already brought Sina with me on a previous trip to South Africa. It owed more to a generational mother-daughter obligation of wanting to share my love of working with communities in need, in hope that one day she might remember our shared experiences.

Through my work with the UN, I have come to love Kenya and Ethiopia. Through my marriage I now have family in Nigeria. But South Africa, Biko, the insistent antiapartheid movement, Nelson Mandela, Jacob, Bantu, and Sis. Bessie were now the faces that peopled the blind spots on the map of the continent of my origins. If there is genetic memory in my DNA, let it be the collective memory of these people, this struggle, these manifestations of who I am. And so with the plane banking above the hills of South Africa, I am forging a bond with my daughter, the first such bond in over three hundred years.

This is not to say I brought Sade without some misgivings. But Sade had recently shown her mettle at school in Bethesda. She had gotten into a scuffle after school with a classmate while they were waiting for the school bus. I'm sure he was a very nice boy, and I know Sade is a very nice girl. These things happen, no big deal. I didn't even know any of it had happened until a few days later, when I picked Sade up from school and she was visibly upset. She was sitting on a bench in front of the school with a scowl on her face and her arms folded in front of her as if I had forbidden her to ever have ice cream again. She got in the car without saying a word. She held the same posture almost all the way home. I finally had to ask her, "Sade, what's wrong, honey? You seem so angry."

"I am not going to sit on that bench again tomorrow!" she insisted, without looking at me.

"What do you mean, Sade? What bench?"

"The one I was just sitting on while everyone else was laughing and having fun." She continued looking straight ahead. "Including him."

"Sweetie, what are you talking about?"

"I'm talking about I got in a fight with this boy the other day, and now I have to sit all by myself on that bench in front of the school and he doesn't have to. He can run around and laugh and play games."

I pulled the car over and shut off the engine. "Why don't you tell me what happened, sweetie."

"The counselor says I have to sit on that bench all by myself for two weeks because I got into a fight with Jason. But I went to the library and found the rules that say that I have rights and they can't do that to me if they don't do the same thing to Jason. So I'm not going to sit there tomorrow."

I called the school counselor and told her of Sade's decision. The counselor made arguments against this—it wouldn't be fair to Sade, it wouldn't be fair to the other children, it would cause more commotion, and on and on. But I told the counselor that Sade's decision was final, and she should instruct the patrol guard not to harass my daughter.

The next time I arrived to collect Sade from school, she was standing tall and proud, her head held high. She gave the boy a victorious look out of the corner of her eye and climbed into my car. Once I had turned the corner, I pulled the car over, and we gave each other a high five. It was the first time Sade had asserted her rights as a student and a human being, and I was proud that she had prevailed.

A week before the Barnard students came, I conducted some initial interviews and made final preparations for their arrival. My first trip was to Brits to meet with a group of vanadium victims. Jacob had arranged for me to meet with Garrison. Garrison had spent years—literally—sucking sulfuric acid into a glass ferule with his mouth. Inevitably, he ingested some of the acid, which caused burning of his mouth, throat, and digestive and respiratory tracts. The sulfuric acid was used to test the potency of the various chemicals in the soup required to refine vanadium. Garrison had complained of spitting up blood and of seeing blood in his urine and stool.

Jacob Ngakane had first introduced me to Garrison during my private visit to South Africa in 1998. During that trip Garrison had skillfully interpreted my interviews with victims of vanadium poisoning. Garrison acted as our interpreter during my interviews with a group of about twenty mine workers, their wives, and widows, in the open space inside the little church. We traveled to Brits via a short caravan. In addition to Sade and myself, Danny Glover provided a South African film crew of two cameramen, a sound man, two directors, and the scriptwriter, Joslyn Barnes from New York.

I had met Danny Glover about one year prior to our trip to South Africa through a mutual friend, James Early, the director of cultural studies for folklife programs at the Smithsonian Institutions. James had briefed Danny about my struggle at the EPA and the passage of the No FEAR Act, and told him of the plight of vanadium workers. After our first meeting, Danny and I started discussions about producing a movie based on the passage of the No FEAR law and the crisis in Brits, with the goal of telling the world about vanadium workers. I was impressed with his total commitment to the struggle of working class and poor Africans and his willingness to place his stature and resources at the disposal of those in need.

He instantly expressed interest in helping in any way that he could in documenting the ongoing atrocities, and started preproduction for a movie about the miners and the No FEAR story, hiring Joslyn to write the script.

Danny Glover's involvement brought a high profile to the issue. What was more important, he brought eyewitnesses—and cameras.

||||||||||||

I was keenly aware that while the interviews were being conducted in the postapartheid era, the miners were still risking everything in speaking with me. There was a new government in place in South Africa to be sure, but there was also the economic reality that the only jobs in Brits were largely in Western-owned mining operations and other extractive businesses, chemical plants, and tire production facilities. Word of troublemaking spread fast, and because so many more people were in need of work than jobs were available, the companies were in the driver's seat. Every one of the people I interviewed had already been fired from the mine, so any reasonable expectancy that they might be hired elsewhere was nearly delusional. Still, they had to hold on to something, and hope is that much more powerful when it is the only thing a person has left. That these desperate people were willing to speak meant that their need to tell their stories was stronger than the hope of employment they were still clinging to. Despite all the suffering, sickness, and death related to mine work, there were still lines of men queued outside the gates every day seeking work.

And, for the first time, I also saw women seeking employment. My research indicated that there were significant gaps in research on the relationship between vanadium and health risks in women. For example, given the known effects on men, how did vanadium exposure impact female reproductive health? Could exposure to vanadium trigger uterine, cervical, or breast cancers? The exploitation of these innocent women reminded me of similar circumstances reported to me in Beijing.

If women were now being employed in the mines, this would expand the pool of disposable human resources the mining companies had to draw from among the surrounding townships. To the unfortunate inhabitants of places like Alexandra or Brits, any work was better than no work—even if it meant becoming gainfully employed in a sacrifice zone.

I started by saying how happy I was to be back in South Africa again and that I had met some of them in my previous trip to Brits. Through the commission we had organized some study tours in the United States.

Garrison touched my arm, indicating that I should slow down so that he could translate. But the miners seemed uneasy in their chairs. They made no eye contact with me. Garrison started reacting in Setswana to the objections the miners raised. They did not know me, and for all they knew, I could be exposing them to risk.

"What about the deal you made?" one of them asked in Setswana, looking directly at me. "Where are the scientists you promised?"

"The resolution passed, and the United States was supposed to conduct independent research," I explained. I waited for Garrison to finish. The miners looked at me. "That didn't happen. And so what we eventually did was return to South Africa with a group of women doctors, who some of you met, and we started to do our own independent research on vanadium exposure."

The miners watched Garrison as he spoke in their language, and then they looked back toward me and listened.

"You are the experts. You work with the substance. What we need to do is to have you tell us what is happening to your bodies, what is happening to your families, and what is happening to your communities as a result of coming in contact with this substance."

I still hadn't connected.

"I deeply regret that the promises were not kept. I was removed from my position because I kept insisting that the United States honor its commitments. I am here now at my own expense. The film crew is here at Danny Glover's expense. We are going to help you, and the only way for us to do that now is to tell your story to the outside world. I need you to trust me."

Some of the men nodded as Garrison translated. Some smiled, looking at me. After Garrison finished translating, we decided to tape outside where the light was better, where there was fresh air. The interviews were not expansive, particularly detailed, or mind blowing, but a light of recognition danced in the victims' eyes as they spoke. They opened themselves to me. These first exploratory conversations were the most important of them all. We were connected now. Everything else we did during the trip would couple with that.

The research project was divided into two phases: initial interviews with miners that I conducted with the video assistance of Danny Glover's crew and more in-depth interviews, and compilation of interdisciplinary data with recommendations from the Barnard research team.

Garrison's demeanor was relaxing. We had broken through the resistance.

I ended by thanking them for having the courage to step forward and share their experiences and health concerns from exposure to vanadium. We discussed their symptoms individually. I was impressed with their calm when describing the indescribable.

One by one they spoke of green tongues, blackish-blue tongues, black tongues—their battle scars from working in and around vanadium. They spoke of bleeding from every place imaginable in the body, and their fear of death. While the miners were polite and respectful, their eyes pled.

I had gotten engrossed in the Brits victims' plight when a commotion broke out behind us. Joslyn cried out, "It's Sade!"

I dropped everything and ran with Joslyn. A group of miners stood in a corner of the church grounds. I heard shouting and some kind of ruckus. There was a man in the center surrounded by the others, and there with him was my Sade. I worked my way through the cluster of people, shouting, "What's going on?" and calling to my daughter. Suddenly, the man in the middle whirled and broke free, running.

"Sade! Sade!" I ran to her. "Sade, what happened?"

"I don't know," she said. "This man told me to come with him."

"But who was he, sweetie? What did he want?"

"I don't know! He was friendly. He just seemed like he was an official or something. Like he needed me for something."

There was near pandemonium as the miners yelled after the fleeing man. A mineworker broke in and said something to Garrison, who conveyed what the man was saying to me.

"He says he knows who it was. It was a company man. One of us, but one of them. He had been milling about near your daughter." Garrison listened and then spoke to me while looking at the miner who continued to talk excitedly.

"Suddenly, we saw him leaving with the little girl. We ran to him and stopped him and called for others to come. Before he could get away, we had him surrounded. He would have kidnapped your daughter."

I could hear no more as I threw my arms around Sade. I felt as though a chasm had opened under my feet. I was shaking. I wanted to run—but I didn't want to run away, I wanted to run after someone. I wanted to run after that man. I wanted to bite him and put his eyes out with my nails. I felt like I could see everyone and everything, down to the last blade of grass. I could hear what the assailant was hearing as he ran. My heart was racing.

After a break, while everyone regrouped, I took Sade aside, and we hugged, cried, yelled, and apologized.

Afterward the group reconvened outside the church. I now understood in the pit of my stomach, in the roots of my teeth, how these people could feel violated and trampled upon by a corporation that would stop at nothing to intimidate, including abducting an innocent girl. In the turmoil of that assault, in the terrible gnashing of raw emotion, a primal opening and release took place in me. My hair stood on end. My eyes flashed. For no more than five minutes, I was the teeth mother. And every South African in that churchyard saw it. We now shared a common enemy. I was no longer the stranger from the United States Environmental Protection Agency who had come to South Africa and told them a bunch of pretty lies—I was one of them. My daughter was now their daughter.

Everyone decided that we were done for the day. The mine owners had made their point. This informed our decision not to return to the community once the students had arrived but to confine ourselves to the conference site outside of Brits, with one brief field trip to the mining site. Many of the former and current miners attended the vanadium conference and participated in interviews away from the immediate vicinity of the mine.

Breathing African Air

"Victor is he that runs first and last."
—Aeschylus, *from* Agamemnon, *inscribed on the* Runner,
Spirit of the Greek Games, *in the Barnard College courtyard*

The Barnard women and faculty arrived to find a film crew documenting their every move. "Excuse me, Dr. Coleman?" Alexandria is a tall woman. Because of her soft voice, I was surprised when I turned and saw it was her. She was smiling. "I wonder if I could ask a favor of you?"

"Of course."

"I have dreamed of coming to Africa all my life." She hesitated. "I wonder if I could step outside with you to have my first lungful of African air."

We found an exit and slipped outside together without being noticed by any of the others. Alexandria took my hand. She eased her head back, and the air she had been holding burst from her mouth. Then, with a contented and easy smile, she breathed in slowly through her nose with her eyes closed. I stood drinking it in and then took her other hand and joined in, my eyes closed. We stood in silence, breathing in South African air. When I opened my eyes, she was still smiling, still standing with her head tilted back. Her eyes were still closed, and a path of tears had run down her cheeks. She opened her eyes, smiling, and whispered, "Thank you."

This was the Barnard students' first trip to Africa. They were excited. They were anxious. They were wide eyed with the look of a team headed for a big tournament. Sade was barely a teenager. So a certain fear crept into my heart, knowing that we were all entering a darkness for which experience, innocence, compassion, and exuberance were poor preparation. That human instinct would soon be engaged in all who encountered the vanadium victims. What we would do with it and who would listen were the two questions none of us could answer.

By the end of the evening it was clear that Vivian Taylor and her colleague Rosalind Rosenberg had sent me the best of their legions, and it was also clear that they were all out of gas. I have always found that the day after a cross-Atlantic journey I was OK, because I could still run on empty. But the day after that I'd be starting on empty. These girls, as good as they were, were way past empty. If we were going to get the best out of them, they all needed to get some sleep.

Morning came as soon as I had closed my eyes and laid my head on my pillow. I woke up tired. A cold shower helped, and by the time we left for the conference I felt much better. The morning found us all outside the township of Brits with our operation in full throttle. The camera crew, the directors, Joslyn, the Barnard team, and a host of students and faculty from Smith College were all rested, all focused, all fired up. We decided to divide our efforts between one camera crew capturing the interviews of the miners and their families and survivors speaking at the conference, and the second camera crew capturing the more generalized and unpredictable impromptu moments whatever they might be. It was good seeing Heeten again, in his element, his dark eyes flashing with intensity. Jacob was energetic and calm (for him) and seemed to know that his job that day was to provide a comforting welcome to his American guests.

When I first came into the room, Jacob was arranging a sprawling bouquet of bright orange and red lilies and exotic flowers. There were several of these around the tables, which were arranged around the perimeter of the room along with chairs lining the walls so that we would all be facing the center. There were pitchers of water and orange juice, sliced fresh fruits, pineapple, and pastries. The east-facing room was bright with the morning sun; the flowers, fruit, and pitchers, vibrant. This was my first experience of Jacob as host, and he was perfect. His smile was genuine, his demeanor inviting.

The four Barnard students came in, all energy and enthusiasm. Ah, youth. They carried piles of notebooks and papers and books. Their excitement, warmth, and good humor as they introduced themselves to some of the South African students reminded me of my first trips to Africa not that long ago. There had been a vast transformation in my attitudes in little more than a decade. As I observed these bright young women, I saw something of myself displayed in each of them: Alexandria, reserved, pensive, but aware that there were elements of this moment that she could not access for years; Alexandra, immediate and bright, with a clarity that reminded me of a bird's keen eyesight; Hayley, radiant, quick to a fault with just the right amount of circumspection to atone for it; and Kendra, who burned a low, smokeless fire underneath a calm liveliness. This early in the day they were all college girls, bubbly, laughing, and excited.

A tall, blond man entered the room. He was in his forties, wearing a loose green sweater, his face turning bright red as he shook Heeten's hand with a robust grip, smiling broadly. He used some South African expression I couldn't get, but it was a familiar, friendly greeting. As they stood and talked, the strange similarity between Australian English and the speech of Afrikaners struck me. This must be Richard Spoor, I thought. That he was an Afrikaner had not occurred to me.

After opening comments and a welcome by Jacob, several miners made brief statements thanking the Americans for coming. Then two people took turns speaking. The first was Frederick Bagone. The next was Richard Spoor.

Frederick's voice had the raspy quality that so many of the miners had from damage to their vocal chords. Its depth fluctuated with the bobbing of his Adam's apple, between something just shy of a harsh rasping and the deep glugging sound of a ceramic jug pouring water. It was almost like he was choking several times in each sentence and would not be able to finish it. It gave a suffering quality to his words along with a stilted hesitancy.

But his words, though they almost tripped and stumbled forward, came together in complicated, well-organized, and structured sentences. It was a combination of the depth of his intelligence and the struggle to find the right word and then execute it around the damage in his throat. He also had large, round, expressive eyes that looked frightened at a fundamental level, the way someone who suffers from emphysema has a panicked look while struggling through speech. Yet Frederick's faltering was rhythmic, it had a musical phrasing, and he came off as being altogether fearless. He had a vulnerability that was wound in grace and courage. On more than one occasion his voice seemed like prophesy, shooting out in quick bursts as his ears listened to a sound that was coming to him from another place or perhaps even another time. Frederick described the processing of vanadium.

Richard Spoor was an occupational health attorney with particular emphasis on mine workers and lung disease. He began his presentation by admitting to having had "a bit of a contemptuous regard for the fashionable field of environmental health and environmentalists and bunny huggers and game reserves and whatever." He stopped and enjoyed the room's laughter, comfortable with poking fun at himself. "But I've come to realize that as much as I'd like to focus on occupational health, you can't do that. Workers live around the factory. Their families themselves are affected. The problems they experience in the plant are experienced outside. So reluctantly, I'm having to bring environmental issues back on board."

Richard looked much taller standing alone at the easel than when he had first walked in. His tenor voice continued. "The lives of miners are pretty short. When you hit the fifteen-, twenty-, twenty-five-year period—maximum twenty-five—you are finished." He waved his hand in a dismissive manner. "You have lung disease, back problems, caused by the hard physical labor, most likely degenerative back disease."

He held his hands beside his head as if he were looking at a model in front of him. "The miner is now forty years; if he's lucky, he's forty-five years old. Thereafter you get sent back home. He's unemployed and impoverished for the rest of his life. He brings home tuberculosis, he cannot contribute to the rural economy in which he lives, he needs care, he has hospital expenses, he's going to the hospital and back, and he sucks in his wife and other family members to support and help him, he gives tuberculosis to his wife, he passes it to his kids, because of poverty and malnutrition they become more susceptible to these diseases, and you generate poverty."

David Shapiro would have been proud of the way Richard was laying out the case.

"Let's make no mistake," said Richard. "Migrant people, gold miners in this country, they are professional miners, they are career miners, they are lifelong miners—no different from your Kentucky coal miners. It's generation, after generation, after generation, spending their working lives in the mines."

Richard drew two maps on an easel behind him, both rough sketches of the Southern Cape, representing South Africa. On the first he darkened the poorest areas in the country. On the second map he darkened the parts of South Africa that had been supplying labor to the gold mines—five generations of men for the last hundred years.

"Surprise, surprise. There's a very close overlap. And these mining areas are among the highest paid in all of Africa. So, why all the poverty? This poverty map is caused by the burden of disease, and to a very substantial extent, it's the burden of occupational lung disease. These communities have become poorer and poorer as each generation has worked in the mines. Hundreds of billions of rand have been lost to these communities. And it's operated as a subsidy of industry. Industry has not borne those costs. They just walk away from those costs. It's not their cost. It's not their problem."

Richard's face had become red. It was not easy for him to relive the instrument of such injustice with its telling. I could see the four Barnard women nodding in recognition. He continued, his voice subdued.

"I've seen enough to know that all South Africans would be richer, healthier, and happier if we'd never mined the stuff in this country. Whatever benefits they brought in terms of money and employment and infrastructure and roads, it pales—it's nothing—compared to the enormous social and environmental cost that that industry has inflicted on this country. We are impoverished by it. We're getting poorer with every ton of vanadium that they export.

"That's a notion that takes some getting used to. It helps if you understand that the real measure of how well you're doing as a society is your health. The real test is not how much money you've got in the bank but how healthy you are. If you are healthy and you live to seventy-five, eighty—my God! If I'm healthy I am per se rich. I am per se happy. It's that simple. It doesn't matter how rich or poor you are; it matters how healthy you are. It is impossible to be healthy mentally, physically, and deprived. The two just don't work together. There's a popular perception that we need to be rich to be healthy, and we need to be rich to be happy. That's simply not true. We should be looking at ways to stay healthy and to live long and happy lives."

As soon as Richard completed his presentation, everyone surged forward to ask questions.

᎗᎗᎗᎗᎗᎗᎗᎗᎗᎗

"Rachel? Rachel, is that you?"

I looked out the window at the woman slowly twisting her neck from left to right searching for the vanadium conference room. When I had first met Rachel the last time I was in South Africa, she had been so much in grief that she could not communicate with me or Joanne. I had affectionately called her the "cloak woman" in my report. Instead of answering my questions, she had simply and eloquently placed the cloak that she had worn to her husband's funeral around her shoulders as her statement.

I was so heartened to see her again, especially since it had taken me seven years to return. Rachel had come as a widow of a mineworker. She was wearing a turquoise hat and a colorful blouse of bright orange, green, yellow, and blue squares. She was animated and laughing with the others.

This time, she was ready to talk; she had traveled a great distance to tell her story. Rachel was born in 1942. She had met her husband, and they had struggled through poverty during the early years, right up to 1980, when he started working in the vanadium mines.

"He was always busy, always doing something, and he enjoyed every little thing," Rachel said. "But very soon after he started working he started to change. He lost his appetite. He had soreness in his back. He became lonely. He had no energy. He urinated blood."

I had learned by then that women, especially when in the presence of men, didn't use phrases like "sexual dysfunction." They were delicate with the feelings of the men who might have been suffering from the same thing, so they said instead he "had no energy" or "he was always tired," to spare them. But it was one thing after another from the beginning, and it was always something. His body changed. His tongue turned green. He bled from his eyes. His sweat in the night would stain the sheets black.

"His tongue would be green when he got home, and then it would be gone in the morning. Or it would sometimes last a few days. Sometimes it would be black. Sometimes it would be blue."

Rachel's husband died in 1996. Sixteen years—within the work span Richard Spoor had identified. I asked if she could describe how that had affected her life.

"O-o-o-o," she cried, like a descending birdcall, with a soft warble. "My life was destroyed. I missed him. I missed everything about him. His smile. The way he woke up. Everything. Everything."

"And were your children affected? Did they get sick?"

"They were not sick as children. They have bronchitis now. But my granddaughter lived with my husband and me for eight years. She had asthma and eye problems. My granddaughter would play a little bit, go inside and spray. Then come out, play a little bit, go inside and spray. After she sprayed," Rachel said, gesturing like she was holding an inhaler, "then she would be open.

"I got involved in the struggle because I could see no one was getting help from the mines. What I see about joining with the union is that by the end of the day we are going to get something out of it. Vametco only wants people to work for them. When they are finished, they won't do anything for them."

Rachel had waited her turn to speak among the others who had come from all over Brits to tell their stories. I suggested that she might allow me to come back to her home. Before we left, she told me that she was hungry, and I gave her a few dollars to help out. The next day, when I arrived at her home, she asked again for money. I could see that her cupboards were completely empty.

"What did you do with the money I gave you yesterday?" I asked. I had never seen cupboards with not so much as a single bottle of ketchup. "I thought you were going to buy food with it."

"I put it toward my rent," she told me. "I would rather be hungry than homeless." Homelessness would have exposed her to all kinds of dangers, from the weather to predators both wild and human. She felt that if she had a home, she could at least keep the predators at bay.

This became the pattern we followed. We interviewed those who had made their way to our location based on Jacob's publicizing our presence or as part of the initial interviews carried out with the film crew. The crew and I then made follow-up visits to people's homes. Seeing where they lived, their food supplies, and their hygiene could be more instructive than their testimonials.

One of these people was Jobob, a man in his sixties, who lived in a single-floor trailer that may have been all of twenty feet by twenty feet. Jobob had painted the majority of the building bright orange, without cutting the paint in tight to the doors, window, or eaves, so that the original white of the metal was still exposed. On the side of the building facing the road he had written "Jobob" in large dark letters. He sat on a metal folding chair in a purple madras plaid shirt, navy blue sweater vest, and a purple baseball cap that was filthy from sweat stains and dirt. Many, many years had blended the Nike logo in with the hat's dark stains. The afternoon sun's low angle heightened the deep lines in Jobob's face and sharpened his purple clothes against the sun-drenched orange of his house.

"I had six children. Three are still alive. I don't remember their ages." Jobob seemed wary of the camera, of recording his words. His eyes moved from me, to the cameraman, to the boom man, and back to me or the interpreter, while he listened to my questions. He didn't move his head.

"In 1987 I started working for Vametco at age forty-three. I was a tractor operator. I cleaned the streets inside Vametco, worked from seven to four Monday through Friday, sweeping spillage, driving over the dust, creating more dust. People with shovels put the spillage in dustbins. On Saturday and Sunday I would work later and could go places inside the facility that I couldn't go into during the week because of all the traffic and workers. On the weekend I could go wherever I needed to clean, because there wouldn't be as many people working then."

I asked him about safety equipment.

"I was given a disposable mask. Thin, dust would go through. They only gave one mask. About a year after I was hired I started experiencing shortness of breath. I went to a private doctor. I was coughing and wheezing. And my feet were always sore. I was given an aspirator, other medications, and one mask.

"My wife moved away." He looked away toward the distance, pointing. Referring to his impotence, he continued, "It started after a year. After seven years there was nothing. I don't see properly, just a very short distance. When I was still working in the mine my tongue turned to green for a week, and sometimes they gave me medication. My private doctor confirmed I had inhaled vanadium dust, that it was creating sores in my chest. Vametco X-rayed my chest once, but they didn't tell me what it showed. They kept the films."

As was the case with the interviews we conducted in 1998, the South Africans we interviewed during the Barnard trip in 2005 were notable for the similarities in the afflictions noted by the miners and their families. Jobob was not an isolated example.

This trip was corroborating the testimonials of the victims and charges I had learned of in 1996 from Jacob Ngakane during the Gore-Mbeki study tours and reported to my government. There was the appearance of deliberate, systematic endangerment and disregard for the lives of South African vanadium mineworkers. It appeared that, by reneging on its pledge to send scientists to investigate the claims I had reported, the United States government was complicit in these crimes.

|||||||||||

The Barnard team had scheduled decompression time in the Kruger National Park, a wildlife preserve, in Mpumalanga, at the conclusion of the conference, so that we could reflect and process what we had heard and seen. It seemed a good place to go where we could all rest, relax, and ask one another if we'd really just seen what we had seen. We were surprised and relieved when our girls had "womaned up" on us. They had not gone to pieces and did not therefore need our shoulders to cry on or an expansive reach to absorb their primal screams.

Still, there was a distance in all of our eyes, a quiet reserve that belied our easiness. Of all of us, it was not the students but the rest of us who were most in need of comfort. More than a few times I found myself looking inward as I gazed across grasslands. Or I'd catch Diane, as if in trance, listening to something only she could hear. "You know, Marsha," she said as if she were still listening, "if I have to devote the rest of my life to the cause of bringing justice to these people, I could die happy."

Tim, a sweet man and Irish to his bones, was never far from that mix of melancholy and joy that so marks Irish poets. At the park, Tim repeated himself many times. "I'm appalled, as a scientist, that people can be treated as though they are parts of a machine. Wear them out, get another part." He walked around shaking his head. "It's horrifying."

But the girls. I have said it before, but it's worth repeating: ah, youth. It may have been their psyches protecting them from awareness of what they were feeling, but there were no overt signs that these young women were suffering. Kendra Tappin was perhaps the best barometer of the young Barnard women's mindsets. Kendra kept searching for an answer with a freshness and energy that bespoke both her years and the measure of her fight.

"I'm trying to find a way—there must be some way to draw the American public in," she said over and over. She was not angry. She was not obsessed. She was determined. As were Alexandra, Hayley, and Alexandria. The girls were remarkably in the moment, in both the crucible of Brits and the overwhelming beauty of Kruger. A week in either environment could have given one the wrong impression of what South Africa, in its entirety, was. I did not want these young Americans to come out of Brits thinking it was representative of the whole of South Africa any more than I wanted them to think that the exotic endless expanse of Kruger was the place.

The week we spent in Kruger was a blessing. Sha-Sha, as the Barnard team called Sade, had found four older sisters who took her to heart. I could see so much of myself in them. I could see what life had once been like before I was lowered into the smelting tank. For Sade, it was a time to hang with some older sisters who delighted in her, but more, it was a time when Sade observed the best of some very gifted young women up close. Wheels were turning with all of them. I could see it in the down times, between trips to different parts of the park. Something had touched us all.

And then it was time to go.

Sade and I were on our way through customs. We had stayed a few more days after we had stood waving good-byes while the Land Rover pulled away from Kruger with the arms of Barnard girls flailing outside the windows and becoming rhythmic the farther away they got. Standing in line, I smiled, thinking of the sunlight flooding the room earlier that morning as the words, "Thank you for bringing me to South Africa, Mommy," woke me with the early sounds of birds. Sade and I had shared a bed in Jacob Ngakane's home in Johannesburg during the last two nights of our stay. And now we were one customs officer away from being able to sit back in our seats on a plane for the long trip home.

I handed our passports to the customs officer, a black South African man around forty, sitting behind a desk.

"And where are you from, young lady?"

"America."

He opened his eyes wide. "America!" He smiled warmly at Sade. "Step around the desk, please."

I stayed on the side of the desk opposite him. The officer swung his chair around to face Sade, and as she neared him he leaned forward, putting his elbows on his thighs with his hands resting between his knees. This had been the way that Daddy sat when he quizzed me on his sermons.

"Well, you may have been born in the United States of America as some accident of fate"—he smiled with his face level to Sade's—"but now you have breathed and eaten and slept under the South African stars. Do you know what that means?"

Sade shook her head and smiled.

"It means that from now on you are South African." His smile could not have been more kind. "Don't forget to come back and see us, my daughter."

iiiiiiiiiiiii

Dean Taylor called me after my return from South Africa to say that she had found funding for a conference on vanadium at Barnard. "Marsha, we're going to see this through."

For those of us in the States, this was straightforward. We had to review our notes, organize a conference, and show up. For Frederick Bagone, it would not be so simple. The US Mission in South Africa denied Frederick's request for a visa, citing concerns that he could be coming to the United States under false pretenses and was a risk to disappear once he had entered the country. The reasoning was that with the economic realities in South Africa, Frederick was a prime candidate to go underground seeking a better life in America.

This struck all of us—those who had worked with Frederick and come to know him as a man who had dedicated his life to improving the conditions for his fellow South Africans—as being patently ridiculous. To us it seemed far more likely that the knowledge Frederick had about the working conditions in the mines, coupled with his ability to articulate this to the American public and his thorough understanding of the extractive process, were what the US government really viewed as dangerous. So while we went ahead with the planning for the conference on vanadium, we also launched into full mobilization of applying pressure on the US Mission to grant Frederick a visa.

We wrote letters to the mission in South Africa, refuting their claims. Reporters in New York received our press releases with curiosity and interest and began reporting about the upcoming conference. Questions were asked that suggested the denial of a visa to Frederick was an attempt by the US government to prevent the release of any information that might disparage US policy toward the new South Africa.

We appeared on radio call-in programs to announce a conference where the Barnard students would report their findings from the trip. People at the grassroots level were becoming interested in the story, largely because of how it flew in the face of the US government's purported support of the Mandela government. Despite our campaign, the mission continued to deny Frederick a visa. Reluctantly, we resigned ourselves to having to hold the conference without Frederick, while still holding out some hope that the mission would come around.

We scheduled the speakers so that Barnard president Judith Shapiro could be given the honor of introducing the participants, the sponsors, and the rationale for the program. I would follow Dr. Shapiro, and then Alexandra, Hayley, Alexandria, and Kendra would present their findings. We had publicized the event with Jacob Ngakane and Frederick Bagone as the featured speakers. But as of the morning of the symposium, we still had no idea if Frederick would arrive.

"Good evening. It is my pleasure to welcome you to tonight's symposium, 'A Journey to South Africa,'" Dr. Shapiro began.[2] "We have gathered here to celebrate and learn about the work done during a very important research project on the impact of vanadium mining in South Africa, specifically in a small mining town north of Johannesburg called Brits." Dr. Shapiro went on to thank Vivian Taylor, who had helped pull together the funding and the Barnard team.

Dr. Shapiro turned the mic over to Professor Tim Halpin-Healy. Tim served as the master of ceremonies for the night and introduced Joslyn Barnes, the screenwriter who was working with Danny Glover on a script for the No FEAR movie.

"Danny is filming and could not attend," Joslyn said. "But he is definitely here in spirit and asked that I read this statement for him: 'I was pleased to provide resources for the conference held in Brits and for taping of interviews with the miners themselves. I am personally committed to ensuring that the story of the mining in Brits gets told.'"

Then Tim introduced me. All through the years of struggle within the EPA, within the US court system, and within the very limited context in which the corporate media framed my civil rights case, I had been waiting for a moment to arrive when the soapbox David Shapiro had forecast for me would present itself. That night at Barnard was my soapbox.

"It is time to tell the truth about what is going on in Brits, South Africa," I began. "I have given so many talks about vanadium, and no one seemed to care about it. . . . Well, I came to Barnard, and Vivian Taylor cared.

"Many of you know that the US Embassy in South Africa denied Frederick Bagone a visa last Thursday. Because of the enormous effort that was put forth by the mass media, members of Congress, through the Barnard community, Frederick is sitting right over here today."

The auditorium burst into applause.

"And Jacob Ngakane. Jacob is a freedom fighter. He was one of the members of the liberation front in South Africa. He went through all the things that you read about. He was imprisoned because he was fighting for freedom in South Africa. He was tortured in the prisons. He still fought for the rights of vanadium workers as a union leader.

"Crimes against humanity are taking place at Vametco Mine in Brits, South Africa, only one hour from the capital, Pretoria. There are reports that people have died from vanadium poisoning, while others are chronically ill from exposure. After suffering the indignities of apartheid, vanadium workers and their families continue to pay the ultimate price. Our trip to South Africa was a life-saving mission, but not in the traditional sense of bringing doctors and medicines to a place. What we brought was hope and the promise that we would carry the message back to the United States and the global community and tell the stories of the men, women, and yes, children, who are very ill or dying anonymous deaths from vanadium poisoning.

"Peace is not simply the absence of war. In its most organic state it is the presence of justice. We have an opportunity to make a difference and, in our own small way, change the world one community at a time."

I returned to my seat and listened to the presentations of the Barnard students, Hayley, Alexandra, Kendra, and Alexandria; they laid out their cases surgically and were brilliant in their analysis of the facts surrounding the Brits community. Hayley called upon the US government to keep the commitments it had made to the Brits community under the Gore-Mbeki Commission and to conduct an independent investigation. But what brought me back to the present was an anecdote Kendra told.

"While we were in South Africa, we met with members of the African National Congress Youth League, and at dinner one night"—Kendra began, her bright yellow sweater so hopeful against her very dark skin—"one of the gentlemen we had dinner with leaned over to me after I had asked him what they do there, and he said, 'Well, what we do in here is we teach our lions,' referring to their young people. 'We teach them, and if they're ready, they roar.'"

Kendra paused, placing her dark hands against her chest. "To me, that was the most profound thing, the most valuable thing, this man could ever have said to me. And so I feel as women returning to Barnard we're continuing that tradition of South Africa, of young people who are learning to roar. That's what I hope we accomplish tonight."

There was a burst of applause. I could see heads nodding and people in the audience turning to speak to one another. Kendra had hit home.

It was then time for the South Africans to speak. First, Jacob Ngakane strode to the podium.

"Good evening," Jacob said in a clear voice. Jacob spoke rapidly, his mastery of English readily apparent in his articulate delivery. "I'm quite impressed by the quality of the research by the Barnard students while they were there. And I am also deeply touched that within that short period of time they could demonstrate such good understanding of our situation so accurately. I was deeply moved, as I was sitting here listening, that I spent two weeks with them and they came up with these findings.

"I salute Barnard College for producing useful citizens for sustainable development. We all know the difference between paying a visit to a defenseless, impoverished people who cannot afford a decent meal and those who are affluent and well to do. It is difficult to afford a smile when you have visited such people. Your trip to my country, South Africa, was a different mission—a mission of support and a need to understand our success as well as our challenges. On behalf of the many people you met, we thank you very much. America is fortunate to have citizens like you. Barnard College must be very proud to produce citizens that represented its country properly."

Then Jacob said, "Brits holds two vanadium groups doing vanadium mining in South Africa: the USA's Strategic Minerals and Swiss-based Xstrata Mines. This Swiss company recently resolved its case with its former and current workers and the surrounding communities. This settlement was made with the help of attorney Richard Spoor. Stratcor [Strategic Minerals Corporation], a USA-based company, has continuously closed their ears. They don't want to listen. They're not prepared to enter into negotiations. They are just displaying the terrible arrogance of saying, 'We don't care, we don't understand, it was not us, we don't want to enter into any constructive engagement.' And this really worries everyone who is saying, 'Can't they just learn that it pays to listen and just engage in constructive negotiations?' This matter can be resolved better than that."

Jacob looked up from his statement and surveyed the room. "Let us use this symposium as a forum to declare our commitment to serve humanity.

"And so let me introduce Frederick. Frederick worked in Vametco Vanadium Company. He has seen it all. He understands all the processes. I was very fortunate to be drawn into the miners' confidence, to share their painful experiences with them, but I think it is better to hear it from the horse's mouth. But Frederick Bagone is here, and he can tell you much better than I can. Many thanks. Frederick."

Where Jacob was quick and decisive in both his language and movements, Frederick was slower and more wary. He was wearing a dark brown jacket and walked to the podium with deliberation, placing his statement down self-consciously.

"Good evening, everybody. I would like to thank you for inviting me to your country for this important occasion." Frederick's speech was much slower than Jacob's, but the quality of his voice penetrated the room, softer, disjointed, and hoarse, with words issuing from deeper in his throat, many of them getting caught there before he had to nearly expel them so they would clear his mouth.

"I am Frederick Bagone, and I am from South Africa. I am a former worker at Vametco Minerals Corporation that was owned by Union Carbide, and it is now owned by Stratcor Minerals Corporation, headquartered in Danbury, Connecticut, USA."

English was not Frederick's native tongue, and he didn't have the polish Jacob had developed through years of education. Frederick read each word syllabically; his speech had a stilted quality. He rolled his *r*'s. Frederick had never been to America before. He was not accustomed to speaking in front of an audience. He took a half step backward, crossed his arms in front of his chest, and read, "Alexandria, Hayley, Alexandra, and Kendra, you will never know how much your research and visit to Brits meant to all of us. We felt that the world had forgotten us, and then you came to our rescue." Loud applause interrupted him.

"I started to work for Union Carbide vanadium mine in Brits on the twenty-eighth of May, 1979, first as a temporary worker, and later became permanent. While I was a temporary worker, I worked in an area that was exposed to extreme heat, of degrees ranging between a thousand degrees to fifteen hundred degrees Celsius. The heat was so intense that it could melt the steel. Not long after I started working full-time, I saw a horrible accident where two of my colleagues were critically injured and one died instantly when a concrete slab of magnetite fell on them."

Frederick shuffled his feet, wiping his brow with the palm of his hand and recrossing his arms before continuing.

"And now my story. In 1986, Union Carbide changed its name to Vametco, after the Bhopal tragedy, and to avoid criticism of supporting the racist regime. I started experiencing terrible effects of contacting vanadium that doctors referred to as bronchitis. I coughed up blood. My tongue used to turn green. When I worked in the smelting and refinery plants, I developed sores caused by minute vanadium and carbon particles that penetrated my skin.

"Sometimes I would wake up and find my white sheets totally blackened by the vanadium coming out of my skin. In addition, my eyes were affected, and I am still suffering from that effect today. After realizing what was happening to me and seeing my colleagues becoming ill and die, I became scared that I was also going to die. I became desperate and decided to join my colleagues in demanding improved working conditions and better salary, which management vehemently rejected. At that time I was earning ZAR 8.60, which in today's dollars is equal to $1.25 per hour. Our demand was an increase of two rand per hour for all employees, which would have brought my salary to ZAR 10.80, or equivalent to $1.50 per hour."

There were looks of shock, people shaking their heads. "Approximately 360 workers were dismissed. Some are still unemployed, like myself. Others are deceased. And approximately 270 are living miserable lives but still united and striving for our cause. Numerous diseases are common among workers and communities residing in the nearby vicinity; chronic bronchitis and eye problems abound. Workers in extraction plants like the precipitation, reactor, and refinery plants develop green tongue; some experience erectile problems that cause marital splits like divorce and misery to occur. Yes, we have a long list of diseases among former workers. Most of them, their deaths are similar. Lung cancer, kidney failure, and liver cancer—these problems seem to be the main causes of their death.

"Vanadium powder and its sister chemicals can stay for a long time in the human body, causing irreparable damage to soft tissue that in the end leads to death. The modern ablution facilities were built late, when major damage has been caused to workers who used to take their working clothes home to be washed by their children and wives, thus poisoning them without their knowing.

"During dusty months magnetite would be carried far by the wind and land on the roofs of communities who used to rely on rainwater for drinking and washing purposes. The drinking water was contaminated. The chemicals that were in the water flowed from the plants and poisoned the water and killed livestock that drank it. One nearby community has a large number of men and women who are now infertile. Many children as young as three years old have to wear glasses, as the magnetite dust has affected their eyes.

"The common suffering caused by the same source kept my workers together. We tried and are still trying to find solutions that will bring our suffering to an end. Therefore, unity is the weapon that will help us survive."

Frederick shifted his weight back and forth on his feet before continuing. He looked briefly at the audience as he reached forward and turned the page.

"I really want to thank the Barnard College students for coming to our country to do some research of our misery. We are faced with a terrible dilemma of working in a situation that has killed so many of my friends and colleagues or being unemployed. No one should have to choose between feeding their family or ruining their health for the sake of a job. But that's the situation we find ourselves in.

"As a small, impoverished community fighting a huge, rich American multinational corporation, we request your help. Despite our suffering I believe that, if we work together and commit ourselves to a path of justice and a workplace that is healthy and fair, we can make a difference in the lives of my community. I firmly believe, as Dr. Martin Luther King Jr. once said, we shall overcome.

"I thank you all."

Frederick collected his papers to thunderous applause. He stepped back and stood with his statement in both hands lowered in front of his waist. The room rose to its feet. Frederick started to return to his seat but was stopped by Jacob who touched his elbow and then stood aside, applauding. Cheers went up in the room for both of them. Many people were weeping.

||||||||||||

Perhaps it was the sound of a voice that was injured.[3] Or the sound of an innocence that remained despite his experience. Perhaps it was the presence of such dignity, in a setting ten thousand miles from the scene of the crimes. Whatever it was, it was clear Frederick was a man whose suffering had not hardened him but instead had brought forth his humility and a purpose not bent on vengeance but justice. That was what fed the audience at Barnard that night.[4] While Jacob and Frederick spoke that evening, the United States and other industrial nations were exacting their terrible demand for vanadium on innocents in South Africa. Frederick had come as the prophet of Brits—whose people, lives, families, and community were entombed as unknown soldiers without so much as a trumpet playing "Taps"—appealing to our better angels for us to stop.

It would be foolhardy to believe that captains of commerce would voluntarily relinquish their addiction to this strategic mineral.[5] Add to this the new technologies of the twenty-first century that are developing vanadium batteries that will hold their charges for a hundred years, and it is difficult to see how the green revolution will proceed without the vanadium industry continuing its legacy of green crimes.

Perhaps our meeting was just random chance. Or maybe it was something closer to fate. But at the triumphant end of the long struggle against apartheid, Jacob and Frederick stood as symbols marking a stunning victory of the meek over the powerful.

Toward the end of one century, Frederick, Jacob, and I were drawn into an economic and political vortex where our countries merged a new millennium with vanadium's well-entrenched pipeline. Through our activism, our resistance, and our refusal to submit, we three walked away—injured but alive. Their victory inspired the beginning of another struggle that culminated in the passage of the No FEAR Act.

Giants and Grasshoppers

*And there we saw the giants. . . . And we became like grasshoppers
in our own sight, and so were we seen by them.*
                                        —Numbers 13:32–33

Mom had always warned me as a kid about looking at the grasshoppers
in my life and mistaking them for giants. I see my mother taking me, as
a child, between her knees and looking me in the eye.

"They're just bullies, Marsha. They can only hurt you if you let them.
You must punch through the fear. You can fight it now or fight it later.
But you will some day have to fight it."

Giants. Their later disguises included a professor, EPA managers, an
obstinate congressional member, and the federal government itself. To
me they were intimidating, but Mom always saw these giants as the
grasshoppers they were.

As I was leaving the conference at Barnard after Jacob and Frederick
had spoken, the sky was turning from blue to gray. It struck me that this
idea of mistaking grasshoppers for giants was precisely what Steve Biko
had meant when he said, "The most powerful weapon of the oppressor
is the mind of the oppressed." How terrifying must a hippo, the South
African slang expression for an armed personnel carrier, have been to
a black man it could crush under its tracks like an ant? Or shred with

machine-gun fire? How paralyzing was it for antiapartheid resisters to see in all the newspapers, on all the telecasts, the images of Hector Pieterson being carried away from the Soweto massacre, dying while his teenage sister ran alongside sobbing? Or the corpse of Steve Biko's mutilated and tortured body?

And yet, like Jacob and Frederick, millions of black South Africans kept on striking and kept on fighting, sacrificing themselves—not to the open maw of industry—but as a willful offering of themselves to the cause of their people's freedom, laid on the altar of their race's dignity. Bullets and clubs do not frighten that kind of person.

Dogs cannot intimidate that kind of determination. If anything, those with guns, tanks, and armament—provided in large part by the United States—the armed forces of Africa's mightiest military must have recoiled when their weapons fell asleep in their hands. To them, the swarms of people they had never seen as anything more than ants must have suddenly looked like giants. Giants filled with a fierce resolve.

A breeze slipped through the courtyard, piercing the industrial smell of New York, lifting the ancient words "Victor is he who runs first and last," before giving way to the sweet scent of African hibiscus and linden, a calypso-like timpani of traffic and wind carrying the allure of everything that rises from the streets. We had opened our arms to fellow human beings. We had heard of their pain, their struggle, and embraced it as our own. It is the sound freedom makes.

Grasshoppers no longer looked like giants. We had mastered what my mom had long ago identified as the most imposing grasshopper of all: fear.

Like a Landscape from the Book of Time

When it was over and the day laid down beside us like a landscape from the book of time, nameless, orphaned, mute, there was a presence in the room that closed down around us and listened. It did not care about the heads of state. It did not care about the slip of time. It was a moment that any man, any woman, every person to have ever lived, would have listened into and heard. It had been a day for the ages, and already it was falling away. It was the end of a time and an effort that took everything we knew to give, and now it left us alone. Segun, Olusegun, so far from the cool mountains of Nigeria and its deep African nights. And me, Ngozi, after so many years, after so much unknown, and with so much at stake—a moment's blessing. All of it falling away, where I am, alone, with my husband who touches me. My gift is his tears.

"You did it, sweetheart. You saw it through." His voice is quaking. The power in his arms and shoulders now whisper-touches my skin.

"Was it enough?"

"Yes, Marsh. It is enough." I can see the slope of his cheek-bones glistening, the slow rise and fall as he breathes. "It is a lifetime."

"I could not have . . ."

He leans his forehead to mine, rocking. No, no. Our noses barely touch. "I am here. I am always here." How I know is in showing. He does not need words.

It is still with us when I ease my hand away and his slips onto the sheet. The peepers trill through the window. I listen. I listen down the hall to my children. Listen outside their doors. And go in where Sina is listening. He is lying on his side. I see his eyes as they follow me.

"Olusina?"

I bend over him and kiss his cheek. I place my hand on his forehead.

Jesu a se amona ati alakoso re.

"Do you know what I said?" I am whispering.

"I think so. . . . 'Jesus will be my guide and guardian'?"

"Thank you, Olusina. Thank you for your patience. It will be better now."

He takes my hand and kisses the knuckles. I feel his beardless skin.

Then on to Sade. Folasade. The quiet of the room deepens with her breathing.

In Yoruba her name means "God has given me a crown." I whisper into her dream.

O ni ri iponju.

You will never encounter hardship.

"Sleep, little one. We did this for you."

There is a heartbeat, a pulsing, the sound of footsteps, barefoot, and the settling in of sheets.

It is here now.

It is always here.

For now . . . I can go to sleep.

Afterword

|||||||||||||

by Rev. Walter E. Fauntroy

Mostly, it went the way all rehearsal-strategy sessions go. There were staffers who had researched the issues confronting the nation's air and water. There were politicos who knew the opposition party's position better than the opposition did. Still others had sharpened their knives while reviewing an opponent's record and then plied their skills taking nominees apart. This was Washington. Everyone entering a Senate confirmation hearing—especially for EPA administrator, where so much commerce is at stake—expects some bloodletting.

The difference was about holdover litigation from the preceding administration of Carol Browner and the Democratic Party. All the eyes in the room were trained on Christine Todd Whitman, who at the time was still the Republican governor of New Jersey and was also president-elect George W. Bush's nominee for EPA administrator. It was her standing up suddenly when asked what she would do about the agency's ongoing appeal of the verdict in *Coleman-Adebayo v. Carol Browner*, soon to become *Coleman-Adebayo v. Christine Todd Whitman* were she to be confirmed, that raised everyone's eyebrows. She did not want a court case to be among her options when she sat before the Senate Committee on Environment and Public Works at her confirmation hearings.

Those present would later learn that Whitman had placed a call to the one person she trusted above all others on matters of race in America, the Reverend DeForest Blake "Buster" Soaries Jr. Rev. Soaries was a next-generation Baptist preacher who held divinity degrees from both Princeton Theological Seminary and the United Theological Seminary. His twin sons were named Malcolm and Martin. Soaries had served as Whitman's secretary of state and enjoyed a special confidence with the governor.

In this instance Whitman had not sought his spiritual guidance nor even his legal counsel. She needed his insight into the nuanced labyrinth of deep African American politics and a clear understanding of the cultural implications of the case. To Rev. Soaries it was a cut-and-dried discrimination issue where the powerful had gotten called on long-standing structural abuses within the government. His advice was simple: get rid of it. Everyone in the African American community was aware that Carol Browner and Attorney General Janet Reno were bent on protecting the agency's reputation, the criminal behavior of EPA managers notwithstanding, and had vowed to continue pushing the appeal process through the courts. This would have sentenced Marsha to another ten years of legal jujitsu in the federal court system, where she would remain outmanned and out-financed, exhausted emotionally and financially. Whitman, however, made an unequivocal healing gesture: in her first act as EPA administrator, Whitman announced the agency would not appeal the verdict in *Coleman*.

Now, Coleman-Adebayo's first problem was having won her case. To agency loyalists, the judgment against the agency was an embarrassment brought by a highfalutin black troublemaker, and the danger to the agency was that her victory would encourage other troublemakers to start standing up for themselves too. Marsha was marked and had to go. The agency began negotiating with Dr. Coleman-Adebayo on a severance package. The new administrator was happy to hang the judgment on a Democratic administration.

Later, Whitman would distinguish herself, bucking the political current as EPA administrator by refusing to go along with President Bush's desire to back away from carbon dioxide emissions control. That ended the EPA tenure of Christine Todd Whitman. In walking away with her head held high, Whitman also walked away with the conciliatory tone she brought to the agency. Negotiations broke off between the agency and Dr. Coleman-Adebayo, despite having come close to closure on the ramifications of her discrimination case. Following Michael Leavitt as EPA administrator was Stephen Johnson. Johnson was an old EPA insider, having come from the ranks of EPA's Senior Executive Service. Any hope of amicability died with Johnson's confirmation.

Through eight long years of George W. Bush, we saw the systematic dismantling of EPA oversight, particularly in the area of pollution reporting requirements. We saw the same managers who had acted so callously toward Dr. Coleman-Adebayo get promoted. But we did not see the long, slow, continued persecution of Dr. Coleman-Adebayo carried out by those same managers. We did not see the toll stress took on a decent family, on a loving husband, on a woman of conscience whom the government left dangling over the abyss while it pared its nails and strung her out in court. Notably, under all the promise and hope that emerged during the transition from Mr. Bush to Mr. Obama, we did not see her illegal firing.

It was a cruel game. One side with infinite resources, the other a parody of the American myth of the valiant individual at odds with a system. In our folklore the individual triumphs, as Marsha triumphed in her life, in her career, and in the courts by suffusing the civil rights movement with the moral ballast that stabilized the push for the first civil rights and whistleblower legislation of the twenty-first century. But winning against the United States bears bitter fruit that piles up through institutional retaliation. The stress is intense.

Every war has casualties. In this war, stress is the killer. Some, like Lillian Pleasant and Pat Lawson, do not live through it. Their suffering and loss is only so much collateral damage. Others, including Dr. Coleman-Adebayo, got sick. Seeing what was happening, several congressional members wrote to Administrator Johnson, offering Dr. Coleman-Adebayo reasonable accommodation if EPA would detail her to their office. They reasoned that the government might still benefit from her many talents. And the EPA's response? It refused to detail Marsha in every instance until the end of the Bush years.

This was where Rev. Buster Soaries once again was called on to assist a female nominee from New Jersey. This time, I asked Rev. Soaries to approach Barack Obama's EPA nominee, Lisa Jackson. In addition to my personal appeal, I provided letters from the NAACP, the Black Ministers Conference of Montgomery County Maryland, National

Whistleblowers Center, and from Congressman Chris Van Hollen, who was the congressional liaison to the White House during Mr. Obama's transition. We asked that the incoming administration make a highly visible gesture to all federal employees by making Marsha whole again after she had endured nearly a decade of agency reprisals.

Surprising would be an understatement for Lisa Jackson's response. Unlike her New Jersey predecessor, Jackson would not be magnanimous. But with Carol Browner playing a key role on President-elect Obama's transition team and operating out of EPA headquarters again, perhaps Lisa Jackson's deaf ear was not surprising after all.

Just as America had not seen Rosa Parks coming in 1955, in 1995 America did not see another black woman, this one named Marsha, coming either. This time, a Barnard College graduate and MIT-trained social scientist who had benefited from Rosa's stand stepped forward. This time the means of transportation was not the back of a segregated bus but Air Force Two, and the scene of the discrimination was in the highest reaches of the American government. This time, the jurisdiction would not be a single white judge in the Deep South; it would be the federal court system in Washington, DC.

How ironic, then, that the named defendant in the case Marsha brought under the 1964 Civil Rights Act would be a white woman, Carol Browner, who proclaimed in sworn testimony before Congress that she was the beneficiary of affirmative action that laid the foundation for her eventually assuming the position as EPA administrator. And that the person defending Ms. Browner was a black, female assistant US attorney named Wyneva Johnson, who was from—of all places in America— Mississippi was enough to make one cynical.

Such are the depths of the forces of racism. In a case alleging racial, sexual, and color discrimination by the US government against a black woman, the government reached into its bag of tricks, rummaging through the bloody history and broken bones of Mississippi that included the ghosts of Medgar Evers and Emmett Till, and produced a black woman to perform as a modern equivalent of Bull Connor. "Was this discrimination," Wyneva would ask the jury in spite of the facts, "or was this disappointment?" In classic form, the government blurred the lines between its public narrative and internal realities. Cancer with a smiling face is still cancer.

I had first encountered an instance of this when in 1979 I acquired a copy of a policy memo written by President Carter's national security advisor, Zbigniew Brzezinski, National Security Council Memorandum 46, "Black Africa and the U.S. Movement." The document detailed an orchestrated plan to create antagonisms between Africans and African Americans and exacerbate animosity between educated and poor blacks. I was livid at the arrogance of the document and alarmed by the potential harm to the African American community it represented. I consulted with Randall Robinson, the young man whom the late Congressman Charles Diggs and I had given the task of organizing Trans-Africa. We called a press conference, in my capacity as chair of the Congressional Black Caucus Brain Trust on Black Voter Participation and Network Development, to present the document to the media, and were delighted that the press conference was well attended—standing room only. I went to bed that evening satisfied that I had done my conscientious duty. To my shock and dismay, when I checked the news the next day, not one mention of this egregious memo had made any of the press. I now know, after having served in Congress for twenty years, that the only way for a story of that magnitude to have been quashed was for the White House to have leaned very heavily on decision makers in the nation's editorial boards to have them kill it.

But why would the free press in the land of the free so uniformly and systematically kill a story with such profound implications for so many? It is because the interests served by the media are the same ones that benefit from the suppression of a politically informed and active African American community like the one that thrived during the 1960s.

The confluence of media acquiescence and the cynical front-loading of AUSAs of color in discrimination cases are illustrative of how the government manipulates opinion and outcomes. It is not difficult to see why so few of the thousands of federal workers experiencing injustice rebel and why, of those courageous enough to formally seek redress in the courts, so few prevail.

This only accentuates the significance of Marsha's stance. Against these tremendous odds and at great peril to herself, personally, and to her family, Marsha did not ask, "Is it safe?" She did not ask, "Is it politic?" When it came to witnessing US complicity in crimes against humanity as it was happening in the vanadium mines of South Africa, she asked the only question of import: "Is it right?" The jury considering the merits of her case asked itself if EPA was right and answered with a resounding "No!"—awarding Marsha the largest judgment against EPA in its history.

The media, the EPA, the Congress, and the president could not deny this story. And when word of it reached the general body of federal workers, there was an adamant and spontaneous outpouring of support for Marsha, with corroboration of her allegations. For the first time since the 1960s, a significant burst of life issued once again from the civil rights movement, and that burst culminated in the enactment of the No FEAR Act of 2002—the first civil rights and whistleblower protection legislation of the twenty-first century.

In a variation on the theme the government employed at Marsha's trial, two African American women now run the two offices that were pivotal during Marsha's struggle at EPA: Lisa Jackson is EPA administrator, and Michelle De Pass is the assistant administrator of the Office of International Activities. Both of these women are wont to quote civil rights heroes. It is easy to quote the dead. But neither has acknowledged their own indebtedness to the African American woman who preceded them at EPA and made their appointments not only necessary but—from the perspective of the status quo—inevitable. Contrary to all decency, on April 1, 2011, EPA administrator Lisa Jackson sent a memorandum to all 17,800 of her employees:[1]

> I appointed Rafael DeLeon as our new director for the Office of Civil Rights; he is someone I knew would bring energy and experience to the post. Under his leadership, the EPA set a record for training its employees under the No FEAR Act.

Rafael DeLeon orchestrated Marsha's termination from the EPA. The message sent by Jackson to thousands of EPA employees was clear—reward, promotion, and upward mobility is not based on merit and hard work but patronage, corruption, and an unquestionable commitment to following orders, no matter how despicable. DeLeon was a key player in Browner's office of civil rights and human resources during the time period that the violations occurred that the No FEAR Act sought to eradicate; this promotion was his reward. This man is now responsible for implementing the law that Marsha and others watered with their sweat and sacrifice.

Tragically, the larger story of the systematic poisoning of vanadium mine workers in South Africa has never been fully told. This is not just a case of racism—it is at the very least one of criminal negligence. But as we saw with the civil rights movement in the last century, sparks provided by individuals like Rosa Parks and Dr. King can light an entire revolution. The flame that rose out of Marsha's victory was only the beginning. Let no amount of propaganda or the stunning silence of the media fool you into believing that we are anywhere near a post-racial America. The further protections before Congress today in proposed No FEAR II and III legislation are vitally important to everyone's civil rights. So too is oversight of a government where corrupt managers, political appointees, and politicians would prefer to have none.

The federal government has yet to honor Marsha Coleman-Adebayo's contribution toward helping establish a more perfect union that celebrates, cherishes, and protects the least among us. And far from elevating the very managers and SES officials who were implicated for wrongdoing in her case, the Justice Department should be actively adhering to the letter and spirit of the No FEAR Act to ensure that the federal workplace is worthy of its monuments to liberty, equality, and justice.

Congress and the president should monumentalize the contribution whistleblowers have made by enacting No FEAR Acts II and III, which would hold federal managers personally responsible for wrongdoing committed under their supervision and strengthen the protections guaranteed to ordinary workers so that they could report malfeasance occurring above them in the chain of command without fear of reprisal. Imagine the benefit to all of us who have been saddled with the bailout of high-ranking and highly paid executives who abused the financial markets with impunity and without oversight, if the whistleblower protections of No FEAR II and III had already been in place to safeguard federal workers who are everywhere in place to witness—and call out—waste, fraud, and abuse.

And lastly, Congress and the president of the United States should approve the tasks and funding of the No FEAR Institute as an educational vehicle and watchdog organization to educate federal workers on their inalienable rights and to blow the whistle on any federal employee, whether an EPA administrator or a groundskeeper, who uses antiquated and illegal institutional practices that have been resolutely rejected by the courts, the Congress, the executive, and—most notably—the people.

That is what the sixties taught us about the power of the people. What the nineties and early 2000s have taught us is that the top-down model has reasserted itself with a vengeance and that, for vast numbers of federal employees, the federal government represents a sacrifice zone to any who challenge, expose, or resist its corrupt, illegal, and self-perpetuating status quo. If we want whistleblower protection, accountability for wrongdoers, and justice for all of us, it is time once again for the same kind of grassroots organizing that worked so effectively for the general good of the people in the 1960s. It is time for the common people to recognize who in government are our friends and who, our foes. And it is time to bring a concerted effort against the forces of darkness that have consolidated power behind secrecy and the tyranny of a ruling elite who demonstrate nothing but contempt for the masses and obeisance to their corporate masters. When we have built those necessary foundations, it will be time for the people to hit the streets in demand of justice.

A lot has happened since a night in 1952 at Virginia Union University when I struck up a conversation on theology with a newly ordained Baptist minister I had just met. It wasn't until the windows started showing the first gray of morning that we realized we had talked all night. We only knew that there was magic and mystery and power in what we had explored about the cosmos and a deep sense of hope and determination we both had found in ourselves. It was a fleeting moment between two young men who were sharing their souls, and if we had learned nothing else, from that moment on we knew we were brothers. Neither one of us knew that next morning that our conversation would continue through the rest of our lives or that his life and work would become the benchmark for the American voice for justice, on par with those of Frederick Douglass and Abraham Lincoln. That young minister's name was Martin.

Neither did we know at the time that his time with us on earth would be curt or that his triumph and challenge would be so enduring. Yet as I write this, now approaching my eighties, Dr. Martin Luther King Jr. is as alive now and pertinent to the struggle for justice today as he was when at the height of his prowess his body was silenced. As the poet said, "You can burn the oboe, buddy boy, but you can't touch the notes!" Still, one cannot be a person of color in America—even today—without noticing profuse smoke.

By the heady days of the early 1960s, through a long series of successes that came with a heavy toll in lives and blood and beatings, people of color could look back with pride at a growing catalogue of instances where righteous defiance had braved dogs and clubs and water hoses and had advanced the cause another inch, another step, another mile, toward another milestone. *Brown v. the Board of Education*, Rosa Parks, the Freedom Rides. There was momentum gathering along two fronts that Martin saw and talked about—one in public, on the growing momentum for the forces of justice—and one in private, on the race against time and the convergence of the justice movement with violent forces gathering to protect the status quo. Even as we stood beside Lyndon Johnson during the signing of the 1964 Civil Rights Act—a triumph unimaginable only a decade earlier—everyone in the room knew it was JFK who had sent the bill to Congress. Seven months after that signing, Malcolm X would be the next voice to be silenced. The storms raged. During a speech titled "Beyond Vietnam," delivered on April 4, 1967, Martin linked the war in Vietnam to systemic racism within our own government and culture, saying, "Injustice anywhere is a threat to justice everywhere." He linked the killing of brown babies in Vietnam to the systematic disenfranchisement of black babies in America.

Two weeks after delivering that speech, Martin called me. The speech had ignited a firestorm, with cartoons and editorials charging that Martin was a danger to the American way of life and a tool of Ho Chi Minh. There was a stinging rebuke from Roy Wilkins of the NAACP, Whitney Young, and other civil rights funders. As a consequence, contributions dropped precipitously, with the criticism directed at Dr. King charging that he was out of his element in trying to become a foreign policy leader.

When he called me, he was despondent, feeling he had to do what his conscience demanded. I quoted him an old eighteenth-century English clergyman I had been reading at the time, words that have now become widely attributed to Martin: "Cowardice asks the question, 'Is it safe?' Expediency asks the question, 'Is it politic?' But conscience asks the question, 'Is it right?' And there comes a time when one must take a position that is neither safe, nor politic, nor popular but because conscience tells one it is right."

Martin was buoyed by the power of that quote. He thanked me, saying it was just what he needed, and used it in response to the criticisms leveled against him from that day forward. One year—to the day—after delivering his "Beyond Vietnam" speech, Martin was murdered. He was thirty-nine.

I cannot say I've never regretted encouraging him to stay with the themes we had developed for that speech. The thought of what may have been haunts me to this day. But that is only in moments of doubt, moments when I let fear creep back into me, when I forget that I am more than just one man. Perhaps the timing of his execution contained a message. But even without his "Beyond Vietnam" speech, Martin was a marked man. During President Kennedy's funeral in Washington, DC, as Martin and I stood watching from the top floor of what was then the International Hotel, Martin had said to me, "If they will kill a president, I won't live to be forty." He knew it. Coretta knew it. We all knew it. It was a race against that convergence that saw the Democratic National Convention in 1968 draw heavy curtains closed on a decade that had started with so much optimism and that ended in the kitchen of the Ambassador Hotel in Los Angeles.

My last conversation with Martin was on a plane when we were coming up from an all-day Saturday meeting on March 30, 1968, that had been marked by a long and contentious discussion of whether we should abandon the poor people's campaign idea, because of the violent rhetoric of some of the young Student Nonviolent Coordinating Committee people. Some of the young people who were part of our team had said that nonviolence had run its course. They thought we needed to come up with a more threatening approach. They liked the slogan, "Burn, baby, burn!" Martin remained adamant, telling me afterward, "If every one of them turns to violence, I will not. If you haven't found a cause you're willing to die for, you're not fit to live."

Yet having lived it and knowing even then that this was an inspired period that was sparking the imagination not only of black Americans but of all Americans and people the world over, we still didn't know then what we have since come to cherish about how bright the flame was that burned in all of our hearts. And how rarely that flame burns. Its light flooded America, and civil rights became the beacon for others who picked up the torch. The women's movement, the environmental movement, César Chávez with his grassroots support, all advanced the cause for human rights that had been enabled by the civil rights movement. The inspired time of the civil rights movement had come and left its indelible mark and then began a long, slow smoldering that still flashes occasionally, but since the sixties the spark has waned. There is only so much even the most magnificent can do.

Convergence and divergence dance between the poles of good and evil. Through the end of the nineties, despite all of the community organizations, churches, and millions of people who contributed to the light of the civil rights movement of the sixties, the intervening decades have seen the cumulative effects of the forces of evil that took Martin. Crushing poverty, staggering rates of incarceration among black men, whole generations and communities left beneath burgeoning anger. Yet its counterpart—imagination and the words to transform that anger—is building up.

Dr. Marsha Coleman-Adebayo has given us a testimonial to courage in the example of her life, and now with her book we have a blueprint for how powerful and undemocratic forces work within the US government—as well as a guide to what we all can do to change it.

Endnotes

Foreword

1. "U.S., South Africa plan to improves trade, fight crime," CNN.com, February 18, 1999, www.cnn.com/WORLD/africa/9902/18/us.sa.talks. All CNN citations refer to this article.
2. Interagency Working Group on International Exchanges and Training, IAWG Country Studies: South Africa, www.iawg.gov/rawmedia_repository /3fd49561_6f66_4752_88f0_f7c120972851.
3. Jack White, "How the EPA Was Made to Clean Up Its Own Stain—Racism," *Time*, February 23, 2001, www.time.com/time/nation/article/ 0,8599,100423,00.html; Marsha was awarded the Good Housekeeping Award for Women in Government 2003. "Just Saying No to Discrimination," ivillage.com, http://web.archive.org/web/20030620180855 /magazines.ivillage.com/goodhousekeeping/myhome/friends/articles /0,,287164_583490-2,00.html.
4. "About Us," US Diplomatic Mission to South Africa, http://southafrica .usembassy.gov/about-us.html.

Preface and Acknowledgements

1. Diane Dittrick, "Failure Is Not an Option: The Plight of Vanadium Mine Workers in South Africa," video, 62:55, Barnard College, 2004, http:// beatl.barnard.columbia.edu/beatldb/videodb/view_holding.asp?holding _id=328; "A Journey to South Africa—Symposium and Multimedia Exhibition Highlights Barnard Students' and Faculty Mission to South

Africa's Hazardous Vanadium Mines," Barnard College News Center, www
.barnard.edu/newnews/news032204.html.

Introduction

1. The US delegation included three representatives from industry—one
   Dow senior vice president and two IBM officials—a science and technology executive, and the South African manager of governmental programs.
2. Jonathan Rosenthal, "Dow Faces Suit Over South African Pollution: Farmers
   Claim Herbicides Destroyed Land, Lawyer Says," *Bloomberg News*, September 23, 2003. For more details on the IBM and Dow apartheid litigation, see:
   www.mindfully.org/Pesticide/2003/Dow-African-Pollution23sep03.htm.
   See also: www.haguejusticeportal.net/eCache/DEF/8/541.html.
3. Office of F. James Sensenbrenner, chairman of the Judiciary Committee,
   "House Passes Sensenbrenner/Jackson Lee No FEAR Civil Rights Legislation: 'First New Civil Rights Law of the 21st Century' Now Sent for President Bush's Signature," press release, April 30, 2002; "Racism & Retaliation
   at EPA 2 of 3," YouTube video, 4:13, posted by "Brownermustgo," March
   18, 2009, www.youtube.com/watch?v=N1UKJJF3Pss.
4. Linda Halpern, letter to Carol Browner, EPA administrator, March 3, 1997;
   Environmental Protection Agency, response to letter from Linda Halpern,
   March 21, 1997.
5. Heeten Kalan, director, South African Exchange Program on Environmental Justice, letter to Carol M. Browner, EPA administrator, and Albert
   Gore Jr., vice president (on behalf of Shaking Alston, Robert Bullard,
   Deeohn Ferris, Cindy Ko, Pam Tau Lee, Ng'ethe Maina, Vernice Miller,
   Richard Moore and Beverly Wright), October 3, 1996; Environmental
   Protection Agency, response to letter from Heeten Kalan, December 13,
   1996. Also see: Heeten Kalan, director, South African Exchange Program
   on Environmental Justice, letter to Carol M. Browner and Mr. William
   Nitze (on behalf of Richard Moore, National Environmental Justice Advi-
   sory Council; Shaking Alston, representative, Northeast Environmental
   Justice Network; Maria Mbengashe, chief director, Ministry of Environ-
   mental Affairs and Tourism, Eastern Cape; Chaka Ntsane, director, Agri-
   culture Department, Free State; Jacob Ngakane, coordinator, Congress of
   South African Trade Unions) and copied to Vice President Al Gore, South
   African ministers Pallo Jordan and Peter Mokaba, TransAfrica president
   Randall Robinson, US members of Congress, and civil leaders, November
   19, 1996; Rev. Eugene Rivers to Carol Browner and Al Gore, copied to Lily
   Lee, October 28, 1996; EPA response to Eugene Rivers, copied to Carol
   Browner and the Deputy Administrator and Enforcement and Compliance

Assurance, December 13, 1996. It should also be noted that Ms. Deeoi Ferris wrote a letter to the agency, dated October 3, 1996, expressing he. concerns about the direction of the Gore-Mbeki Commission. The agency responded to her letter on October 31, 1996; Randall Robinson, president, TransAfrica, letter to EPA administrator Carol Browner, Vice President Al Gore, US Department of Labor secretary Alexis Herman, EPA assistant secretary William Nitze, Lily Lee of the EPA Office of the Administrator, South Africa deputy minister of the environment Peter Mokaba, Heeten Kalan of the South African Exchange Program on Environmental Justice, October 28, 1996. Response by White House to EPA on October 30, 1996. EPA responded to Mr. Robinson, December 13, 1996, and copied the administrator, the deputy administrator, and Enforcement and Compliance Assurance.

6. Naomi Klein, *The Shock Doctrine: The Rise of Disaster Capitalism* (New York: Metropolitan Books, 2007). For more about the South Africa/Western Cape Anti-Eviction Campaign, see Wendy Willems, "Social Movement Media, Post-Apartheid (South Africa)," Anti-eviction campaign, Western Cape, South Africa, website, http://antieviction.org.za/; Sampie Terreblanche, *A History of Inequality in South Africa 1652–2002* (Pietermaritzburg: University of Natal Press, 2002); Alex Russell, *Bring Me My Machine Gun: The Battle for the Soul of South Africa from Mandela to Zuma* (New York: Public Affairs, 2009).

7. EPA statement, "EPA's International Programs: Serving U.S. Environmental, Economic, Foreign Policy and National Security Interest," regarding EPA's International Programs: "EPA's technical assistance programs overseas . . . have led to commercial opportunities for U.S. environmental businesses, thereby improving the U.S. trade balance and creating high-wage jobs for American citizens." http://nepis.epa.gov/Exe/ZyPURL .cgi?Dockey=5000126P.txt.

8. *Coleman-Adebayo v. Browner* (Civil Case 98-926 and 98-19 39) was decided August 18, 2000; Jack White, "How the EPA Was Made to Clean Up Its Own Stain—Racism," *Time*, February 23, 2001, www.time.com/time /nation/article/0,8599,100423,00.html. Regarding the No FEAR Act, White wrote, "Congress will soon debate the first new civil rights law of the 21st century."

Chapter 1: Welcome to EPA

1. Brooks Hamlin, EPA chapter president, Blacks in Government, letter to Kathy Aterno, chief of staff to Administrator Browner, September 27, 1993. Mr. Hamlin wrote: "In our Agency of over 17,000 employees with

300 Senior Executives, there are only 12 African-Americans in the Senior Executive Service." This letter was copied to Browner and six members of Congress.

2. The EPA helped draft Section K of the Platform for Action developed at the Fourth UN World Conference on Women in Beijing, China, September 4–15, 1995. See: www.un.org/womenwatch/daw/beijing/platform/environ .htm#diagnosis.

3. See Environmental Protection Agency, *EPA InSight*, February 1993, p. 6, http://nepis.epa.gov/Exe/ZyPURL.cgi?Dockey=2000U8ZT.txt. "'I hope EPA employees will introduce themselves to me,' said the new Administrator. 'I don't care if I'm in the elevator or buying lunch, I want to meet them.'"

4. Carol Browner, memorandum to be circulated to all EPA employees regarding Beijing Conference, April 28, 1995. "To: Assistant Administrators, General Counsel, Inspector General, Associate Administrators, Regional Administrators, Staff Office Directors. Dr. Marsha Coleman-Adebayo . . . will be the Agency coordinator for this conference."

5. The U.S. Environmental Protection Agency sponsored this meeting ("Women Thinking Globally, Acting Locally: On the Road to Beijing and the 21st Century," held November 16, 1994) in conjunction with the Department of Labor and other agencies. For thoughts from those who attended this conference: www.lwv-hawaii.com/alohavoter/av9410-pres .htm.

6. Alan Hecht to Carol Browner, EPA administrator, decision memorandum regarding EPA participation in the 1995 United Nations World Conference on Women in Beijing, China, September 4–15, 1995, and related preparatory work, February 22, 1994. Kim Tilley, deputy chief of staff to Administrator Browner, response memorandum to Alan D. Hecht, April 11, 1994. Resistance from senior male managers to agency participation in the Beijing Conference was so virulent that Browner had to send Alan Hecht a handwritten declaration. "I really want this," Browner wrote.

7. "Browner Statement at Oakland," YouTube video, 2:20, Carol Browner speaking at the Oakland preparatory conference to the Beijing Conference, posted by "Brownermustgo," March 21, 2009, www.youtube.com /watch?v=aTD2tEQVvqo.

Chapter 3: Ultimatum to Public Service

1. "[Mandela's] successor famously said, 'I am a Thatcherite.'" See Bob Carty, "Whose Hand on the Tap?: Water Privatization in South Africa," Canadian Broadcasting Corporation News, February 2003, www.cbc.ca/news /features/water/southafrica.html.

2. Bill Nitze, letter to the Dan Glickman, secretary, Department of ⌐
culture, June 26, 1996. Nitze wrote: "Ms. Coleman-Adebayo will ser
as the EPA point of contact and will be available to attend working leve
meetings."

Chapter 4: The Gore-Mbeki Commission

1. Davidson, Joe. "Reagan: A Contrary View." www.msnbc.com/id/5158315
/ns/us_news_life.
2. Democracy Now, "Allied with Apartheid: Reagan Supported Racist South
African Government," June 11, 2004, www.democracynow.org/2004/6/11
/allied_with_apartheid_reagan_supported_racist.
3. Steve Biko, *I Write What I Like* (Chicago: University of Chicago Press,
2002).

Chapter 7: Why Waste MIT on People Like That?

1. Environmental Protection Agency, International Update, September 1992,
http://nepis.epa.gov/Exe/ZyPURL.cgi?Dockey=2000YF37.txt. There is no
debate whether South African officials, General Bantu Holomisa, or Peter
Mobaka endorsed ETI—they did not. Kathy Washburn, Franklin Moore,
and I all testified to this fact. A letter from Kasman to Bill Nitze, "Technology Cooperation in South Africa," November 19, 1996, also confirms this.
2. This information is excerpted from an unclassified cable from the American Embassy, Pretoria, dated August 25, 1995, regarding USAID funding
for exchanges to support the US-South Africa Binational Commission.
3. Kathryn Washburn, Department of the Interior, Office of the Secretary,
memorandum to BNC Staff members, November 12, 1995.
4. Bantu Holomisa, South African deputy minister of environmental affairs,
fax to Ken Thomas, US Embassy counselor, and cover letter to William
Nitze, EPA assistant administrator, February 21, 1996.
5. Patricia Koshel, memorandum ["hold the draft letters"] to Marsha Coleman-
Adebayo, copied to Alan Hecht and Alan Sielen, April 1, 1996.

Chapter 10: Breathing College Air

1. Martin Luther King Jr., "I Have A Dream," speech delivered at Cobo Hall,
Detroit, Michigan, June 1963.
2. *Frontline*, Public Broadcasting Service, *The Long Walk of Nelson Mandela*,
airdate May 25, 1999, producers, David Fanning and Indra deLanerolle;
director, Clifford Bestall; interviewer and writer, John Carlin, series #1716:
www.pbs.org/wgbh/pages/frontline/shows/mandela/etc/cron.html.

William Blum, "How the CIA Sent Nelson Mandela to Prison for 28 Years," *Third World Traveler*, www.thirdworldtraveler.com/Blum/CIAMandela _WBlum.html; Seymour M. Hersh, "U.S. Is Said to Have Given Pretoria Intelligence on Rebel Organization," *New York Times*, July 23, 1986; David Johnston, "C.I.A. Tie Reported in Mandela Arrest," *New York Times*, June 10, 1990, www.nytimes.com/1990/06/10/world/cia-tie-reported-in-mandela-arrest.html; Jeff Stein, "Our Man in South Africa," *Salon.com*, November 14, 1996, www.salon.com/news/news961114.html; Tim Weiner, *Legacy of Ashes* (New York: Penguin Group, 2007); *The Times* (London), "Times Diary: Mandela a CIA Victim?" August 4, 1986; Michael White, "CIA Linked to Arrest of Nelson Mandela," *Guardian*, August 15, 1986.

Chapter 11: Barnard College

1. Barnard College, Office for Multicultural Affairs, "Attallah Shabazz, Daughter of Malcolm X, Reflects on the Life of Her Father, at Barnard College, Feb. 18," Barnard Campus News, February 17, 2001. On February 18, 1965, Malcolm X delivered a speech at Barnard titled "The Black Revolution and Its Effects on the Negro of the Western Hemisphere."

Chapter 12: MIT

1. Noam Chomsky, *For Reason of State* (New York: Pantheon Books, 1973); Noam Chomsky, *American Power and the New Mandarins* (New York: Pantheon Books, 1969); Noam Chomsky, with Edward Herman, *The Washington Connection and Third World Fascism* (Boston: South End Press, 1979).
2. Margalit Fox, "Carol Chomsky, 78, Linguist and Educator," *New York Times*, December 20, 2008.

Chapter 14: Retaliation at EPA

1. "Blacks in Government," Obituary of Patricia Lawson, February 21, 2006, www.bignet.org/Memorial/PatriciaLawson.htm.
2. The MIT Series on Technology and the Corporation conference "Proactive Environmental Strategies for Industry: Anticipating the Future in Environmental and Sustainability Driven Problems" was held on May 8, 1996.
3. "The World Factbook—Field Listing: Natural Resources," Central Intelligence Agency, www.cia.gov/library/publications/the-world-factbook/fields /2111.html. The listing for South Africa includes natural gas, coal, many strategic minerals, gem diamonds, platinum, copper, vanadium, and salt.
4. Foreign Policy Study Foundation, Inc., *South Africa: Time Running Out: The Report of the Study Commission on U.S. Policy Toward Southern Africa* (Berkeley: University of California Press, 1981).

5. National Oceanic and Atmospheric Administration, Database of Ha~
   ous Chemicals, Cameochemicals, "Vanadium Pentoxide," cites as sou~
   "EPA report, 1998," http://cameochemicals.noaa.gov/chemical/4757.
6. Open Letter from NEJAC concerning South Africa, June 12, 1996.
7. Kenneth A. Thomas, memorandum to William Nitze, concerning "The
   Role of EPA in the Gore-Mbeki Conservation, Environment and Water
   Committee," April 17, 1996.

Chapter 16: President of the United States

1. Letter from Peter Mokaba, deputy minister of environmental affairs,
   South Africa, to William Nitze, EPA assistant administrator, copied to
   Carol Browner, EPA administrator, and Bruce Babbitt, secretary of the
   department of interior, October 7, 1996.
2. During the apartheid years, more than a dozen attempts were made to kill
   Mokaba. See: Official Site of the City of Durban, South Africa, Sharen Thim-
   boo, Content Editor, www.durban.gov.za/durban/government/renaming
   /bios/fiery-visionary.
3. Sandy Hurnall, Executive Office of the President of the United States, Council on Environmental Quality, memo to Peter Umhofer, October 30, 1996.
4. TransAfrica Forum website publication, " Our History," www.transafri-
   caforum.org/about-us/our-history; Charlie Rose, "A Conversation with
   Author Randall Robinson," December 26, 2007, www.charlierose.com
   /view/interview/8852; Randall Robinson, *An Unbroken Agony* (New York:
   Basic Civitas Books, 2008).
5. Democracy Now, "'We Made a Devil's Bargain': Fmr. President Clinton
   Apologizes for Trade Policies that Destroyed Haitian Rice Farming," April
   1, 2010, www.democracynow.org/2010/4/1/clinton_rice.
6. Mark Kasman, memorandum to Alan Hecht, "South Africa reply," October 8, 1996.

Chapter 17: Last Obstacle to the End Run

1. Rev. Eugene Rivers, letter to Carol Browner, EPA administrator, and Al
   Gore, vice president, October 28, 1996.
2. Randall Robinson, letter to Carol Browner, EPA administrator, copied to
   Vice President Al Gore, Alexis Herman, William Nitze, Lily Lee, South African Deputy Minister Peter Mokaba, and Heeten Kalan, October 28, 1996.
3. Lily Lee, EPA Office of the Administrator, memo to Peter Robinson, chief
   of staff, EPA Office of the Administrator, regarding "Environmental Justice Letters to the Administrator and the Vice President on South Africa,"
   October 3, 1996.

Alan Hecht, memo to Mark Kasman, Pat Koshel, Alan Sielen, and Marsha Coleman-Adebayo, November 25, 1996.

. Mark Kasman, memo to Bill Nitze, regarding "Technology Cooperation in South Africa," November 19, 1996.

6. Ibid.

7. Ibid.

8. Ibid.

9. United States-South Africa Binational Commission, "Terms of Reference: Conservation and Environment Committee, United States-South Africa Binational Commission," Tab 3, Article VI, included in the Environmental Management and Pollution Working Group, 2nd Meeting, December 1, 1995, South Africa.

10. AmEmbassy Pretoria ECON Section, memo to Marsha Coleman-Adebayo, concerning "Operation of the U.S.-South Africa Bilateral Relations," November 7, 1996.

11. "Open Letter to the NEJAC Concerning South Africa," June 12, 1996.

12. Pat Koshel, memorandum to Marsha Coleman-Adebayo regarding unsatisfactory performance, December 13, 1996.

13. William Nitze, memorandum to Carol Browner, EPA administrator, concerning "Office of International Activities 1996 Report," January 13, 1997. The memo informs Ms. Browner that "OIA signed agreements with . . . the US Environmental Training Institute for work in South Africa." It should be noted that the study was actually conducted at Howard University in Washington, DC, not Harvard, as Mr. Nitze wrote to the administrator.

14. An example of an EPA playbook: Wendy Lawrence, "Addressing and Resolving Poor Performance: Practical Application for OPP Front Line Managers," Labor and Relations Staff Office of Human Resources, July 29, 2010. Diane Lynne, president, NTEU Chapter 280, and Bill Evans, senior vice president, wrote in response: "We are concerned that managers are using presentations like this to target employees who are nearing retirement or going through personal problems."

15. Marsha Coleman-Adebayo, letter to Patricia Koshel, copied to William Nitze, Alan Hecht, Alan Sielen, and Donald Sadler, titled "Response to Your December 13, 1996 Memo," March 4, 1997.

Chapter 18: Yes, Clarice

1. Trenton High, EPA Security, incident report memorandum to Ernie Howe, "Incident Report/Theft of Computer Information," January 16, 1997.

2. Marsha Coleman-Adebayo, ed., *EPA Environmental Justice Monitor Newsletter*, Office of Environmental Justice, June 1997 and October 1997.

3. Frank Wilderson III, *IncogNegro: A Memoir of Exile and Apartheid* (Cambridge, MA: South End Press, 2008).

Chapter 19: The 1998 Trip to South Africa

1. "Toxicological Profile for Vanadium," US Department of Health and Human Services, Public Health Service Agency for Toxic Substances and Disease Registry, September 2009, www.atsdr.cdc.gov/ToxProfiles/tp58.pdf.
2. "Chemical Information Review Document for Oral Exposure to Tetravalent and Pentavalent Vanadium Compounds Supporting Nomination for Toxicological Evaluation," National Institutes of Health, National Institute of Environmental Health Sciences, National Toxicology Program, January 2008, http://ntp.niehs.nih.gov.
3. "Environmental Health Criteria 81: Vanadium," World Health Organization, International Programme on Chemical Safety, 1988, www.inchem. org/documents/ehc/ehc/ehc81.htm.
4 Foreign Policy Study Foundation, Inc., *South Africa: Time Running Out: The Report of the Study Commission on U.S. Policy Toward Southern Africa* (Berkeley: University of California Press, 1981).
5. Ibid.
6. Trevor Johnson, "Swiss Company Accused of Poisoning Workers in South Africa," World Socialist Web Site, April 7, 2001, www.wsws.org/articles /2001/apr2001/pois-a07.shtml.
7. Ibid.
8. Interviews conducted with vanadium workers, Brits, South Africa.

Chapter 20: Death Threats and Missed Opportunities

1. F. James Sensenbrenner, chairman of the Committee on Science, letter to Carol Browner, EPA administrator, referencing the assignment, December 15, 2000.

Chapter 21: *Coleman-Adebayo v. Carol M. Browner*

1. *Marsha Lynne Coleman-Adebayo v. Carol M. Browner*, CA No. 98-CV-926 and 98-CV-1939, Washington, DC. I referred to the transcript of the trial record before Judge Colleen Kollar-Kotelly and a jury. Testimony was excerpted from volumes one through twelve of the court transcript.

Chapter 25: Can You Hear Me

1. Michael A. Fletcher, "Rampant Bias at EPA Is Alleged—Agency Chief Urged to Take Action; Class-Action Suit Planned," *Washington Post*,

August 31, 2000, www.washingtonpost.com/ac2/wp-dyn?pagename=article&contentId=A52624-2000Aug30&language=printer.

2. Carol Browner, EPA administrator, and W. Michael McCabe, EPA assistant administrator, signed a mass mailer to all EPA employees, regarding "Report on Diversity and Fairness in the EPA Workplace," January 19, 2001.

3. Dwight Welch, Marsha Coleman-Adebayo, and Anita Nickens, "The Toxic Environment at the Environmental Protection Agency (A Report on Diversity 'Progress' at EPA)," *Inside the Fishbowl*, March 21, 2001.

4. "Racism & Retaliation at EPA 1 of 3," YouTube video, 5:29, posted by "Brownermustgo," March 18, 2009, www.youtube.com/watch?v=rKXFdsKaEL8.

5. Michael A. Fletcher, "Rampant Bias at EPA Is Alleged," *Washington Post*, August 31, 2000.

6. Marsha Coleman-Adebayo, "Toward a Fair Federal Workplace," *New York Times*, May 27, 2002, www.nytimes.com/2002/05/27/opinion/toward-a-fair-federal-workplace.html.

7. *Good Housekeeping*, "They've Changed Your Life," July 2003.

8. *Inside the Fishbowl*, edited and authored by Dwight Welch, president, National Treasury Employees Union 280. May 2000 articles include: "Smashing Irongate," by Dwight Welch and Marsha Coleman-Adebayo, p. 1; "Victors not Victims—Smashing Iron Gate," p. 12, "The Cleaning Lady," p. 12; "Smashing the Iron Gate: NAACP Rally" p.13; March 2002, Vol. 18, No. 2. articles include: "Sharpton Led Rally," "Environment of Plantation Attitude," and "War on Managers Who Terrorize Employees." May 2002, Vol. 18, No. 3: "President Bush Signs No FEAR Bill into Law," See: www.nteu280.org.

Chapter 27: Congressional Hearings

1. Leroy Warren Jr., letter to Al Gore, vice president, copied to William Clinton, president, and F. J. Sensenbrenner, congressman, June 29, 2000.

2. House Committee on Science, "Intolerance at EPA—Harming People, Harming Science?," 106th Cong., 2nd sess., 2000, 106–103. See also: "Racism & Retaliation at EPA 2 of 3," YouTube video, 4:13, posted by "Brownermustgo," March 18, 2009, www.youtube.com/watch?v=N1UKJJF3Pss.

Chapter 29: Journey to No FEAR

1. Dwight Welch to Christine Whitman, memorandum, September 13, 2001, regarding "Unacceptable Response to Act of War."

2. *Jet*, "EPA Worker's Battle Against Bias Sparked Recent Signing of Century's First Rights Bill," June 10, 2002.

Chapter 30: Al Sharpton

1. *Jet*, "Major Civil Rights Battle Erupting on Capital Hill Over Federal Employees 'No FEAR Act,'" March 25, 2002.
2. President Bush signed the Notification and Federal Employee Anti-discrimination and Retaliation Act in the Oval Office on May 15, 2002. See photo in insert section for attendees.

Chapter 31: Vanadium

1. Barack Obama speaking to business leaders at a brainstorming forum in Cleveland, Ohio. www.resourceinvestor.com/News/2011/3/Pages /Obama_hails_vanadium_energy_breakthrough.aspx.

Chapter 32: Breathing African Air

1. Diane Dittrick, "Failure Is Not an Option: The Plight of Vanadium Mine Workers in South Africa," video, 62:55, Barnard College, 2004, http:// beatl.barnard.columbia.edu/beatldb/videodb/view_holding.asp?holding_ id=328; "A Journey to South Africa—Symposium and Multimedia Exhibition Highlights Barnard Students' and Faculty Mission to South Africa's Hazardous Vanadium Mines," Barnard College News Center, www .barnard.edu/newnews/news032204.html.
2. Ibid.; "Barnard Delegation Heads to South Africa on Research and Humanitarian Trip," Barnard College News Center, www.barnard.edu/newnews/ news090803.html; "Diane Dittrick: Senior Associate in Environmental Science, Co-Director of the Environmental Science Laboratory," Barnard College, www.barnard.edu/faculty/profiles/dittrick_d.html; "Turned Away in 1929, Civil Rights Leader Dorothy Height Is Embraced by Barnard as 'Honorary Alumna' 75 Years Later," Barnard News Center, www.barnard .edu/newnews/news060404.html.
3. I interviewed Jacob Ngakane, former COSATU representative, by e-mail on April 29, 2010, regarding the health of vanadium workers. The interview is presented here as a reference for material in this chapter:
"In respect of company doctors, workers were always complaining about white racist Afrikaner doctors who were used only to ensure that workers don't go to black doctors. Many black doctors and workers were vocal about the state of Vametco workers' health. The workers were forced to submit their medical records to these racist company doctors. The company doctors had the authority to approve or reject the medical reports. It was rare for a white doctor to approve the work of a black doctor—these decisions were made based on color lines. This was a practice which black

workers under apartheid system were subjected to. It was common. When I got involved (as a union representative), I could not believe the pattern of illnesses and death were the same, the set up was so organised. When I studied the report from the SA National Institute of Occupational Diseases, their report stated that workers were ill and dying because of their lifestyles i.e. smoking, drinking and sexual activities, it was insulting, and for me sitting at meetings with these white doctors representing the apartheid system (who with a clear conscience insulted our people) was the worst you could expect from a doctor.

"The fact of the matter is the multinationals from the West and Europe use Africa for dumping their dangerous operations. They know that in their own countries they will not get away with murder. That is why countries (western) foreign policies amongst others will protect atrocities committed in the so-called third world countries because we are their perfect guinea pigs.

"The issue of using milk to control dangerous work places is one of the worst tools the apartheid doctors used to give to black workers who were exposed to poisonous chemicals. There is no scientific evidence that milk will take care of such situations. Many workers died because of this 'treatment.'

"What I recall the President of Vametco in the USA was called on the same day and informed of your presence and he instructed that we should be removed, that's what abruptly stopped our mine tour after it was approved by local management."

4. Diane Dittrick, "Failure Is Not an Option: The Plight of Vanadium Mine Workers in South Africa," video, 62:55, Barnard College, 2004, http://beatl.barnard.columbia.edu/beatldb/videodb/view_holding.asp?holding_id=328. The video includes footage of the Barnard College symposium.

5. National Oceanic and Atmospheric Administration (NOAA), Database of Hazardous Chemicals, Cameochemicals, "Vanadium Pentoxide," cites as source: "EPA report, 1998," http://cameochemicals.noaa.gov/chemical/4757; And the work continues, see: "Whistleblower Week in Washington."

Afterword

1. Lisa Jackson, "Strengthening and Revitalizing the EPA's Civil Rights and Diversity Programs." Memorandum to all EPA employees, April 1, 2011.

Bibliography

Biko, Steve. *I Write What I Like*. Chicago: University of Chicago Press, 2002.

Blacks in Government. "Patricia Anne Lawson." www.bignet.org/Memorial /PatriciaLawson.htm.

Blum, William. "How the CIA Sent Nelson Mandela to Prison for 28 Years." *Third World Traveler*, May 26, 2008.

Bullard, Robert D. "BP's Waste Management Plan Raises Environmental Justice Concerns." *Dissident Voice*, July 29, 2010.

Carson, Rachel. *Silent Spring*. New York: Houghton Mifflin, 1962.

Carty, Bob. "Whose Hand on the Tap?: Water Privatization in South Africa." Canadian Broadcasting Corporation News, February 2003.

Chomsky, Noam. *American Power and the New Mandarins*. New York: Pantheon Books, 1969.

Chomsky, Noam. *For Reason of State*. New York: Pantheon Books, 1973.

Chomsky, Noam and Edward Herman. *The Washington Connection and Third World Fascism*. Boston: South End Press, 1979.

Coleman-Adebayo v. Carol Browner. Civil Case 98-926 and 98-1939, transcripts.

Coleman-Adebayo, Marsha, ed. *EPA Environmental Justice Monitor Newsletter*. Office of Environmental Justice. June 1997–October 1997.

Coleman-Adebayo, Marsha. "Toward a Fair Federal Workplace." *New York Times*, May 27, 2002.

Democracy Now. "Allied with Apartheid: Reagan Supported Racist South African Gvt." June 11, 2004.

Democracy Now. "'We Made a Devil's Bargain': Fmr. President Clinton Apologizes for Trade Policies that Destroyed Haitian Rice Farming." April 1, 2010.

Dittrick, Diane. "Failure Is Not an Option: The Plight of Vanadium Mine Workers in South Africa." Barnard College presentation, http://beatl.barnard .columbia.edu/beatldb/videodb/view_holding.asp?holding_id=328.

Durban (City of). "Peter Mokaba." www.durban.gov.za/durban/government /renaming/bios/fiery-visionary.

Environmental Protection Agency. *EPA InSight*. February 1993.

Fletcher, Michael A. "Rampant Bias at EPA Is Alleged—Agency Chief Urged to Take Action; Class-Action Suit Planned." *Washington Post*, August 31, 2000.

Foreign Policy Study Foundation, Inc. *South Africa: Time Running Out: The Report of the Study Commission on U.S. Policy Toward Southern Africa*. Berkeley: University of California Press, 1981.

Fox, Margalit. "Carol Chomsky, 78, Linguist and Educator." *New York Times*, December 20, 2008.

Good Housekeeping. "They've Changed Your Life." July 2003.

Hersh, Seymour M. "U.S. Is Said to Have Given Pretoria Intelligence on Rebel Organization." *New York Times*, July 23, 1986.

Jet. "Major Civil Rights Battle Erupting on Capital Hill Over Federal Employees 'No FEAR Act,'" March 25, 2002.

Johnson, Trevor. "Swiss Company Accused of Poisoning Workers in South Africa." World Socialist Web Site, April 7, 2001. www.wsws.org/articles /2001/apr2001/pois-a07.shtml.

Kinnell, Galway. "Under the Maud Moon." *The Book of Nightmares*. New York: Mariner Books, 1973.

Kirkpatrick, David A. "E.P.A. Halts Florida Test on Pesticides." *New York Times*, April 9, 2005.

Klein, Naomi. *The Shock Doctrine: The Rise of Disaster Capitalism*. New York: Metropolitan Books, 2007.

Meredith, Martin. *Nelson Mandela: A Biography*. New York: St. Martin's/Griffin Press, 1997.

Ngakane, Jacob. Interview by Dr. Marsha L. Coleman-Adebayo. E-mail. April 29, 2010.

Robinson, Randall. "A Conversation with Author Randall Robinson." By Charlie Rose. *Charlie Rose*. PBS. December 26, 2007.

Robinson, Randall. *An Unbroken Agony*. New York: Basic Civitas Books, 2008.

Russell, Alex. *Bring Me My Machine Gun: The Battle for the Soul of South Africa from Mandela to Zuma*. New York: Public Affairs, 2009.

Stein, Jeff. "Our Man in South Africa." Salon.com, November 14, 1996.

Terreblanche, Sampie. *A History of Inequality in South Africa 1652–2002*. Pietermaritzburg: University of Natal Press, 2002.

White, Michael. "CIA Linked to Arrest of Nelson Mandela." *Guardian*, August 15, 1986.

Washington Post. "Chemical Industry Funds Aid EPA Study: Effect of Substances on Children Probed." October 26, 2004.

Times (London). "Times Diary: Mandela a CIA Victim?" August 4, 1986.

U.S. Congress. House of Representatives. Committee on Science. "Intolerance At EPA—Harming People, Harming Science?": Hearing Before the Committee on Science. 106th Cong., 2nd sess., October 4, 2000.

Weiner, Tim. *Legacy of Ashes.* New York: Penguin Group, 2007.

Welch, Dwight, Marsha Coleman-Adebayo, and Anita Nickens. "The Toxic Environment at the Environmental Protection Agency (A Report on Diversity 'Progress' at EPA)." *Inside the Fishbowl*, March 21, 2001.

Welch, Dwight. "The Cleaning Lady." *Inside the Fishbowl*, May 2000.

Welch, Dwight. "Environment of Plantation Attitude." *Inside the Fishbowl*, March 2002.

Welch, Dwight. "President Bush Signs No FEAR Bill Into Law." *Inside the Fishbowl*, May 2002.

Welch, Dwight. "Sharpton Led Rally." *Inside the Fishbowl*, March 2002.

Welch, Dwight. "War on Managers Who Terrorize Employees." *Inside the Fishbowl*, March 2002.

White, Jack. "How the EPA Was Made to Clean Up Its Own Stain—Racism." *Time*, February 23, 2001.

Wilderson, Frank, III. *IncogNegro: A Memoir of Exile and Apartheid.* Cambridge, MA: South End Press, 2008.

Appendix

Legislative Stages to the No FEAR Public Law

from the Library of Congress Records H.R.169

Title: Notification and Federal Employee Antidiscrimination and Retaliation Act of 2002

Sponsor: Rep Sensenbrenner, F. James, Jr. [WI-9] (introduced 1/3/2001) Cosponsors (26)

Related Bills: S.201

Latest Major Action: Became Public Law No: 107-174 [GPO: Text, PDF]

House Reports: 107-101 Part 1; Senate Reports: 107-143

ALL ACTIONS:

1/3/2001: Sponsor introductory remarks on measure. (CR E13)

1/3/2001: Referred to the Committee on Government Reform, and in addition to the Committees on Energy and Commerce, Transportation and Infrastructure, and the Judiciary, for a period to be subsequently determined by the Speaker, in each case for consideration of such provisions as fall within the jurisdiction of the committee concerned.

1/3/2001: Referred to House Government Reform

2/13/2001: Referred to the Subcommittee on the Civil Service and Agency Organization.

1/3/2001: Referred to House Energy and Commerce

2/7/2001: Referred to the Subcommittee on Environment and Hazardous Materials, for a period to be subsequently determined by the Chairman.

1/3/2001: Referred to House Transportation and Infrastructure

1/4/2001: Referred to the Subcommittee on Water Resources and Environment.

1/3/2001: Referred to House Judiciary

5/9/2001: Committee Hearings Held.

5/23/2001: Committee Consideration and Mark-up Session Held.

5/23/2001: Ordered to be Reported (Amended) by Voice Vote.

6/14/2001 12:51pm: Reported (Amended) by the Committee on Judiciary. H. Rept. 107-101, Part I.

10/2/2001 2:18pm: Mr. Sensenbrenner moved to suspend the rules and pass the bill, as amended.

10/2/2001 2:18pm: Considered under suspension of the rules. (consideration: CR H6071-6076)

10/2/2001 2:18pm: DEBATE—The House proceeded with forty minutes of debate on H.R. 169.

10/2/2001 2:31pm: At the conclusion of debate, the Yeas and Nays were demanded and ordered. Pursuant to the provisions of clause 8, rule XX, the Chair announced that further proceedings on the motion would be postponed.

10/2/2001 6:01pm: Considered as unfinished business. (consideration: CR H6100)

10/2/2001 6:24pm: On motion to suspend the rules and pass the bill, as amended Agreed to by the Yeas and Nays: (2/3 required): 420—0 (Roll no. 360). (text: CR H6072-6073)

10/2/2001 6:24pm: Motion to reconsider laid on the table Agreed to without objection.

10/3/2001: Received in the Senate and Read twice and referred to the Committee on Governmental Affairs.

3/21/2002: Committee on Governmental Affairs. Ordered to be reported with amendments favorably.

4/15/2002: Committee on Governmental Affairs. Reported by Senator Lieberman with amendments. With written report No. 107-143. (text of measure as reported in Senate: CR 4/23/2002 S3226-3228)

4/15/2002: Placed on Senate Legislative Calendar under General Orders. Calendar No. 346.

4/23/2002: Measure laid before Senate by unanimous consent. (consideration: CR S3226-3231)

4/23/2002: Passed Senate with amendments by Unanimous Consent. (text: CR S3229-3231)

4/24/2002: Message on Senate action sent to the House.

4/30/2002 2:08pm: Mr. Sensenbrenner moved that the House suspend the rules and agree to the Senate amendments.

4/30/2002 2:08pm: DEBATE—The House proceeded with forty minutes of debate on the motion to suspend the rules and agree to the Senate amendments to H.R. 169.

4/30/2002 2:26pm: At the conclusion of debate, the Yeas and Nays were demanded and ordered. Pursuant to the provisions of clause 5, rule I, the chair announced that further proceedings on the motion would be postponed.

4/30/2002 6:32pm: Considered as unfinished business. (consideration: CR H1745)

4/30/2002 6:56pm: On motion that the House suspend the rules and agree to the Senate amendments Agreed to by the Yeas and Nays: (2/3 required): 412—0 (Roll no. 117). (consideration: CR H1691-1696, H1745-1746; text as House agreed to Senate amendments: CR H1691-1693)

4/30/2002 6:56pm: Motion to reconsider laid on the table Agreed to without objection.

4/30/2002: Cleared for White House.

5/7/2002: Presented to President.

5/15/2002: Signed by President.

5/15/2002: Became Public Law No: 107-174.

The No FEAR law may be viewed at:
http://thomas.gov/cgi-bin/query/F?c107:11:./temp/–c107jRfyM1:e865:

Index